THE BOOK OF
SEALS & AMULETS

THE BOOK
OF
SEALS & AMULETS

Shadow Tree Series
Volume 3

Jacobus G. Swart

THE SANGREAL SODALITY PRESS
Johannesburg, Gauteng, South Africa

First edition, 2014
Second printing, 2014

Published by The Sangreal Sodality Press
74 Twelfth Street
Parkmore 2196
Gauteng
South Africa
Email: jacobsang@gmail.com

ISBN 978-0-620-59698-5

Dedicated to Gloria Swart

"O Love! O Life! O Light! May we truly be Conceived and Live according to Thy Will within the Womb where we await Thy Word! .....Welcome indeed are they that enter with entitlement our closest circles of companionship."

—William G. Gray (*The Sangreal Sacrament*)

Shadow Tree Series

Volume 1: The Book of Self Creation
Volume 2: The Book of Sacred Names
Volume 3: The Book of Seals & Amulets

Contents

Illustrations

Hebrew Transliteration

There are transliterations of Hebrew words and phrases throughout this work. In this regard I have employed the following method. The Hebrew vowels are pronounced:

"a" — like "a" in "f**a**ther";

"e" — like the "e" in "l**e**t" or the way the English pronounce the word "Air" without enunciating the "r";

"i" — like the "ee" in "s**ee**k";

"o" — like the "o" in "n**o**t" or the longer "au" in "n**au**ght"; or again like the sound of the word "**Awe**";

"u" — like the "oo" in "m**oo**d";

"ai" — like the letter "y" in "m**y**" or "igh" in "h**igh**" or like the sound of the word "**eye**"; and

"ei" — like the "ay" in "h**ay**."

The remaining consonants are as written, except for:

"ch" which is pronounced like the guttural "ch" in the Scottish "Lo**ch**" or the equivalent in the German "I**ch**," and "tz" which sounds like the "tz" in "Ri**tz**" or like the "ts" in "hear**ts**."

In most cases an apostrophe (') indicates a glottal stop which sounds like the "i" in "bit" or the concluding "er" in "father," otherwise it is a small break to separate sections of a word or create a double syllable. For example, I often hear people speak of *Daat* (Knowledge), sounding one long "*ah*" between the "*D*" and the concluding "*T*." The correct pronunciation is however *Da'at*, the apostrophe indicating that the term comprises actually two syllables, "*dah*" and "*aht*." In this word a quick glottal stop separates the first syllable from the second. As a vowel it is the same sound made when one struggles to find the right word, and say something like "*er.....er.....er.....*"

One further rule is that the accent in Hebrew is, more often than not, placed on the last syllable of the word. Of course there are numerous instances which disprove this rule, but it applies almost throughout Hebrew incantations, e.g. those found in Merkavistic literature, etc.

"He put his vessel on his table. Upon opening it, he found a second vessel inside, and within it there was a frog.....Haninah built a room for the frog.....He fattened him up with the best and finest foods until he had spent all he possessed... ... .

INTRODUCTION

As mentioned in the previous volumes of the "Shadow Tree Series," I have devoted myself for more than four decades to both a serious investigation, as well as to the practical implementation, of Kabbalistic teachings in my everyday life. For me "Kabbalah" is like a pair of old slippers, i.e. absolutely comfortable and easily slipped into, and it has remained so for the entire period that I have been associated with it. There are certainly times when I battle with the obscurities of the doctrines found in some of the primary texts, but, in the main, Kabbalah has served me well on many levels, whether these be physical, mental, emotional or spiritual. In terms of my everyday existence, I have found the teachings of "Practical Kabbalah" especially meaningful, despite the endless warnings about these being "bad," and that I might incur "the wrath of the Almighty."

Of course, it is worth noting that "Kabbalah" and orthodox Judaism have always been uneasy bedfellows. Sometimes they would be more or less comfortable in their relationship and need of each other, but at other times they would burst into open conflict. The strong messianic tendencies of certain Kabbalists, like for example Shabbetai Tzvi, Jacob Frank, or, much further back, of Abraham Abulafia,[1] contributed to the notion amongst the orthodoxy that the tradition is a blasphemous quagmire out to snare the gullible. Yet, should the same Messianic tendency shine forth in what appears to be a most godly and sanctified individual, such as Rabbi Isaac Luria and his "official" successor, Chaim Vital,[2] then we can relax and bask in the glory of their unique "spiritual light" without any trepidation of being led up the garden path, so to speak.

i

We know that mysticism goes hand in hand with Judaism, as it does with other faiths, provided it stays on the "thin and narrow" and manages to dress its visions, miracles and what can only be termed "magical activities," in the garb of the formal and accepted religious views of the day. If anyone should step a fraction out of line, that individual, who was deemed into manifestation in order to be redeemed into eternity, will be doomed by his peers unto the aeons. To put it simply, certain concepts of Kabbalah entered mainstream Judaism, and have comfortably remained there to this very day. These pertain mainly to the speculative side of the Tradition.

Many Rabbis were both Kabbalists and orthodox religious leaders of their communities, as are some still today, with no particular problem one way or the other. Having said that, I should also mention that some of them kept their more "controversial" experiences and activities quite hidden for fear of rejection, as for example the case of Rabbi Joseph Karo and his *Maggid* clearly indicates.[3] However, the more individualistic aspects of the tradition, such as "Practical Kabbalah," which patently involves magical practices, often led to a fracas everywhere, and yet there were again many orthodox Rabbis who beneficially utilised this forbidden zone of the tradition.[4] In fact, many still do with their *Kameot* (Hebrew amulets), *Segulot*, *Terufot*, and magical uses of holy writ.

Naturally we need to recognise that the rise of pseudo-messiahs, such as the earlier mentioned Shabbetai Tzvi and Jacob Frank, contributed enormously to the fall of Kabbalah from grace in the eyes of mainstream Judaism. Even more so after Shabbetai Tzvi's conversion to Islam, following the Jewish authorities denouncement of him as a blasphemer to the Muslim authorities. He caused a lot of havoc with his enormous influence over thousands of Jews across the then "civilized" world, and naturally this was more than worrying to the rabbinical authorities who wanted to protect their flocks, and who saw Tzvi's appeal as spelling disaster for Jewry as a whole. This was certainly a very dark period for both Kabbalah and Judaism alike. However, today Shabbetai Tzvi and his approach to both Kabbalah and Judaism, are understood in a much more open manner, and he appears less of a threat. The same cannot be said for "Practical Kabbalah," which is still drawing vehement condemnation from mainstream religious authorities.

A while back I responded to a post on the internet in which it was claimed that Joseph Karo, the great 16th century legalist and Kabbalist, referred to "*Kabbalah Ma'asit*[5] (Practical Kabbalah) in his *Shulchan Aruch*[5] as "black magic." Seeking clarification I wrote: "In the numerous pre-Lurianic Kabbalistic texts, as well as several subsequent works of the same genre penned by East European Baalei Shem, the term '*Kabbalah Ma'asit*' referred to 'Practical Kabbalah' exclusively. There is no specific indication in these writings that the appellation '*Kabbalah Ma'asit*' referred to 'Black Magic' *per se*. When exactly did it acquire the adverse connotation you are referring to?" To this I received the following response: "*Shulchan Aruch Yoreh De'ah*.....laws of *Avoda Zerah*. The *Shulchan Aruch* makes very clear that *Kabbalah Ma'asit* is what the *Torah* was referring to when it spoke about magic. There are a few rare exceptions, but by and large that is the status."

Since I could not find any reference to *Kabbalah Ma'asit* being "black magic" in the reference provided, I continued quizzing lest it appeared somewhere else in that authoritative legalistic tome, asking: "Does the *Shulchan Aruch* use the specific appellative 'Black Magic' in reference to '*Kabbalah Ma'asit*,' and does this turn astute and highly revered Kabbalists like Rabbi Eleazar of Worms, Rabbi Moshe Cordovero, Rabbi Moshe Zacutto, Rabbi Avraham Chamui, *et al*,[6] who openly shared techniques belonging to the '*Kabbalah Ma'asit*' arena, into heretics who pandered what is forbidden? By the same token are 'Practical Kabbalistic' writings like the *Sefer Raziel*, *Brit Menucha*, *Shorshei ha-Shemot*, amongst others,[7] considered 'black magic' texts?"

In response I was told that "Actually the *Sh"A* refers to black magic and all other forms of forbidden sorcery as *Kabbalah Ma'asit*. As well as enumerates the practices that are forbidden. Considering that R' Cordovero was actually a teacher of R' Karo, I would assume that R' Karo learned what was forbidden from him. Receipt and knowledge of Kabbalah ma'asit is not forbidden, its usage is. Read the introduction by R' Zecuto (who is post-Lurianic by the way), he specifically warns against the usage of what he has written. There are exceptions to this within the bounds of *halacha*, but one first must be a competent Rav versed in the applicable *halachot* to know what they are and when they can be properly applied."

Realising the "deflective" nature of this response, the lack of direct textual references, the absurdity of the claim that it is in order to read and learn about Practical Kabbalah, but not to put such knowledge to practical use, and that I am not likely to get a clear answer to my query, I did not press for further details. It quickly became abundantly clear that pursuing the matter any further would just result in me listing more and more of those astute rabbis who not only wrote about, but actually employed that which the individual in question termed "Black Magic." Likewise he will come back with a list of equally as many astute rabbis who denigrated "Practical Kabbalah." So why bother?

I thought the statement that Moses Cordovero was the teacher of Joseph Karo, and that the respondent assumed that accordingly "R' Karo learned what was forbidden from him," to be indeed most curious, since Cordovero himself freely shared techniques of the *Kabbalah Ma'asit* (Practical Kabbalah) genre in his *Pardes Rimmonim* (*Garden of the Pomegranates*).[8] Joseph Karo was certainly not unfamiliar with the more "extreme aspects" of Practical Kabbalah. After all, he diligently kept a diary, albeit a secret one, of his clairvoyant channelling of a *Maggid*, a heavenly spirit mentor,[9] and he apparently left his mark in the local lore of Nikopolis, the town in which he grew up, where visitors are still being shown Karo's *Kan Gishmi* (Fountain of Blood), a spot where it is said he "performed miracles."[10] One wonders if the latter were of the "Practical Kabbalah" variety?

Regarding Moses Zacutto's warning "against the usage of what he has written," we know that he personally employed many of the magical techniques he listed so openly and enthusiastically in his *Shorshei ha-Shemot* (*Roots of Names*)[11] and *Sefer ha-Sodot she-Kibbalti mi Rabbotai* (*The Book of Secrets I Received from My Masters*).[12] In fact, in many instances he affirmed the efficacy of these procedures with the phrase "tested by me," and hence J.H. Chajes appears to be correct in his observation that Zacutto "assembled this magical material for practical and not merely theoretical purposes."[13] It is also curious that Chaim Vital and his son Samuel, both of Lurianic fame, did not hesitate to consult with Muslim magicians when they felt it necessary to do so![14]

I recently had to face a challenge and was called upon to put my money where my mouth is, i.e. back a claim I made in "*The Book of Sacred Names*"[15] regarding "Practical Kabbalah" techniques in "*Sefer Pardes Rimmonim*" (*Garden of Pomegranates*) by Moses Cordovero.[16] My opponent maintained that there is not a single instance of anything pertaining directly to "Practical Kabbalah," or "Jewish Magic" for that matter, to be found in this text written by the father-in-law of the Holy Ari. Hence he felt it necessary to challenge me to either "own up" or face public exposure of my "deceit".....no less!!

I would not normally bother with uninformed challenges, but I thought I might face the "truth of the matter" and satisfy the "questing spirit" of my challenger with an example of Practical Kabbalah penned by the very hand of the great Moses Cordovero, who wrote in his *Pardes Rimonnim: Gate Ten Chapter 1*, that "[t]here is no doubt that the colours can introduce you to the operations of the *Sefirot* and the drawing down of their overflow. Thus, when a person needs to draw down the overflow of Mercy from the attribute of Grace, let him imagine the name of the *Sefirah* with the colour that is appropriate to what he needs, in front of him. If he [applies to] Supreme *Chesed*, [let him imagine] the outmost white.....Likewise when he will operate a certain operation and he will be in need of the overflow of the [attribute of] Judgement, let him then dress in red clothes and imagine the form [of the letters of] the *Tetragrammaton* in red, and so on in the case of all the operations causing the descent of the overflows..... Certainly in this manner [we may explain] the meaning of the amulets. When a person prepares an amulet for the [*Sefirah* of] *Chesed*, let him imagine the [divine] name in a bright white, since then the operation of that name will be augmented.....

We have seen someone who designed amulets which refer to the [attribute] of [stern] judgement [using the colour of] red, and those which refer to Grace in white and those which refer to Mercy in Green, and everything [was done] in accordance with what [was revealed] by true [angelic] mentors, which taught to him the preparation of the amulets. All this [was done] in order to introduce him to the subject of the colours and the operations which derive from the above....."[17]

Considering the subject matter addressed in this quote, you might well wonder what exactly comprises "*Practical Kabbalah*." My personal stance is that it incorporates a lot more than simply "magical applications," such as those addressed in my "*Book of Sacred Names*."[18] Besides those specific details, I personally include:

1. meditational techniques like those of Eleazer of Worms,[19] Abraham Abulafia,[20] the *Tzerufim* of Albotini,[21] as well as the *Kavvanot* and *Yichudim* of Lurianic Kabbalah,[22] etc.
2. worshipful invocations and prayers such as those found in Kabbalistic *Siddurim* (prayer books), etc.;[23]
3. practical applications of the ten *sefirot*, the latter having been termed "the spiritual energies of Mind and Emotion" by Rabbi Laibl Wolf,[24] and of which there are a number of wonderful and well-known "practical" studies such as those by my late mentor, William G. Gray,[25] or the more recent very innovative and equally well written work of R.J. Stewart,[26] etc.

Notwithstanding this, the underlying intentions of "Practical Kabbalah" are the same as those of "Ritual Magic." In fact, the two appellatives could be employed interchangeably. However, what I find personally bothersome, is the rarity of commonsense views on magic and allied subjects in contemporary writings dealing with this topic. People still espouse the most absurd views on what magic is, and what it is supposed to do for them. In this regard I often get letters from people who demand communication with a deceased family member or friend, wanting powerful talismans against witchcraft, etc., and if one could throw in a good book on "powerful prayers" to accompany candle and incense rituals, plus a very good, huge and detailed dream book, they would consider themselves to be in "occult heaven."

Naturally I do understand that such letters derive from the sheer necessity to find solutions to the obstacles and disasters besetting ones life, and that what we need to know is how to keep ourselves together under the pressure of perdition itself, and how to survive in body, mind, soul and spirit whilst the "forces of darkness and destruction" are hammering us into the ground, and proving by every means how helpless, futile and ineffective we are. Plainly we need *solid* stuff which will relieve us from pain and destruction, rather than all the "pretty-pretty" decorative trash which looks good when nothing threatens our essential existence. I have had quite enough of the rubbish which has been doing the rounds on the mystical market for years and years.

What does it matter who or what the "Elemental Spirit" of the Moon is, or how one might construct a "Talisman of Venus," unless such matters support our essential existence in what is a very dangerous world for most of its denizens? That is what I am hoping to address in this third volume of *"The Shadow Tree Series,"* which is devoted to an important aspect of Practical Kabbalah, i.e. *Kameot* (Hebrew amulets) and "Magical Seals." Of course, I do not believe anybody should fully rely on amulets or talismans to solve all the difficulties they may meet in life. It is vitally important to understand the fundamental factors within ones own being, which attract and align with the problems one encounters in ones life. In other words, the techniques of "Practical Kabbalah," i.e. amulets, etc., should be a support in ones attempt to create the right sort of balance one needs in order to live a meaningful life, but they certainly should not be an end in themselves, or considered the ultimate solution to all problems in life.

I am reminded of the saga of Rabbi Elazar Abuchatzeira, the grandson of the famed 20th century Kabbalist Baba Sali, who was killed by a fundamentalist religious fanatic. I was greatly perturbed when I learned the motive behind the murder. As it is, a lot of controversy surrounded the Rabbi, and I have been reflecting on the role of this in his murder. He was basically accused of charging exorbitant fees for spiritual services rendered. I am perfectly aware that there is a powerful religious faction out there who condemns *anyone* receiving *any* reward for *segulot*, etc., however this simply does not make sense in a world where you have to "earn your keep," and where you need cold hard cash to keep body and soul together. Personally speaking, my only objection is against those who are fleecing their clients, and in this regard it was said that the Rabbi took hundreds of thousands of dollars from a very gullible public, who were buying into what was termed his "superstitious promises." Critics called it "a hair raising tale," and accused Rabbi Abuchatzeira of being a swindler.

I should make it clear that having been on the most beneficial receiving end of *Segulot* and *Kameot* myself, I am disinclined to glibly dismiss such items as being superstitious nonsense. This notwithstanding, I certainly would not condone robbing the poor of their hard earned money, and this would seem to be the major issue at play here. As it is, believing with every fibre of my being in the process of "self creation," i.e. that all humans are constantly creating their own personal life circumstances, it appears to me that the "reality" which the Rabbi had been "living" in recent years, and was seemingly unable to recognise or change, turned into a roller coaster ride which lead to that tragic inevitable finality.

Now, "realities" do have a tendency of being "reinterpreted" with hindsight, and subsequent to the funeral of Rabbi Elazar Abuchatzeira, a headline read "*Rabbi Abuhatzeira Bore the Burden of Evil Decrees*," and the subheading continued "Rabbi Abuhatzeira saved the people of Israel from evil decrees through his brutal death, leading rabbis say." The brother of the deceased affirmed that "harsh punishments were decreed on the people of Israel, and he wanted to nullify them," and continued "as he nullified many harsh decrees for us.....We ask you, Rabbi Elazar: go before the Throne of Glory and pray there for the people of Israel. Pray for the entire family. Pray for your sons, your daughters, your grandchildren and wife."[27]

How very curious! According to all reliable sources, the Rabbi was slain by a frequent visitor, Asher Dahan, a 42 year old resident of the Haredi city of Elad, who was constantly seeking blessings and advice from the Rabbi, and whose motive for murder was reported to have been solely based on the fact "that Abuhatzeira had failed to solve his marital problems,"[28] similar sentiments having been expressed at the time by the ever growing list of detractors of the Rabbi around the globe.

Underlying this situation is a most serious matter. Firstly, whilst one may employ special spiritual techniques and practices in support of ones aim to solve problematic situations, i.e. a failing marriage, I believe the fundamental failing here is the essential instruction of the "disappointed killer" in the necessity of changing those "obstacles" within himself, which lead to the failing of his marriage in the first place. It is no good to simply lay the blame at the feet of your life partner. The witty May West was perfectly right in claiming that "it takes two to get one into trouble"![29]

Secondly, I believe the major dilemma pertains directly to these "*Tzadikim*," who have a predilection for placing themselves on pedestals of self-aggrandisement. Their perceived "infallibility" is positioning them so way beyond criticism and the recognition of their "*fallibility*" as beings of flesh and blood, that they are being viewed by their compatriots as being virtually the "mouthpiece" of the Divine One on earth, if not the very incarnations of the Almighty in person.....God forbid! It is always "*I* will heal you"! "*I* will solve your marriage problems"! When will they realise that you can no more live anyone else's life, than you can eat or defecate for them?

Again, don't get me wrong, I am a firm believer in the doctrines and magical techniques of "*Practical Kabbalah*." However, what I find fundamentally flawed is the cultivation of total reliance on the person of the *Tzadik*, or anybody else for that matter, to solve all life problems. Most people are unable, or even unwilling, to work changes within their own beings, i.e. establishing the right mindset, which would afford at least the possibility for a lasting implementation of the new "reality" they seek. Instead they would expect a *Tzadik*, especially one who is a "mini-Messiah," to "do it" for them. This is extremely dangerous, and all "*Tzadikim*," and especially would-be "Messiahs," should note that if they dare allow anything like that to continue in their lives, there is bound to be many more incidents akin to the sorry saga of the now "martyred" Rabbi Elazar Abuchatzeira!

Now, before there are any misconceptions about the current tome, I had better explain what it is and what it is not. It is not a definitive encyclopaedia of Hebrew amulets created to grant readers' every desire and solve all the difficulties they may encounter. In fact, it is both an investigation in the mystical interpretations of magical seals, and a practical guide in which I share primary information on Hebrew amulets, which the reader might employ beneficially for personal intentions in their daily lives. Despite the fact that I am fully convinced of the effectiveness of the practices shared in all volumes of my "*Shadow Tree Series*,"[30] I hold out no guarantees regarding the success or failure of their employment. Nothing more.....nothing less!!

✳✳✳

As in the case of the previous two volumes of this series, I would once again recommend to everyone perusing and investigating the material shared in this volume, to consider commencing any study of Kabbalistic material by sitting in a restful, peaceful manner, and then, with eyes shut for a minute or so, to meditate on these words:

> "Open my eyes so that I may perceive the wonders of Your teaching."

In this regard, it is important to whisper the phrase repeatedly as you allow yourself to sense, as it were, in a "feeling" manner, the meaning of the words you are uttering. It is important not to attempt any mental analysis or deliberation on the meaning of the actual words being contemplated. Again, they should be simply repeated several times, whilst allowing yourself to "feel" the meaning of the phrase within yourself. As stated previously,[31] it is a good idea to read a section in its entirety, without trying to perceive any specific meaning, then to pause for a few seconds, and afterwards attempt to understand within yourself the general meaning of what was being said. In this way you begin to fulfill an important teaching of Kabbalah, which tells you to unite two "worlds"—the inner and the outer within your own Being. By allowing yourself to "feel" the meaning of what you are reading, you learn to surrender to the words. You open yourself, again fulfilling one of the requirements of Kabbalistic study, which is to surrender the "me," the ego, and to remove arrogance and bias. You simply attempt to sense with your being what is being portrayed in the section you are perusing. This act is a serious step on the path of perfecting ones personality, because it stops the expansion of the ego, and increases chances of obtaining "True Knowledge."

✳✳✳

I simply cannot conclude this introduction to *The Book of Seals and Amulets*," without offering due acknowledgment to my dear Friends and Companions for the enormous input I have received over the two years of writing this text. This volume is dedicated to my wife Gloria, "*Orelima*," "Light of the Mother God," to whom

I offer my deepest gratitude for the enormous love and thoughtfulness that characterise her life and being. For more than three decades I have benefitted from the loving care my body, mind, soul and spirit have received from this remarkable lady who brought me to the full realisation that the "Chalice of the Mysteries" is indeed her heart!

I need to again acknowledge my beloved mentor, William G. Gray, who opened my inner eyes to "esoteric mysteries," and offer again my most heartfelt appreciation to my South African Friends and Companions, in Johannesburg Norma Cosani, Gidon Fainman, John Jones, Geraldine Talbot, Francois le Roux, Ian Greenspan, Gerhardus Muller, Ryan Kay, Simon O'Regan; in Durban Marq and Penny Smith; and in Pretoria Carlien Steyn, Magriet Engelbrecht, Helene Vogel and Gerrit Viljoen, all of whom have illuminated my darkness with their insightful comments and queries. I further offer my profound appreciation to my fellow Sangreal Sodality Companions living around the globe, Marcus Claridge in Scotland, Hamish Gilbert in Poland, Bence Bodnar and little Vilmosh Bodnar in Budapest, Elizabeth and Warwick Bennet in Australia, and all my Companions everywhere "whose Identities are known unto Omniscience alone," as well as my "Fellow Questers" on our internet forums whose curiosity greatly contributed to the material shared in this volume.

I would once again like to offer my heartfelt thanks to my very dear friend Jonathan Helper who again helped me translate obscure Hebrew writings, and to Uri Raz who shared with me his knowledge of "Practical Kabbalah." In conclusion, I wish to express my most profound gratitude to Simon O'Regan whose insightful questions inspired much of the material shared in this tome, and who participated directly in the creation of several of the illustrations employed in this work, and to Norma Cosani who perused "the draft" in the greatest detail, corrected that which needed "rectification," and who once again rid this work of ambiguities.

Happy Reading!

Jacobus Swart
Johannesburg
January 2014

. ...Haninah and his wife went into the frog's room and said to him: 'Dear friend, to our great sorrow we can no longer keep you'... ... .

Chapter 1
Levanah — Moon
SACRED NAMES
IN
HEBREW AMULETS

The employment of amulets for protection against malevolence of all sorts; or to promote physical, mental and spiritual health; or to generate happiness in matters of the heart; etc., is a global phenomenon. It is not restricted to one nation or, for that matter, to single religious communities, but can be viewed to be quite central to the spiritual traditions of the world since the earliest days of human "self awakening."[1] Furthermore, amulets and talismans have maintained their central position in global religions, despite the vociferous protestations of the clergy, be they Jewish, Christian or Muslim.

One simply cannot inform all and sundry regarding the primary holiness of a sacred text, i.e. the Bible, etc., and then attempt to stop a mother considering that declared "holy book" to be a most powerful talisman and employing it as such, e.g. placing written portions of it in the cot of her baby in times of desperate need. In this regard, it was reported that amongst the North African Jewish communities the *Sefer ha-Zohar*, virtually the "bible" of Kabbalah, was employed "as an infallible remedy for their ills" which they placed "under the pillow of a sick patient or under the bed of a barren woman."[2] Furthermore, one cannot expect that a Divine Name, the holiness of which inspires the greatest awe, should not be considered powerful enough to banish the greatest evil which might beset humankind.

We might also note that there has been a lot of, as it were, "cross fertilisation" of ideas amongst the nations, especially when they reside in close proximity of one another. Hence, we find great similarity between the "talismanic traditions" of Jewish and Islamic magic. A commentator noted laconically that the "rabbis

1

were powerless to control these manifestations of ideas that had grown out of the centuries-long interaction of Berber, Jewish and Arab credulity and superstition." He further noted that all believed "in the efficacy of talismans and in all the protective devices against the occult powers such as ritual phrases that included the mention of God's name, of fishes, of the protective hand and the figure five."[3] I hope to address these and other devices employed in Hebrew amulets, and, in this regard, commence with a perusal of some of the important Divine Names employed in *Kameot* (amulets).

A. אדני—*Adonai*

The Divine Name *Adonai* is employed in a variety of ways in Jewish mysticism, magic and meditation, but in the current instance we will focus specifically on its use in Hebrew amulets. In this regard, it is worth noting that this Divine Name corresponds to *Malchut* (Kingdom) on the sefirotic tree,[4] and there are further interesting considerations regarding this attribution which are addressed elsewhere in this tome.

Now, whilst the Divine Name אדני (*Adonai*) is rarely employed on its own in Hebrew amulets, it often appears conjointly with other Divine Names, e.g. the Ineffable Name (*YHVH*); *Ehyeh*; portions of the "Forty-two Letter Name of God" and the "Name of Seventy-two Names," etc.[5] Amongst the few occurrences in which this Divine Name is singularly employed in a *chotam* (magic seal), is in the following *Kamea* (amulet) in which the twenty-four permutations of *Adonai* are combined into a magic seal for the purpose of alleviating infertility in women. The said permutations appear in various formats of which the following order is correct:

אידנ	אינד	אניד	אנדי	אדין	אדני
דאני	דאינ	דיאנ	דינא	דנאי	דניא
נדיא	נדאי	נאדי	נאיד	נידא	ניאד
ינאד	ינדא	ידנא	ידאנ	יאנד	יאדנ

As said, this magic seal is employed as an aid in curing a barren woman of her sterility, and in this regard, the instruction is to inscribe the square comprising the twenty-four permutations in the format of the listed magic "word square."[6] Since this *chotam* (magic seal) is understood to receive an influx of "power" from the "Name of Seventy-two Names," we are informed to state the purpose of the amulet below the magic seal, and to do this in the name of the "Seventy-two Names of *Chesed*" (Loving-kindness). Hence the latter Divine Name should be listed in full in the item.

We are further told to also reference the combination ריו in the *Kamea*. This special "Name," pertaining to both *Chesed* (Mercy) and *Gevurah* (Strength), is said to battle the *Klipot* (demonic shards). The *gematria* of this peculiar Hebrew letter combination is 216, which we are told relates to the 216 letters of the "Name of Seventy-Two Names." It is also said that the entire construct comprising the magic seal, pertains to the word עיבור (*Ibur*—"impregnation" or "gestation"), this being the fundamental purpose of the amulet in question. As it is, the *gematria* of this word is 288, i.e. 4 x 72, hence this term is also included in the amulet we are addressing.

In conclusion, there are further instructions to add *Genesis 21:1* as well as *Genesis 30:22* to the amulet, these verses being traditionally employed in Jewish magic to promote fertility and to ease childbirth. Respectively they read:

(*Genesis 21:1*) ויהוה פקד את שרה כאשר אמר ויעש
יהוה לשרה כאשר דבר

Transliteration:

v'YHVH pakad et Sarah ka'asher amar va'ya'as YHVH l'Sarah ka'asher diber.

Translation:

And *YHVH* remembered Sarah as He had said, and *YHVH* did unto Sarah as He had spoken.

(*Genesis 30:22*) ויזכר אלהים את רחל וישמע
אליה אלהים ויפתח את רחמה

Transliteration:

va'yizkor Elohim et Rachel va'yishma eileha Elohim va'yiftach et rach'mah

Translation:

> And *Elohim* remembered Rachel, and *Elohim* hearkened to her, and opened her womb.

Whilst this amulet against infertility in women is perhaps somewhat difficult to construct, the following simpler *Kamea* is equally employed to encourage fertility as well as pregnancy:

יו	יטש מר כך	אה חגז לגב	דכלה מי אליד	אהבה בחנוני יהו
קהלא				

יו הן הלא	רעוש מה בן	אה חנה ולגד	מלה מ אלידי	אבא באנונה יהי

In this instance we are told that if a woman should find herself battling to fall pregnant, the said amulet should be written and suspended on her person, e.g. like a pendant. It is said she will get pregnant in no time at all.[7]

It is somewhat difficult ascertaining the exact meaning of the words and Hebrew letter combinations in each section. The first terms in the two upper rightmost columns read אהבה דכלה (*Ahavah d'Kalah*—"love for the bride"), whilst the first two words similarly located in the lower construct read אבא מלה, perhaps *Aba milah* ("the word (promise or circumcision) of the father"). Be that as it may, the upper construct clearly pertains to the empowerment of a woman, whilst the lower one is doing the same for the man in her life.

B. אהיה – *Ehyeh*

The Divine Name אהיה (*Ehyeh*), as well as the full biblical expression אהיה אשר אהיה (*Ehyeh asher Ehyeh*—"I am that I am" or "I will be what I will be") (*Exodus 3:14*), appear in Hebrew amulets. The letters comprising this Divine Name are sometimes arranged in the shape of letter squares, as shown in the following two versions of the *Ehyeh* square:[8]

ה	י	ה	א
י	ה	א	ה
ה	א	ה	י
א	ה	י	ה

ה	י	ה	א
א	ה	י	ה
י	ה	א	י
ה	א	י	ה

I am addressing "letter" and "word" squares in greater detail in the next chapter, and the *Ehyeh* square is equally discussed elsewhere in this work in terms of its usual employment in conjunction with other Divine Names, magic squares, etc. In this regard, it should be noted that the four letters comprising אהיה (*Ehyeh*) are often combined in a *chotam* (magic seal) with the four letters of the Ineffable Name for amuletic purposes:

ה	י	ה	א
י	ה	ו	ה
ה	ו	ה	י
א	ה	י	ה

This letter square is sometimes employed singularly on the front of an amulet, whilst the back of the construct would comprise the name of the owner. It is understood that the special magical qualities of these Divine Names employed conjointly in this magic square will benefit the one whose name is written on its rear. However, the said magic square is often employed conjointly with the Name אהיה (*Ehyeh*), holy writ, etc., as shown in the following *Kamea* for the promotion of pregnancy:[9]

We are informed the *Kamea* should be written by a *Sofer* (scribe) who is pure in mind, body and soul. The amulet should be inscribed in clean, clearly written Hebrew lettering on a kosher scroll, and the following statement is vocalised prior to writing the *Kamea*:

הריני כותב קמיע הזעת בשעתא טבתא טבתא בגדא טבא
לאסותא מן שמיא עבור האשה [פלונית בת פלוניּת]
אשת [פלוני בן פלוניّ]

Transliteration:

> *Hareini kotev kamea ha-zot b'sha'ta tovta b'gada tava l'as'vata min sh'maya avur ha-ishah [.....Plonit bat Plonit.....] eshet [.....Ploni ben Ploni.....]*

Translation:

> I am writing this amulet in an auspicious time, for good health from heaven for this woman [.....fill in the name of the female recipient.....], wife of [.....fill in the name of her husband.....]

This is followed by writing the *Kamea* in question, of which the adjuration at the top reads:

יהי רצון מלפניך אהיה אשר אהיה שתרחם על האשה
[פלונית בת פלוניׁת] ותתן לה בקרוב הריון מבעלה
[פלוני בן פלוני] בזרע של קימא בכח השמות הקדושים
האלה על ידי המלאך שמשיאל

Transliteration:

> *Y'hi ratzon milfanecha Ehyeh asher Ehyeh shet'rachem al ha-ishah [.....Plonit bat Plonit.....] v'titen la b'karov herayon miba'alah [.....Ploni ben Ploni.....] b'zera shel kayama b'koach ha-shemot ha-kadoshim ha-eleh al y'dei ha-malach Shamshi'el*

Translation:

> May it be your will *Ehyeh asher Ehyeh* [I am that I am] to have mercy on the woman [.....fill in the name of the female.....] and soon grant her pregnancy from her husband [.....fill in the name of the male.....] with his existent seed [sperm], in the power of these Holy Names through the angel *Shamshi'el*

Below this incantation we trace a set of Divine Names which, whilst I have yet to find an elucidation of their origin, appear to be derived from biblical phrases in the usual manner, i.e. the capitals or concluding letters of words, these being in the current instance:

ואא הבבא באז ובא ואא ולא פוו אהו ובה והו ההעה

אכהלייה יצהבואהות אמן סלה נצח ועד ה ה ה הלז

The concluding phrase in the third line plainly reads *Omein Selah Netzach Va'ed* (*Amen*, Enduring (Victory), *Selah*, Forever). This is followed by the triple presentation of the letter ה, the *monogrammaton* or "Single Letter Name of God," of which we are told "in kabbalistic amulets is often repeated,"[10] each being a representation of the Ineffable Name. This is in turn succeeded by the concluding name הלז (vocalised *heilaze*). This Name was derived from three words in *Genesis 47:23* reading הא לכם זרע (*hei lachem zera*— "here is seed for you").[11]

In conclusion we are instructed that when the construction of the *Kamea* is concluded, the object should be located in a little metal container which is in turn to be placed in a small leather pouch. This item should then be suspended around the neck of the woman in such a way, that it rests between her breasts. However, it should be noted that this item is to be carried on her person only during her so-called "pure days." In other words, it has to be removed from her person during menstruation.[12]

The earlier mentioned Divine Name הלז (*heilaze*) is considered to have in itself the power to aid a barren woman to fall pregnant. In this regard, we are told that another *Kamea* can be constructed from sixteen silver coins collected from sixteen women who have not suffered any difficulty during childbirth, and of whose male offspring none has perished. The sixteen coins are passed on to a Jewish silversmith or jeweller, who has to convert them into a single round plate comprising no impurities.[13]

However, prior to working the coins into the mentioned round silver disc, the jeweller himself must be purified, i.e. visit a *Mikveh* (ritual bath), wear a fresh clean garment, and it is stated that his clothing is not to touch the silver plate at any time. Having prepared himself in this manner, the silversmith has to engrave on the front side of the silver plate a single, large letter ה (*Heh*), i.e. the *Monogrammaton* which is said to have "a peculiar holy status,"[14] and which is extensively employed in Hebrew amulets. On the rear of the disc is engraved the full phrase הא לכם זרע (*hei lachem zera*). Elsewhere in this tome we refer to the same phrase and procedure being applied for the very same purpose in terms of the "Magic Square of the Seventh Order."

In the current instance the silver disc is afterwards located inside three bags. The first is made from white silk, the second from linen, and the third again from white silk, all sewn up with white cotton thread. Having located the *Kamea* inside the white silk bag, which is in turn placed inside the linen bag, and then located inside the third white silk bag, it is afterwards hung around the neck of the barren woman on the third (Tuesday) or the sixth day (Friday) of the week.[15]

C. יהוה —*Ineffable Name*

In the *Sefer Raziel*, יהוה (*YHVH*), the שם המפורש (*Shem ha-Meforash*—"Ineffable Name"), the most sacred Divine Name, is termed "the beginning of all the Divine Names," whether the latter refer to the most elevated, i.e. Divine Names which cannot be "erased," or to the lower, secondary type.[16] The "secret" of the Ineffable Name is said to pertain to *Adam*, the primordial male (זכר—*zachar*), and *Eve*, the primordial female (נקבה—*n'keivah*) of *Genesis*. In fact, we are told that the four letters comprising יהוה (*YHVH*), the lofty and awesome Name, afford us knowledge of our primordial ancestral origination.[17]

I believe the real "secret" of the Ineffable Name is the concept of אהבה (*Ahavah*—"love"). The numerical value (*gematria*) of the latter term is 13 [א = 1 + ה = 5 + ב = 2 + ה = 5 = 13]. Regarding the "nature of love" we are told that "one 'love' added to another — two lovers — equals 26."[18] This is the *gematria* of יהוה [י = 10 + ה = 5 + ו = 6 + ה = 5 = 26]. Truly it has been said that "two people in love participate in a Divine experience."[19]

Since it is considered the most powerful Divine Name in existence, the Ineffable Name is included in numerous amulets for a variety of purposes of both the constructive and destructive kind. In this regard, the following magical activity may be considered a misapplication of the *Tetragrammaton*, yet it should be understood that this Unique Name is considered the most potent force determining the outcome of any honourable purpose, so why should it not be employed for purposes of effective resistance to, for example, the military might of crazed dictators, etc.? Whilst such a defensive measure might turn out to be destructive, it could equally be enormously beneficial in the preservation of the life and limb of oneself and ones kin. Hence it should come as no surprise that the magical applications of the Ineffable Name include the following *chotam* (magical seal) employed as a defense against an enemy at war:

This seal appears to be the Ineffable Name written in magical script, but I have not been able to ascertain the exact magical alphabet it might have been derived from. However, in terms of the talismanic use of this magical image, we are told it has the power to destroy the camp of the enemy in war situations.[20]

To affect this outcome, one has to collect four fairly large stones from a dirt road or cobblestone track. On each of these stones is inscribed the magical seal conjointly with specific phrases. On the first stone is written (*Exodus 15:3*):

יהוה איש מלחמה יהוה שמו לעולם ועד יה אא״א סס״ס

Transliteration:

> *YHVH ish milchamah YHVH shemo l'olam va'ed Yah Omein Omein Omein Selah Selah Selah*

Translation:

> *YHVH is a man of war, YHVH is His Name throughout eternity Yah Amen Amen Amen Selah Selah Selah*

On the second is written the portion from *Isaiah 41:2* reading יתן כעפר חרבו (*yiten ke'afar charvo*—"his sword maketh them as the dust"), whilst on the third is inscribed another portion of the same verse reading כקש נדף קשתו (*K'kash nidaf kashto*—"his bow as the driven stubble"), and on the fourth stone the opening phrase from *Psalm 11:2* reading כי הנה הרשעים ידרכון *(Ki hineh har'sha'im yid'r'chun*—"For, lo, the wicked bend the bow"). Having written the magical seal on all four stones conjointly with their respectively associated biblical phrases, the task is completed by casting the rocks into the arena of the enemy.[21] *Curiouser and curiouser! cried Alice.....!*

Curiously enough, the letters comprising the opening portion of *Exodus 15:3,* are intertwined with a portion of the "Forty-two Letter Name of God," and a section of *Numbers 21:14*, in order to create the following *Kamea*, utilised for the purpose of bringing about "justice" in the most powerful manner possible:[22]

הַשֵׁן	וְעֶכׇ	הרֹלׄ	יׇקֻעַ
מִגֶר	שְׁנַמ	יִנׇא	אׇטִי
הָשֵׁר	מֶכׇפׇ	חִיֶם	לׇדִב
הַצֶמׄ	וֹרֹחׇ	הַטֶל	יבׇמׄ

Starting with the top row reading horizontally from right to left, the first letters in each block spell the opening phrase from *Exodus 15:3* reading יהוה מלחמה איש יהוה (*YHVH ish milchamah YHVH*—"*YHVH* is a man of war *YHVH*"). Reading the second letters similarly spells a portion of the "Forty-two Letter Name of God," i.e. קרע שטנ נגד יכש בטר צ (*karo' satan' nagida yeicheisha bitaro tza*). Lastly, the third letters in each block, when again read horizontally from right to left, reveal the segment of *Numbers 21:14* reading על כן יאמר בספר מלחמ[ת] (*al ken ye'amar b'sefer milcham*[ot]—"wherefore it is said in the book of the war[s]*"*).

We are informed that the Hebrew characters מ and ח, appearing in the words מלחמה (*milchamah*—"war") and מלחמת (*milchamot* —"wars"), and which conjointly spell the Hebrew word for "hot" (חם—*Cham*), are particularly potent in triggering the "intense heat" (מחום—"*michom*") of Divine Judgment. Furthermore, the sixteen tri-letter Divine Names formed from the intertwining of the said verses and the "Forty-two Letter Name," are said to indicate the sixteen edges of the "correcting sword" of "the Holy One, blessed be He."[23] I have previously made some reference to "the remarkable powers of the sixteen-edged divine sword," with particular reference to its special potency to "diminish the powers of the pestilence and other *mazikin* (malevolent forces) and the granting of a meaningful life."[24]

Be that as it may, another interesting application of the *Tetragrammaton* in Hebrew amulets, pertains to the so called "Twelve Letter Name of God," i.e. the twelve permutations of the Ineffable Name, or "Twelve Banners," which is in this instance arranged in a magic square.[25] In this regard, the following order is correct:

יוהה	יההו	יהוה
הדיו	הויה	הוהי
ויהה	וההי	והיה
ההוי	היוה	היהו

We are informed that this magical glyph has wondrous powers, amongst which is said to be great pleasure and joviality; strengthening of virility; and special protection against injurious forces.[26] Curiously enough, this very magic square was incorporated in a Hebrew-Christian amulet which we are told was amongst a number of amulets employed in the 17th century by Jewish converts to Christianity.[27] It appeared in publication in the following two variant formats:

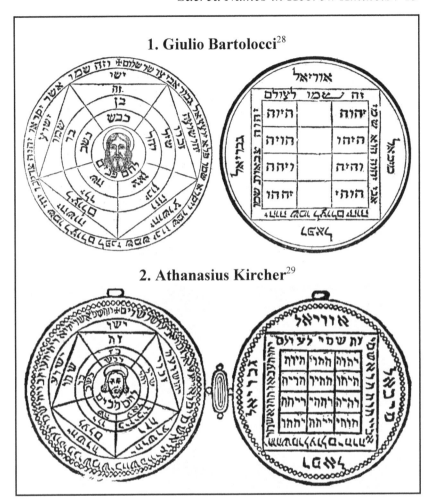

1. Giulio Bartolocci[28]

2. Athanasius Kircher[29]

The presentation of the twelve permutations are clearly faulty in both illustrations. Theodor Schrire analysed a very poor cast-lead copy of this amulet, which he mentioned was dug up in France.[30] Since portions of the inscription were illegible, and he appeared to be unaware of the published versions, Schrire's analysis of the item is incomplete. I had the good fortune of perusing an excellent cast-bronze copy of this item held in a private American numismatic collection. In that instance the twelve permutations were correct and arranged in perfect order.

As far as the remainder of the inscription on the amulet is concerned, we notice that the front portion comprises the haloed head of the Christian Saviour located in the centre of a pentagon with the subscript פנים לחם (*lechem panim*—"shew bread"). Christian tradition considers the twelve loaves of "Shew Bread" in the biblical Tabernacle/Temple, to be a prefiguration of the "Body of Christ" as represented in the bread/wafers of the Mass/ Communion Service. The remainder of the front portion of the amulet in question, is divided into three further layers, and the whole enclosed in an outer circle. The inscription in the outer border is easily traced in Bartolocci's presentation, reading:

וזה שמו אשר יקרא יהוה צדקנו (*Jeremiah 23:6*)

יהי שמו לעולם לפני שמש ינון שמו (*Psalm 72:17*)

ויקרא שמו פלא יועץ אל גבור אבי (*Isaiah 9:5* [6])

עד שר שלום

Transliteration:

> (*Jeremiah 23:6*) *v'zeh sh'mo asher yikra YHVH tzid'keinu*
> (*Psalm 72:17*) *y'hi sh'mo l'olam lifnei shemesh yinon sh'mo*
> (*Isaiah 9:5* [6]) *vayikra sh'mo pele-yo'etz-el-gibbor-abi-ad-sar-shalom*

Translation:

> (*Jeremiah 23:6*) and this is his name whereby he shall be called, *YHVH* is our righteousness
> (*Psalm 72:17*) May his name endure for ever; may his name be continued as long as the sun.
> (*Isaiah 9:5* [4]) and his name is called *pele-yo'etz-el-gibbor-abi-ad-sar-shalom*

Below the outer circle and external to the pentagon we trace five names assigned to the Christian Saviour at the time, i.e. ישו (*Yesu* [?]); ישוע (*Yeshua*); יהשוה (*Yeh'shua* [?]); יהושוע (*Yehoshuah*); and יהושועה (*Yehoshuah* [?]). Of the five appellatives only two are actually proper names in Hebrew. I have previously addressed the construct יהשוה, a Renaissance invention to which some fanciful mystical attributions were made.[31] Some consider this a "great invention," whilst it is totally phoney.

Now, the first layer of the hexagon portion comprises a five worded phrase reading זה שמו לעולם וזה זכרי (*zeh sh'mo l'olam v'zeh zichrei* [זכרו—*zichro* according to Bartolocci]—"this is his eternal name and this is my memorial"). The five words comprising the second layer, i.e. בן (*ben*—"son"); בר (*bar*—"son"); ילד (*yeled*—"boy"); ינון (*Yinon* according to Bartolocci, which is one of the appellatives traditionally employed in reference to the Messiah),[32] and שיל (probably שלה—*Shilah* or *Shiloh*), appear to be references to the "sonship" of the Christian Saviour, but the concluding two terms are somewhat difficult to ascertain. As indicated, the concluding term could read *Shilah* or *Shiloh*. The latter term is particularly relevant, since Kabbalists ascertained some connection between this word and the Messiah.[33]

The third layer of the amulet in question appears to comprise five Hebrew words referring to a lamb or sheep, i.e. כבש (*Kevesh*—"Lamb"); כשב (*Keshev*—"Lamb"); שה (*Sheh*—"Lamb"); צאן (*Tzan*—"Sheep"); and רחל (*Rachel*—"Sheep [Ewe lamb]"). All of these are understandable in terms of the Christian Saviour being called the "Lamb of God."

As noted earlier, the reverse of the amulet comprises the twelve permutations of the Ineffable Name, as well as the Names of the four main archangels, i.e. אוריאל (*Ori'el*) [top]; רפאל (*Rafa'el*) [bottom]; מיכאל (*Micha'el*) [right] and גבריאל (*Gavri'el*) [left]. The inscriptions along the four borders of the central construct read: (top) זה שמי לעולם (*zeh sh'mi l'olam*—"this is my name forever") (*Exodus 3:15*); (left) יהוה צבאות שמו (*YHVH Tzva'ot sh'mo*—"*YHVH* of Hosts is His Name*") (*Jeremiah 10:16; 51:19*); [bottom] יהוה שמו לעולם יהוה (*YHVH sh'mo l'olam YHVH*—*YHVH* is His Name forever *YHVH*), and [right] אני יהוה הוא שמי (*Ani YHVH hu Sh'mi*—"I am *YHVH*, that is My name*") (*Isaiah 42:8*).

In addressing the extensive employment of the Ineffable Name in Hebrew amulets, we need to consider two very important Divine Names which comprise the conjunction of יהוה (*YHVH*) and אדני (*Adonai*), i.e. יאהדונהי and איהדיונהי.[34] To understand the uniqueness of these Divine Name combinations, we need to consider that in Kabbalah the Ineffable Name is employed with

specific reference to the sphere of *Tiferet* (Beauty) on the sefirotic
Tree, whilst the Name *Adonai* pertains to the sphere of *Malchut*
(Kingdom). We are often reminded of the particular fascination
Kabbalists have with the relationship between *Tiferet* and *Malchut*
in Jewish Mysticism. Respectively these two *sefirot* represent:

Tiferet	*Malchut*
יהוה (*YHVH*)	אדני (*Adonai*)
Sun (Direct Light)	Moon (Reflected Light)
King	Queen
Upper	Lower
Male Principle	Female Principle
Beloved	Lover
Husband	Bride

Engendering a "sacred marriage" between *Tiferet* (King) and
Malchut (Queen-*Shechinah*), or the male and female aspects of the
Divine One, is understood to be "the most important task that the
mystic assumes in his quest."[35] In this regard, the sexual act itself
is a physical expression of the "sacred union" of the Divine Male
and Female Principles, i.e. when undertaken with the fully
focussed intention of unifying the "Eternal One" (Divine Father)
and the *Shechinah* (Divine Mother).[36] We have been reminded that
"*sexual intimacy* within the life of God is the paradigmatic
expression of divine wholeness."[37] Also, whilst we note the sexual
act being employed with the intention of encouraging a "Sacred
Marriage" between the masculine and feminine aspects of the
Divine One, the visualisation and mental expression of יאהדונהי
(*Yahadonai* or *Yahadonahi*) is equally understood to facilitate the
said "Sacred Marriage."

This topic needs careful investigation, which cannot be
accommodated within the scope of this tome in which we are
considering the talismanic uses of Hebrew Divine Names. Hence,
it has to be assigned to a future volume in this series, and we have
to return to a perusal of יאהדונהי, sometimes called the "Eight
Letter Name of God," which, as indicated in the following table,
is portrayed in *Shiviti* plaques, *Kameot*, Kabbalistic *Siddurim*
(prayer books), etc.,[38] in a variety of decorative ways:

As noted earlier, two Divine Name constructs result from the conjunction of the Ineffable Name and *Adonai*, i.e. יאהדונהי and איהדונוה. The first combination, considered to be "solar," aligns with "*B'rachot*" (Blessings), i.e. the channeling of "Direct Light" from *Tiferet* (Beauty) to *Malchut* (Kingdom), whilst the second combination, understood to be "lunar," pertains to "*Kadishim*" (Sanctifications), i.e. the redirection of the Reflected Light back from *Malchut* (the "Lower Splendour") to *Tiferet* (the "Supernal Splendour"). This interplay between the mentioned *sefirot* refers to our relationship with the "Eternal Living Spirit." It is a kind of "inner sexuality" between the "Infinite One" and our "Selves," in which there is a continuous flow of "Divine Light" generated and projected by Divinity to us, which we then have to refocus and return for renewal in the "wholeness" of the "One-Beyond-All-Being," from whence it is reprojected to us, and so forth.

Contemplation of the said two Divine Name constructs in the following simple *Kamea*, is not only understood to facilitate the union of the Divine One and the *Shechinah*, but is said to facilitate the process of "opening the heart" in alignment with the "Spiritual Powers" inherent in the Divine Names. The fundamental motive is to literally infuse oneself with "Divine Force," in order to engender the unencumbered flow of "Divine Abundance" not only in ones life, but also outwards into the wider realm of physical manifestation.

As can be clearly seen, this *Kamea* is mainly comprised of the Ineffable Name/*Adonai* conjunction. The header reads:

אדון הכל היה הוה ויהיה

Transliteration:
> *Adon ha-kol hayah hoveh v'yiyeh*

Translation:
> Lord of all that was, is and will be.

Located centrally in bold decorative glyphs is the Ineffable Name, which includes the Divine Name *Adonai* in its concluding *Heh*. Centrally above the Ineffable Name, and below it at the right margin is located the combination יאהדונהי. In turn, on the same level at the left margin we trace אידהנויה. Next, positioned directly below the listed two Divine Name constructs, we read to the right ברוך הוא (*Baruch hu*—"Blessed be He") and to the left

וברוך שמו (*u-varuch shemo*—"and blessed be His Name). The first "blessing" statement is aligned with the first two letters of the Ineffable Name (יה), whilst the second is associated with the concluding two letters (וה). The *Kamea* is concluded with the curious Divine Name combination עששייצ, which I will be addressing in greater detail shortly.

In conclusion, it is worth noting that the יאהדונהי (*Yahadonai*) Divine Name construct, also known as the "Eight Letter Name of God,"[39] features particularly prominently as a superscript in Hebrew amulets from Kurdistan.[40] We are reminded that the *gematria* of this Divine Name [י = 10 + א = 1 + ה = 5 + ד = 4 + ו = 6 + נ = 50 + ה = 5 + י = 10 = 91], which is equivalent of that of the word אמן (*Amen* [א = 1 + מ = 40 + נ = 50 = 91]). This is said to "reinforce" the sanctity of the "Eight Letter Name."[41]

D. שדי—*Shadai*

As noted in my "*Book of Sacred Names*," the Name שדי (*Shadai*) refers to the "All-sufficient Unlimited One," and whilst there has been much debate and speculation as to what this very ancient Divine Name really signifies, "it is generally accepted that it means 'Almighty'." I also noted that "some scholars conjectured that the Name was derived from *Shadu*, the ancient Akkadian word meaning 'mountain.' Thus the 'Almighty' would be seen to be strong, fortified, immutable....."[42] The power of protection is associated with this Name, hence it appears as the single Divine Name engraved on the surface of small metal *Kameot* of all shapes and sizes.[43] I have inspected several such *Shadai* amulets in the magnificent collection of Hebrew amulets housed in the Magnes Museum in Berkeley.

Be that as it may, שדי (*Shadai*), or at least the initial of this Divine Name, adorns the front of every *Mezuzah*, an item comprised of a biblical inscription which is affixed to the doors of Jewish homes. Whilst it fulfills a religious function in our day, there are many who, like our mediaeval ancestors,[44] still consider it to be a protection amulet of the most potent kind. As in the case of the earlier mentioned *Monogrammaton*, in which a ה (*Heh*) is the single letter abbreviation of the Ineffable Name, the initial שׁ (*Shin*) represents the Name *Shadai*, and both of these Hebrew letters appear in this singular format on many ancient and modern amulets.[45]

The letters comprising the Name שׁדי (*Shadai*) are also sometimes arranged in the form of a letter square. In this regard, I have recently perused an amulet ring the front of which is comprised of the following *Shadai* square:

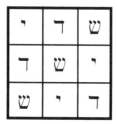

The Divine Name in question comprises six permutations, which can be traced on this *chotam*. However, the listed format of the *Shadai* square is by no means standard. For example, this letter arrangement is very different from the following version presented in the famous *Toldot Adam*:[46]

שׁ	ד	י
ה	י	שׁ
י	שׁ	ה

The six permutations of *Shadai* (שׁדי) are also at times employed in *Kameot*. Consider the following amulet, the intention of which is to save oneself from plagues and epidemics.[47] The amulet comprises the following Divine Names:

וְלָד אָבְוּ יָאָז וַלַל וְלָב
שָׁדִי שִׁיד דִישׁ דְשִׁי יְשַׁד יְדַשׁ

This set of Divine Names was constructed from the initials of the words comprising *Leviticus 26:5* reading:

והשיג לכם דיש את בציר ובציר ישיג את זרע ואכלתם
לחמכם לשבע וישבתם לבטח בארצכם

Transliteration:

> *v'hisig lachem dayish et batzir uvatzir yasig et zara va'achaltem lach'm'chem lasova vishav'tem lavetach b'artz'chem*

Translation:

> And your threshing shall reach unto the vintage, and the vintage shall reach unto the sowing time; and ye shall eat your bread until ye have enough, and dwell in your land safely.

The six permutations of the Name *Shadai* (שׁד״י) in the earlier mentioned Divine Name construct, refer to the word דיש (*dayish*—"threshing") in the associated biblical verse, this term being itself one of the permutations of the Divine Name in question. As it is, the mentioned six permutations relate to the twelve zodiacal periods, of which I have perused two versions. In one version the zodiacal months are aligned in pairs in direct order to the six permutations of *Shadai*, i.e. *Aries/Taurus*—שׁד״י; *Gemini/Leo*—שׁי״ד; etc. I was taught the following order of *Shadai/Zodiacal* affiliations, which was said to be correct. It also agrees with related details addressed in the previous volume of this series:[48]

Permutation	Zodiacal Period	
שׁדי	*Taleh (Aries)*	*Moznaim (Libra)*
שׁיד	*Shor (Taurus)*	*Akrav (Scorpio)*
דיש	*Teomim (Gemini)*	*Keshet (Sagittarius)*
דשׁי	*Sartan (Cancer)*	*Gedi (Capricorn)*
ישׁד	*Aryeh (Leo)*	*Deli (Aquarius)*
ידשׁ	*Betulah (Virgo)*	*Dagin (Pisces)*

We are informed that the Divine Names should be written on a kosher lambskin scroll together with the *Shadai* permutation pertaining to the month or zodiacal period in which you are constructing the amulet. It is understood that the listed Divine Names act in conjunction with the said permutation, in order to protect a home and all within it from an epidemic or plague. It is subsequently located at the entrance of ones own or any other residence.[49]

Should you be in any doubt regarding the correct *Shadai* permutation aligned with the specific period in which you might be composing this amulet, you could simply include all six permutations of the said Divine Name. In this manner, the correct one will be effective at the time, and the rest will, as it were, join the "process of empowerment" over the succeeding months, all depending on how long the amulet remains on your front door.

Be that as it may, the six permutations equally feature in the following protection *Kamea*, in which they are aligned with the six letters of the Name תפתפיה (*Taftafyah*), as well as with the six points of the hexagram:

The inscription in the centre of the amulet reads:

על צבא יהיה לו לצבא על מגן יהיה לו למגן צוה
פחד בשם פחדיאל

Transliteration:

> *Al tz'va yiyeh lo l'tzva al magen yiyeh lo l'magen tzaveh*
> *pachad b'shem Pachdi'el*

Translation:

> The host [forces] will be the host, the shield will be the
> shield commanding fear in the name of *Pachdi'el*

As shown in several instances in this tome, the Name *Shadai* is
often utilised in Hebrew amulets in conjunction with other Divine
Names and magical symbols. In the following instance it is
employed conjointly with the Ineffable Name, for the purposes of
reversing the ill fortune of a woman whose sons die in infancy:[50]

The curious Divine Name construct in the centre comprises the
initials of the words of *Exodus 23:26* reading:

לא תהיה משכלה ועקרה בארצך את מספר ימיך אמלא

Transliteration:

> *Lo tih'yeh m'shakelah va'akarah b'artzecha et mispar*
> *yamecha amalei*

Translation:

> None shall miscarry, nor be barren, in thy land; the number
> of thy days I will fulfil.

The vowels employed in the said Divine Name construct, are exactly those aligned with the initial letters of the words in the biblical phrase. These vowels are also aligned with the four appearances of the Ineffable Name, the order being top right, top left, bottom right and bottom left. As you have probably noticed, the additional concluding two vowels employed in the Ineffable Name bottom left, do not appear in the central Divine Name construct. They were derived from the two vowels of the word אמן (*Omein*—"*Amen*").

We are informed that the angel associated with this *Kamea* is שמעאל (*Shma'el*), however I think this angelic reference pertains to שמעיאל (*Shmai'el*), an angel from the angelic caste of the אופנים (*Ofanim*). Be that as it may, I would personally include the angelic Name in the *Kamea*, perhaps on the rear of the amulet. There are several references to this "Spirit Intelligence" in Jewish magic.[51]

However, to achieve the intended aim of this current *Kamea*, one is instructed to create four copies of the amulet respectively to be hung on the four corners of the house in which the mentioned unfortunate woman resides. Curiously enough, the Divine Name לתמובאמיא, when conjoined with the four letters of the Ineffable Name, affords us a set of three Divine Names, which are equally employed to forfend miscarriage. These are:

$$\text{יִלְהָתוּמָה יִוְהִבְוָאָה יִמְהִיִוָאָה}$$

In order to achieve the stated aim, these Divine Names should be engraved on a silver disk, which is afterwards placed inside a little container, i.e. a locket, to be worn on the person of the individual needing this support.[52]

In another instance the listed initials of the mentioned verse from *Exodus* are formed into the following letter square, which is employed conjointly with the Names of eleven "Spirit Intelligences" for the very purpose of aiding a woman who has suffered a miscarriage or who has lost infant sons:[53]

בְּ	נִ	מְ	תָ	ל
לְ	בְּ	נִ	מְ	תָ
תָ	לְ	בְּ	נִ	מְ
מְ	תָ	לְ	בְּ	נִ
נִ	מְ	תָ	לְ	בְּ

Inscribe the *chotam* (magical seal) at the top of a deerskin parchment or kosher scroll. Next write the following incantation below the letter square:

יהי רצון מלפניך שומר נפשות חסידיו שתשמור פרי
בטנה של נושאת קמיע זה עליה מכל נזק ומקרה רע
ומהפסד היסודות כי אין שומר ורופא מבלעדיך
כדכתיב אם יהוה לא יבנה בית שוא עמלו בוניו בו
אנא מלא רחמים חוס וחמול ורחם עליה ולא תשכל
פרי בטנה עוד אמן נצח סלה ועד אמן כן יהי רצון

Transliteration:

Y'hi ratzon milfanecha shomer nefashot chasidav shetishmor pri bitnah shel noset kamea zeh aleah mikol nezek umikre ra v'mehefsed ha-yesodot ki ein shomer v'rofe mibil'adecha k'dektiv (Psalm 127:1) im YHVH lifneh vayit shav am'lu vonav bo, ana male rachamim chus v'chamol v'rachem aleah v'lo teshakel pri bitnah od Omein Netzach Selah Va'ed Omein ken y'hi ratzon

Translation:

May it be your will, He who protects the souls of His devotees, to safeguard the fruit of her belly with this amulet she is carrying on her, from all harm and bad incidents, from the loss of the foundations, since there is nobody else who protects and heals besides You, as it is written (*Psalm*

127:1) "Except *YHVH* build the house, they labour in vain that build it." Please grant compassion, protect and have pity and mercy on her that she will no more loose the fruit of her belly. *Amen*, Enduring (Victory), *Selah*, Forever. *Amen* thus be it so willed.

Continue by appending to the incantation the following abbreviation with vowels of *Psalm 33*:

רַצָּב לָנָת הֹלָב בְּעָז לֹשַׁל שִׁחָהֶ נַבְכ יָדְי וְמַב אֹצּוּ חֵימָ
הָבִי שָׁנוּ פְּכָצ כֻּכַּם הַנֹב תִּימֶ כָּהָם יָכִי תֶכֹב אָנֹה צֻוִי
הֵעָג הֵמַע עֵיל תַּמַל לְוָא הַאֵי אֶהָב לֹלְם הִירְך אֶכָב הָמֵשׁ
הֹאָב יְהָה יַלֹה אֶכֶּם אֹהֵן בְּחָג לִיֹּב כֻּשֶׁה לֹוֹח לִיֹה עַיָא
יְלַל לְמֵנ וּבָּנ חַלַע וְהֶכ בִּיל כִּבְכָּן בָּיֹח יְעָב יֻחַל

Transliteration:

> *Ratzaba lanat' holab' b'aza losilo sichahei nabiki yad'y'
> v'mabe otz'u che'y'ma habiy' sana'u pichatz' kokamei
> hanob' t'yimei kahami yakayo teikihu avahu tzivay'
> hei'ago heima'a ay'l' tamali l'va'a ha'ay' ehaba l'lomi
> hiy'ra ebab' hamishi hi'eba yohaha yaliha ekama eihano
> b'chagi loyib' koseha li'uchei loy'hi eiy'e y'lal' l'mina
> ubana chila'e uhuki boyili kiv'ka vay'cha y'aka yichala*

As an aside, this abbreviation of *Psalm 33* is equally employed on its own in an amulet to aid women who suffer miscarriages incessantly, or who cannot fall pregnant. In this instance the abbreviation is written on the inside of a bowl, or on a piece of parchment to be placed inside the bowl. The writing is dissolved in water, which is afterwards consumed by the woman seeking spiritual protection or to fall pregnant. This is done on the night of her *Mikveh* (ritual bath).[54]

Be that as it may, the earlier *Kamea*, i.e. the one comprised of the letter square as well as the names of eleven Spirit Intelligences, is concluded with a set of special Divine and Angelic Names, specifically:

סנוי סנסנוי סמנגלף יאהקותה בדפטיאל פדפדס
שמרירון עזרירון אנרנל צמרכד עשציי

Transliteration:

> *Sanoi Sansanoi Semangelof YAHKVTH B'dafti'el Pad'padas Shamriron Azriron Enar'nal Tzamarchad Ashtzei*

Whilst we are addressing some of these Angelic Names and Divine Names elsewhere in this text, it is worth noting the importance of two of those listed here. The first is בדפטיאל (*B'dafti'el* [some say *Badpati'el*])[55] which is termed the "Holy Light."[56] We are informed that the name of the angel *B'dafti'el* prevents miscarriages, and appears "only on amulets that are made to assist women in childbed."[57] However, it is worth noting that it is one of the angelic names employed to banish demonic imps and evil spirits from a residence.[58] We are told *B'dafti'el* is aligned with the term במוכסז (*B'mochsaz*),[59] the latter referring to, as it were, the "severe" (*Gevurah*) aspect of the word אלהינו (*Eloheinu*).

It is said that if you recall the name *B'dafti'el* when you travel around at night, you will have no fear since no harm will befall you, and you will not be beset by any injurious spirits. It is worth noting that the *gematria* of בדפטיאל (*B'dafti'el*) [ב = 2 + ד = 4 + פ = 80 + ט = 9 + י = 10 + א = 1 + ל = 30 = 136] is equal to that of the word קול (*Kol*—"voice," "sound" and "thunder" [ק = 100 + ו = 6 + ל = 30 = 136]). In this regard we are reminded that the *gematria* of the full spelling of the letters comprising the word קול, i.e. קוף, ואו and למד [ק = 100 + ו = 6 + פ = 80 + ו = 6 + א = 1 + ו = 6 + ל = 30 + מ = 40 + ד = 4 = 273], is equal to that of the word גער (*Ga'ar*—"to scold" [ג = 3 + ע = 70 + ר = 200 = 273]). In this regard, it is understood that the "voice" of *B'dafti'el* "rebukes" all evil, including the *Klipot* (demonic shards).[60]

The second Divine Name we have to consider is אנרנל (*Enar'nal*). This Name is good in all *Kameot* created for healing purposes, and was derived from the phrase אל נא רפא נא לה (*El na r'fa na la*—"Heal her now *El*, I beseech Thee") (*Numbers 12:13*).[61] The Divine Name in question appears in a number of amulets.[62]

Now, there is a simpler practice in which the Name *Shadai* is employed to aid a woman who has lost her sons. In this instance seven coins are collected from seven pregnant ladies. These coins are conjoined into a single disc on which the Name שדי (*Shadai*) is engraved, which is afterwards placed in the hand of the sorely afflicted woman.[63] In contrast to other similar practices listed elsewhere in this tome, this specific working does not appear to require any prior purification or, for that matter, any special prior preparation.

The Name שדי (*Shadai*) is also said to alleviate the plight of a woman who has suffered a miscarriage. In this instance one starts the procedure by writing *Psalm 55:9* [8] and *Genesis 21:1* on deerskin parchment, or a sheet of clean good quality paper. It is good to verbalise the words as one writes them. The said verses read:

(*Psalm 55:9* [8]) אחישה מפלט לי מרוח סעה מסער

(*Genesis 21:1*) ויהוה פקד את שרה כאשר אמר

Transliteration:

> (*Psalm 55:9* [8]) *Achishah miflat li meiruach so'ah misa'ar*
> (*Genesis 22:1*) *v'YHVH pakad et Sarah ka'asher amar*

Translation:

> (*Psalm 55:9* [8]) I would haste me to a shelter from the stormy wind and tempest.
> (*Genesis 22:1*) And *YHVH* remembered Sarah as He had said.

Next continue, by writing the following incantation:

בשם שדי תהא קמיע זו ל[פלונית בת פלונית] שלא
תפיל ילדיה ולא מטפת דם המפלת לא יהיה משכל
ומשכלה בשם אהיה אשר אהיה יה יהוה ובשם מיכאל
גבריאל רפאל דניאל כתותיאל פניאל סנוי סנסנוי
סמנגלף אמן נצח סלה ועד

Transliteration:

> *B'shem Shadai tehe kamea zu l'[.....Plonit bat Plonit.....] shelo tapil yeladeiah v'lo mitipat dam ha-mapelet lo yiyeh miskal v'miskalah b'shem Ehyeh asher Ehyeh YH YHVH ub'shem Micha'el Gavri'el Rafa'el Dani'el Katuti'el Pani'el Sanoi Sansanoi Semangelof Omein Netzach Selah Va-ed*

Translation:

> In the Name *Shadai* this amulet will be for [.....fill in the
> name of the sufferer.....] that she will not abort her
> children, and not emit any blood of a miscarriage, and will
> not loose boys or girls. In the Name *Ehyeh asher Ehyeh YH
> YHVH* and in the name *Micha'el Gavri'el Rafa'el Dani'el
> Katuti'el Pani'el Sanoi Sansanoi Semangelof Amen*,
> Enduring (Victory), *Selah*, Forever.

Afterwards the *Kamea* is carried on the arm of the woman in
question.[64]

E. Enigmatic Divine Names

1. אגלא—*Agala'a* (also *Agulo'o, Agula, Agli, Agila*, etc.)

As explained fairly extensively in *"The Book of Sacred Names,"*
whilst the Divine Name אגלא (*Agala'a*) "is generally associated
with the sphere of *Malchut* (Kingdom) on the sefirotic Tree, it has
been claimed that it pertains to *Gevurah* (Might)."[65] This magical
Divine Name is an acronym constructed from a phrase in the
Amidah prayer:

אתה גיבור לעולם אדני

Transliteraton:
> *Atah Gibor l'Olam Adonai*

Translation:
> You are mighty throughout eternity *Adonai*

I have discussed the inherent power of this remarkable Name in
great detail in the previous volume of the Shadow Tree Series. As
noted in that text, the Name *Agala'a* is mainly utilised for security
purposes in Hebrew amulets, and whilst I cited its employment in
amulets meant to calm a stormy sea, avert the "Evil Eye,"
extinguish a fire, alleviate a fever, and for healing in general, etc.,
I also acknowledged its application in amulets intended to cultivate
a good memory.[66]

We are informed that אגלאא (*Agala'a*) is the appellative of the שר של גבורה (*Sar shel Gevurah*—"Prince of Severity [Strength]"), hence this Divine Name is associated with the Element of Fire, and sometimes employed in conjunction with the Name יוהך (*Yohach*), for the purposes of freeing oneself from confinement in a prison. Be that as it may, the Name אגלאא (*Agala'a*) appears in several of the *Kameot* included in this text. As noted, this is mainly for purposes of protection.

2. אזבוגה—*Azbogah* (*Azbugah*)

The Name *Azbogah* is said to be good for rescue or deliverance. Titled the "*Shem ha-Sheminit*" ("The Name of the Eights"), because the *gematria* of each of its three component letter pairs is eight (א [1] + ז [7] = 8; ב [2] + ו [6] = 8; ג [3] + ה [5] = 8), this Divine Name is also said to be one of the seventy Names of *Metatron*, the "Prince of the Face."[68] We are told that the Name אזבוגה (*Azbogah*) was derived from *Exodus 15:1*:

אז ישיר משה ובני ישראל את השירה הזאת ליהוה
ויאמרו לאמר אשירה ליהוה כי גאה גאה

> Transliteration:
>> *Az yashir mosheh uvnei yisra'el et ha-shirah ha-zot la-YHVH va-yomeru leimor ashirah la-YHVH ki ga'oh ga'ah*
>
> Translation:
>> Then sang Moses and the children of Israel this song unto *YHVH*, and spoke, saying 'I will sing unto *YHVH*, for He is highly exalted'

Azbogah has been attributed to *Binah* (Understanding) on the sefirotic tree,[69] and this unique Name is both a Divine Name and the title of an angelic "Prince," and we are informed that the term "*Azbogah*" originated from the words אזר (*izer*—"to gird") and בגד (*beged*—"a garment"). Hence I noted in "*The Book of Sacred Names*" "the divine appointment of this awesome 'Celestial

Prince' to clothe (gird) the 'righteous and pious of the world with the garments of life and wrap them in the cloak of life, that they may live in them an eternal life'," and that these "special 'garments of life,' also called 'garments of glory,' refer to immortal spirit bodies understood to be 'bodies of light'."[70]

Considering these details regarding "garments of glory," we might have a greater sense as to the meaning of the statement that the Name אזבוגה (*Azbogah*) pertains to the twenty-four adornments of the כלה (*Kalah* —"the Bride"),[71] the latter being a reference to the *Shechinah*, the "Divine Bride" or feminine aspect of Divinity. However, it is generally acknowledged that the twenty-four "Adornments of the Divine Bride" comprise the Hebrew Bible, i.e. *Torah* (the five books of Moses); *Nevi'im* (the seven books of the Prophets), and *Ketuvim* (the nine books called "Writings"), twenty-four in all.[72]

In case you wonder why the Hebrew Bible is suddenly reduced to twenty-four books only, it should be noted that in Jewish tradition 1st and 2nd *Samuel* are considered to be one book. The same applies to 1st and 2nd *Kings*, as well as 1st and 2nd *Chronicles*. *Ezra* and *Nehemiah* are also thought of as being one tome, and likewise the twelve minor prophets are said to be a single book.

3. אתניק—*Atneik* (also *Etn'yika*, etc.)

The Name אתניק (*Atneik*) is ranked amongst a set of Divine Names which are collectively titled the "Signature of God."[73] Whilst it is understood that this Divine Name relates to the sphere of *Tiferet* (Beauty) in some measure, we are informed it pertains more to the *sefirah* of *Gevurah* (Severity), hence it is employed to conquer enemies.[74] It is said to have been derived from the a phrase in *Exodus 6:5* reading:

את נאקת בני ישראל

Transliteration:
Et na'akat b'nei Yisra'el
Translation:
The groaning of the children of Israel.

We are informed that the Divine Name in question also pertains to the expression וַתֵּלֶד אֶת קַיִן (*va-teled et Kain*—"give birth to Cain"), the expression אֵת קַיִן being a permutation of אתניק (*Atneik*). Since the biblical personage Cain relates again to *Gevurah* (Severity), this emphasises the direct links of the Name *Atneik* to this *sefirah* on the sefirotic tree. In this regard, it is worth noting that the *Etn'yika* vocalisation of the Divine Name is derived from the respective vowels associated with the component letters of the Name in the expression "*et Kain.*"[75]

However, the Divine Name אתניק (*Atneik*) is also employed in an amuletic procedure to "open your heart," i.e. expand your consciousness to greater comprehension or to embrace a greater whole, so to speak. We are told that the tradition regarding this "opening of the heart" was brought by Moses from Mount Sinai, and that he passed it on to Joshua, his successor.[76] Since then it has been passed on from one individual to the next over a lengthy period, and now I am sharing it with an English readership.

Be that as it may, the procedure necessitates writing the following eight Divine Names respectively on eight myrtle leaves, i.e. one Divine Name per leaf, in the following order:

4.	3.	2.	1.
ורחש] זחש	אחש	גליל	אתניק
8.	7.	6.	5.
אבש	ולס	ילס	אסעפס

Afterwards you have to fill eight small containers with wine, and then dissolve the eight Divine Names respectively in the eight containers of wine. Ensure that you dissolve one Name per container, by dipping the myrtle leaf in the wine and moving it to and fro until it is washed clean of any writing. It is also important to mark the containers in exact numerical order, since the wine is consumed one container a day over an eight day period, and this should occur in the listed order of the said Divine Names.[77]

An important factor here is to keep silent about anything which might be contributing to your subsequent "awakening," even if such "revelation" comes via the written word in a book. The result will be:

ה״ יאיר עינינו בתורתו נצח סלה ועד אמן כן
יהי רצון

Transliteration:

Ha-Shem ya'ir eineinu b'Torato, Netzach Selah Va'ed Omein ken y'hi ratzon

Translation:

The Divine One will light our eyes unto his Law, Enduring (Victory), *Selah*, Forever, *Amen* thus be it so willed.[78]

4. ביט—*BYT*

This Name was derived from *Psalm 91:14* in which the Divine One proclaims כי בי חשק ואפלטהו (*Ki vi chashak va'afalteihu* — "Because he hath set his love upon Me." It is said the Name ביט pertains to Sacred Oil, since the letter combination of the Divine Name is transposed by means of the *Atbash* cipher (א = ה; ב = ש) to read שמן (*Shemen*—"oil"). On the other hand, when we employ another well-known Kabbalistic cipher, i.e. the *Albam* cipher (א = ל; ב = מ), the Divine Name in question indicates an association with the word שמר (*Shamar*) meaning to "keep," "observe," "guard," etc. In this regard we are informed that the Name ביט "guards" or protects us against evil forces, e.g. *shedin* (fiends), *mazikin* (harmful forces), *ruchot* (evil spirits), etc. In fact, the Name in question is said to have been granted the power to protect us against all baneful powers. As it is, the Name ביט can be employed to alleviate physical suffering. In this instance the individual in distress should write the Name with saffron on a piece of paper, then dissolve the writing in a little water, and afterwards drink the infusion.[79]

Curiously enough, the *gematria* (numerical value) of ביט [ב = 2 + י = 10 + ט = 9 = 21] equates with that of the Names אהיה

(*Ehyeh* [א = 1 + ה = 5 + י = 10 + ה = 5 = 21]) and יהו (*IAO* or *Yehu* [י = 10 + ה = 5 + ו = 6 = 21]). The meaning of this is hinted at in *Isaiah 40:11* where we read בזרעו יקבץ טלאים (*Bizro'o y'kabetz t'la'im*— "that gathereth the lambs in his arm." We are also instructed that the Name ביט is etched in the very brain of *Tahari'el* (טהריאל), the angel whose name means "Purity of God," who is said to be in charge of the celestial realm of "white sapphire" in the "World of Creation" (העולם הבריאה—*Olam ha-Bri'ah*), and who supports the ascent of the *Neshamah* (Divine Self) into this lofty sphere.[80]

Now, the name ביט is especially employed in amulets intended to relieve suffering. In this regard, we are informed that anyone suffering from pain, illness, etc., will find relief by writing the Divine Name in question with saffron on a piece of parchment. Afterwards the writing is dissolved in a bowl or glass of water, and the infused liquid consumed.[81]

Certain *Kameot* comprise the six permutations of ביט, specifically:

ביט בטי יטב

יבט טבי טיב

The "secret" of these permutations is said to pertain to the phrase in *Deuteronomy 10:7* reading יטבתה ארץ נחלי מים (*Yotvatah eretz nachalei mayim*—"Jotbah, a land of brooks of water"). The six permutations are employed to aid the recovery of an individual who has lost his speech. To effect this result one has to write down these names on a piece of paper, and then to place them under the tongue of the afflicted individual. There is however a snag, because we are told that the individual in question will either recover his speech forthwith, or drop dead on the spot! We are told the individual will certainly talk even if he or she is going to die. Moses Zacutto informs us that this procedure was tried and tested with full results. We are told that the correct order of these permutations is טבי טיב בטי ביט יטב יבט.[82]

5. טפטפיה—*Taftafyah* (also *Teftefyah, Teftafyah, Tiftufyah* and *Tafitofeiho*)

In *"The Book of Sacred Names"* I addressed in some detail the magical employment of the remarkable and efficacious Divine Name *Taftafyah* (also pronounced *Teftefyah, Teftafyah, Tiftufyah* and *Tafitofeiho*).[83] Whilst having in that volume made some reference to its use in *Kameot*, there are yet some details remaining which need to be addressed here.

It was noted that *Taftafyah* is one of the seventy names of the archangel *Metatron*, and that it is called the "Name of the Thought" (*Shem ha-Machshevah*). In this regard we are informed that it pertains to *Chochmah* (Wisdom) "the source of mind."[84] The Name itself was composed of the first two letters of verses 69, 70 and 76 of *Psalm 119* which read:

(Verse 69) טפלו עלי שקר זדים אני בכל לב אצר פקודיך

(Verse 70) טפש כחלב לבם אני תורתך שעשעתי

(Verse 76) יהי נא חסדך לנחמני כאמרתך לעבדך

Transliteration:

(verse 69) *TaF'lu alai sheker zeidim ani b'chol lev etzor pikudecha.*

(verse 70) *TaFash kachelev libam ani torat'cha shi'asha'ti.*

(verse 76) *Y'Hi na chasd'cha l'nachameini k'imratecha l'avdecha.*

Translation:

(verse 69) The proud have forged a lie against me; but I with my whole heart will keep Thy precepts.

(verse 70) Their heart is gross like fat; but I delight in Thy law.

(verse 76) Let, I pray Thee, Thy loving-kindness be ready to comfort me, according to Thy promise unto Thy servant.

We also noted that the Name *Taftafyah* "is considered amongst the most potent Sacred Names, certainly one which, in combination with the 'Shield of David' (hexagram), was amongst the most popular protective magical charms of the mediaeval world."[85] This Divine Name is extensively employed in *Kameot*, often in the form of a "magic square" as shown below:

ה	י	פ	ט	פ	ט
ט	ה	י	פ	ט	פ
פ	ט	ה	י	פ	ט
ט	פ	ט	ה	י	פ
פ	ט	פ	ט	ה	י
י	פ	ט	פ	ט	ה

This *Chotam* (magic seal) "can be worn by pregnant women as a *Kamea* of protection against the death of infants during pregnancy and during the birth process, or placed in the cradle with babies to keep death at bay."[86]

I have perused a number of metal amulets engraved with this "Magic Square." In some instances the relevant amulet is simply comprised of this word square on one side and the name of the owner on the other.[87] Elsewhere the rear of the same *Kamea* was engraved with the following Divine Names:

Top Right Corner: יהוה
Top Left Corner: אהיה
Bottom Right Corner: אדני
Bottom Left Corner: אגלא

The full name of the owner was located centrally, and below this the Hebrew sentence משליח מגן לבני והיטבך (*mashliach magen livni v'heitivcha*—"I will send a shield to my son and he will do thee good") in two rows. The concluding portion of the phrase derives from *Deuteronomy 30:5*. There were also accompanying details instructing the utterance of the mentioned phrase each time the amulet is worn on ones person, e.g. as a pendant, etc.

It should also be noted that since the utterance of the Name *Taftafyah* itself is understood to grant one command over fear, it is said this Divine Name acts מגן על צבא אל (*al tz'va al magen*—"on the host of the shield"). As it is, the *gematria* of the Name טפטפיה (*Taftafyah* [ט = 9 + פ = 80 + ט = 9 + פ = 80 + י = 10 + ה = 5 = 193]) is equal to that of על מגן (*al magen*—"of the shield" [ע = 70 + ל = 30 + מ = 40 + ג = 3 + ן = 50 = 193]).[88] The "shield" referred to is the "Shield of David," the hexagram, which is the symbol of *Metatron*. In this regard, I stated that "*Taftafyah* is considered amongst the most potent Sacred Names, certainly one which, in combination with the 'Shield of David' (hexagram), was amongst the most popular protective magical charms of the mediaeval world."[89]

Furthermore, we are told that the potency of this Divine Name is such, that if one should find oneself in a situation of war and facing the belligerency of enemies, one needs but call the Name of the "Prince of Protection," *Taftafyah*, in order to be saved.[90]

6. יוהך כלך—*Yohach Kalach*

The יוהך כלך (*Yohach Kalach*) combination is fairly commonly employed in protection amulets. This Divine Name construct was derived from the concluding letters of the words comprising *Psalm 91:11* reading:

כי מלאכיו יצוה לך לישמרך בכל דרכיך

Transliteration:

ki malachav y'tzaveh lach lishmorcha b'chol d'rachecha

Translation:

For He will give his Angels charge over thee, to keep thee in all thy ways.

We are informed that the angels referred to in the verse are יוהך (*Yohach*) and כלך (*Kalach*), they being two companion guardian Spirit Intelligences (angels). In this regard, there is an interesting practice in which one has to visualise the forms of two large "heroic figures," one to the right and one to the left of oneself. They should be envisioned as enclothed in all kinds of arms.[91] יוהך (*Yohach*), the Angel on the right, is "in charge of the *Midot ha-Din*, the 'Qualities of Judgment' who is 'appointed over divine vengeance,' as well as a reference to the 'avenging sword' of God.....We are told that the remarkable powers of the sixteen-edged divine sword include the ability to 'diminish the powers of the pestilence and other *mazikin* (malevolent forces)' and the granting of a 'meaningful life'." It is also said that this Spirit Intelligence, when called upon, will protect us as we journey through life.[92] Elsewhere it is maintained the Name of the Eternal One (יהי) is in יוהך (*Yohach*), thus this unique angel is empowered to escort, protect and save.[93]

7. כוזו במוכסז כוזו—*Kuzu B'mochsaz Kuzu*

This popular Divine Name construct, which is often employed on the reverse side of the *Mezuzah* scroll, is termed the "Fourteen Letter Name." I have addressed this Divine Name to some extent in "*The Book of Sacred Names*."[94] Briefly, כוזו במוכסז כוזו (*Kuzu B'mochsaz Kuzu*) is comprised of the letters succeeding those of the Names יהוה אלהינו יהוה (*YHVH Eloheinu YHVH*) [*Deuteronomy 6:4*] in the Hebrew alphabet, and we are informed that it has the power to "awaken the dead."

We are also told that whereas the combination *YHVH Eloheinu YHVH* pertains to the sphere of Mercy (*Chesed* or *Gedulah*) on the sefirotic Tree, the *Kuzu B'mochsaz Kuzu* transposition relates to Severity (*Gevurah*). In this regard, the Name כוזו במוכסז כוזו (*Kuzu B'mochsaz Kuzu*) is termed the "Strong Hand," as opposed to יהוה אלהינו יהוה (*YHVH Eloheinu YHVH*), its "positive" counterpart, which is termed the "Great Hand."[95]

8. מצפץ—*Matz'patz* (also *Matzapatza; Matzapitza*; etc.)

Matz'patz is a well-known transposition of the Ineffable Name (*YHVH*) by means of the *Atbash* cipher, a popular Kabbalistic cryptographic method applied to the Hebrew alphabet in which the letter *Alef*, the first letter of the Hebrew alphabet, is exchanged with *Tav*, the last letter; the letter *Bet*, the second letter, is exchanged with *Shin*, the second last letter, etc. Applying this to the letters of the Ineffable Name, certain so called "hidden Names" of God are revealed, amongst which is *Matz'patz* (מצפץ).

It was noted that the *gematria* of this Divine Name [מ = 40 + צ = 90 + פ = 80 + צ = 90 = 300] is equal to that of ברחמים (*b'rachamim*—"with compassion" [ב = 2 + ר = 200 + ח = 8 + מ = 40 + י = 10 + מ = 40 = 300]). We are also informed that this Divine Name features in *Genesis 31:49*, reading:

והמצפה אשר אמר יצף יהוה ביני ובינך כי נסתר
איש מרעהו

Transliteration:

> *v'ha-Mitzpah asher amar yitzef YHVH beini uveinecha ki nisater ish merei'ehu*

Translation:

> and Mizpah, for he said: '*YHVH* watch between me and thee, when we are absent one from another.'

The Divine Name can be traced in this verse, and all of this is understood to indicate the inherent benevolent power of *Matz'patz*, and hence this Divine Name is said to mean "God protects."[96] Many readers would again have recognised this Divine Name from its appearance in the famous Christian magical text titled "*The Key of Solomon*," where it is employed in the adjuration of demonic forces.[97] However, in primary Kabbalistic literature the Name *Matz'patz* is said to pertain to "compassion," and whilst it is employed in this Hebrew amulet amongst Divine Names meant to protect the wearer against malevolent spirit forces, it is not primarily used in the adjuration of "demons."

9. עששיי—*Ashtzei* (also *Oshotziyiyi*)

This Divine Name is very important in Hebrew amulets. It comprises the five letters respectively succeeding the five occurrences of the Ineffable Name (*YHVH*) in *Psalm 121*, i.e. ע (*Ayin*) verse 2; ש (*Shin*) and צ (*Tzadi*) verse 5; and the two letters י (*Yod*) from verses 7 and 8. The power of this Divine Name is said to be vast and mighty, i.e. subduing "outsiders" (demonic forces); restraining the mouth that curses; etc. There are also five important angels aligned with the five letters of the Name עששיי (*Ashtzei*), i.e. עזריאל (*Azri'el*); שריאל (*Sari'el*); צדקיאל (*Tzadki'el*); ישראל (*Yisra'el*) and יהדריאל (*Y'hadri'el*).

We are further told the *gematria* of עששיי (*Ashtzei* [ע = 70 + ש = 300 + צ = 90 + י = 10 + י = 10 = 480]) is equal to that of לילית (*Lilit* [ל = 30 + י = 10 + ל = 30 + י = 10 + ת = 400 = 480]). It is said that the "secret" here is the protection of the "*Brit Milah*" (Holy Covenant [circumcised penis]) against impurities and spontaneous seminal flow, i.e. nocturnal emissions.[98] Talking of "seminal flow," I am reminded of the following *Kamea* in which the Name עששי, in this instance vocalised *Oshotziyiyi*, is employed in conjunction with the Divine Name צמרכד (*Tzamarchad*); אנקתם פסתם פספסים דיונסים (*Anaktam Pastam Paspasim Dionsim* ["Twenty-two Letter Name"]); and יוהך כלך (*Yohach Kalach*). The Names of twenty angels are added to the mix, meant to support and protect a woman who suffers miscarriages and whose children are dying.[99] The twenty angels listed in alphabetical order in the *Kamea* are:

דודיאל	גדודיאל	ברוכיאל	אוריאל
חסדיאל	זהוריאל	ותקיאל	הדריאל
מלכיאל	כבודיאל	יופיאל	טוביאל
פלטיאל	עזריאל	סתריאל	נוריאל
שמריאל	רחמיאל	קדושיאל	צדקיאל

Transliteration:

Ori'el	*Baruchi'el*	*G'dodi'el*	*Dodi'el*
Hadri'el	*Vataki'el*	*Zehori'el*	*Chasdi'el*
Tuvi'el	*Yofi'el*	*K'vodi'el*	*Malchi'el*
Nuri'el	*Satari'el*	*Azri'el*	*Palati'el*
Tzadki'el	*K'doshi'el*	*Rachmi'el*	*Shamri'el*

The amulet is written on deerskin parchment in the name of the individual requiring this support, hence the *Kamea* opens with her name written at the top of the amulet. Below the name insert the following written incantation:

יהי רצון מלפניך יהוה אלהי ואלהי אבותי רופא
רחמן רופא נאמן רופא חנם עוזר כל נעזר רופא
כל בשר ומפליא לעשות שתשמור נושאת קמיע
זה עליה היא ופרי בטנה מכל נזקי שידין ולילין
ורוחין בישין בשבתה ובקומה ובלכתה ובבואה
ובשכבה מכל מקרה רע אבי"נ [abbreviation] אמן
כן יהי רצון] (*Psalm 91:10*) לא תאונה אליך רעה
ונגע לא יקרב באהליך בשם לתא רול יבכ מיל
לבד עכי פתב רעש ותת כוב בחו אכי שיו עאב
אוא בישו עתי

Transliteration:

Y'hi ratzon milfanecha YHVH Elohai v'Elohei avotai rofe rachman rofe ne'eman rofe chinam ozer kol ne'ezar rofe kol basar v'mafli l'asot sh'tishmor noset kamea zeh aleiha hi v'pri bitnah m'kol nez'kei shedin v'lilin v'ruchin b'ishin v'shivtah u'b'kumah u'v'lechtah u'v'vo'ah v'b'shichbah m'kol mikreh ra omein ken y'hi ratzon (Psalm 91:10) lo t'uneh alecha ra'ah v'nega lo yikrav b'oholecha b'shem LTA RVL YBK MYL LBD AKY PTB RASh VTT KVK BchV AKY ShYV AAB AVA BYShV ATY

Translation:

May it be your will *YHVH* my God, and God of my fathers, merciful healer, loyal healer, gratuitous healer, helper of all who needs aid, healer of all flesh who works wonders, to save the one who is bearing this amulet on herself and the fruit of her belly from all maleficent *shedin* (demonic fiends), and *lilin* (night demons), and *ruchin* (ghosts), and *ishin* (evil spirits), when she sits and when she rises, and when she goes and when she comes, from all bad incidents, *Amen* thus be it so willed. (*Psalm 91:10*) "There shall no evil befall thee, neither shall any plague come nigh thy tent," in the Name of *LTA RVL YBK MYL LBD AKY PTB RASh VTT KVK BchV AKY ShYV AAB AVA BYShV ATY*

The concluding set of Divine Names was constructed from the initials of the words comprising *Psalm 91:10*. This set of Divine Names are said to have the power to defeat and eliminate all debilitating hindrances and evil situations.[100]

Be that as it may, the *Kamea* is concluded by writing the following letter square, seals, Divine Names and Angelic Names below the incantation:

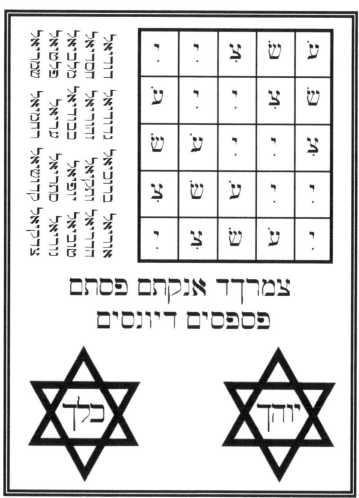

The Name עשציי (*Ashtzei*) is sometimes paired with a companion Divine Name מלכהך (*Melachaheicha*), and, curiously enough, the combined *gematria* of this pair of Divine Names [ע = 70 + ש = 300 + צ = 90 + י = 10 + י = 10 + מ = 40 + ל = 30 + כ = 20 + ה = 5 + כ = 20 = 595] is again equal to the full spelling of the letters comprising the name לילית (*Lilit* [ל = 30 + מ = 40 + ד = 4 + י = 10 + ו = 6 + ד = 4 + ל = 30 + מ = 40 + ד = 4 + י = 10 + ו = 6 + ד = 4 + ת = 400 + א = 1 + ו = 6 = 595]).

The Divine Name מלכהך (*Melachaheicha*) was likewise derived from *Psalm 121*, i.e. from the concluding letters of the five Hebrew words preceding the five appearances of the Ineffable Name in this Psalm, and this important Divine Name combination is employed in a ritual to protect a house against thieves. In this regard, one is instructed to collect five small stones from a road, which have to be washed until they are thoroughly cleansed. Next the entire *Psalm 121* is pronounced five times over the stones whilst keeping the Divine Name construct עשציי מלכהך (*Ashtzei Melachaheicha*) firmly focussed in ones mind. We are informed this action will cancel and exhaust the power of thieves intending to invade ones personal space. *Psalm 121* reads:

[verse 1] שיר למעלות אשא עיני אל ההרים מאין
יבא עזרי

[verse 2] עזרי מעם יי [יהוה] עשה שמים וערץ

[verse 3] אל יתן למוט רגלך אל ינום שמרך

[verse 4] הני לא ינום ולא יישן שומר ישראל

[verse 5] יי [יהוה] שמרך יי [יהוה] צלך על יד
ימינך

[verse 6] יומם השמש לא יככה וירח בלילה

[verse 7] יי [יהוה] ישמרך מכל רע ישמר את נפשך

[verse 8] יי [יהוה] ישמר צאתך ובואך מעתה ועד
עולם

Transliteration:

[verse 1] *shir lama'alot esa einai el heharim me'ayin yavo ezri:*

[verse 2] *ezri me'im YHVH oseh shamayim v'aretz:*

[verse 3] *al yiten lamot rag'lecha al yanum shomrecha:*

[verse 4] *Hinei lo yanum v'lo yishan shomer yisra'el*

[verse 5] *YHVH shomrecha YHVH tzil'cha al yad yeminecha:*

[verse 6] *Yomam ha-shemesh lo yakekah v'yarei'ach balailah:*

[verse 7] *YHVH yishmorcha mikol ra yishmor et naf'shecha:*

[verse 8] *YHVH yishmor tzeit'cha uvo'echa mei'atah va'ed olam.*

Translation:

[verse 1] A Song of Ascents. I will lift up mine eyes unto the mountains: from whence shall my help come?

[verse 2] My help cometh from *YHVH*, who made heaven and earth.

[verse 3] He will not suffer thy foot to be moved; He will not slumber that keepeth thee.

[verse 4] Behold, He that keepeth Israel doth neither slumber nor sleep

[verse 5] *YHVH* is thy keeper; *YHVH* is thy shade upon thy right hand.

[verse 6] By day the sun shall not smite, nor the moon by night.

[verse 7] *YHVH* shall keep thee from all evil; He shall keep thy soul.

[verse 8] *YHVH* shall guard thy going out and thy coming in, from this time forth and for ever.

Afterwards one has to ascend the roof of ones residence or other property, and with all ones power cast four of the stones respectively in the four directions, i.e. one to the East, another to the North, etc. The fifth stone is to be kept in a box.[101]

10. צורטק—*Tzurtak* [also *Tzortak*]

As I indicated elsewhere,[102] it is said the Name צורטק (also צורתק [*Tzurtak*]) was derived from the concluding letters of words in *Deuteronomy 32:3*, and from the initial letters of certain words in *Psalm 119*, as shown below:

הַצוּר תמים פעלו כי כל דרכיו (*Deuteronomy 32:3*)

משפט אל אמונה ואין עול צדיק וישר הוא

צֶדק עדותיך.....וַאדברה בעדותיך.....רְאֵה (*Psalm 119*)

עניי.....טוב טעם ודעת.....קראתי בכל לב

Transliteration:

> (*Deuteronomy 32:3*) ha-Tzur t'mim po'olo ki kol d'rachav
> mishpat El emunah v'ein avel tzadik v'yashar hu.
> (*Psalm 119*) Tzedek eidotecha.....v'adab'rah b'eidotecha
> .....r'eih onyi.....tuv ta'am va-da'at.....karati v'chol lev.

Translation:

> (*Deuteronomy 32:3*) The Rock, His work is perfect; for all
> His ways are justice; a God of faithfulness and without
> iniquity, just and right is He.
> (*Psalm 119*) Thy testimonies are righteous.....I will speak
> of Thy testimonies.....See mine affliction.....Teach me good
> knowledge.....I have called with my whole heart.

It is maintained that the Name *Tzurtak* is an abbreviation of
"*Tzurat ha-Kodesh*" meaning "the form of the holy,"[103] and I noted
previously that this Name is amongst a set of Divine Names
"which the early Merkavists had to utter 112 times, like a mantra,
in preparation of the 'Merkavistic Descent,' which is, as it were, a
meditative inter-dimensional journey."[104] I also noted that *Tzurtak*
"governs the most 'creative' aspect of man, which can engender
the very best of goodness and the greatest evil in this world, i.e. the
tongue, this Name is called upon to guard ones mouth against
uttering bad speech."[105]

Be that as it may, this Divine Name, like so many of the
others listed in this tome, is equally employed in *Kameot* for the
purpose of protecting women in childbirth and also against
premature delivery. In the following *Kamea* the Name צורטק
(*Tzurtak*) is employed conjointly with a set of Divine and Angelic
Names, as well as the *Ehyeh/Ineffable Name* square, intended to
protect pregnant women against miscarriage and other afflictions
which might beset the unborn.[106]

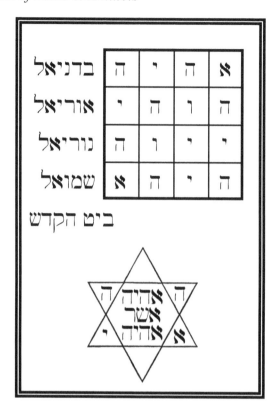

ה	י	ה	א
י	ה	ו	ה
ה	ו	י	י
א	ה	י	ה

בדניאל

אוריאל

נוריאל

שמואל

ביט הקדש

This construct is inscribed on a metal disk conjointly with a set of
Divine Names as well as a written incantation, which is to be
suspended around the neck of the pregnant individual. The
adjuration reads:

צורטק בשם רחמים וחסד בזחות המלאכים הקדושים
והטהורים יאיא הדיה ונאי הייה יהא רעוא מן כדמך
שם יהוה שישמרו אלו השמות לנ]פלוני בן פלוני[
למלאת חדשי עיבורה ולקיים את העובר בבטנה
ויוציאנו חי ויהיה ולד של קיימא בכח אתניק צורת
חותמך שבו נחתמו שמים וארץ בכח השם הגדול
כוזו במוכסז כוזו

Transliteration:

> *Tzurtak b'shem rachamim v'chesed biz'chut ha-malachim
> ha-k'doshim v'ha-tehorim YAYA HDYH VNAY HYYH y'hei
> ra'ava min kadamach shem YHVH sheyishmeru eilu ha-
> shemot l'[.....Ploni ben Ploni.....] lemle'at chod'shei iburah
> v'lekayem et ha-ubar b'bitnah vayotzi'einu chai v'yiyeh*

> *valad shel kayama b'koach Atneik tzurat chotamcha shebo nechtemu shamayim v'aretz b'koach ha-shem ha-gadol Kuzu B'mochsaz Kuzu.*

Translation:

> *Tzurtak* in the Name of mercy and loving-kindness, in the merit of the holy and pure angels, *YAYA HDYH VNAY HYYH*, may your will extend from your name *YHVH*, with these names to protect [.....fill in the name of recipient.....] for the months of pregnancy, keeping the foetus in her stomach and to bring it forth alive, and to be brought into existence by the power of *Atneik*, the pattern of the magical seal signed in heaven and earth in the power of the great name *Kuzu B'mochsaz Kuzu.*

Instructions list the first set of four Divine Names in the written incantation to be יהיא ההיא וניא הדיה, but the current presentation is correct. Closer inspection of what is termed "the great and awesome Name," i.e. יאיא הדיה ונאי היית, clearly reveals these Divine Names to have been created by intertwining the four letters comprising four very potent Divine Names. The first letters of the four Names spell יהוה; the second אדני; the third ייאי; and the four concluding letters spell אהיה. We are told their power is brought to bear by means of prayer and fasting.[107]

The curious Name ייאי comprising the third portion of the Divine Name construct under consideration, was derived from the initials of the opening words of *Psalm 67* verse 4 [5] ישמחו (*yishm'chu*— "be glad"); 6 [5] יודוך (*yoducha*—"thanks unto Thee"); 7 [6] ארץ (*aretz*—"earth"); and verse 8 [7] יברכנו (*y'var'cheinu*— "bless us"). Interestingly enough, the Divine Name in question is the concluding portion of אלייאי, a very special Divine Name constructed from the initials of the first words of *Psalm 67:2* [1] to *8* [7]. In this regard, the three additional letters at the beginning of the Divine Name were derived from verse 2 [1] אלהים (*Elohim*); verse 3[2] לדעת (*lada'at*—"to know"); and verse 4 [3] יודוך (*yoducha*—"thanks unto Thee").

Now, we are told the said Divine Name pertains to the wonders of the sacred incense (*k'toret*).[108] Be that as it may, since *Psalm 67* is of major importance in Hebrew amulets, I will be addressing it in great detail later in this tome.

11. צמרכד—*Tzamarchad* (also *Tzemiroch'da*; etc.)

The Name צמרכד (*Tzamarchad*) was derived from the concluding letters of the first five verses of *Genesis* chapter 1. Readers might recall the misspelled version of this Divine Name on an amulet published in Henry Cornelius Agrippa's "*Occult Philosophy*." He claimed that this Divine Name as well as its sister equivalent, בווווו (*B'v'vavava*) which was derived from the initials of the same verses in the "*Book of Genesis*," are employed "against the affrightments and mischief of evil spirits and men, and what dangers soever, either of journey, waters, enemies, arms.....and by this Ligature they say that a man shall be free from all mischiefes, if so be that he firmly beleeveth in God the creator of all things."[109]

The Name *Tzamarchad* engraved on a silver disk, sometimes conjointly with בוווו (*B'v'vavava*) or גדשנאל (*G'dashni'el*), is indeed good for protection against all sorts of danger.[110] As mentioned elsewhere, this Name is employed, amongst other purposes, "to bring confusion in the mind of the individual against whom it is directed."[111]

As it is, צמרכד (*Tzamarchad*) is called the "Name of the Wing (Edge)" and its "secret" is said to be the beauty of the "Supreme Mother," i.e. the *Shechinah*, and it should be noted that this Divine Name is also employed to encourage fertility in women.[112] However, the Divine Name in question is mainly employed as a protection against attacks from belligerent beings. In this regard, the following *Kamea* is written on a deerskin scroll for this very purpose:

This amulet comprises the Divine Name צמרכד (*Tzamarchad*) located centrally, the Name יוהך (*Yohach*) along the four borders, and כוזו (*Kuzu*) at the cross-borders. In order to affectuate the *Kamea*, it is pinned to the hem or an edge of a garment, which is simply shaken in the direction of whatever possible assailant may come your way.[113]

The following *Kamea* is a more complex version of the amulet under discussion. It is also intended to protect one against physical assault, i.e. from aggressive animals and hostile people. It should be written on a Friday, i.e. the eve of *Shabbat*, on a deerskin parchment or clean sheet of paper, in the name of the intended bearer. As shown below, the item comprises a double border:

We are reminded that the one who intends writing the amulet should be purified in a ritual bath (*Mikveh*). Afterwards the *Kamea* is written in the name of the individual for whom it is intended. In this regard, commence by saying the *Vihi no'am* prayer. This prayer comprises the concluding verse of *Psalm 90* and the whole of *Psalm 91*, reading:

[Psalm 90:17] ויהי נעם **אדני** אלהינו עלינו ומעשה ידינו
כוננה עלינו ומעשה ידינו כוננהו

[Psalm 91 Verse 1] ישב בסתר עליון בצל שדי יתלונן

[Verse 2] **אמר** ליהוה מחסי ומצודתי אלהי אבטח בו

[Verse 3] כי הוא יצילך מפח יקוש מדבר הוות

[Verse 4] באברתו יסך לך ותחת כנפיו תחסה צנה
וסחרה אמתו

[Verse 5] **לא** תירא מפחד לילה מחץ יעוף יומם

[Verse 6] מדבר באפל יהלך מקטב ישוד צהרים

[Verse 7] יפל מצדך אלף ורבבה מימינך אליך לא יגש

[Verse 8] רק בעיניך תביט ושלמת רשעים תראה

[Verse 9] כי **אתה** יהוה מחסי עליון שמת מעונך

[Verse 10] **לא** תאנה אליך רעה ונגע לא יקרב באהלך

[Verse 11] כי מלאכיו יצוה לך לישמרך בכל דרכיך

[Verse 12] על כפים ישאונך פן תגף באבן רגלך

[Verse 13] על שחל ופתן תדרך תרמס כפיר ותנין

[Verse 14] כי בי חשק ואפלטהו אשגבהו כי ידע שמי

[Verse 15] יקראני ואענהו עמו אנכי בצרה אחלצהו
ואכבדהו

[Verse 16] **ארך** ימים אשביעהו ואראהו בישועתי

Transliteration:

[Psalm 90:17] *Vi'hi no'am adonai eloheinu aleinu uma'aseh yadeinu kon'na aleinu uma'aseh yadeinu kon'neihu*

[Psalm 91 Verse 1] *Yoshev b'seter elyon b'tzel Shadai yitlonan*

[Verse 2] *omar la-YHVH machsi um'tzudati elohai evtach bo*

[Verse 3] *ki hu yatzil'cha mipach yakush midever havot*

[Verse 4] *b'evrato yasech lach v'tachat k'nafav techseh tzinah v'socherah amito*

[Verse 5] *lo tira mipachad lailah mechetz ya'uf yomam*

[Verse 6] *midever ba'ofel yahaloch miketev yashud tzohorayim*

[Verse 7] *yipol mitzid'cha elef urvavah miminecha elecha lo yigash*

[Verse 8] *rak b'einecha tabit v'shilumat r'sha'im tir'eh*

[Verse 9] *ki atah YHVH mach'si elyon samta m'onecha*

[Verse 10] *lo t'uneh alecha ra'ah v'nega lo yikrav b'oholecha*

[Verse 11] *ki malachav y'tzaveh lach lishmorcha b'chol d'rachecha*

[Verse 12] *al kapayim yisa'uncha pen tigof ba'even rag'lecha*

[Verse 13] *al shachal va-feten tid'roch tirmos k'fir v'tanin*

[Verse 14] *ki vi chashak va-afaltehu asag'vehu ki yada sh'mi*

[Verse 15] *yikra'eni v'e'eneihu imo anochi v'tzarah achaltzeihu va'achab'deihu*

[Verse 16] *orech yamim asbi'eihu v'ar'eihu bishu'ati*

Translation:

[*Psalm 90:17*] And let the graciousness of the Lord our God be upon us; establish Thou also upon us the work of our hands; yea, the work of our hands establish Thou it.

[*Psalm 91* Verse 1] O thou that dwellest in the covert of the Most High, and abidest in the shadow of *Shadai* [the Almighty];

[Verse 2] I will say of the *YHVH*, who is my refuge and my fortress, my God, in whom I trust,

[Verse 3] That He will deliver thee from the snare of the fowler, and from the noisome pestilence.

[Verse 4] He will cover thee with His pinions, and under His wings shalt thou take refuge; His truth is a shield and a buckler.

[Verse 5] Thou shalt not be afraid of the terror by night, nor of the arrow that flieth by day;

[Verse 6] Of the pestilence that walketh in darkness, nor of the destruction that wasteth at noonday.

[Verse 7] A thousand may fall at Thy side, and ten thousand at Thy right hand; it shall not come nigh thee.

[Verse 8] Only with thine eyes shalt thou behold, and see the recompense of the wicked.

[Verse 9] For thou hast made *YHVH* who is my refuge, even the Most High, thy habitation.

[Verse 10] There shall no evil befall thee, neither shall any plague come nigh thy tent.

[Verse 11] For He will give His angels charge over thee, to keep thee in all thy ways.

[Verse 12] They shall bear thee upon their hands, lest thou dash thy foot against a stone.

[Verse 13] Thou shalt tread upon the lion and asp; the young lion and the serpent shalt thou trample under feet.

[Verse 14] 'Because he hath set his love upon Me, therefore will I deliver him; I will set him on high, because he hath known My name.

[Verse 15] He shall call upon Me, and I will answer him; I will be with him in trouble; I will rescue him, and bring him to honour.

[Verse 16] With long life will I satisfy him, and make Him to behold My salvation.'

In the current instance the *Vihi no'am* prayer is said whilst keeping the name of the name of the angel יוהך (*Yohach*) firmly fixed in ones mind. At the conclusion of the the the prayer add:

ל[נפלוני בן פלוני] בשם יהו

Transliteration:

l'[.....Ploni ben Ploni.....] b'shem Yahu

Translation:

"for [.....fill in the name of recipient.....] in the Name *Yahu*

Then continue by saying *Genesis 1:1–5*:

[*Genesis 1* Verse 1] בראשית ברא אלהים את השמים ואת הארץ

[Verse 2] והארץ היתה תהו ובהו וחשך על פני תהום ורוח אלהים מרחפת על פני המים

[Verse 3] ויאמר אלהים יהי אור ויהי אור

[Verse 4] וירא אלהים את האור כי טוב ויבדל אלהים בין האור ובין החשך

[Verse 5] ויקרא אלהים לאור יום ולחשך קרא לילה ויהי ערב ויהי בקר יום אחד

Transliteration:

[*Genesis 1* Verse 1]_Bereishit bara Elohim et ha-shamayim v'et ha-aretz

[Verse 2] *v'ha-aretz haitah tohu va-vohu v'choshech al pnei t'hom v'ru'ach Elohim m'rachefet al pnei ha-mayim*
[Verse 3] *vayomer Elohim y'hi or va-y'hi or*
[Verse 4] *vayar Elohim et ha-or ki tov vayavdel Elohim bein ha-or u-vein ha-choshech*
[Verse 5] *vayikra Elohim la'or yom v'lachoshech kara lailah va-y'hi erev va-y'hi voker yom echad*

Translation:

[*Genesis 1* Verse 1] In the beginning *Elohim* created the heaven and the earth
[Verse 2] and the earth was unformed and void, and darkness was upon the face of the deep; and the spirit of God hovered over the face of the waters.
[Verse 3] And *Elohim* said: 'Let there be light.' And there was light.
[Verse 4] And God saw the light, that it was good; and God divided the light from the darkness.
[Verse 5] And *Elohim* called the light Day, and the darkness He called Night. And there was evening and there was morning, one day.

Next, the *Kamea* itself is inscribed, commencing with the central portion reading:

כוזו במוכסז כוזו בוווו תמצית קדש קדשים פניאל
אוריאל טפטפיה אגלא מצמצית

Transliteration:

Kuzu B'mochsaz Kuzu B'v'vavava tamtzit Kodesh Kadashim Pani'el Ori'el Taftafyah Agala'a Matzmatzit

Translation:

Kuzu B'mochsaz Kuzu B'v'vavava the essence of the Holy of Holies *Pani'el Ori'el Taftafyah Agala'a Matzmatzit*

I have already addressed most of the listed Divine Names, and have also noted that the combination בוווו (*B'v'vavava*) is the "sister equivalent" of צמרכד (*Tzamarchad*). However, we should briefly consider the concluding Divine Name, i.e. מצמצית (*Matzmatzit*, also *M'tzamtzit*, etc.). We are told this Divine Name is derived from the Hebrew term צמצום (*Tzimtzum*— "Contraction").[114]

The *Kamea* under discussion is completed by writing the Name צמרכד (*Tzamarchad*) four times, respectively along the four borders. Afterwards the *Kamea* is to be carried inside the clothing of the recipient, i.e. in an inside pocket, or pinned to the seam of a garment, etc. If you should encounter ferocious creatures, whether these be of the two or four legged kind, you simply shake the portion of the garment where the amulet is kept towards the approaching danger, as well as in the four directions.[115]

To conclude our investigation into this remarkable Divine Name, consider the following somewhat ornate *Kamea* in which *Tzamarchad* is employed in conjunction with *Taftafyah* and other Divine Name constructs, as well as with a set of magical glyphs, all employed for the purpose of again protecting the unborn against injurious spirit forces:

The Divine Names to the right reads:

צמרכד טפטפיה על צבא על מגן מרומים נער יער

Transliteration:

Tzamarchad Taftafyah al tz'va al magen m'romim na'ar ya'ar

Translation:

Tzamarchad Taftafyah of the host of the shield a wild youth (forest boy).

The concluding two terms of the phrase is somewhat obscure. I have elected to translate it "a forest youth." Considering the fundamental purpose of this amulet, i.e. protection against all sorts of demonic forces, the "forest youth" might be a reference to a "wild spirit, e.g. a satyr. Reference is made in the accompanying adjuration to just such entities.

There is no elucidation as to the meaning of the magical glyphs below this phrase, but the ornate image to the left comprises the names *Tzamarchad* at the top, *Taftafyah* down the right, and the combination קהסמגת in the centre. The latter Divine Name is part of a set of three Divine Names which we will address in greater detail later in this work. Be that as it may, the *Kamea* we are addressing is completed with the inclusion of the following written adjuration:

יהי רצון מלפניך יהוה אלהי ואלהי אבותי אהיה
רופא רחמן שתשמור פרי בטנה של [פלונית בת פלונית]
מכל נזקי שידין ולילין ושעירים ורוחין בישין שלא
יהיה להם יכולת להזיק לפרי בטנה מעתה ועד עולם
בכח שמותיך הקדושים ובעוצם ידך תגן ותסתרהו
בסתר כנפיך מכל מקרה רע כי אתה שומר חסידיך
והבוטחים בך ברוך שומר ישראל

Transliteration:
> *Y'hi ratzon milfanecha YHVH Elohai v'Elohei avotai Ehyeh rofe rachaman sh'tishmor pri bitnah shel [.....Plonit bat Plonit.....] mikol nizkei shedin v'lilin v'se'irim b'ruchin b'ishin shelo yiyeh lahem y'cholet lehazik l'pri bitnah me'atah va'ed olam b'koach shmotecha hak'doshim u'b'otzem yod'cha tagen v'tastirehu b'seter k'nafecha mikol mikreh ra ki atah shomer chasidecha v'ha-botchim b'cha baruch shomer Yisra'el*

Translation:
> May it be your will *YHVH* my God, and God of my fathers, *Ehyeh* the merciful healer, to protect the fruit of the belly of [.....fill in the name of the pregnant woman.....] from all harmful *shedin* (demonic fiends), and *lilin* (night demons), and *se'irim* (satyrs [goatfooted demons]), and *ruchin* (ghosts), and *ishin* (evil spirits), so that they will not have the ability to harm the fruit of her belly from now unto eternity, in the power of Your holy names and with the strength of Your Hand to protect and hide him in secret under Your wings, from all bad incidents because You

protect Your pious followers and who trust You. Blessed be the Protector of Israel.

We are told this amulet also has the power to prevent miscarriage, and is equally effective as protective measure for someone whose children are dying.[116]

F. The Twenty-two Letter Name

The appellative "Twenty-two Letter Name" refers to the traditional expression אנקתם פסתם פספסים דיונסים (*Anaktam Pastam Paspasim Dionsim* [also vocalised *'naket 'ma P'sotam P'sips'yema Dayev'soyam*]), which is extensively employed in Hebrew amulets. This Divine Name is traditionally employed at the conclusion of the "Priestly Benediction" uttered during *Rosh Hashanah*, and is often included in Hebrew amulets. We are informed that this peculiar Divine Name comprises a transposition of the twenty-two letters of the first five words of the "priestly blessing" in *Numbers 6:24–25*, these being:

יברכך יהוה וישמרך יאר יהוה

Transliteration:
>   *Y'varech'cha YHVH v'yishm'recha ya'er YHVH*

Translation:
>   *YHVH* bless thee and keep thee, shine *YHVH*

Now, whilst this Divine Name is a transposition of the twenty-two letters of the first five words of the "priestly blessing," each letter of the Divine Name in question is said to be the initial of a word. In this regard we are informed that the phrase derived from these words, pertains to one being freed from the prison of anxiety and fear. We are further informed that those who generally have a low self-esteem, and who suffer melancholy and depression, can be relieved from such states of confusion and even resentment by means of the "Twenty-two Letter Name" being employed, for example, as a "*Hagah*" (Hebrew mantra).[117]

As indicated in "*The Book of Sacred Names*,"[118] the recognition of the power of this Divine Name to relieve stress and fear, has led to it being employed in a Hebrew amulet to alleviate the terrors and fears a child may be experiencing.[119] In this instance the "Twenty-two Letter Name" is written conjointly with other Hebrew "Names of Power," specifically:

אנקתם פסתם פספסים דיונסים
יוהך כלך צמרכד אזבוגה

(*Anaktam Pastam Paspasim Dionsim
Yohach Kalach Tzamarchad Azbogah*).

Additionally one has to add to the amulet the following phrase:

שמרו לילד הזה מכל דבר רע אמן נצח סלה ועד

Transliteration:
> *Shmoro la-yeled ha-zeh mikol davar ra, Omein Netzach Selah Va-ed*

Translation:
> Protect this child from every evil thing, *Amen*, Enduring (Victory), *Selah*, Forever.

G. The Forty-two Letter Name

אבגיתצ קרעשטן נגדיכש בטרצתג
חקבטנע יגלפזק שקוצית

(*Avgitatz Karastan Nagdichesh Batratztag
Chakvetna Yaglefzok Shakutzit*)

The forty-two letters of this enigmatic Name are divided into seven groups of six letters each, and a variety of ways have been offered as far as the actual pronunciation of this Divine Name is concerned. In this regard, the one listed above is easily employed.

We are told the primary "secret" of the "Forty-two Letter Name" pertains to *Ma'aseh B'reshit*, i.e. the "Workings of Creation." Furthermore, as again noted in *"The Book of Sacred Names,"* "contemplation and meditation on this special Divine Name is said to have the power to elevate the 'Soul,' raising it from '*Olam ha-Asiyah*,' the physical 'Realm of Action,' to '*Olam ha-Yetzirah*,' the higher 'Realm of Formation'." I also noted that "the letters of the 'Forty-two Letter Name' are said to 'manifest' as forty-two 'shining lights' which are expressed in forty-two unique 'spiritual forms'," and that "these 'forms' pertain to sets of

Divine Names and associated 'Spirit Intelligences' directly related to the component letters of the 'Forty-two Letter Name'."[120]

Having addressed these special "Spirit Forces" inherent in the Divine Name in question in great detail in the oft mentioned *"The Book of Sacred Names*,"[121] including having shared a set of practical procedures of aligning with these powers, I only need to add here that the "Forty-two Letter Name" also relates to the sphere of *Gevurah* (Strength/Severity) on the sefirotic tree, hence the inclusion of this Divine Name in *Kameot* again concerns the invocation of the special "powers of protection" inherent within the very letters of this Name.

There is a usage of the "Forty-two Letter Name of God" in Jewish Magic, which might come as a surprise. I am sure you will ascertain from the *Kameot* shared in this tome, the majority of Hebrew amulets pertain to protecting pregnant women, infants and their mothers. In this regard, the magical uses of the "Forty-two Letter Name" also pertain to aiding infants who appear to have difficulties breastfeeding following their emergence from their mothers' womb. To effectuate this special help, we are told to write the complete "Forty-two Letter Name" in normal Hebrew handwritten script on a *kosher* scroll, and, with the writing held towards the child, shake the *Kamea* in front of his or her face. We are informed that with the help of the Almighty One, the infant will commence suckling forthwith.[122]

As noted elsewhere, the seven sectors of the "Forty-two Letter Name" are employed separately for a variety of magical purposes.[123] For example, the יגלפזק portion of the Divine Name in question aligns with the "quality of mercy" associated with the archangel מיכאל (*Micha'el*). Here, to invoke the "quality of mercy," one writes an amulet comprised of this specific portion of the "Forty-two Letter Name."[124] Afterwards, in order to ensure the success of the *Kamea*, one has to face East and, whilst holding the amulet, say:

יהי רצון מלפניך אהיה אשר אהיה ומלפניך המלך
מיכאל ובשם יגלפזק שתצליח בקמיע זה

Transliteration:
Y'hi ratzon milfanecha Ehyeh asher Ehyeh u'milfanecha ha-malach Micha'el v'b'shem Y'galp'zak sh'tatzliach b'kame'a zeh

Translation:

> May it be your will *Ehyeh asher Ehyeh* and with the angel *Micha'el* in front, and in the name of *Y'galp'zak* to succeed with this amulet.

Now, the "Forty-two Letter Name" is often employed conjointly with other Divine Names, as well as Angelic names, "magic squares," etc., as shown in the following representation of a 19th century Hebrew amulet from Iraqi Kurdistan:[125]

Front

יאהדונהי

בשם אבג יתצ קרע שטנ נגד
יכש בתר צתג חקב טנע יגל
פזק שקו צית בשכ מלו ובשם
אלו שמות המלאכים הכתובים
ארגמן אוריאל רפאל גבריאל יהו
מיכאל נוריאל להאר

א	ה	י	ה
ה	א	ה	י
י	ה	א	ה
ה	י	ה	א

וילב סייג וגדר
ומשמרת לנוקזע
מעתה ועד עולם

Rear

יהוה שדי

בשם שלא אעה מיע עמי ע
שו איל ראי שהליוי שיי שיצ
עיי יהליוב יימרי אניי צומו
ע בנפורת יוס פבן פור תעלי
עין בניה צעדה עלי שור
ובשם יוהך כלך לא תאונה אליך
רעה ונגע לא יקרב באהליך
סייג ומשמרת וגדר לנוקזע
מעתה ועד עולם אכיר

The front portion of the *Kamea* comprises the יאהדונהי
(*Yahadonai*) header, which often appears in this format on metal
amulets. Below the header we note the earlier mentioned *Ehyeh*
square located bottom right. We also trace the first of two
incantations comprising this amulet. The latter, written in nine
lines, reads:

בשם אבג יתצ קרע שטן נגד יכש בתר צתג חקב טנע
שם ברוך [abbreviation מלו בשכ צית שקו פזק יגל
כבוד מלכותו לעולם ועד] ובשם אלו שמות
המלאכים הכתובים ארגמן אוריאל רפאל גבריאל
יהו מיכאל נוריאל לתאר וליב (*Psalm 91:10* abbreviation)
זה קמיא לנושא [abbreviation לנוקזע ומשמרת וגדר סייג
עליון מעתה ועד עולם

Transliteration:

> *B'shem AViGe YaToTzi KaRo' SaTaN' NaGiDa
> YeiCheiSha BiTaRo TzaTaG' CheKeVa Tin'I YaGaLi
> P'Z'Kei ShuKoVa TzoYaT' Baruch Shem K'vod Malchuto
> l'Olam Va'ed u'b'shem eilu shemot ha-malachim ha-
> k'tuvim Argaman Ori'el Rafa'el Gavri'el YHV Micha'el
> Nuri'el LTAR VLYB (Psalm 91:10) siyag v'geder
> v'mishmeret l'nose kamea zeh alav me'atah va'ed olam*

Translation:

> In the name *AViGe YaToTzi KaRo' SaTaN' NaGiDa
> YeiCheiSha BiTaRo TzaTaG' CheKeVa Tin'I YaGaLi
> P'Z'Kei ShuKoVa TzoYaT'* Blessed be the Name of His
> glorious Kingdom throughout eternity, and in the written
> names of these angelic messengers *Argaman Ori'el Rafa'el
> Gavri'el YHV Micha'el Nuri'el LTAR VLYB* (*Psalm
> 91:10*), a fence and boundary and safeguard for the bearer
> of this amulet from now unto eternity.

The rear portion of the amulet equally commences with a header,
i.e. יהוה שדי (*YHVH Shadai*), and below we read the second of
the mentioned incantations, also written in nine lines. It reads:

בשם שלא אעה מיע עמי ע שו איל ראי שהליוי שיי שיצ
עיי יהליוב יימרי אניי צומו ע (*Psalm 121* abbreviation)

בנפורת יוס פבן פור תעלי עין בנית צעדה עלי שור
ובשם יוהך כלך לא תאונה אליך רעה (*Genesis 45:10*)
ונגע לא יקרב באהליך (*Psalm 91:10*) סייג ומשמרת וגדר
לנוקזע [abbreviation] לנושא קמיע זה עליון מעתה ועד
עולם אביר [abbreviation] אמן כן יהי רצון]

Transliteration:

> B'shem ShLA AAH MYA AMY A ShV AYL RAY ShHLYVY
> ShYY ShYTz AYY YHLYVB YYMRY ANYY TzVMV A (*Psalm
> 121*) BNPVRT YVS PBN PVR TALY AYN BNYT TzADH
> ALY ShVR [Divine Names constructed from *Genesis 45:10*]
> ub'shem Yohach Kalach lo t'uneh alecha ra'ah v'nega lo
> yikrav b'ahalecha (*Psalm 91:10*) siyag v'mishmeret
> v'gader l'nose kamea zeh alav me'atah va'ed olam Omein
> ken y'hi ratzon

Translation:

> In the name *ShLA AAH MYA AMY A ShV AYL RAY
> ShHLYVY ShYY ShYTz AYY YHLYVB YYMRY ANYY
> TzVMV A (Psalm 121) BNPVRT YVS PBN PVR TALY AYN
> BNYT TzADH ALY ShVR* [Divine Names constructed from
> *Genesis 45:10*] and in the name *Yohach Kalach* "there
> shall no evil befall thee, neither shall any plague come nigh
> thy tent," (*Psalm 91:10*) a fence and safeguard and
> boundary for the bearer of this amulet from now unto
> eternity, *Amen* thus be it so willed.

In this instance, the inclusion of the most important Divine Names
affording Divine Blessing and the strongest spiritual protection,
with additional support from the five great archangels, etc., affords
us a very special Hebrew amulet.

H. The Name of Seventy-two Names

I have addressed the "Name of Seventy-two Names" previously.[126]
In the current instance we will focus essentially on the use of this
enigmatic Divine Name in Hebrew amulets. To commence this
investigation we will briefly review the origins and format of the
"*Shem Vayisa Vayet*." Herewith the lay-out of the seventy-two tri-
letter portions comprising the entire construct:

6 ללה	5 מהש	4 עלם	3 סיט	2 ילי	1 והו
12 ההע	11 לאו	10 אלד	9 הזי	8 כהת	7 אכא
18 כלי	17 לאו	16 הקם	15 הרי	14 מבה	13 יזל
24 חהו	23 מלה	22 ייי	21 נלכ	20 פהל	19 לוו
30 אום	29 ריי	28 שאה	27 ירת	26 האא	25 נתה
36 מנד	35 כוק	34 להח	33 יחו	32 ושר	31 לכב
42 מיכ	41 ההה	40 ייז	39 רהע	38 חעם	37 אני
48 מיה	47 עשל	46 ערי	45 סאל	44 ילה	43 וול
54 נית	53 ננא	52 עממ	51 ההש	50 דני	49 והו
60 מצר	59 הרח	58 ייל	57 נמם	56 פוי	55 מבה
66 מנק	65 דמב	64 מחי	63 ענו	62 יהה	61 ומב
72 מום	71 היי	70 יבמ	69 ראה	68 חבו	67 איע

As explained previously, the "*Shem Vayisa Vayet*" was constructed from the letters comprising *Exodus 14:19–21* reading:

(Verse 19) ויסע מלאך האלהים ההלך לפני מחנה ישראל
וילך מאחריהם ויסע עמוד הענן מפניהם ויעמד
מאחריהם

(Verse 20) ויבא בין מחנה מצרים ובין מחנה ישראל ויהי
הענן והחשך ויאר את הלילה ולא קרב זה אל זה כל
הלילה

(Verse 21) ויט משה את ידו על הים ויולך יהוה את הים
ברוח קדים עזה כל הלילה וישם את הים לחרבה
ויבקעו המים

Transliteration:

> (Verse 19) *vayisa malach ha-elohim ha-holech lifnei machaneh yisra'el vayelech mei'achareihem vayisa amud he-anan mip'neihem vaya'amod mei'achareihem*
>
> (Verse 20) *vayavo bein machaneh mitz'rayim uvein machaneh yisra'el vay'hi he'anan v'hachoshech vaya'er et ha-lailah v'lo karav ze el ze kol ha-lailah*
>
> (Verse 21) *vayet mosheh et yado al ha-yam vayolech YHVH et ha-yam b'Ru'ach kadim azah kol ha-lailah vayasem et ha-yam lecharavah vayibak'u ha-mayim*

Translation:

> (Verse 19) And the angel of God, who went before the camp of Israel, removed and went behind them: and the pillar of cloud removed from before them, and stood behind them;
>
> (Verse 20) And it came between the camp of Egypt and the camp of Israel; and there was the cloud and the darkness here, yet gave it light by night there; and the one came not near the other all the night.
>
> (Verse 21) And Moses stretched out his hand over the sea; and the Lord caused the sea to go back by a strong east wind all the night, and made the sea dry land, and the waters were divided.

Each of these verses comprises exactly seventy-two letters, and in constructing the "Name of Seventy-two Names," the seventy-two letters of the first verse are arranged in the standard manner from right to left, whilst those of the second verse are located in reverse order underneath. In turn, the seventy-two letters of the third verse are located underneath the second row in the standard manner from right to left. By reading the entire construct in columns of three letters each, we arrive at the "*Shem Vayisa Vayet.*"

This remarkable Divine Name is employed in Hebrew amulets, sometimes in portions and sometimes even engraved in full on small silver trays, as shown in the following *Kamea*:[127]

Front

והו	ילי	סיט	עלם	מהש	ללה	אכא	כהת
הזי	אלד	לאו	ההע	יזל	מבה	הרי	הקם
לאו	כלי	לוו	פהל	נלך	ייי	מלה	חהו
נתה	האא	ירת	שאה	ריי	אום	לכב	ושר
יחו	להח	כוק	מנד	אני	חעם	רהע	ייז
ההה	מיך	ול	ילה	סאל	ערי	עשל	מיה
והו	דני	החש	עמם	גנא	נית	מבה	פוי
נמם	ייל	הרח	מצר	ומב	יהה	ענו	מחי
דמב	מנק	איע	חבו	ראה	יבם	היי	מום

Rear

אבג יתצ קרע שטן נגד יכש בתר
צתג חקב טנע יגל פזק שקו צית
אנקתם פסתם פספסים דיונסים
מצפץ שמעיה יוהך כלך כוזו במוכסז
כוזו מטטרון שמריאל אוריאל מהש
רפאל גבריאל מיכאל נוריאל
רזיאל סנדלפון יופאל ענאל שפי
אדירירון גבורתיאל אתנק שדי
צדקיאל ענאל קפציאל עזריאל
הדריאל סנוי סנסנוי סמנגלוף
לשמירת נקז

In this instance the front portion of the construct comprises nine rows, each of which is made up of eight tri-letter portions of the "*Shem Vayisa Vayet*." The rear portion reads:

אבג יתצ קרע שטן נגד יכש בתר צתג חקב טנע
יגל פזק שקו צית אנקתם פסתם פספסים דיונסים
מצפצ שמעיה יוהך כלך כוזו במוכסז כוזו מטטרון
שמריאל אוריאל מהש רפאל גבריאל מיכאל נוריאל
רזיאל סנדלפון יופאל ענאל שפי אדיררון גבורתיאל
אתנק שדי צדקיאל ענאל קפציאל עזריאל הדריאל
סנוי סנסנוי סמנגלוף לשמירת נקז [נושא קמיע זה]

Transliteration:

> *AViGe YaToTzi KaRo' SaTaN' NaGiDa YeiCheiSha BiTaRo TzaTaG' CheKeVa Tin'I YaGaLi P'Z'Kei ShuKoVa TzoYaT' Anaktam Pastam Paspasim Dionsim Matz'patz Sh'ma'ayah Yohach Kalach Kuzu B'mochsaz Kuzu Metatron Shamri'el Ori'el Mahash Rafa'el Gavri'el Micha'el Nuri'el Razi'el Sandalfon Yofi'el An'el Shefi Adiriron G'vurti'el Atneik Shadai Tzadki'el An'el Kaftzi'el Azri'el Hadri'el Sanoi Sansanoi Semangelof l'shmirat nose kamea zeh*

Translation:

> *AViGe YaToTzi KaRo' SaTaN' NaGiDa YeiCheiSha BiTaRo TzaTaG' CheKeVa Tin'I YaGaLi P'Z'Kei ShuKoVa TzoYaT' Anaktam Pastam Paspasim Dionsim Matz'patz Sh'ma'ayah Yohach Kalach Kuzu B'mochsaz Kuzu Metatron Shamri'el Ori'el Mahash Rafa'el Gavri'el Micha'el Nuri'el Razi'el Sandalfon Yofi'el An'el Shefi Adiriron G'vurti'el Atneik Shadai Tzadki'el An'el Kaftzi'el Azri'el Hadri'el Sanoi Sansanoi Semangelof* for protection, this being the purpose of this amulet.

As noted the rear portion of the amulet incorporates several of the earlier addressed Divine Names, as well as the Names of a number of Angelic Intelligences, all acting conjointly in the task of guarding and benefitting the owner of the said *Kamea*.

It might come as a surprise to learn that the "Name of Seventy-two Names" is also employed in a variant format in Jewish magic.[128] In this regard the arrangements of the letters of the three verses comprising this Divine Name are in the exact same order, i.e. as written from right to left, the result being as follows:

6	5	4	3	2	1
לִיֵה	מֵבֵשׁ	עָאֹם	סְבֵט	ייִי	וֵוּ
12	**11**	**10**	**9**	**8**	**7**
הַמֵע	לְהוּ	אֵנֵד	הֵחֵי	כְמֵת	אֲנֵא
18	**17**	**16**	**15**	**14**	**13**
כְבֵי	לֵוּו	הֵמֵם	הַיֵי	מֵרֵה	יֵצֵל
24	**23**	**22**	**21**	**20**	**19**
חֵדֵרִי	מֵנֵה	יֵחֵי	נְמֵכ	פְנֵל	לִיו
30	**29**	**28**	**27**	**26**	**25**
אוֹמֵ	רְלִי	שֵׁאֵה	יֵרֵת	הֵשֵׂא	נֵיה
36	**35**	**34**	**33**	**32**	**31**
מֵנֵד	כֵעֵק	לְהֵח	יֵיו	וְהֵר	לִיב
42	**41**	**40**	**39**	**38**	**37**
מֵכְב	הֵשֵׁה	יֵחֵז	רְהֵע	חֵוֹמֵ	אֵנִי
48	**47**	**46**	**45**	**44**	**43**
מֵתֵה	עֵאֵל	עֵרִי	סֵאֵל	יֵיה	וַוֻל
54	**53**	**52**	**51**	**50**	**49**
נְוֹת	נֵהֵא	עֵלֵם	הֵישׁ	דֵלִי	וֵהוּ
60	**59**	**58**	**57**	**56**	**55**
מֵזֵר	הֵבֵח	יֵרֵל	נֵקֵם	פֵאִי	מֵלָה
66	**65**	**64**	**63**	**62**	**61**
מֵכֵק	דֵהֵב	מֵזִי	עֵלוּ	יֵאֵה	וְהֵב
72	**71**	**70**	**69**	**68**	**67**
מֵהֵם	הֵלִי	יֵימֵ	רֵלֵה	חֵדֵו	אֵלֵע

As indicated, these combinations are presented with vowels, since some magical applications require these in certain instances. In this regard, the vowels are directly related to their order of appearance as aligned with the letters comprising the three biblical verses from whence the *Shem Vayisa Vayet* was derived. We are told that both the standard and variant seventy-two tri-letter units can be employed for exactly the same talismanic purposes, which in the current instance require the tri-letter units to be arranged into thirteen *Kameot* comprised of five units each, and one *Kamea* of seven units.

As it is, such employment of the "Name of Seventy-two Names" necessitates precise knowledge regarding the exact days when these *Kameot* should be composed. In this regard:

> 1. the first amulet is written on the third day of any Hebrew month;
> 2. the second is written on the seventh day of the month;
> 3. the third on the tenth day of the month;
> 4. the fourth on the twentieth of the month;
> 5. the fifth on the twenty-third of the month; and
> 6. all of the remaining *Kameot* are written on the twenty-ninth day of the month.[129]

The actual mental/emotional stance of the one composing these *Kameot* plays a primary role in the efficacy of each amulet. Hence the instruction to acquire a most harmonious mindset prior to commencing the creation of a *Kamea*, and, whilst the Divine Names are being written, to recite the component Divine Names in a pleasant voice. In fact, we are told the power of these amulets necessitates cleanliness of body, great mental and emotional purity, devotion, fasting, as well as abstinence from any sexual activities for at least three days prior to commencement of these magical procedures.[130]

Of the fourteen *Kameot* under discussion, some are constructed for benevolent purposes, e.g. love, etc., and quite a number are employed for nefarious outcomes, e.g. deeds of hatred, psychic restraint of unwilling victims, intimidation and causing people to fear you, attacking an individual at a distance, etc. In my estimation indulgence in such vile activities deserves the strongest condemnation. It should be noted that the term "vile" is but a permutation of the word "evil."

Since the volumes of the *Shadow Tree Series* are devoted to spiritual and magical practices meant to improve and uplift on all levels of existence, the life of the serious and devoted practitioner of these arts, as well as impacting the larger community and environment, I will not share any activities pertaining to expressing hate, seeking vengeance, working acts of destruction on ones fellow humankind, or anything of that ilk. Hence we will inspect only amulets which benefit us in the most meaningful manner, without detracting in any manner from anything or anyone. In this regard, I have selected the following *Kameot* to be included here:

KAMEA 1

וזו ייי סבט עאם מבש

The first *Kamea* is composed to generate love. Whilst the instruction is to write this amulet on a *kosher* deerskin scroll, it is equally good to employ a good, clean sheet of plain parchment, i.e. the kind used by scribes to write *mezuzot* or those employed in the construction of *tefilin* (phylacteries). We are informed that if these items are not readily available when required, that one may write the Divine Names and magical seals on a day old egg of a black chicken. Afterwards the egg is incinerated in a fire and its ashes stored inside a small pouch, locket or other tiny container to be carried on ones person.[131]

As noted, the five tri-letter Names and accompanying magical seals are to be written on the third day of a Hebrew month, and it is important that the said day should be bright, clear, free from cloud and rain.[132] A Hebrew calendar will indicate the exact day in terms of the standard dates employed globally.

KAMEA 3

לחו המע יצל מרה היי

This *Kamea* is created to "open the heart," i.e. expand ones consciousness to comprehend the greater whole in terms of sacred studies, etc. We mentioned that this amulet should be written on the tenth day of the month, however further instruction maintains that it should be composed in the seventh hour on *Rosh Chodesh* (first day) of the Hebrew month *Sivan*, or as close to this day as possible, if the appropriate time should fall on *Shabbat* (Sabbath).

The *Kamea* should again be written on kosher parchment.[133] The listed five tri-letter portions are penned on the front of the parchment, and the following set of Divine and Angelic Names in conjunction with a short adjuration, are written on the rear portion of the amulet:

הוי בריאל רפאל עניאל יה והו שרפיאל תפתחו לבי
תמהרו ותפתחו לבי למילף אולפן דאורייתא

Transliteration:
> *HVY Bari'el Rafa'el Ani'el YH VHV Sarfi'el tiftechu libi temaharu v'tiftechu libi l'milaf ulpan d'oraita*

Translation:
> *HVY Bari'el Rafa'el Ani'el YH VHV Sarfi'el* open my heart, hurry and open my heart, open my heart to spiritual teachings (Higher Laws [Torah instruction])

Afterwards the amulet is placed in a glass of wine in order to dissolve the writing. However, here is another important point to consider. The wine itself is to be placed in the earth for the period of two weeks between *Rosh Chodesh* (first day) of the month *Sivan* to *Erev Shavu'ot* (Eve of the Festival of Weeks), or for the period of two weeks between *Rosh Chodesh* (first day) of the month *Nisan* to *Erev Pesach* (Eve of Passover).[134]

After dissolving the writing on the parchment in the wine, the procedure is concluded by the liquid being consumed. Then, we are told, "you will see wonders."

KAMEA 4

המם לוו כבי ליו פנל

This amulet is employed to "shut the mouth" of a slanderer. Whilst this action is somewhat belligerent, it is clear that its use may well be required by those who are suffering the unpleasant effects of *lashon ha-ra* (the "evil tongue"). This being said, it is perfectly clear that we are all "self creators," and that time could be far better spent focussing on that which "empowers" ones being into a full recognition of "oneness," which would reduce the defamatory behaviour of a perceived "enemy" into absolute meaninglessness.

Of course, humanity has a long way to go before this is fully realised, and I am perfectly aware that each one of us is struggling to cope with personal vulnerabilities in terms of physical, mental and emotional survival. In this regard, "magical self defence" may well be necessary in certain situations, and this is where there is a *Kamea* designed to control defamatory speech. To achieve this, you have to write the listed five tri-letter portions of the "*Shem Vayisa Vayet*" on a small square of parchment made from calfskin. It has also been suggested that the amulet could be written on the placenta of a cow.[135]

Afterwards the amulet is to be carried on your person. On encountering the perfidious storyteller, the amulet is to be held tightly in your hand. When you come face to face with the individual in question, you are to expose without any sign of fear the *Kamea* to the individual whilst looking that person straight in the eye. The trick is to expose the vilifier to the amulet in a sort of hidden manner, e.g. he/she must not actually physically see the magical object. The individual will not be able to make any malicious remarks regarding your person whilst you are present.

There is further instruction regarding exposing the individual to the amulet a second time prior to departing his/her company. In this instance you are to reveal both the front and the back of the parchment, whilst fearlessly looking the said individual straight in the eye, and then depart with confidence and faith in Divine support. Bear in mind that in all circumstances the exposition of this *Kamea* should always be in the mentioned hidden manner.[136]

On sharing this a while back with a fellow "magical Companion," who was suffering the brunt of a slanderous tongue, I was queried as to the possibility of working the procedure in the imagination, i.e. whilst the individual is not physically present. On considering the much abused saying that "the thought is as good as the deed," I suggested he give it a try. To our great surprise, the magical action applied mentally produced equally great results. In this instance, my friend faced his detractor mentally, and whilst looking fearlessly and with great confidence into the eyes of the envisioned individual, he exposed to that character the physical amulet he had been clasping in his hand.

KAMEA 5

נמכ יחי מנה חהו ניה

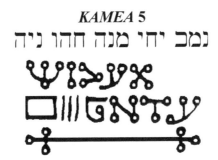

These Divine Names and accompanying seals are employed in instances necessitating some or other request having to be presented to a higher authority, i.e. a governmental administrator, judiciary, or another in high office who might impact ones life benevolently. In this instance the original instruction requires one to write the listed five tri-letter Names and accompanying magical seals on parchment made from the skin of an aborted animal.[137] I am aware that this *Kamea* was employed to great effect with the said Divine Names and seals written on plain good parchment, hence I suggest you spare yourself the gory task of having to skin an aborted animal. Voodooistic actions such as these might have impressed mediaeval mindsets, but more recent experience clearly indicates the task at hand to be well executed with great effect by means of the many good parchments available in our day.

As said, the instruction is to write the Divine Names and seals on parchment, which is held in your hand or carried in your belt during the time when you have to face the higher authority with a personal request. However, since this action requires great purity to ensure a beneficial outcome, it is necessary to fast and to perform prayers and ritual submersion in a sacred bath (*Mikveh*). Regarding the latter activity, we are informed that if such is not at your disposal, then you must be careful to abstain from any sexual activity for around two days prior to seeking a specific service from an individual in high office.[138]

KAMEA 10

ערי עאל מתה והו דלי

This portion of the "Name of Seventy-two Names" is employed in an amulet to work *Kefitzat ha-Derech* ("Shortening the Way," i.e.

magical travel or teleportation).[139] We are instructed that the first time you work this technique, you have to enter into a ritual bath (*Mikveh*). This portion of the procedure is not required when you repeat the procedure, however you should always perform some self purification prior to working this procedure.

Afterwards, write the relevant five Divine Names conjointly with an adjuration on deerskin parchment. The latter reads:

משביע אני עליכם החמשה שמות הקדושים והטהורים
בשם הכתר הנורא אלהי האלהים ואדוני האדונים האל
הגדול הגיבור והנורא שתוליכוני ממקום זה שאני עומד
עליו עד מקום פלוני בנחת ולא בצער בהשקט בבטח
ובמנוחה בבריאות גופי ובשלימות איברי בכל הדרך
הזה אשר אנכי רוצה לילך עד מקום פלוני ותביאוני
למחוז חפצי ותנחוני בנחת רוח בדרך כדי שלא אצטער
ולא אתבלבל ותהיה הליכתי בטח כחפצי וכרצוני ולא
תתנו רשות לשום בריה להזיקני בכל עניין בעולם ולא
לקטרג ולא לערער עלי ואל יעכבוני בשום מקום שלא
ברצוני והזדמנו אלי לעשות בקשתי ורצוני אמן סלה

Transliteration:

> *Mashbi'a ani aleichem ha-chamishah shemot ha-k'doshim v'ha-t'horim b'shem ha-keter ha-nora Elohei ha-Elohim v'Adonai ha-Adonim ha-El ha-gadol ha-gibor v'ha-nora shetolichuni mimakom zeh she'ani omed alav ad makom ploni benachat v'lo b'tzar b'ha-shket b'vetach u'b'menuchah b'bri'ut gufi v'beshlimut everai b'chol ha-derech ha-zeh asher anochi rotzeh leleach ad makom ploni v'tavi'uni l'machoz cheftzi v'tanuchuni b'nachat ru'ach ba'derech kedei shelo etzta'er v'lo etbalbel v'tihyeh halichati betach kecheftzi u'kerotzoni v'lo titnu r'shut l'shum bri'ah lehazikeni b'chol inyan ba'olam v'lo l'katreg v'lo l'ar'er alai v'al ya'ak'vuni b'shum makom shelo birtzoni v'hizdamnu elai la'asot b'kashati v'r'tzoni Omein Selah*

Translation:

> I adjure you with these five holy and pure Names, in the
> Name of the awesome Crown, God of Gods and Lord of
> Lords, the great, strong and awesome God, that you
> transport me from this place I am standing on, to a certain
> place gently, not in distress but calmly, securely and
> restfully, in health of my body and completeness of limbs
> throughout this entire journey to the place I wish to visit,
> unto a certain place, and guide me satisfactorily on the way
> that I will suffer no regret and no confusion, and the course
> of my journey secure in accordance with my wish and my
> will, and do not grant permission to any creature to harm
> me in any manner in the world, and not denounce and not
> appeal against me and not delay me in any place which is
> not within my will and which passes my way, but act
> according to my wish and my will. *Amen Selah.*

When you have concluded writing this incantation, the scroll is
placed inside a bamboo tube. We are informed the bamboo
segment must comprise seven knots, and should be *"arba amot"*
(four cubits). The length of one cubit is from the elbow to the tip
of the middle finger which, we are told, is around 20 inches. Four
cubits would then be 80 inches, i.e. 6 feet 8 inches or 203.2
centimetres. Following the insertion of the scroll, the two ends of
the bamboo staff are sealed with fresh white wax.

You have to purify yourself, refrain from all sexual activity,
and practice a fast during which you restrict yourself to consuming
bread and water only, all of this taking place for a period of
twenty-four hours prior to performing magical travel. When the
time arrives to work the technique, your entire body needs to be
washed, after which you have to put on a clean white garment. You
must then exit the city, the instruction being that you walk the
length of a bowshot out of town. Whilst raising the bamboo wand

in front of your body, and without speaking, turn your head to look backwards momentarily, after which continue walking until you arrive at your destination. The instruction is not to allow your eyes to wander in any way whatsoever, i.e. looking sideways, but to proceed straight ahead. In this regard, there have been suggestions elsewhere that your face be covered with a kerchief during the magical travel.

It is said you will have no physical sensory experiences of anything during the magical journey, i.e. whether there be mountains or rivers along the way, you will not have any direct experience of these. It is said that you will "fly like an eagle," and that the destination you seek will be in the very first town or city you arrive at. After having arrived at your destination, you are to lower the bamboo wand and proceed into the town as you carry the lowered wand, and to fulfil the fundamental purpose of your visit.

Further instruction reads that should you wish to overnight in the location, that you need to remove the scroll from the bamboo tube and place it where it can be guarded whilst you are sleeping, e.g. under your pillow. On waking you may relocate the item inside the wand should you wish to employ it again, i.e. to effect the return journey.[140]

Next, let us consider the conjoined utilization of several Divine Names in Hebrew amulets.

I. Compounded Employment of Divine Names

It was inevitable that certain fundamental Kabbalistic doctrines regarding Divine Names would have come to be considered to embody "amuletic" virtues. In this regard we might consider the four "*milui*," i.e. the full spellings of the letters comprising the Ineffable Name, aligned with the "Four Worlds" concept, as featured in the following *Shiviti* amulet for "purity of thought" (*Machshavah*):[141]

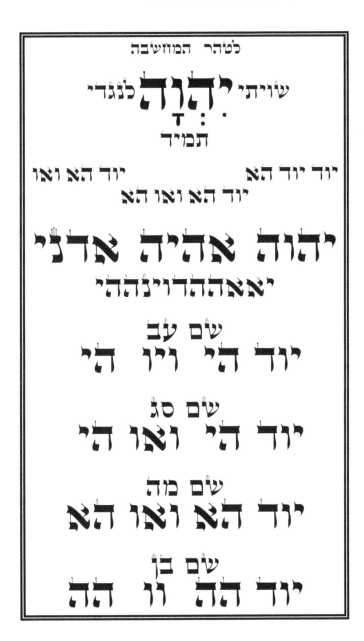

We are informed that the attainment of great understanding necessitates "purity of thought," and that it is good to work with *Kavvanah*, i.e. powerful attention conjoined with willful intention. These qualities of mind are generally understood to be powerfully engendered by *Shiviti* amulets and plaques, the latter being large sacred wall-hangings comprised of arrangements of Divine and

Angelic Names, often beautifully illuminated with a selection of artistic adornments specifically meaningful to the composer of the item.

As indicated in *"The Book of Sacred Names,"*[142] in which I have analysed one such construct titled the "Universal *Shiviti* Amulet," all such articles are named after the inscription usually located in the upper portion of the item. In this regard, we note top centre the four large letters comprising the Ineffable Name, *YHVH*, directly below the words לטהר המחשבה (*l'tahar ha-machshevah*—for the purification of thought), this being the fundamental purpose of the amulet under consideration. Conjoined with the words on either side and directly below the Ineffable Name, we read the biblical phrase after which the construct is named:

שויתי יהוה לנגדי תמיד (*Psalm 16:8*)

Transliteration:

Shiviti YHVH l'negdi tamid

Translation:

I have set *YHVH* before me always

Beside the fundamental intention of all *Shiviti* plaques, which is for us to daily keep our heart/mind focus on the Ineffable Name, the *Kamea* requires the owner to not only read, but to actually enunciate the Divine Name with the vowels indicated, i.e. *chirik* (*ee*) and *patach* (*ah*), thus sounding the Name "*YiH'VaH*" during the reading of the opening phrase. This action is followed by tracing and contemplating the displayed arrangements of component letter combinations and *milui* ("fillings"—full spellings) of יהוה (*YHVH*), as well as the two Divine Names here affiliated and conjoined with the *Tetragrammaton*.

Whilst having addressed this important Kabbalistic concept extensively in a previous volume of my "Shadow Tree Series,"[143] I thought to revisit it here for the sake of clarity. The reasoning here is that the different spellings of the names of two of the three letters comprising the Ineffable Name, i.e. וה, are fundamental in ascertaining the "levels of expression" of יהוה in which the letters ה (*Heh*) and ו (*Vav*) have different "fillings" (spellings).

Traditionally the letter ה (*Heh*) can be spelled הא (*Heh-Alef*), הה (*Heh-Heh*) or הי (*Heh-Yod*), and ו (*Vav*) can be spelled ואו (*Vav-Alef-Vav*), ויו (*Vav-Yod-Vav*) or וו (*Vav-Vav*). The three variations of spelling are termed:

> *Milui d'Alfin* (*Alef* filling);
> *Milui d'He'in* (*Heh* filling); and
> *Milui d'Yodin* (*Yod* filling).

Applying this to the relevant letters in יהוה (*YHVH*), the Sacred Name can be expanded into what is traditionally termed the "Forty-Five Letter Name of God," "Fifty-Two Letter Name of God," "Sixty-Three Letter Name of God," and "Seventy-Two Letter Name of God." In fact, each of these expanded Names are understood to pertain to one of the "Four Worlds" of Kabbalah, respectively the worlds of *Asiyah, Yetzirah, Bri'ah* and *Atzilut*, as shown below:

> הה וו הה דוי (*Yod-vav-dalet Heh-heh Vav-vav Heh-heh*) comprises the "Fifty-Two Letter Name of God," and in *gematria* the combination בן (*Ben* [ב = 2 + ן = 50 = 52]), which is representative of the "Fifty-Two Letter Name of God."
>
> הא ואו הא דוי (*Yod-vav-dalet Heh-alef Vav-alef-vav Heh-alef*) comprises the "Forty-Five Letter Name of God," which corresponds in *gematria* to מה (*Mah* [מ = 40 + ה = 45]).
>
> הי ואו הי דוי (*Yod-vav-dalet Heh-yod Vav-alef-vav Heh-yod*) comprises the "Sixty-Three Letter Name of God," represented by the combination סג (*Sag* [ס = 60 + ג = 3 = 63])
>
> הי ויו הי דוי (*Yod-vav-dalet Heh-yod Vav-yod-vav Heh-yod*) comprises the "Seventy-Two Letter Name of God," which is related to the "Name of Seventy-Two Names." This *milui* of the Ineffable Name is appropriately represented by the combination עב (*Av* [ע = 70 + ב = 2 = 72]).

It should be noted that the important "Sacred Marriage" of the "higher" and the "lower" as expressed in the Divine Name יאהדונהי (*Yahadonahi*), the earlier mentioned conjunction of the Ineffable Name and *Adonai*, is also fundamental to the four expansions of *YHVH*. In this regard we are told that

1. the "*Av*" (72) expansion "motivates the union of *Chochmah* (Wisdom/Father) and *Binah* (Understanding/Mother)";

2. the "*Sag*" (63) expansion is associated with *Binah* (Understanding) and "elevates the Feminine Waters through the *Neshamah*"[144] (Higher Self) of the *Tzadik* (righteous individual);

3. the "*Mah*" (45) expansion "motivates the union between Tiferet (Beauty/Male [King]) and *Malchut* (Kingdom/ Female [Queen]); and

4. the "*Ben*" (52) expansion "elevates the Feminine Waters through the *Nefesh* (Instinctual Self) of the *Tzadik* (righteous individual).[145]

Keeping these considerations in mind, it is apparent that, the expansions in the "*Machshavah Kamea*" we are addressing, reflect the sacred union of the "centre" and the "circumference," i.e. the "All" with and the "All-in-All." It should be noted that extended spellings of a number of Divine Names, e.g. יהוה (*YHVH*), אהיה (*Ehyeh*), אלהים (*Elohim*), אדני (*Adonai*), etc., are employed in Hebrew amulets.

Be that as it may, the design of the current *Kamea* is comprised of three basic sectors. The upper portion encompasses the earlier mentioned opening biblical phrase, below which is located three sets of full spellings of the letters of the Ineffable Name (*milui d'alfin*) as follows:

(Left)   (Right)

יוד הא ואו   יוד יוד הא

(Centre)

יוד הא ואו הא

Yod-vav-dalet Heh-alef Vav-alef-vav He-alef

As clearly indicated, the full spelling in this instance is *Milui d'Alfin*, the expanded format of the *Tetragrammaton* titled the "Forty-Five Letter Name of God" or "*Mah*"-expansion. Contemplating the entire combination we read the full spelling of י יה יהו יהוה (*Yod Yod-Heh Yod-Heh-Vav Yod-Heh-Vav-Heh*), a format of letters comprising the Ineffable Name which is sometimes depicted:

Referring to this image as the *"Tetragrammaton Tetractys,"* I noted in *"The Book of Sacred Names"* that "this image was often engraved on silver triangles and worn on the body as protective amulets," and further mentioned that "the four layers of Hebrew glyphs represent the 'Four Worlds,' four principles of manifestation, and four aspects of ones being, i.e. *Tzelem* or *Guf*, *Nefesh*, *Ru'ach* and *Neshamah*."[146] Hence tracing the expanded spellings of this pattern in our amulet, is said to not only align the practitioner with the universal order of the "Four Worlds," but to actually trigger within every aspect of his being the Divine Power inherent in the mentioned expansion of the *Tetragrammaton*. After all, the *"Mah"*-expansion of the Ineffable Name pertains to ones own hands—the organs of conscious action or of giving and receiving which should be governed by mindfulness.[147]

    The second and central portion of the amulet comprises the listing of three Divine Names and their unification into one great name in the following manner:

יהוה אהיה אדני

יאאההדוינההי

In Kabbalah these three special Divine Names are considered instrumental in the flow of Divine Abundance from *Keter* (Crown), the loftiest sphere on the sefirotic Tree, via *Tiferet* (Beauty) the central sphere, down into *Malchut* (Kingdom), the earthly realm of physical existence. Each of these spheres are aligned with one of the three listed Divine Names, specifically:

אהיה (*Ehyeh*) —   *Keter* (Crown)

יהוה (*YHVH*) —   *Tiferet* (Beauty)

אדני (*Adonai*) —   *Malchut* (Kingdom)

In seeing these three primary Divine Names and their ultimate union displayed centrally in the amulet under consideration, I am reminded of the Kabbalistic doctrine regarding the outpouring of "Divine Abundance" from its source in the Ultimate Unmanifest, and its flow into physical manifestation down the "Central Pillar" on the sefirotic Tree. In this regard, we are informed that the initial א (*Alef*) of both the Names אהיה (*Ehyeh*) and אדני (*Adonai*) is a reference to the "Divine Essence" of אין סוף (*Ain Sof*) being funnelled as infinite *Shefa* (Abundance) into the realms of manifestation. In delineating this unique force-flow from *Ehyeh* via *YHVH* and *Adonai* into the whole of physical manifestation, Joseph Gikatilla wrote: "Know that the activity of the upper Name which is *Ehyeh* is the activity of absolute mercy, and that this is the Name that brings good and gives for free and has mercy not out of judgment but out of absolute mercy....."[148]

Of course, as noted in a previous discussion on this very topic, "in the entire concept of *Ain Sof* (the Infinite No-Thing) pouring out *Shefa* (divine abundance), the basic idea is infinity without any limitation whatsoever. There is simply no underlying motive for God to be obliged to pour out *Shefa* because of a sense of pity for that which He emanated into existence. The basic function of divine creative emanation is *Chesed*, an enormous loving-kindness, not for any specific reason as such, but simply for itself alone."[149]

In this regard, I believe what is of paramount importance here is the location of the Ineffable Name, aligned as it is in this instance with *Tiferet* (Beauty). Again it was noted that the concept of Beauty should "not be perceived in a limited manner" since it "has something to do with things being harmoniously related together."[150] Underlying this concept is a sense of absolute "oneness," as I noted "What I find so amazing about the way *Shefa* is being funneled down into manifestation is that, whilst it is being expressed in all the realms of manifestation in an infinite, 'all-possible-possibilities' number of ways, the 'many ways' are harmoniously related in a universal 'oneness,' and this is called 'Beauty'."[151]

As I gaze at the three unique Divine Names listed in the centre of a *Kamea* created with the intention of not only clarifying (purifying) mind, but also to "open the heart" to greater understanding, I am again brought to the realisation of how our sense of "separateness" in this world has led to the loss of our primordial recognition of the divine unity between all aspects of incarnate existence, and how, "in order to restore the flow of 'Divine Abundance,' we have to realign ourselves with the perfect unity of the 'All,' i.e. re-establish balance with the 'Beauty' and 'Loving-kindness' of the Eternal One."[152]

In being mindful of this, it is clear to me that as I trace the third portion of the amulet, which is comprised of the four expansions of the Ineffable Name, indicating the "strengths" of the Divine One in manifestation listed in exact order below the great Unified Name, i.e. the composite of *YHVH*, *Ehyeh* and *Adonai*, I am again reminded that every individual "must return to 'oneness' within him or herself, and to restore and keep the balance micro-cosmically between body, mind, soul and spirit, as well as align with the forces of 'Divine Abundance' macro-cosmically" throughout the "Four Worlds." Here then, in this very special "*Shiviti* Amulet" said to "purify mentality," we find an incredible *Yichud* (unification) the contemplation of which will not only facilitate clarity of mind, but bring the necessary inner alignment which will "afford the free flow of *Shefa*, Divine Abundance, into oneself and ones world."[153]

Whilst we have been perusing an amulet intended to "purify the mind" and "open the heart," I thought it would be worthwhile investing *Kameot* aiding good recollection. In this regard, the Divine Name אהדי (*Ahadi*) is employed in Hebrew amulets for the purpose of improving memory. The Name אהדי (*Ahadi*) was derived from three sources:

1. the expression יהוה אחד (*YHVH echad*—"*YHVH* is One*");

2. the phrase וימלא כבוד יהוה (*v'yimalei kavod YHVH*— "shall be filled with the glory of *YHVH*") (*Numbers 14:21*); and

3. the sentence הדברים האלה היה דבר יהוה אל אברם אחר (*Achar ha-d'varim ha-eleh hayah d'var YHVH el Av'ram*—"After these things the word of *YHVH* came unto Abram") (*Genesis 15:1*).[154]

I am not at all certain as to the reason why the component letters comprising the Name אהדי were arranged in the order employed in Jewish magic, however we are informed that the letters were mainly derived from the initials of four words in the third listed source, i.e. אל יהוה דבר היה.[155]

The Name אהדי (*Ahadi*) is included in a magical seal drawn in a variety of formats on deerskin parchment, or again on clean good quality paper, in order to achieve good memory recall. To achieve this end, we are informed the following *Kamea* should be written on the 17th day of the month *Tamuz*, i.e. the minor fast day commemorating the destruction of the Temple in Jerusalem. The amulet is then kept until the "ten days of repentance," i.e. the period between *Rosh Hashanah* (New Year) and *Yom Kippur* (Day of Atonement), when it is rolled up, bound three times, and afterwards carried on ones person inside a small silver locket, tube or talisman holder.[156]

The phrase written along the outer rim of the inner square is *Genesis 48:3* reading:

אל שדי נראה אלי בלוז בארץ כנען ויברך א(ו)תי

Transliteration:

El Shadai nir'ah elai b'luz b'eretz k'na'an vaivarech oti

Translation:

El Shadai appeared unto me at Luz in the land of Canaan, and blessed me.

The four Hebrew terms located above this verse are מזרח (*Mizrach*—"East"); צפון (*Tzafon*—"North"); מערב (*Ma'arav*—"West") and דרום (*Darom*—"South"). The vowels employed with the four letters of the Divine Name אהדי (*Ahadi*) are, from right to left, a *Sh'va*; *Patach*; *Kamatz*; and a *Chirik*. Apparently this has some unspecified special significance.

Whatever that may be, we are told that after completion of the *Kamea* and throughout the year, whenever one needs to remember or having to recall anything whatsoever, one only needs to put the silver locket comprising the amulet inside ones mouth, and the required recollection will be achieved forthwith.[157]

Elsewhere we find a related amulet, i.e. also an *Ahadi* amulet employed for the very same purpose, however the format of the *Kamea* is somewhat more complex:

In this instance the amulet is employed in conjunction with the "Twenty-two Letter Name of God." In this regard, we are informed the אָנְקְתָּם פַּסְתָּם פַּסְפַּסִים דְיוּנְסִים ('naket'ma p'sotam p'sips'yema dayev'soyam) vocalisation of the "Twenty-two Letter Name," is based on the vowels employed in the word יְהַבְךָ (y'hav'cha—"your burden"). The latter term appears in *Psalm 55:22 [23]* reading הַשְׁלֵךְ עַל יהוה יְהַבְךָ (*Hashlech al YHVH y'hav'cha*—"Cast thy burden upon *YHVH*").[158] As in the case of the previous *Kamea*, the current amulet is likewise, as it were, enhanced by *Genesis 48:3*.

The construction of this *Kamea* again takes place on the 17th day of *Tamuz*, however, one is instructed to pay a visit to the *mikveh* (ritual bath), where one has to do a ritual submersion whilst wearing a hat on ones head and a belt around the waist. This is done prior to writing the amulet on a deerskin, or similarly prepared hide of any kosher animal which did not fall prey to a carnivorous animal.

Furthermore, the writing of the amulet should be done in *ashurit*, i.e. the formal Hebrew lettering employed in writing biblical scrolls, all written with a new quill or pen with the special ink employed in the writing of a biblical scroll. We are instructed to commence the composition of this amulet with the "Twenty-two Letter Name" written at the top of the scroll, then to write the *Ahadi* portion of the amulet, as it were, from the centre outwards — *Ahadi* with vowels in the centre; the same term without vowels written along the four borders of the inner square; etc.[159]

We will next consider a few of the large, extensive amulets composed of complex aggregates of biblical verses, Divine and angelic Names, "Magic Squares," etc. There are numerous examples of such amulets readily available, and in this regard I would like to share here a very weathered 17/18th century *Kamea*, which was constructed in Germany, and is now housed in the Israel Museum, Jerusalem.[160] The amulet is virtually illegible in part, however, by carefully investigating its component sectors, I was able to work a full reconstruction.

This item is comprised of several of the standard Divine Names often employed in *Kameot*, i.e. the Ineffable Name, the "Name of Seventy-two Names," the "Forty-two Letter Name," etc., as well as verses and abbreviations of sections of the Hebrew Bible relevant to the fundamental intention behind its construction. In terms of the latter, we might note that there is an extensive tradition surrounding the abbreviation of sacred writ on Hebrew amulets. Titled ראשי תיבות (*Roshei Teivot*—Acronyms/ Abbreviations [lit. "Heads of Boxes"]).[161] Their purpose is not only to save space on relatively small writing surfaces, but also to form a number of highly specialised Divine Names.

Be that as it may, finding this amulet most intriguing, I decided to restore and correct the image with the convenient facilities of a modern day computer. As shown below, the format of the final image is virtually identical to that of the original handwritten *Kamea*:

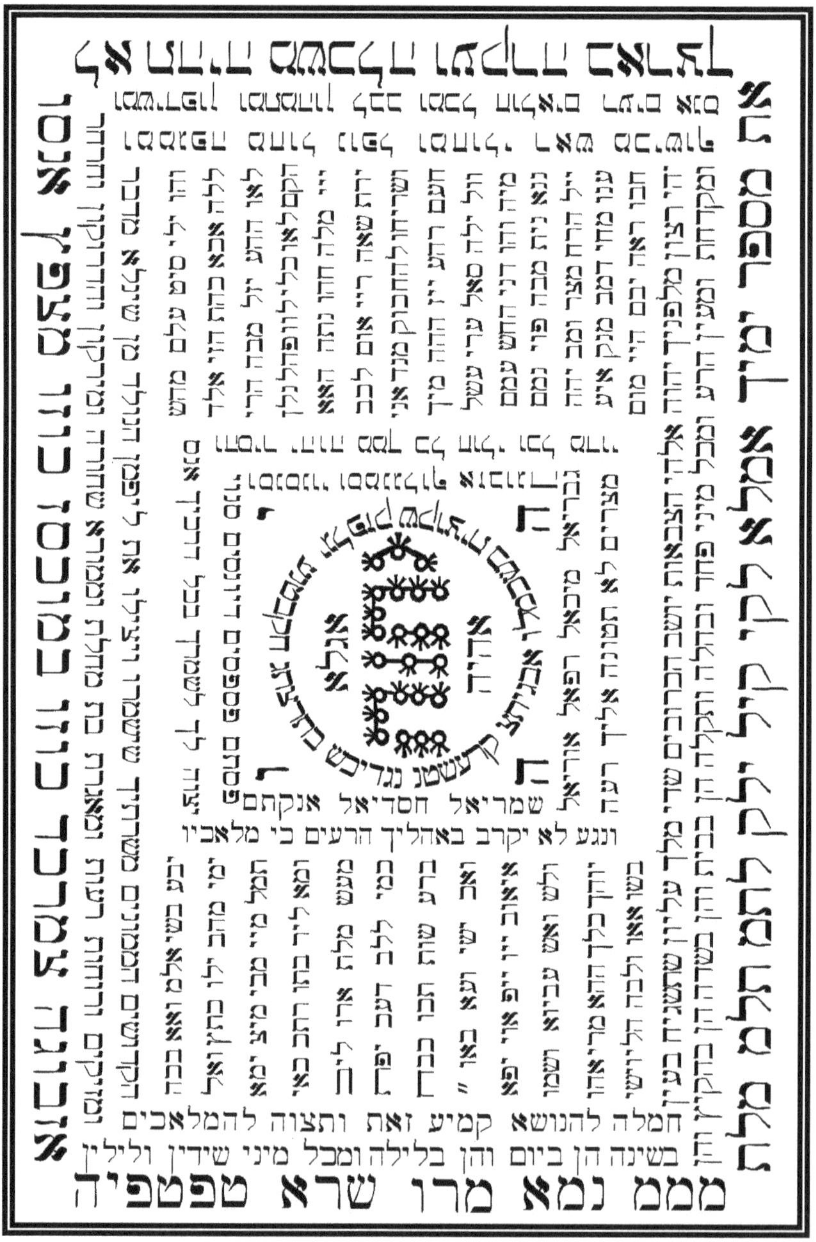
שמריאל חסדיאל אנקתם
ונגע לא יקרב באהליך הרעים כי מלאכיו
חמלה להנושא קמיע זאת ותצוה להמלאכים
בשינה הן ביום והן בלילה ומכל מיני שידין ולילין
ממם נמא מרו שרא טפטפיה

Commencing at the top right corner of the *Kamea* the outer border reads:

Right Down

לֹא תִהְיֶה מְשַׁכֵּלָה וַעֲקָרָה בְּאַרְצֶךָ..... (*Exodus 23:26*)

Transliteration:

Lo Tihyeh m'shakelah va'akarah b'artzecha.....

Translation:

None shall miscarry, nor be barren.....

Bottom

אֶת מִסְפַּר יָמֶיךָ אֲמַלֵּא (*Exodus 23:26* cont.)

לקי קיל ילק (*Genesis 49:18*)

לתמ תלמ מלת (*Exodus 22:17* [18])

Transliteration:

.....*et mispar yamecha amalei* (*Exodus 23:26* cont.)

LKY KYL YLK (abbreviation and permutations of the initials of לִישׁוּעָתְךָ קִוִּיתִי יהוה [*Lishu'atcha kiviti YHVH*]) (*Genesis 49:18*)

LTM TLM MLT (abbreviation and permutations of the phrase מְכַשֵּׁפָה לֹא תְחַיֶּה [*m'chashefah lo t'chayeh*]) (*Exodus 22:17* [18])

Translation:

.....in thy land; the number of thy days I will fulfil.

I wait for Thy salvation *YHVH* (*Genesis 49:18*)

Thou shalt not suffer a sorceress to live. (*Exodus 22:17* [18])

Left

ממם נמא מרו שרא טפטפיה

Transliteration:

MMM NMA MRV ShRA Taftafyah

In the bottom border the curious abbreviation לקי (*LKY*) derived from *Genesis 49:18*, is particularly important and extensively employed in Hebrew amulets.[162] Regarding the left border, the concluding portion of the outer construct of the amulet, we have already addressed the Divine Name *Taftafyah* in some detail earlier. I am not at all sure however as to the meaning of the four three letter constructs employed in this portion of the amulet. Having consulted a number of sources on Hebrew acronyms which might possibly be employed in *Kameot*, I am yet at a loss as to what the said abbreviations might mean.

Top

אזבוגה צמרכד כוזו במוכסז כוזו מצפץ אנסו

Transliteration:

Azbogah, Tzamarchad, Kuzu B'mochsaz Kuzu, Matzapatza, ANSV [Omein Netzach Selah Va'ed]

As indicated, the upper border of the *Kamea* comprises four earlier addressed Divine Names, i.e. *Azbogah, Tzamarchad, Kuzu B'mochsaz Kuzu*, as well as *Matz'patz*. Additionally, we note the outer border concluding with the four letter combination in the upper border of the amulet under discussion, this being the abbreviation of אמן נצח סלה ועד (*Omein Netzach Selah Va'ed* [*Amen*, Enduring (Victory), *Selah*, Forever]), a concluding formula fairly extensively employed in Hebrew incantations and amulets.

Next we turn our attention to the inner border of the *Kamea* comprising a written incantation in two lines. To read the invocation, commence bottom right, following the innermost line of the two and trace around the entire amulet. Conclude by perusing the outermost line in the same manner. The invocation reads:

יהי רצון מלפניך יהוה אלהי הצבאות יושב הכרובים
שדי מלך עליון שתשגיח בעין חמלה להנושא קמיע זאת
ותצוה להמלאכים הקדושים הממונים משרתיך שישמרו
ויצילו את ליפמן הנולד מן שינלא מדבר וממגפה מחול
נופל ומחולי ראש מכישוף ומקדחת ומעין הרע ומכל
מיני פחד ובהלה ותקלה הן בבית והן בשדה הן בהקיץ
והן בשינה הן ביום והן בלילה ומכל מיני שידין ולילין
ומזיקים ורוחות רעות ומאגרת בת מחלת וממורא
שחורה ומירקון והדרוקון וחרחר ומשידפון ומתמהון
לבב ומכל חולאים רעים אנס

Transliteration:

> *Y'hi ratzon milfanecha YHVH elohei ha-tzva'ot yoshev ha-k'ruvim shadai melech elyon shetashgiach b'ayin chemlah l'hanose kamea zot v'tetzaveh ha-malachim ha-kadoshim ha-memonim meshartecha sheyishmeru v'yatzilu et Lipman ha-nolad min Shinla midever v'mimagefah michol nofel v'micholi rosh mikishuf v'mikadachat v'mi'ayin ha-ra v'mikol minei pachad v'behalah v'takalah hen babayit v'hen basadeh hen b'hakitz v'hen b'shenah hen b'yom v'hen b'lailah v'mikol minei shedin v'lilin v'mazikim v'ruchot ra'ot v'mi'agrat bat machalat v'mimorah sh'chorah v'miyarkon v'hadrokon v'charchar v'mishidafon v'm'timahon l'vav v'michol chola'im ra'im ANS [Omein Netzach Selah].*

Translation:

> May it be your will *YHVH*, God of Hosts, enthroned on the *Kerubim, Shadai*, lofty King, to oversee with your merciful eye the one who carries this amulet, and will command the holy messengers (angels), those who are charged with serving you, will guard and save Lipman born of Shinla from pestilence and from plague, from sand falls[?] and from sickness of the head, from sorcery and from fever, and from the evil eye, and from all manner of fear and terror and hindrance, whether at home and whether in the field, whether awake and whether asleep, whether in the day and whether at night; and from all kinds of *shedin* (fiends), and *lilin* (demonic forces), and *mazikim* (harmful forces), and evil spirits, and from *Agrat bat Machalat*, and from melancholy, and from jaundice and the dragon, and wheezing and skin rashes, and heart shock, and from all bad diseases. *Amen* Enduring *Selah* Forever.

It appears this *Kamea* was written for a certain Lipman born of Shinla, in order to protect him against a variety of spiritual foes and diseases. In several instances it is difficult to ascertain the exact meaning of some of the Hebrew terms referring to specific ailments, the meanings of several Hebrew words being in many instances quite different in the 17/18th century, when this amulet was written, from the modern usage of the same words. In this regard, I find translating the following terms in the incantation to be somewhat problematic:

1.　חול נופל (*Chol Nofel*—"sand falls") do not appear to align with the context of the amulet. It was suggested the term refers to "quicksand." However, as the term חול employed as a verb also means "writhing in pain," I suspect that the correct reading of the expression in question might be "collapsing with searing pain." On the other hand, considering the succeeding and associated term in the amulet referring to "sickness of the head," the problematic expression might be referring to "falling sickness," i.e. epilepsy.

2.　דרקון (*drakon*). The word refers to a "dragon." Considering again the context, and the preceding term ירקון (*yarkon*) meaning "jaundice," i.e. the yellow sickness, I tend to think the word in question to be a reference to the "green sickness," i.e. chlorosis, a very common disease in Europe at the time when the amulet was written. Otherwise the term in question might even be referring to hepatitis.

3.　חרחר (*charchar*) is one of those wonderful onomatopoeic words meaning "wheezing," i.e. the sound of breathing when the lungs are congested. Whilst I have translated it thus, I believe the underlying intention here pertains to protecting the bearer of the amulet against all problematic lung conditions, i.e. asthma, emphysema, etc.

4.　שידפון (*shidafon*). Considering the context and fundamental protective function of the amulet being addressed, I am inclined to think the term *shidafon* refers to all manner of debilitating skin conditions, i.e. blisters, chronic eczema, etc.

5.　תמהון לבב (*timahon levav*). Literally "heart shock," I believe this expression is indicating in this instance conditions ranging from palpitations to heart attacks, etc.

It should also be noted that the fundamental meaning of the expression מורה שחורה (*morah sh'chorah*) is really black depression.

As indicated, several members of the infernal hosts against whom protection is being sought in Hebew amulets, are equally listed in the current amulet, i.e. *shedin*, *lilin*, *mazikin*, etc. There is one amongst these malevolent denizens whose appearance in amulets is fairly rare. I am referring to אגרת בת מחלת (*Agrat* [also *Igrat*] *bat Machalat*), consort of *Ashmodai* and queen of the demons, of which more anon.

Having perused the two sets of borders of this *Kamea*, we now turn our attention to the very centre of the amulet in which we note the peculiar presentation of the Ineffable Name adorned with twenty-four little circles, each of which is comprised of three "rays," so to speak. We are told the twenty-four circles pertain to the twenty-four permutations of the Ineffable Name, and, the "rays" (24 x 3 = 72) refer to the "*Shem Vayisa Vayet*," i.e. the "Name of Seventy-Two Names." Presentations of the Ineffable Name in the same format can be found in several primary Kabbalistic texts, sometimes only indicating the twenty-four circles without the additional three-rayed "crowns." As mentioned in "*The Book of Sacred Names*," this image of the Ineffable Name "became particularly popular amongst Hermetic Kabbalists, especially with those who marvel at the 'mysteries' of the '*Shemhamforash*' referred to in works like the '*The Key of Solomon*'."[163] I noted that "the author, purportedly King Solomon, tells us that he had 'done great things by the virtue of the *Schema Hamphorasch*, and by the Thirty-two Paths of *Yetzirah*. Number, weight, and measure determine the form of things; the substance is one, and God createth it eternally."[164] We are also informed in this text that:

> "Happy is he who comprehendeth the Letters and the Numbers. The Letters are from the Numbers, and the Numbers from the Ideas, and the Ideas from the Forces, and the Forces from the *Elohim*. The Synthesis of the *Elohim* is the *Schema*. The *Schema* is one, its columns are two, its power is three, its form is four, its reflection giveth eight, which multiplied by three giveth unto thee the twenty-four Thrones of Wisdom.

Upon each Throne reposeth a Crown with three Rays, each Ray beareth a Name, each Name is an Absolute Idea. There are Seventy-two Names upon the Twenty-four Crowns of the *Schema*. Thou shalt write these Names upon Thirty-six Talismans, two upon each Talisman, one on each side. Thou shalt divide these Talismans into four series of nine each, according to the number of the Letters of the *Schema*.

Upon the first Series thou shalt engrave the Letter *Yod*, symbolised by the Flowering Rod of Aaron. Upon the second the Letter *HE*, symbolised by the Cup of Joseph. Upon the third the Letter *Vau*, symbolised by the Sword of David my father. And upon the fourth the *HE* final, symbolised by the *Shekel* of Gold. These thirty-six Talismans will be a Book which will contain all the Secrets of Nature. And by their diverse combinations thou shalt make the Genii and Angels speak."[165]

As mentioned, in the case of the *Kamea* we are investigating, the seventy-two "rays" align with the earlier addressed "Name of Seventy-two Names," these being listed in full on the centre-right portion of the amulet. As it is, the employment of the "Name of Seventy-two Names" in the *Kamea* in question, certainly does not require any verbal expression on the part of the owner, who simply has to carry it on his or her person to reap the benefit thereof. Hence, let us turn our attention back to the Ineffable Name in the centre of the amulet.

Continuing with the details surrounding the Ineffable Name in the centre of the *Kamea*, we recognise the Names אגלא (*Agala'a*) and אהיה (*Ehyeh*) respectively located above and below the special "magical" presentation of the Ineffable Name. We should note that these two Divine Names have a great deal of special significance in Jewish magic and mysticism. The Name אהיה (*Ehyeh*) is attributed to both *Keter* (Crown) and *Binah* (Understanding) in the primary literature of theoretical and practical Kabbalah. I noted in "*The Book of Sacred Names*" that related, as it is, to the loftiest sphere on the *Etz Chaim* (Tree of

Life), "*Ehyeh* has a special relationship via *YHVH* in *Tiferet* (Beauty) with *Adonai* in *Malchut* (Kingdom)," a connection which benefits our existence "in the most abundant manner."[166] In this regard Joseph Gikatilla informs us in his "*Gates of Light*" to "Know that the activity of the upper Name which is *Ehyeh* is the activity of absolute mercy, and that this is the Name that brings good and gives for free and has mercy not out of judgment but out of absolute mercy....."[167] So now we also understand that the two Names *Agala'a* and *Ehyeh*, respectively located above and below the Ineffable Name, are positioned so in order to invoke the protective powers of might and the forces of absolute mercy, in harmony with the all encompassing dominion of the most Holy Name of the Divine One in the very centre of the amulet.

Next, we see that the *Agala'a/YHVH/Ehyeh* combination is encompassed by the "Forty-two Letter Name," the latter concluding with the six-letter abbreviation often accompanying this Divine Name in Hebrew amulets, this being:

ברוך שם כבוד מלכותו לעולם ועד

Transliteration:
    Baruch Shem K'vod Malchuto l'Olam Va'ed
Translation:
    Blessed be the Name of His glorious Kingdom throughout eternity.

In turn we note that the core of the amulet includes the four letters of the Ineffable Name located in the four corners of the central square containing the Divine Name construct we have been addressing, i.e. י (*Yod*) in upper right corner, ה (*Heh*) in the lower right, ו (*Vav*) upper left corner, and the concluding ה (*Heh*) lower left. Plainly, the omnipotent dominion of the Ineffable Name is being emphasized here, equally asserting this *Kamea* to be a most potent "power object," so to speak.

The middle portion of the amulet is completed with a set of Divine and Angelic Names which are in turn enclosing the central construct we have been addressing. These can be traced:

(Bottom) גבריאל מיכאל רפאל אוריאל.....

(Left) שמריאל חסדיאל אנקתם.....

(Top) פסתם פספסים דיונסים סנוי.....

(Right) וסנסנוי וסמנגלוף אזבוגה

Transliteration:

(Bottom) *Gavri'el Micha'el Rafa'el Ori'el.....*

(Left) *Shamri'el Chasdi'el Anaktam.....*

(Top) *Pastam Paspasim Dionsim Sanoi.....*

(Right) *v'Sansanoi v'Semangelof Azbogah*

Translation:

(Bottom) *Gabriel Michael Rafael Oriel.....*

(Left) *Shamriel Chasdiel Anaktam.....*

(Top) *Pastam Paspasim Dionsim Sanoi.....*

(Right) *and Sansanoi and Semangelof Azbogah*

The opening set of six Angelic Names is well-known. This is succeeded by the earlier addressed "Twenty-two Letter Name," which is in turn followed by the names of three curious Angelic personages, who are often depicted in the form of bird-like images on Hebrew amulets in order to protect mothers and infants against *Lilit*, the "mother of all demons." These angels, named *Sanoi*, *Sansanoi* and *Semangelof*, is addressed in greater detail elsewhere in this text. As shown, the set of Divine and Angelic Names under consideration is concluded with a repeat of the earlier addressed Divine Name *Azbogah*.

Next we note that all the mentioned central Divine and Angelic Names are, as it were, enveloped in an outer square commencing with the first portion of *Deuteronomy 7:15* and continuing with *Psalm 91:10—11*. This portion of the *Kamea* is concluded with a Hebrew abbreviation, the whole reading:

(Right) [*Deuteronomy 7:15*] והסיר יהוה ממך כל

חלו]לי וכל מדוי.....

(Bottom) לא תטונה [*Psalm 91:10—11*] מצרים

[correctly תאנה] אליך רעה.....

(Left) ונגע לא יקרב באהלו]ך [הרעים] כי מלאכיו

(Top right to left) יצוה לך לשמרך בכל דרכיך

אנ׳ס]אמן נצח סלה[

Transliteration:

> (Right) [*Deuteronomy 7:15*] *v'hesir YHVH mimcha kol choli v'chol madvei.....*
>
> (Bottom) *mitzrayim.....* [*Psalm 91:10*] *lo t'tuneh* [should read *t'uneh*] *alecha ra'ah.....*
>
> (Left) *v'nega lo yikrav b'ahalecha* [*ha-ra'im*] *ki malachav.....*
>
> (Top) *y'tzaveh lach lishmarcha b'chol d'rachecha ANS* (*Omein Netzach Selah*)

Translation:

> (Right) [*Deuteronomy 7:15*] And *YHVH* will take away from thee all sickness; and He will put on none of the evil diseases of.....
>
> (Bottom) Egypt..... [*Psalm 91:10—11*] There shall no evil befall thee.....
>
> (Left) neither shall any plague come nigh thy tent [evil diseases], For He will give His angels.....
>
> (Top) charge over thee to keep thee in all thy ways *ANS* [*Amen*, Enduring (Victory), *Selah*]

It should be noted, and as indicated elsewhere in this tome, *Deuteronomy 7:15* is extensively employed in a variety of Hebrew protection and healing amulets. Be that as it may, our investigation into this remarkable amulet concludes with the complete *Shem Vayisa Vayet* written over fourteen lines in the right column, and twelve lines of mainly three-letter combinations comprising the left column of the *Kamea*. The complete construct incorporates:

1.   in the main the initials of the words comprising *Psalm 91*:

יבע בשי אלמ ואא בכה ימי מהב ילו כתן ואל תמל

מיי מבי מיצ ימא ומא ליר בתו רתכ כאי מעש מלת

ארו ליב כמי ללב דעכ יפת ברע שות תכו כבח ואכ

ישי ועא באו ״ איאוב

2.　　the initials of the words comprising the "Priestly Blessing" in *Numbers 6:24—27*:

ייו ייפ אוי יפא ולש ואש עביוא

The Priestly Blessing reads:

(Verse 24) יברכך יהוה וישמרך

(Verse 25) יאר יהוה פניו אליך ויחנך

(Verse 26) יסע יהוה פניו אליך וישם לך שלום

Transliteration:

(Verse 24) *Y'varech'cha YHVH v'yishm'recha*

(Verse 25) *Ya'eir YHVH panav eilecha vichuneka*

(Verse 26) *Yisa YHVH panav eilecha v'yasem l'cha shalom*

Translation:

(Verse 24) *YHVH* bless thee, and keep thee,

(Verse 25) *YHVH* make His face to shine upon thee, and be gracious unto thee,

(Verse 26) *YHVH* lift up His countenance upon thee, and give thee peace.

3.　　The famous Divine Name combination:

ושמו יוהך כלך

Transliteration:

v'shemo Yohach Kalach

Translation:

And his Name is *Yohach Kalach*.

As noted earlier, the Divine Name *Yohach Kalach* comprises the concluding letters of the words of *Psalm 91:11*.

4.　　The initials of the words comprising *Genesis 48:16*:

ההא מרי אהו בשו ואו ולבה

The verse itself reads:

המלך הגאל אתי מכל רע יברך את הנערים ויקרע

בהם שמי ושם אבתי אברהם ויצחק וידגו לרב בקרב

הארץ

Transliteration:

> *ha-mal'ach ha-go'el oti mikol ra y'varech et ha-n'arim*
> *v'yikarei vahem shmi v'shem avotai Avraham v'Yitzchak*
> *v'yidgu larov b'kerev ha-aretz*

Translation:

> the angel who hath redeemed me from all evil, bless the
> lads; and let my name be named in them, and the name of
> my fathers Abraham and Isaac; and let them grow into a
> multitude in the midst of the earth.

5. and the concluding abbreviation formed from the initials of
    Psalm 121:4:

הליוישי

The original verse reads:

הנה לא ינום ולא יישן שומר ישראל

Transliteration:

> *Hinei lo yanum v'lo yishan shomer Yisra'el*

Translation:

> Behold, He that keepeth Israel doth neither slumber nor
> sleep.

It is worth noting that the Divine Name constructs comprising
abbreviations of Biblical verses are often employed in Jewish
Magic, and have been extensively delineated by Moses Zacutto in
his *Shorshei ha-Shemot*.[168]

Now, I believe it expedient to conclude this chapter with a
perusal of the employment of some of the "exotic" Divine Names
in conjunction with the more standard ones presented in letter
square format. In this regard, consider the following presentation
of an 18th/19th century Persian protection *Kamea*:[169]

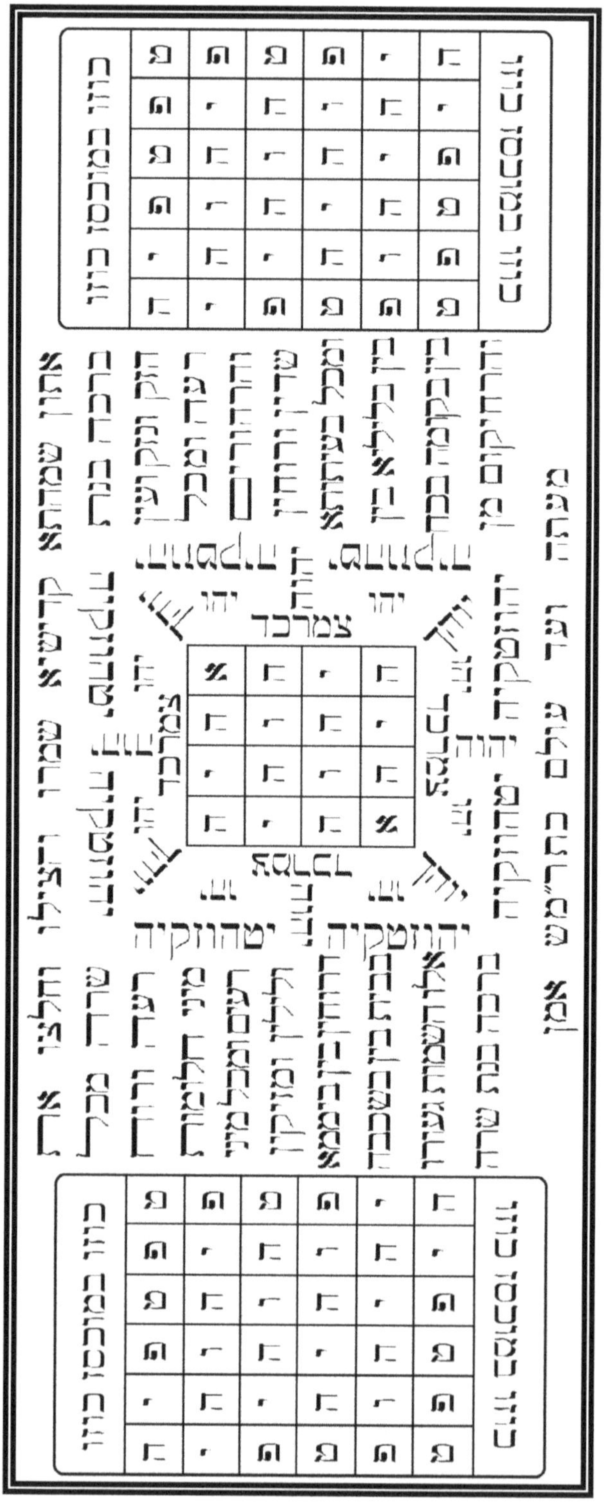

Here the Name *Taftafyah* is combined with the ineffable Name in a *Chotam*. A header and footer comprised of the "Fourteen Letter Name of God," i.e. כוזו במוכסז כוזו (*Kuzu B'mochsaz Kuzu*), is added to the magical seal, and two exact copies of this construct are respectively located to the right and leftmost portion of the *Kamea*. I have elsewhere addressed a similar word square comprised of *Taftafyah*, *Agala'a* and the Ineffable Name.[170]

The reason for the conjoint employment of *Taftafyah* and the Ineffable Name is Divine Protection. Add to this the "Fourteen Letter Name," i.e. *Kuzu B'mochsaz Kuzu*, a Divine Name assigned to *Gevurah* (Strength) on the sefirotic tree which is employed to overcome fear, and the combination will make a most potent magical device, one which is understood to afford the greatest protection in all sorts of dangerous circumstances. This is clearly emphasized in the Aramaic/Hebrew incantation inscribed around the central *Ehyeh/Tetragrammaton* "letter square" reading:

אתון שמהתא קדישיא שמרו והצילו וחלצו את ברכה
בנת שרה מכל הזן'ק ונזק ועין רעה ורוח רעה ומכל
מיני חלומות והרהורים רעים ומכל מיני שדין ורוחין
ולילין ומזיקין ומכל בעיתותא דרוחין בין ביממא בין
בליליא בין בבית בין בשכבה בין בקומה בכח אלו
השמות גערו יהרחיקום מן ברכה בנת שרה
מעתה ועד עולם כתר''מש אמן

I am uncertain as to the pronunciation of the Aramaic terms, however the translation could be read:

"You Holy Names guard and save and deliver the sanctity of the daughter of Sarah from all harm and injury, and evil eye and evil spirit, and from all bad dreams and evil thoughts, and from all kinds of *shedin* (fiends), and *ruchin* (spirits), and *lilin* (demonic forces), and *mazikin* (harmful forces), and from all spirits of terror, whether by day, whether at night; when at home, when she is lying down, when she rises up; in the power of these Names rebuke [these forces], dismiss them from the sanctity of the daughter of Sarah, from now unto eternity, Crown of the Messiah (כתר משיח—*Keter Moshiach*), Amen.

Located in the very centre of the amulet is the earlier addressed *Ehyeh*/Ineffable Name "letter square." As shown in the following detail from the amulet, the entire magic seal is encircled by a number of specialized Divine Names:

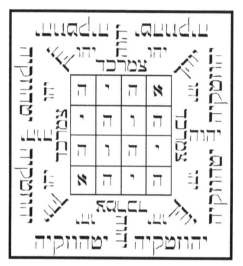

Adjacent the four borders of the central *chotam* of the *Kamea* we trace the earlier addressed Name צמרכד (*Tzamarchad*). Located on all four sides of this Divine Name at right angles to the square, is the Ineffable Name which is, as it were, "braced" on either side by יהו (*YHV*), the basic letters of the *Tetragrammaton*, and which is considered a Divine Name in its own right. The pattern here is: four quarters – *Tzamarchad*; four times – Ineffable Name; four times – *YHV* eight times.

Next we notice the Name יוהך (*Yohach*) inserted four times in the amulet, and located angularly at the four corners of the central seal. Finally four sets of a very peculiar Divine Names יהוזמקיה יטהוזקיה are positioned along the four outer borders of the central construct. Whilst these Divine Names comprise the Ineffable Name conjoined with the letters זמקי and their permutation טזקי, we are told that their origination is obscure.[171] The same Divine Name combination is employed in a magical activity, the intention of which is to take advantage of an enemy.[172]

The magic seal under discussion is employed elsewhere with some variations, as shown in the next, somewhat complex *Kamea* for the alleviation of smallpox, chicken-pox, etc.[173]

This *Kamea* opens with the following incantation written at the very top of the scroll or page:

יהי רצון מלפניך יהוה אלהי ואלהי אבותי עשה למען
קדושת שמותיך אנקתם פסתם פספסים דיונסים אבגיתץ
קרעשטן נגדיכש בטרצתג חקבטנע יגלפזק שקוצית
ובזכות שם עשציי שתחוס ותחמול ותחון ותגן אל [פב״פ]
נקד״ע [נושא קמיע זה עליין מכל מרעין בישין ומחולי
אבעבועות אנס״ו [אמן נצח סלה ועד]

Transliteration:

Y'hi ratzon milfanecha YHVH Elohai v'Elohei avotai aseh l'ma'an k'dushat shmotecha Anaktam Pastam Paspasim Dionsim Avgitatz Karastan Nagdichesh Batratztag Chakvetna Yaglefzok Shakutzit v'biz'chut shem Ashtzei shetachus v'tachmol v'tachon v'tagen al [.....Ploni ben Ploni.....] nose Kamea zeh alaiv m'chol mere'in b'ishin u'm'cholei aba'abu'ot Omein Netzach Selah Va'ed.

Translation:

May it be your will *YHVH* my God, and God of my fathers, act for the sake of the holiness of Your Names, *Anaktam Pastam Paspasim Dionsim, Avgitatz Karastan Nagdichesh Batratztag Chakvetna Yaglefzok Shakutzit*, and in the merit of the Name *Ashtzei*, to spare and have mercy and pity and protect [.....insert the name of the recipient.....], the bearer of this amulet, from all evil doers and bad spirits, and the illness of pox, *Amen*, Enduring (Victory), *Selah*, Forever.

Below the incantation is the *Kamea* construct proper, which includes again the "Twenty-two Letter Name," the "Forty-Two Letter Name," this time with the standard phrase employed at the conclusion of incantations ברוך שם כבוד מלכותו לעולם ועד (*Baruch shem k'vod malchuto l'olam va'ed*—"Blessed be the Name of His glorious Kingdom throughout eternity").

Next, underneath the said Divine Names, the three listed seals are to be written with their associated Divine Names, as indicated in the illustration. The upper *chotam* (seal) comprises a birdlike figure, such images being often employed in conjunction with the names of the acclaimed three child protecting angels. In this instance the form is aligned with סמנגלוף (Semangelof), the other two, סנוי (Sanoi) and סנסנוי (Sansanoi) being respectively located to the right and left of the central image. Adjacent to the head of this figure, we trace respectively right and left the Divine Names שדי (Shadai) and אהיה (Ehyeh). In turn, we read below the mentioned two angelic names located on either side of the image, the earlier addressed Divine Name יוהך כלך (Yohach Kalach).

The central seal is a hexagram comprised of the Name שדי (Shadai) in its centre, and encircled by the six permutations of לקי (LKY), the earlier mentioned abbreviation of *Genesis 49:18*, which is often employed in amulets as a call for Divine aid. The six permutations are usually listed in the order presented in the *Kamea*, i.e. לקי ליק קלי קיל ילק יקל (LKY LYK KLY KYL YLK YKL). The combination וימכח is one of three Divine Names, i.e. וימכח וממהאי ליבובש, which were constructed from the initials of the words comprising *Deuteronomy 7:15*, reading:

והסיר יהוה ממך כל חלי וכל מדוי מצרים הרעים
אשר ידעת לא ישימם בך ונתנם בכל שנאיך

Transliteration:

> *V'hesir YHVH mim'cha kol choli v'chol mad'vei mitzrayim ha-ra'im asher yada'ta lo y'shimam bach un'tanam b'chol shon'echa*

Translation:

> And *YHVH* will take away from thee all sickness; and He will put none of the evil diseases of Egypt, which thou knowest, upon thee, but will lay them upon all them that hate thee.

The mentioned three Divine Names are employed in amulets which safeguard one against plagues.[174]

The third seal at the bottom of the *Kamea* is the one we addressed earlier, and which is employed in the current instance with some variation in terms of associated Divine Names. The central *Ehyeh/Ineffable Name* square remains the same, likewise the fourfold presentation of the Ineffable Name and the Name צמרכד (*Tzamarchad*). However, instead of employing the Divine Name יוהך (*Yohach*) singularly on each of the four corners of the mentioned "magic square," the full combination יוהך כלך (*Yohach Kalach*) is utilised.

The main difference between the current concluding seal and the one addressed earlier, pertains to the Divine Names forming the four outer borders. In the earlier instance it comprised the listed Divine Name pair יהוזטקיה יטהוזקיה only. In the current instance these Divine Name constructs are located along the upper and lower borders only. The right, lower bottom, and left borders comprise (right) וייהעומהד פייהנוחהס, (lower bottom) וייהפולהל ויתהעוצהר, and (left) הימהגופההה יישהרואהל. The first five Names comprise the words of *Psalm 106:30* conjoined with the four letters of the Ineffable Name. This verse employed in this manner is of particular importance in "Practical Kabbalah," and I am addressing this in great detail later in this work. The mentioned verse itself reads;

ויעמד פינחס ויפלל ותעצר המגפה

Transliteration:
  va-ya'amod Pinchas va-y'falel va-te'atzar ha-magefah
Translated:
  Then stood up Phinehas, and wrought judgment, and so the plague was stayed.

The sixth Name in the set, i.e. יישהרואהל, comprises the name ישראל (*Yisra'el*) conjoined with יהוה.[174] However, it has been suggested that the name of the individual requiring the support of this amulet, should be conjoined with the four letters of the Ineffable Name in the same manner, and included in lieu of the latter concluding Divine Name combination. Whilst I am not sure how "kosher" this recommendation is, it will certainly personalise the *Kamea* in a most powerful manner.

Be that as it may, the amulet is concluded with the following written adjuration, repeating some of the sentiments expressed in the opening incantation:

אסותא מן שמיא תיהוי ל[פב״פ] נקז״ע נושא קמיע זה
עליון מעין הרע ומכל מרעין בישין ומחולי אבעבועות
ומכל מיני חולאים ומבכיה בעגלא ברחמי שמייא מאן
דאמר והוה עלמא אנס״ו [אמן נצח סלה ועד]

Transliteration:

> *Asuta min shmaya tihavi l'[.....Ploni ben Ploni.....] nose
> Kamea zeh alaiv m'ayin ha'ra v'm'kol mera'in b'ishin
> v'micholi aba'abu'ot u'm'kol minei chola'im u'mib'chiah
> ba'agala b'rachamei shmaya me'ein d'amar vahava alma
> Omein Netzach Selah Va'ed*

Translation:

> May there be Healing from Heaven for [.....insert the name
> of the recipient.....], the bearer of this amulet, from the Evil
> Eye, and from all evil doers and bad spirits, and the
> sickness of pox, and from all bad illness and from all
> lamentation speedily, with mercy from heaven and who
> speaks unto eternity *Amen*, Enduring (Victory), *Selah*,
> Forever.

. ...The frog opened his mouth and began to speak. 'Dear Haninah, don't grieve. Since you've been taking care of me and feeding me all this time, you can now ask something of me.....' Haninah said: 'There is only one thing I desire. Teach me the entire Law'... ... .

Chapter 2
Kochav — Mercury
LETTER, WORD
&
NUMBER SQUARES

A. Letter Squares

There are literally hundreds of "Letter," "Word" and "Number Squares" to be found in Jewish Magic and Practical Kabbalah. Whilst a very large number of these peculiar items are addressed in primary literature, e.g. *Shorshei ha-Shemot* by Moses Zacutto,[1] etc., many "Magic Squares," unlisted in these texts, were written or engraved on Hebrew amulets.[2] Such items range from simple squares comprising nothing more than a couple of Hebrew glyphs, to very complex constructs comprised of entire biblical verses. They are used as *Kameot* for an equally great variety of purposes, ranging from the most sacred to the most mundane.

The employment of "Letter," "Word" and "Number Squares" for magical purposes necessitates certain procedures. Firstly, such items are written on a variety of clean surfaces, e.g. pottery; deerskin; "virgin parchment"; clean paper; cloth, in some instances even secretly on the hems of garments; etc. Otherwise they are engraved on metal surfaces, e.g. pendants, rings, bracelets, etc.[3] Secondly, depending on the fundamental intentions behind the use of a specific *Kamea*, these items are carried around the neck, wrist, or tied to the upper arm; pinned inside clothing; wrapped in cottonwool, the latter having been "magically enhanced" with fragrant oils; hung inside a room or affixed to the front entrance of a residence; etc. Sometimes the writing is dissolved in a glass of water, to be consumed afterwards by the individual requiring their aid; burned with incense; etc. However, more often than not written *Kameot*, or those inscribed on thin metal plates, are carried rolled up inside "talisman holders," the latter often comprising beautifully handtooled metal tubes.[4]

We might also note that in some instances there are instructions regarding the "empowerment" of amulets. In this regard, I have perused details pertaining to the "personalisation" of these objects by placing a small drop of blood from its bearer on the back of the amulet. I am equally aware of special spiritual techniques in which *Ruchaniyyut* (spiritual force) is directed into an amulet via ones body and hands.

Now, to commence our perusal of "letter squares," let us consider two interesting examples. The opening *Kamea* comprises the first, third, fifth, seventh and ninth letters of the Hebrew alphabet arranged in a five by five grid. In this instance the four letters comprising the second amulet, were respectively added to the upper and lower corners of the construct. This *Kamea* is utilised as protection against epidemics, but I am aware of an instance in which it was used to calm a raging fever.

ד				ב
ט	ז	ה	ג	א
ז	ט	ז	ה	ג
ה	ז	ט	ז	ה
ג	ה	ז	ט	ז
א	ג	ה	ז	ט
ה				ו

I understand the original version of this consisted of only the letter square comprised of the first five odd letters of the Hebrew Alphabet, and that the four alternate even letters, i.e. ב, ד, ו and ח, were later added to the four corners of the construct.[5]

A somewhat more elaborate version of the same letter square locates the names of the four great Archangels of the "quarters," i.e. *Gavriel* (top), *Michael* (bottom), *Rafael* (right) and *Oriel* [*Auriel*] (left), along the edges of the construct. As shown below, the letter pairs adjacent the front and rear of the names of the angels *Ori'el* and *Rafa'el*, respectively read האמת (*ha-emet*) and המלך (*ha-melech*), conjointly translating "the Truth of the King."

We are informed that this *Kamea* should be written on a kosher scroll in *ashurit*, and that it should be located with a bit of the herb Rue inside a red silk pouch. The herb should be cut with a golden coin or disc on a Wednesday prior to sunrise while the moon is still shining, and during a period when the moon is in the ascent, i.e. from New Moon to Full Moon.

Prior to cutting the herb, one has to recite *Deuteronomy 6:4–9* reading:

(Verse 4) שמע ישראל יהוה אלהינו יהוה אחד

(Verse 5) ואהבת את יהוה אלהיך בכל לבבך ובכל נפשך ובכל מאדך

(Verse 6) והיו הדברים האלה אשר אנכי מצוך היום על לבבך

(Verse 7) ושננתם לבניך ודברת בם בשבתך בביתך ובלכתך בדרך ובשכבך ובקומך

(Verse 8) וקשרתם לאות על ידך והיו לטטפת בין עיניך

(Verse 9) וכתבתם על מזזות ביתך ובשעריך

Transliteration:

(Verse 4) *Shmah Yisra'el, YHVH Eloheinu, YHVH Echad*

(Verse 5) *v'ahavta et YHVH eloheicha b'chol l'vav'cha uv'chol nafsh'cha u'v'chol m'odecha*

(Verse 6) *v'hayu ha-d'varim ha-eleh asher anochi m'tzav'cha ha-yom al l'vavecha*

(Verse 7) *v'shinan'tam l'vanecha v'dibarta bam b'shivt'cha b'veitecha uv'lecht'cha va-derech uv'shochb'cha uv'komecha*

(Verse 8) *uk'shartam l'ot al yadecha v'hayu l'totafot bein einecha*

(Verse 9) *uch'tavtam al m'zuzot beitecha uvish'arecha*

Translation:

(Verse 4) Hear, O Israel, *YHVH* our Lord, *YHVH* is One.

(Verse 5) And thou shalt love *YHVH* thy God with all thy heart, and with all thy soul, and with all thy might.

(Verse 6) And these words, which I command thee this day, shall be upon thy heart;

(Verse 7) and thou shalt teach them diligently unto thy children, and shalt talk of them when thou sittest in thy house, and when thou walkest by the way, and when thou liest down, and when thou risest up.

(Verse 8) And thou shalt bind them for a sign upon thy hand, and they shall be for frontlets between thine eyes.

(Verse 9) And thou shalt write them upon the door-posts of thy house, and upon thy gates.

This is followed by the recitation of the earlier mentioned *Vihi No'am* prayer. Then, whilst cutting the rue, say:

אני לוקט אותך בשם יאי לשמירת [פלוני בן פלוני]
מן הדבר ומן המגפה

Transliteration:

Ani loket otcha b'shem YAY l'shmirat [.....Ploni ben Ploni.....] min ha-dever v'min ha-magefah

Translation:

I am collecting you in the Name *YAY* for the protection of [.....fill in the name of the recipient.....] from the pestilence and from the plague.

Afterwards the amulet and the rue are placed in the mentioned silk pouch, and suspended around the neck of the individual for whom it was constructed, and as long as that person is carrying the item, he or she need have no fear of any prevailing epidemic.[6] It is also noted that this *Kamea* cannot be employed repeatedly, or by anyone other than the one for whom it was written. In this instance, it is believed that each individual and every recurrence of the malady require a separate amulet.[7]

However, whilst this specific letter square is employed as a protection against epidemics, I am aware of a fairly recent instance in which it was successfully employed to eliminate a raging fever.

It should be noted that the Divine Name combination יא״ is comprised of the initials of the expression יהוה אלהי ישראל (*YHVH Elohei Yisra'el*).[8] As might be expected, there is a sister letter square to those addressed above. This one is comprised of the second, fourth, sixth and eighth letters of the Hebrew Alphabet, all arranged in the following manner:[9]

ה	ו	ד	ב
ו	ה	ו	ד
ד	ו	ה	ו
ב	ד	ו	ה

Curiously enough, the set of letters comprising this magical seal, spells the term בדוח (*Baduach*) which can mean a "statement" or "report," and also to be "jolly" or "amused." Be that as it may, arranged within a square of sixteen boxes, this *chotam* (magical seal) is said to have great power, not only employed to conquer and defeat enemies, but also to achieve success. For these purposes this letter square is often employed in conjunction with other magical squares and seals.

B. Word Squares

Probably the most well known magical "Word Squares" are those appearing in "*The Book of the Sacred Magic of Abramelin the Mage*," originally translated from a French manuscript by Samuel Liddell MacGregor Mathers of the Hermetic Order of the Golden Dawn fame.[10] In recent years we have seen a new version of this text titled simply "*The Book of Abramelin*," which was translated from German manuscripts by Georg Dehm.[11] The original title of the German manuscript reads "*The Mystical Kabbalah of the Egyptians and the Patriarchs, which is the Book of the True Old Divine Magic*," which we are informed was written by "Abraham Son of Simeon for His younger Son Lamech."[12] We are also told that the author grew up in the house of his father in Worms, and hence the translator/editor of the recent version of this text lists the author as "Abraham of Worms," whom he, after wading through some uncertain documentation, and a lot of careless and forced cerebral conjecture, ascertained with the most "uncertain certainty" to have been the "*Maharil*," i.e. Rabbi Yaakov ben Moshe Levi Moelin, the 14/15th century Talmudist who was Rabbi of Mainz.[13]

Beside the many glaring differences which can be found between the author of the work in question and the "*Maharil*," there is one which the late Raphael Patai referred to in his "*The Jewish Alchemists*,"[14] and which all and sundry appear to have missed. The style of the "word squares" would seem to indicate the text was not written by an *Ashkenazi* (German) hand. In this regard Raphael Patai wrote ".....a scrutiny of the magic squares that form the concluding part of the manuscript in both the German and French versions reveals, I believe, important information concerning the original language of the book. In general, Hebrew magical texts abound in non-Hebrew magical names and words used in conjurations..... In Abraham's book, too, there are many non-Hebrew magical words inscribed in the squares, but by far the largest number of such words is in Hebrew, transliterated in Latin capital letters.

These magic squares usually consist of a basic word appearing in the first horizontal line of the square, then the same word written on the left side perpendicularly from the first letter; at the bottom of the square the same appears written backward, and on the right side the same word is written from the bottom up. Finally, the spaces left inside these four words are filled in with words also written back and forth and down and up. The significant feature for our consideration is that the basic words in the great majority of the squares (there are several hundreds in the book) are, in both the German and French versions, Hebrew words transliterated in Latin capital letters, mostly correctly. These Hebrew words have in every case a direct relationship to the purpose subserved by the magic square as stated in the manuscript. Here are a few examples of the basic words, given precisely as they appear in the German manuscript (in the French they are in most cases identical), followed in parentheses by the correct transliteration and the translation, and by the purpose of the magic square as stated in the manuscript.....

The sum total of the rich Hebrew vocabulary appearing in the magic squares attests not merely to a thorough knowledge of both biblical and post-biblical Hebrew, but also to a familiarity with the nuances of living Hebrew as used by the learned elements in the Jewish communities in books, treatises, letters, and other forms of written expression.

An additional important point emerges from a consideration of these transliterated Hebrew words: in both the German and French manuscripts the words are transliterated in accordance with the Sephardic pronunciation of Hebrew. Had the author written in German, he would have transliterated the Hebrew words following the Ashkenazic pronunciation that had become prevalent in Central and Eastern Europe from the thirteenth century on.....

The occasional addition of the Spanish plural *s* allows us to conclude that the person who translated the book from the Hebrew manuscript into German was a Sephardi Jew who transliterated the Hebrew words as he pronounced them, and where he felt that the plural was more appropriate than the singular added the spanish plural ending. After the Spanish expulsion the presence of Sephardi Jews in German lands was not unusual."[15]

Be that as it may, when it comes to "word squares" achieving great publicity, the following one assuredly ranks amongst the most "famous" (some say "infamous") ever constructed. It was written by the well-meaning Rabbi Yehonatan Eybeschütz whose "talismanic" services to his congregants led to unfair derision, prosecution and ultimate censure. The fact of the matter is that this Rabbi was a most dedicated servant to everyone in his community.[16] In fact, his service extended to the whole of Jewry globally. In this regard we are told in the 1755 edition of his *"Luchot Edut,"*[17] that he was once confronted by a prince of the church who intended expelling all the Jews from the domain under his jurisdiction. It is said the church official challenged the Rabbi to come up with an action which might benefit the Jewish people as a whole.

We are informed that Rabbi Eybeschütz instructed him to write the following sentence on a piece of paper:

עם ישראל חי לעולמי עד

Transliteration:
Am Yisra'el chai l'olmei ad
Translation:
The people of Israel live forever.

The full instruction was that the phrase should be written in a manner in which it could be read in more than twenty thousand ways. On querying how this might be achieved, Rabbi Eybeschütz composed the following amulet:[18]

ד	ע	י	מ	ל	ו	ע	ל	ע	ו	ל	מ	י	ע	ד
ע	י	מ	ל	ו	ע	ל	י	ל	ע	ו	ל	מ	י	ע
י	מ	ל	ו	ע	ל	י	ח	י	ל	ע	ו	ל	מ	י
מ	ל	ו	ע	ל	י	ח	ל	ח	י	ל	ע	ו	ל	מ
ל	ו	ע	ל	י	ח	ל	א	ל	ח	י	ל	ע	ו	ל
ו	ע	ל	י	ח	ל	א	ר	א	ל	ח	י	ל	ע	ו
ע	ל	י	ח	ל	א	ר	ש	ר	א	ל	ח	י	ל	ע
ל	י	ח	ל	א	ר	ש	י	ש	ר	א	ל	ח	י	ל
י	ח	ל	א	ר	ש	י	ם	י	ש	ר	א	ל	ח	י
ח	ל	א	ר	ש	י	ם	ע	ם	י	ש	ר	א	ל	ח
י	ח	ל	א	ר	ש	י	ם	י	ש	ר	א	ל	ח	י
ל	י	ח	ל	א	ר	ש	י	ש	ר	א	ל	ח	י	ל
ע	ל	י	ח	ל	א	ר	ש	ר	א	ל	ח	י	ל	ע
ו	ע	ל	י	ח	ל	א	ר	א	ל	ח	י	ל	ע	ו
ל	ו	ע	ל	י	ח	ל	א	ל	ח	י	ל	ע	ו	ל
מ	ל	ו	ע	ל	י	ח	ל	ח	י	ל	ע	ו	ל	מ
י	מ	ל	ו	ע	ל	י	ח	י	ל	ע	ו	ל	מ	י
ע	י	מ	ל	ו	ע	ל	י	ל	ע	ו	ל	מ	י	ע
ד	ע	י	מ	ל	ו	ע	ל	ע	ו	ל	מ	י	ע	ד

Commencing at the large ע (*Ayin*) in the centre and reading outwards towards the concluding letters ד (*Dalet*) located in the four corners of the *Kamea*, it is said the phrase in question can be traced in twenty-five thousand seven hundred ways. I was taught that tracing amulets in this manner, executing this task with appropriate *Kavvanah*, i.e. intention and attention fully focussed on the meaning of the *Kamea*, will empower the fundamental essence and purpose of the amulet contemplated in this manner.

C. Number Squares

Number squares, generally considered "Magic Squares" proper, are fairly well known, and the saga of their origins and development have been traced from the ancient Far East to Near Eastern magical literature, to their employment in the astrological and alchemical literature of Mediaeval Europe, and numerous examples of these items abound in these locales.[19]

As mentioned earlier, there are an inordinate amount of "word" and "number" squares in Jewish Magic. Yet, when one considers the seven standard "Magic Squares," e.g. those traditionally associated with the seven planets, it would seem that despite the hype in mediaeval magic ritual texts, such as those penned by Cornelius Agrippa von Nettesheim and others inspired by his work on this topic,[20] very few of this specific variety of magic squares are actually extensively employed for magical purposes in "Practical Kabbalah." As can be expected, all the mentioned squares do appear in Kabbalistic writings, and despite the supposition that the association of the seven planets with the seven *chotamot* commenced with Agrippa exclusively, such planetary attributions can be found in primary Jewish alchemical and mystical texts.[21] However, it is worth noting, as the late Aryeh Kaplan pointed out, that the seven standard magic squares were mainly employed for meditative purposes.[22]

1. Magic Square of the Third Order

Regarding the seven so-called "traditional" magic squares, it is widely believed that they follow a definite format, and are always arranged in the same order. However, closer inspection of these items in primary literature reveals many variants. Even as far as the very basic square of the third order is concerned, we notice that whilst the format never alters, the presentation varies in several instances, sometimes even in the same source, as shown below:

A[23]

ד	ט	ב
ג	ה	ז
ח	א	ו

B[24]

ב	ט	ד
ז	ה	ג
ו	א	ח

C[25]

ו	ז	ב
א	ה	ט
ח	ג	ד

4	9	2
3	5	7
8	1	6

2	9	4
7	5	3
6	1	8

6	7	2
1	5	9
8	3	4

D[26]

ו	א	ח
ז	ה	ג
ב	ט	ד

E[27]

ד	ג	ח
ט	ה	א
ב	ז	ו

6	1	8
7	5	3
2	9	4

4	3	8
9	5	1
2	7	6

As a matter of fact, the following four formats of this "magic square" were aligned with the Four Elements:[28]

Air

ב	ז	ו
ט	ה	א
ד	ג	ח

Fire

ד	ט	ב
ג	ה	ז
ח	א	ו

Water			Earth		
ו	ז	ב	ו	א	ח
א	ה	ט	ז	ה	ג
ה	ג	ד	ב	ט	ד

Regarding the "magical" employment of the numerical "Magic Squares," it is interesting that the square of the third order outranks all others in both Jewish and Islamic Magic in terms of popularity. It is attributed to Saturn, and linked to the metal lead.[29] The numerical value of each of the rows, columns and diagonals of the "Magic Square" of the third order is 15, which is the *gematria* of the Divine Name יה (*Yah*).[30] Calculating the numerical value of the three rows, or three columns, indicates the total value of this *chotam* to be 45, i.e. three times *Yah*, which is said to pertain to the third full spelling of the Ineffable Name:

$$\text{יוד הא ואו הא}$$

*Yod-vav-dalet **H**eh-alef **V**av-alef-vav **H**e-alef*

The total numerical value of the letters comprising this expanded spelling of the Ineffable Name is 45, hence it was titled the "Forty-five Letter Name of God" or simply מה (*Mah*), the *gematria* of the latter appellative being also מ = 40 + ה = 5 = 45.[31] Further attributions to this magic square, based on numbers, are אב (*Av*—"father" or "ancestor" [א = 1 + ב = 2 = 3]), this number indicating the threefold format of the square;[32] זאזל (*Zazel* [ז = 7 + א = 1 + ז = 7 + ל = 30 = 45]), and אגיאל (*Agi'el* [א = 1 + ג = 3 + י = 10 + א = 1 + ל = 30 = 45]). The numerical value of the latter two names refers again to the full value of the square in question,[33] and a further *gematria* based suggestion in terms of the threefold square is said to be the word הד (*Hed*—a "shout" or "noise" or "echo" [ה = 5 + ד = 4 = 9]) which equates with the number of blocks comprising the Saturn square.[34] I suppose this word could, with the aid of some fanciful philosophical/mystical jargoning, be force-fitted to the threefold square.

Cornelius Agrippa also listed the Divine Name יה (*Yah* [י = 10 + ה = 5 = 15]), as well as the term הוד (*Hod*—"splendour" or "glory" [ה = 5 + ו = 6 + ד = 4 = 15]), referring to these terms as being aligned with the "Saturn Square" in accordance with certain *gematria* associations.[35] As it is, when it comes to numerical values of Hebrew words, there are numerous Hebrew terms and concepts which will align with the different layers of *gematria* to be found in magic number squares, i.e. enough with which to waste away your time unto eternity.

Be that as it may, both Agrippa and the author of the *Shorshei ha-Shemot* informed us that the "serving spirit" of this *chotam* is אגיאל (*Agi'el* [א = 1 + ג = 3 + י = 10 + א = 1 + ל = 30 = 45]), and its "subservient spirit" is זאזל (*Zazel* [ז = 7 + א = 1 + ז = 7 + ל = 30 = 45]),[36] both again numerically aligned with the total value of the magic square. In the writings of Agrippa these Spirit Intelligences are respectively termed the "intelligence" and "spirit" of Saturn. However he considered the planetary "spirit" to be of the "demonic" variety, the suggestion being that the "intelligence" is employed to effect "good" intentions, whilst the "spirit" (planetary demon) is employed to fulfil "evil" objectives.[37]

I have seen similar opinions expressed in a most interesting scholarly investigation into Hebrew amulets. However, whilst I agree with the authors of this study that "in Practical Kabbalah all the planets have special features,"[38] I have to date not yet chanced upon any references in primary Jewish magical literature in which the two "Planetary Intelligences" associated with each of the "seven planets," are respectively termed an "angel" and a "demon." In the oft mentioned "*Shorshei ha-Shemot*," the subtle forces aligned with the threefold square are simply considered "servants."[39]

I am acquainted with magical actions aimed at direct employment of the subservient planetary intelligences for the engendering of magical aims pertaining to "good intentions" rather than to the so-called "evil" kind. Be that as it may, there are also a set of magical seals, termed "sigils," affiliated with each of the planetary magic squares and their associated Spirit Intelligences. In the current instance these are:[40]

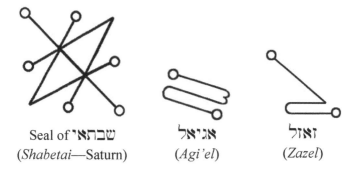

Seal of שבתאי
(*Shabetai*—Saturn)

אגיאל
(*Agi'el*)

זאזל
(*Zazel*)

It is worth noting that the term "sigil" originates from the Latin "*sigillum*," meaning a "seal." It has been suggested that the Latin term was derived from the Hebrew term "*segulah*," the latter referring to a unique word, phrase, sign, seal, action, etc., considered to have special magical efficacy, and is hence considered a unique spiritual "treasure."

The listed "sigils" are not the only ones associated with the "Saturn square." The following pair appear in a manuscript titled "*Mazalot v'Goralot*":[41]

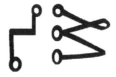

These seals are akin to the following symbol of Saturn which is listed in the Arabic *Picatrix*, the latter text having at one time played a great role in Western magic:[42]

There are certainly many interesting magical practices associated with the "Magic Square of the Third Order," and the first I have selected to share here pertains to *She'elat Chalom* (Dream Questioning), i.e. facilitating requested answers in "Dream Questioning."[43] In this regard the following procedure is worked in a state of holiness and purity on *Erev Shabbat*, the eve of the Sabbath, which in this instance means that you should work the procedure on a Thursday evening.

Write the "magic square" in question on a piece of parchment, ensuring that you inscribe the letter/numbers comprising this *chotam* in their exact letter order in *ashurit* (the Hebrew letters employed by scribes). This is considered an important action in the process of, as it were, "triggering the spiritual powers" behind the magical seal. In this regard we are told the letter ח (*chet*) should be written in the form of a

"hunchback," i.e. ח, which is the manner in which it appears in the Bible. If you employ *sofer* script, the traditional Jewish scribal calligraphy, i.e. letters with "*tagin*" (crownlets), the magic square would appear thus:

ד	ט	ב
ג	ה	ז
ח	א	ו

When you are ready to retire to bed for the night, the completed *chotam* is tied to your forehead in such a manner that the writing is facing outwards. Afterwards you have to recite *Psalm 23* seven times. In this instance we are told to include שדי רוע (*Shadai ro'i*) after the Ineffable Name in the first and last verse of the Psalm, and to utter the two Divine Names as well as the succeeding phrase of the first verse seven times. We are also instructed to insert the Divine Names אל אלהים (*El Elohim*) after the word אתה (*atah*) in verse 4. The entire Psalm would thus read:

(Verse 1) מזמור לדוד יהוה שדי רעי לא אחסר

יהוה שדי רעי לא אחסר יהוה שדי רעי לא אחסר

יהוה שדי רעי לא אחסר יהוה שדי רעי לא אחסר

יהוה שדי רעי לא אחסר יהוה שדי רעי לא אחסר

(Verse 2) בנאות דשא ירביצני על מי מנחות ינהלני

(Verse 3) נפשי ישובב ינחני במעגלי צדק למען שמו

(Verse 4) גם כי אלך בגיא צלמות לא אירא רע כי
אתה אל אלהים עמדי שבטך ומשענתך המה ינחמני
(Verse 5) תערך לפני שלחן נגד צררי דשנת בשמן
ראשי כוסי רויה
(Verse 6) אך תוב וחסד ירדפוני כל ימי חיי ושבתי
בבית יהוה שדי רוע לארך ימים

Transliteration:

(Verse 1) *Mizmor l'david YHVH Shadai ro'i lo ech'sar, YHVH Shadai ro'i lo ech'sar, YHVH Shadai ro'i lo ech'sar, YHVH Shadai ro'i lo ech'sar, YHVH Shadai ro'i lo ech'sar, YHVH Shadai ro'i lo ech'sar, YHVH Shadai ro'i lo ech'sar*

(Verse 2) *bin'ot deshe yarbitzeini al mei m'nuchot y'nahaleini*

(Verse 3) *nafshi y'shoveiv yan'cheini b'ma'g'lei tzedek l'ma'an shemo*

(Verse 4) *gam ki eleich b'gei tzalmavet lo ira ra ki atah El Elohim imadi shivt'cha umish'antecha heimah y'nachamuni*

(Verse 5) *ta'aroch l'fanai shulchan neged tzor'rai dishanta vashemen roshi kosi r'vayah*

(Verse 6) *Ach tov vachesed yird'funi kol y'mei hayay v'shavti b'veit YHVH Shadai ro'i l'orech yamim*

Translation:

(Verse 1) A Psalm of David. *YHVH Shadai* is my shepherd; I shall not want, *YHVH Shadai* is my shepherd; I shall not want, *YHVH Shadai* is my shepherd; I shall not want, *YHVH Shadai* is my shepherd; I shall not want, *YHVH Shadai* is my shepherd; I shall not want, *YHVH Shadai* is my shepherd; I shall not want, *YHVH Shadai* is my shepherd; I shall not want.

(Verse 2) He maketh me to lie down in green pastures; He leadeth me beside the still waters.

(Verse 3) He restoreth my soul; He guideth me in straight paths for His name's sake.

(Verse 4) Yea, though I walk through the valley of the shadow of death, I will fear no evil, for Thou *El Elohim* art with me; Thy rod and Thy staff, they comfort me.

(Verse 5) Thou preparest a table before me in the presence of mine enemies; Thou hast anointed my head with oil; my cup runneth over.

(Verse 6) Surely goodness and mercy shall follow me all the days of my life; and I shall dwell in the house of *YHVH Shadai* my shepherd for ever.

Continue the procedure by saying seven times:

צופיאל צדקיאל רפאל רזיאל

Tzofi'el Tzadki'el Rafa'el Razi'el

Ensure that you have the *kavvanah*, the focussed intention, of your question, i.e. keeping the question powerfully in your mind, whilst verbalising it seven times. Afterwards place both your hands on the "magic seal" on your forehead, and say:

בזכות החותם הזה הנקרא חותם יה ובזכות השמות שהזכרתי שתודיעני הלילה הזה תשובת שאלתי בבירור שהי כך וכך

Transliteration:

> *Biz'chut ha-chotam ha-zeh ha-nikra chotam Yah v'biz'chut ha-shemot shehizkarti shetodi'eini ha-lailah ha-zeh tshuvat she'elati b'beirur shehi kach v'kach.*

Translation:

> In the merit of this seal, called the seal of *Yah*, and in the merit of the Names I mentioned, that you reveal to me this night the answer to my question, in a manner which is clear and certain.

Finally go to bed and ensure that you sleep on your left side, and, if you should wake up after midnight, turn over onto your right side.[44]

There are certainly much simpler procedures in the "magical pantry" of Practical Kabbalah to get answers in dreams, like the following word square which is also constructed from a biblical verse, i.e. *Psalm 4:2 [3]*:

ללש	עהו	בקי
היה	נרע	קים
יחת	נחל	רבכפ
צנה	יבי	אצי
דנה	אתה	ירו

Commencing with the right letters in the rightmost column, then tracing these letters downwards; repeating the process with the rightmost letters in the centre and left columns; then continuing by reading the middle letters in the right, centre and left columns, and concluding with the left letter in the right-top block of the right column; the first eight words in the mentioned verse are revealed. The remaining two words are traced, by reading the remaining letters horizontally, i.e. the third letter of the top centre block, then the third letter of the top left block, followed by the third letters of the blocks comprising the second and third rows, and concluding with the third letter in the right block of the fourth row. The remaining five letters spell the Ineffable Name with an additional letter *Heh* concluding the phrase. The entire phrase reads:

בקראי עניני אלהי צדקי בצר הרחבת לי חנני ושמע
תפלתי יהוה ה

Transliteration:
B'kor'i aneini Elohei tzidki batzar hirchavta li choneini ushma t'filati YHVH H

Translation:
Answer me when I call, God of my righteousness, Thou who didst set me free when I was in distress; be gracious unto me, and hear my prayer *YHVH H*

After writing this square on a piece of parchment , i.e. a fragment of clean white paper, the amulet is placed under your head when you retire to sleep.[45] This is certainly a much easier method than the previous, however an even simpler method employed for

She'elat Chalom (Dream Question) pertains to the idiosyncratic pterygomas listed in Jewish magical literature, specifically the magical use of the name *Adoniram*. The formula reads:

אדונירם
דונירם
ונירם
נירם
ירם
רם
ם

Transliteration:

ADVNYRM
DVNYRM
VNYRM
NYRM
YRM
RM
M

This word/letter combination is considered a "Name of Power" which is written on the palm of the left hand prior to retiring to sleep, in order to elicit a clear answer to any query one might have.[46] It seems the basic reasoning behind this specific use of the word combination in question, is that it serves as a screen through which the sought after answer could be perceived in the most direct manner.

I am particularly curious as to why the word *Adoniram*, the personal name of a biblical personality who was responsible for forced labour in ancient Israel, and who was stoned to death when he acted as a collector of compulsory tax, should have this special power? As it is, the name in question means "My Lord is Lofty," and I am well aware that it is associated in *Chabad* teaching with the Kabbalistic doctrines pertaining to the "sparks" of Divine Light trapped in this world of "Fallen Shards." In this regard, it is maintained that the name *Adoniram*, meaning "My Master is Exalted," alludes "to the elevation of sparks which reconnects the Godliness trapped in this world, where God is the 'Master,' to the sublime 'exalted'."

This peculiar reasoning is backed with further ruminations on the "compulsory tax" referred to in the biblical phrase "*Adoniram* was in charge of the levy," which is purported to indicate that, from the "perspective" of the earlier mentioned "Divine Sparks," "elevation must occur," and that "it follows that the only obstacle to this elevation is to be found within the person himself."[47] Notwithstanding this, I am still curious as to the real reason why the name *Adoniram* is employed in this singular manner in Kabbalistic "Dream Questioning" procedures, and as to why it should be considered a particularly powerful way in which direct responses can be facilitated from "Spiritual Sources."

Getting back to the "Magic Square of the Third Order," we are informed that as a *Kamea* in which its component letter-numbers were written in exact alphabetical order, it has the power to free prisoners from jail speedily,[48] and another curious use of the threefold square is the alleviation of fear. In this instance the instruction is to write the *chotam*, once again in exact numerical order, on the inside of a new pottery bowl, and then to regularly consume liquid from the inscribed side of the container over a period of forty days.[49]

As might be expected, this specific number square is put to great use in Hebrew amulets. In this regard the following amulet is employed to "harden," i.e. strengthen, an infant during a difficult childbirth.[50]

The amulet is constructed in the following manner:

1. Take a kosher scroll, i.e. clean parchment or paper, and write the threefold number square in exact numerical order in the centre of the page.
2. This is followed by writing the three columns of letter/number combinations comprising the *chotam*, respectively directly above, to the right and to the left of the square.
3. In turn the *Digrammaton* (יה), the *gematria* of which we earlier noted is equal to each row and column of the "magic square," is placed directly below.
4. Next, commencing at the bottom, and writing from right to left, encircle the square with the words of *Psalm 142:8 [7]* reading:

הוציאה ממסגר נפשי להודות את שמך בי יכתרו
צדיקים כי תגמל עלי

Transliteration:

Hotzi'ah mimasger nafshi l'hodot et sh'mecha bi yachtiru tzadikim ki tigmol alai

Translation:

Bring my soul out of prison, that I may give thanks unto Thy name; the righteous shall crown themselves because of me; for Thou wilt deal bountifully with me.

5. In conclusion the entire construct is located with the writing against the stomach of the woman in labour.

Moses Zacutto commented that this amulet was tried and tested.[51] Curiously enough, I am aware of the very same amulet having been employed similarly, i.e. tied to the solar plexus of individuals (both adults and children), in order to "strengthen" the wearers in times of great trouble and stress.

It should be noted that there is yet another manner in which this number square is employed for the purpose of easing childbirth during difficult confinements, as shown in the following amulet:[52]

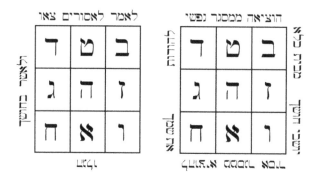

In this instance you have to select a new piece of earthenware which has not yet been exposed to water or fire. A flat raw ceramic or pottery platter will do nicely. This object is then broken into two and the two *chotamot* depicted in the image above respectively written or inscribed on the two pieces. This is followed by writing the following portions of holy writ around the two squares in the following manner:

Right Square

Psalm 142:8 [7] (top) הוציאה ממסגר נפשי (left top down) להודות (left bottom up) את שמך

Isaiah 42:7 (bottom) להוציא ממסגר אסיר (right top up) יושבי חושך (right bottom up) מבית כלא

Transliteration:

Psalm 142:8 [7] (top) *hotzi'ah mimasger nafshi* (left top down) *l'hodot* (left bottom up) *et sh'mecha*

Isaiah 42:7 (bottom) *l'hotzi mimasger asir* (right top) *mibeit kele* (right bottom) *yoshvei choshech*

Translation:

Psalm 142:8 [7] (top) Bring my soul out of prison (left top down) that I may give thanks unto (left bottom up) Thy name

Isaiah 42:7 (bottom) to bring out the prisoners from the dungeon (right top) out of the prison-house (right bottom) them that sit in darkness.

Left Square

Isaiah 49:9 (top) לאמר לאסורים צאו (left
down) הגלו (bottom) לאשר בחושך

Transliteration:

Isaiah 49:9 (top) *leimor la'asurim tzei'u* (left down)
la'asher b'choshech (bottom) *higalu*

Translation:

Isaiah 49:9 (top) saying to the prisoners: "Go forth" (left
down) to them that are in darkness (bottom) "Show
yourselves."

On conclusion of this task, the two pieces of pottery are
respectively placed under the soles of the feet of the woman in
labour, and, it is said, she will rapidly give birth.

It should be noted that the power of the "Magic Square of
the Third Order" is sometimes enhanced by its conjoint
employment with other Divine Name letter squares, i.e. the
Ehyeh/Ineffable Name letter square, i.e.

ה	י	ה	א
י	ה	ו	ה
ה	ו	ה	י
א	ה	י	ה

In this instance the "Magic Square of the Third Order" is inscribed
on the front of the amulet, whilst the Divine Name square is
written on the reverse. We are informed that this action could be
applied to all the threefold number squares we are addressing, the
power of which would be greatly enhanced by the divine qualities
of the *Ehyeh*/Tetragrammaton square.[53]

Elsewhere the threefold square is employed conjointly with
the Divine Name עשצ"יי (*Ashtzei*) in a letter square again meant to
protect and support a women in labour:

י	י	צ	ש	ע
י	ד	ט	ב	ש
צ	ג	ה	ז	צ
ש	ח	א	ו	י
ע	ש	צ	י	י

In this instance the "magic square of the third order" is located centrally, and enclosed on all four sides by the Name *Ashtzei*. The one who writes the amulet is again required to purify himself in a *Mikveh* (ritual bath). Afterwards the *Kamea* is written on *Kosher* parchment or paper, the letters being in the manner of those employed in the writing of a *Torah* scroll. I would recommend the amulet be constructed from the centre outwards, i.e. commence with the threefold square, ensuring that the letters are inscribed in exact alphabetical order. Afterwards write the עשצײ (*Ashtzei*) border, commencing at the upper right corner and writing the Divine Name horizontally right to left, then vertically along the upper right border. Conclude this latter action with the Divine Name written horizontally from left to right along the bottom border, and then vertically from bottom to top up the left border. The finished product is placed between two sheets of paper, and located in the bed near the pregnant woman.[54]

Now, whilst the threefold square is employed in Jewish Magic in fairly straightforward and not too complex ways, e.g. to aid "Dream Questioning"; alleviate fear; strengthen the unborn child; ease the birthing process; etc., its applications in medieval Christian magical literature demand more complex "astral" and other related considerations. In this regard one commentator noted that an "extraordinary belief in astrology and amulets prevailed in Europe during the sixteenth and seventeenth centuries, but especially during the period from 1550 to 1650. The amulets of that time were usually made under the special influence either of the constellations, the fixed stars, or the planets. Those made under the influence, and, as it was termed, in the Seal of the Planets....., were either made under the influence of them altogether, of one single planet, or of two or more combined. They were made of the metals, each of the seven planets having one peculiar to itself. The symbol, therefore, of the planet became also the symbol of the metal; thus there was a close connexion between astrology and alchemy. The metals employed were all purified and employed in a particular manner and also at particular seasons."[55]

The same commentator wrote that the threefold square was to be engraved on lead, and "worn suspended round the neck covered in black silk, and its virtue was to promote success in building and architecture, the cure of saturnine diseases, and ease in childbirth."[56] In a magical text titled "*Liber de Angelis*," which is attributed to a fifteenth century translator named Osbern Bokenham, and which is more about demons than angels, we are informed regarding the "saturn square" that "when you wish to do magic by this figure to help a woman in childbirth, write the figure on the day of Saturn (Saturday) and in its hour (that is the first hour, or eight), when Saturn is fast on course, that is direct, and the Moon is rising in Mercury; write it on silk and tie it to the right hip."[57]

This text also lists malevolent uses of this magic square written in times when Saturn is "unfavourable," i.e. to halt the construction of a building, and to depose high ranking members of the clergy, e.g. bishops, cardinals and popes. On the other hand, we are informed that when it is written in a period when Saturn is favourable and carried on your person, you will fear no one and get whatever you want from all and sundry.[58] A later text succinctly summarizes the magical purpose of the "Saturn Square," informing us that "this Table engraved on a plate of Lead and worn about you, Saturn being fortunate, helps childbirth, makes a man safe and powerful in his petitions to great persons, but if Saturn be unfortunate, it casts a man down from honours and dignities, increases strife and discord."[59]

Be that as it may, it should be noted that these somewhat "coercive" magical uses of the "Magic Square of the Third Order," in the Latin "grimoires," are quite out of sync with its much more simple benevolent employment in Jewish magic.

2. Magic Square of the Fourth Order

As might be expected, it becomes a lot more complex with the larger squares, and what the general readership of western magical literature might consider to be "standard" formulas, could turn out to be quite different. As a case in point, consider for example the square of the fourth order, which is again presented in Cornelius Agrippa's ever popular "*Three Books Of Occult Philosophy*"[60] in the following manner:

4	14	15	1
9	7	6	12
5	11	10	8
16	2	3	13

ד	יד	טו	א
ט	ז	ו	יב
ה	יא	י	ח
יו	ב	ג	יג

Agrippa attributed the following sigils pertaining to the planet Jupiter, as well as the associated serving spirit and subservient spirit to the fourfold square.

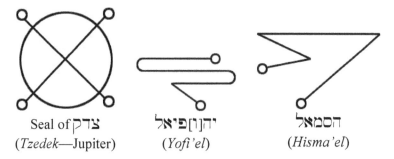

Seal of צדק
(*Tzedek*—Jupiter)

יהן[ן]פיאל
(*Yofi'el*)

הסמאל
(*Hisma'el*)

Whilst it is quite easy to see how the "Saturn Seal" was derived from its associated "Magic Square," it is somewhat more difficult to similarly trace the derivations of the remainder of the seven planetary sigils. This being said, recent analysis affords us some insight into the origins of these curious glyphs.[61]

As shown below, there are again a variant set of magical seals associated with the "Jupiter square," these being listed in the earlier mentioned "*Mazalot v'Goralot*":[62]

The rightmost seal is listed as the symbol of Jupiter in the earlier mentioned *Picatrix*,[63] and is employed in conjunction with the standard fourfold square in the following amulet delineated in the *Toldot Adam*:[64]

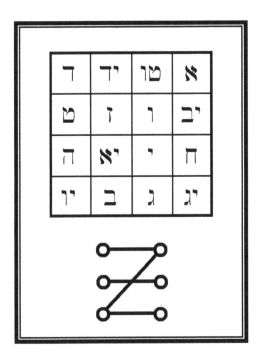

In this regard, we are instructed to inscribe the magic square as well as the mentioned symbol on a plate constructed from tin or lead. According to the instruction the metal plate must not comprise a mix of metals, but must be absolutely pure. Likewise, the individual creating the amulet should be purified by taking a ritual bath prior to writing the *Kamea*. The writing should be *ashurit*, and these should be embossed in exact Hebrew letter-number order. In fact, the entire construct must be embossed on both sides of the amulet. All of this is done on the fifth day of the week, i.e. Thursday the day of Jupiter, preferably not on the ninth or tenth day of the month, and definitely not after the fourteenth day. The *Kamea* is afterwards located inside a little pouch, which is then hung on the wall above the bed.

Now, the author of the alchemical *"Esh M'tzaref,"*[65] the *"Toldot Adam"* by Elijah Baal Shem Tov,[66] and many amulets of both the paper and metal varieties, such as those presented in *"Hebraeische Amulette mit Magischen Zahlenquadraten"* by W. Ahrens;[67] etc., are in total agreement with Agrippa's presentation of the current "magic square." However, there are so me variants like the following example from the earlier mentioned manuscript titled *"Mazalot v'Goralot."*[68] The same format also appears in *"Hebraeische Amulette mit Magischen Zahlenquadraten."*[69]

16	3	2	13
5	10	11	8
9	6	7	12
4	15	14	1

יו	ג	ב	יג
ה	י	יא	ח
ט	ו	ז	יב
ד	טו	יד	א

As generally conceded, numbers are written in "magic squares" in exact numerical order, hence in the case of the fourfold square, which is comprised of the first 16 numbers, each row adds to 34, and the total value of the square is 136. Even in this regard, so-called "standards" are not maintained throughout, and there are alternative "Magic Squares" of the fourfold variety in which only certain numbers are employed. This would naturally result in differing values, which would be in accordance with the mindset, i.e. the "magical intentions," of the one employing these magical items. As a case in point, consider the following example:

8	13	18	1
16	3	6	15
2	19	12	7
14	5	4	17

ח	יג	יח	א
יו	ג	ו	טו
ב	יט	יב	ז
יד	ה	ד	יז

In this instance the numbers 17 to 19 have been added and 9 to 11 excluded, hence each row would now add to 40, and the total numerical value of the square is 160. This "Magic Square" is employed against smallpox, especially in the protection of youngsters, who have not yet been impacted by the disease. However, it is also utilised in curing those who are suffering under the onslaught of the pox. In this regard, the instruction is to write the "magic square" and to suspend it on the persons of those requiring this service.

This "Magical Seal" appears in Chaim Vital's "*Shaar Ruach ha-Kodesh*,"[70] and also features in a number of Jewish magical texts, i.e. "*Refuah v'Chayim b'Yerushalayim*,"[71] etc., and again in a variety of Hebrew Amulets.[72]

One might consider such variant squares to be quite rare, but they are employed fairly extensively. The following is another interesting alternative version of the fourfold "Magic Square" which is aligned with the *Tetragrammaton*:

8	7	10	1		ח	ז	י	א
9	2	7	8		ט	ב	ז	ח
3	12	5	6		ג	יב	ה	ו
6	5	4	11		ו	ה	ד	יא

In this "Magic Square," which is addressed, amongst others, in the "*Shorshei ha-Shemot*" by Moses Zacutto,[73] only the numbers 1 to 12 are employed. To complete the fourfold square, numbers 5 to 8 are repeated, hence, in this instance, the total of the square is 104, and each row adds to 26. The total numerical value of the repeated numbers is likewise 26, hence this "Magic Square" aligns with the Ineffable Name (יהוה), the numerical value of its letters being also 26. In the case of this alternative of the four-fold square, there are further variants as shown below:

8	6	11	1
9	3	6	8
2	12	5	7
7	5	4	10

ח	ו	אי	א
ט	ג	ו	ח
ב	יב	ה	ז
ז	ה	ד	י

12	3	2	9
5	6	7	8
5	6	7	8
4	11	10	1

יב	ג	ב	ט
ה	ו	ז	ח
ה	ו	ז	ח
ד	אי	י	א

The first variant is discussed in "*Shorshei ha-Shemot*,"[74] and the second was addressed in the earlier mentioned "*Mazalot v'Goralot*."[75]

Now let us turn our attention to one of the magical applications pertaining to two of the alternative fourfold "Magic Squares," these being quite different from the one traditionally attributed to Jupiter and popularised by Agrippa.[76] Both of the following *chotamot* belong to the same category, and the second is purely a variant of the first:[77]

8	13	18	1
16	3	6	15
2	19	12	7
14	5	4	17

ח	יג	יח	א
יו	ג	ו	טו
ב	יט	יב	ז
יד	ה	ד	יז

8	14	17	1
16	2	7	15
3	19	12	6
13	5	4	18

ח	י"ד	י"ג	א
י"ו	ב	ז	ט"ו
ג	י"ט	י"ב	ו
י"ג	ה	ד	י"ח

In both instances the numbers 9 to 11 are not included in the "Magic Square," and the numbers 17 to 19 added. The numerical value of each row comprising these squares is 40, and the total value is 160. We are reminded that the total value of this "Magic Square" is equal to the *gematria* (numerical value) of the words עץ (*Etz*—"tree" [ע = 70 + צ = 90 + 160]) and צלם (*Tzelem*—"image" or "likeness" [צ = 90 + ל = 30 + ם = 40 = 160]).[78]

Regarding their usage for magical purposes, these variants, as can be expected, are employed for the same magical purpose in Practical Kabbalah. We are informed that when there is an outbreak of smallpox, measles, or anything of that ilk, all children, and anyone else for that matter who is yet unaffected by the epidemic, can be protected from contracting the virus inadvertently from those infected, by simply carrying either or both of these "Magic Squares" on their person. In this regard we are told to write these "magic seals" on a metal plate or on a "*kosher* parchment," the latter being simply clean parchment or unused sheet of paper.[79]

We are further instructed that if you prefer to engrave the "Magic Square" on a small gold plate, that this should be done in the zodiacal period of *Taleh* (*Aries*) during the first hour of the day at daybreak. On the other hand, if your intention is to write the *chotam* on parchment, this can be done any time on a Thursday afternoon. We are again reminded that what is important about writing any of these "Magic Squares" for magical purposes, is that the Hebrew letter/numbers should be written in *ashurit*, and that their component letter/numbers should be inscribed in exact numerical order.[80]

As mentioned, both squares can be employed conjointly. In some instances the two *chotamot* are respectively engraved on either side of a metal *Kamea* (amulet), or written next to each other on the same parchment, one to the left and the other to the right, or again one at the top and the other at the bottom of the page. Thereafter the amulet is carried like a pendant around the neck.[81]

   The two forms of the fourfold square, i.e. the one in which each row totals 34 and the other in which the same totals 40, are also sometimes employed conjointly.[82] It should also be noted that the threefold and fourfold squares are equally employed conjointly as shown in the following *Kamea*:[83]

אל	סִיהָ	אָאִי	רִיךָ	וַהוּ	חניאל
אלהי	פִלִן	תִצֶת	הָמֵב	יִשָׁח	חסדיאל
ישראל	וַיִה	יִין	וָחו	הִין	רחמיאל
אגלא	יִנה	וִחִי	הִוד	יְתֵן	אהביאל

ד	ו	ה
ה	ד	ו
ו	ה	ד

ח	ו	יא	א
ט	ג	ו	ח
ב	יכב	ה	ז
ז	ה	ד	י

ד	ט	ב
ג	ה	ז
ח	א	ו

The central four columns of the upper square comprise Divine Names constructed from portions of sacred writ reading:

(Genesis 39:2) ויהי יהוה את יוסף ויהי איש מצליח

(Genesis 39:21) ויתן חנו (Psalm 84:12 [13]) חן וכבוד

יתן יהוה

Transliteration:

   (Genesis 39:2) Vay'hi YHVH et Josef vay'hi ish matz'liach
   (Genesis 39:21) vayiten chino (Psalm 84:12 [13]) chen
   v'chavod yiten YHVH

Translation:

   (Genesis 39:2) And YHVH was with Joseph, and he was a prosperous man; (Genesis 39:21) and gave him favour; (Psalm 84:12 [13]) YHVH giveth grace and glory.

The right column of the upper square comprises the appellatives of four Spirit Intelligences, these being חניאל (*Chani'el*); חסדיאל (*Chasdi'el*); רחמיאל (*Rachmi'el*);and אהביאל (*Ahavi'el*). On the opposite side, we trace along the leftmost column the four Names, i.e. אל (*El*), אלהי (*Elohei*), ישראל (*Yisra'el*) and אגלא (*Agala'a*).

As indicated, there are three "magic squares" below the upper magical seal, i.e. the regular threefold square to the right, the earlier mentioned fourfold square which is arranged with the *gematria* of each of its horizontals, columns and diagonals rows totalling 26, thus aligning with that of the Ineffable Name. The letter square to the left is comprised of the term הוד (*Hod*—"Splendour" [ה = 5 + ו = 6 + ד = 4 = 15]), the numerical value of which we noted earlier aligns with the threefold square.

The "*Hod* Square" appears in the following two formats on Hebrew amulets:

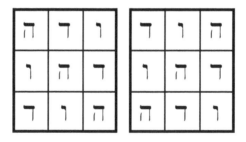

These letter squares are employed for both protection and the increase of personal glamour, and are drawn directly on the four walls of a room. The one to the right is placed on the east and west walls, whilst the other on the left is located on the north and south walls. We are told that these may also be drawn on clean paper, which is similarly positioned. It is further said that these amulets do not require a covering, but some sort of envelope would be necessary when accompanying the owner on a journey.[84]

Now, the compounded amulet comprising the threefold, fourfold, "Hod" square, etc., is said to have the power to increase the charm and respect of the one who carries it. It is said to impact anyone who is touched by this individual. In order to achieve the said aim, we are instructed to draw and write the listed construct at the top of a kosher scroll. Below it is written the following adjuration:

חסדיאל חניאל אהביאל רחמיאל אל אלהי ישראל
אגלא אהיה אשר אהיה הבו חן וכבוד וחסד ורחמים
ל[פלוני בן פלוני] בעיני כל רואיו או בעיני [פלוני
בן פלוני]

Transliteration:

> *Chasdi'el Chani'el Ahavi'el Rachmi'el El Elohei Yisra'el Agala'a Ehyeh asher Ehyeh havu chen v'kavod v'chesed v'rachamim l'[.....Ploni ben Ploni.....] b'einei kol ro'av o b'einei [.....Ploni ben Ploni.....]*

Translation:

> *Chasdi'el Chani'el Ahavi'el Rachmi'el El Elohei Yisra'el Agala'a Ehyeh asher Ehyeh* bring charm and respect and mercy and lovingkindness to [.....fill in the name of bearer.....] in the eyes of all who see this person or in the eyes of [..... fill in the name of a specific individual to be impressed in this manner.....]

It is said that all will be forthwith impacted as they are touched by the bearer of this *Kamea*, who must do so whilst reciting *Proverbs 5:19* three times. This verse reads:

אילת אהבים ויעלת חן דדיה ירוך בכל עת באהבתה
תשגה תמיד

Transliteration:

> *Ayelet ahavim v'ya'alat chen dadeha y'ravucha v'chol eit b'ahavatah tishgeh tamid*

Translation:

> A lovely hind and a graceful doe, let her breasts satisfy thee at all times; with her love be thou ravished always.

Now, we note that the "Magic Square of the Fourth Order" is attributed to the Planet Jupiter, and there is also a set of concepts,

Divine Names and angelic appellatives aligned with the fourfold square, of which, amongst others, Agrippa and company[85] listed אבא (*Aba*—"Father" [א = 1 + ב = 2 + א = 1 = 4]); אל אב (*El Av*—"Father God" [א = 1 + ל = 30 + א = 1 + ב = 2= 34]); יהפיאל (*Jofi'el* [י = 10 + ה = 5 + פ = 80 + י = 10 + א = 1 + ל = 30 = 136]); and הסמאל (*Hisma'el* [ה = 5 + ס = 60 + מ = 40 + א = 1 + ל = 30 = 136]).

The numerical values of these terms are meaningfully related to the Jupiter square, i.e. the *gematria* of the term *Aba* pertains to the fourfold nature of the square, and that of *El Av* to the numerical value of each row, column and diagonal. As indicated earlier, the latter two Angelic names refer to the two Spirit Intelligences associated with Jupiter. However, there is a slight impasse. The *gematria* of the Hebrew names of the listed Celestial Intelligences aligns with the total value of the "Magic Square" of the fourth order, but in the case of the appellative of the main Planetary Spirit, the *gematria* fitted only after the standard spelling of the angelic name, i.e. יופיאל (*Jofi'el*) was "adjusted" to יהפיאל. In this regard, I have been informed that the two spellings refer to different Spirit Intelligences. I doubt that very much, and it is curious that the listed pronunciation is *Jofi'el* in both instances.

Be that as it may, we are told "Jupiter is the source of *growing power*,"thus an amulet comprised of the Jupiter magic square and associated symbol(s), will afford "the ability of obtaining wishes easily and keeping away dreadful sicknesses and diseases."[86] Regarding the Jupiter Square, Agrippa maintains that "if it be impressed upon a Silver plate with Jupiter being powerfull, and ruling, it conduceth to gain, and riches, favor, and love, peace, and concord, and to appease enemies, to confirm honors, dignities, and counsels, and dissolve enchantments if it be engraven on a corall."[87] Further elaboration elsewhere instructs us to "take a thin piece of silver made on its day (Thursday) and hour, and let Jupiter be in a favorable position." The fourfold square is then engraved on the metal, and we have to "suffumigate it with aloe wood and ambrosia." The item is then carried on ones person, and it is claimed that all "who see you will love you, and you will succeed in whatever you ask of them. And if you put this figure between the feet of merchants, their business will grow. And if you put it in a dove-cot or in a place where bees gathered, they will thrive. And if you carry it with you, your fortune will go from good to better. And if you place it in the seat of some prelate, his rule will last and he will not fear his enemies."[88]

3. Magic Squares of the Fifth & Sixth Order

Having perused the various formats of the "Magic Squares" of the third and fourth order, we might as well take a closer look at the remaining "planetary" squares and their variants.

The "Magic Square" of the fifth order, commonly called the "Mars square," is depicted in Agrippa's "*Occult Philosophy*"[89] in the following manner:

11	24	7	20	3
4	12	25	8	16
17	5	13	21	9
10	18	1	14	22
23	6	19	2	15

יא	כד	ז	כ	ג
ד	יב	כה	ח	טז
יז	ה	יג	כא	ט
י	יח	א	יד	כב
כג	ו	יט	ב	טו

The same "Mars" square was also published in the "*Esh M'tzaref*,"[90] and is also addressed by W. Ahrens in "*Hebraeische Amulette mit Magischen Zahlenquadraten.*"[91] In this instance each row of the "Magic Square" adds to 65, and its total value is 325. The *gematria* of a set of letters, words, Divine and other names are again associated with the total numerical values of the "Mars Square." According to Agrippa these are ה (*Heh* [5]); יהי

(*Y'hi*—"there is" [' = 10 + ה = 5 + ' = 10 = 25]); יֽאדֿ (*Adonai* [א = 1 + ד = 4 + נ = 50 + ' = 10 = 65]); גראפיאל (*Grafiel* [ג = 3 + ר = 200 + א = 1 + פ = 80 + ' = 10 + א = 1 + ל = 30 = 325]); and ברצאבאל ([correctly ברצבאל] *Bartzabel* [ב = 2 + ר = 200 + צ = 90 + ב = 2 + א = 1 + ל = 30 = 325]).[92] The latter two names refer to the serving and subservient spirits attributed to this "Magic Square."

The following magical seals pertain to the associated planet:[93]

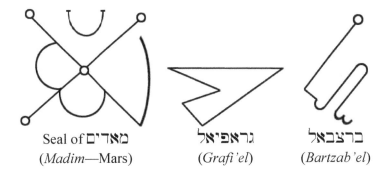

Seal of מאדים
(*Madim*—Mars)

גראפיאל
(*Grafi'el*)

ברצבאל
(*Bartzab'el*)

To date I have seen very limited practical application of the "Magic Square" of the Fifth Order in Jewish Magic. However, Agrippa and his followers has it that the Mars Square "engraven on an Iron Lamen or Sword, makes him that bears it valiant in war and terrible to his adversaries, and shall conquer his enemies. And if it be cut in Cornelian stone it stops bleeding and the menstrua. But if Mars proves unfortunate let it be graven on a Lamen of red brass. It casts down the potent from dignities and honours and riches, breeds discord and contentions and hatred of man and beast, makes unfortunate those that go a hunting and to the wars, causeth sterility or barrenness in men, women and other creatures."[94]

A later manual in the tradition of Cornelius Agrippa elaborates on the fivefold square, saying that it "is made for war and battles and destruction." However, it suggests that the Mars square be engraved on "a thin piece of copper in its hour and day

(Tuesday), when it is falling with respect to Mercury or the Moon, or malefic, or retrograde." This is followed by a rather unsavoury task in which one has to "suffumigate" the item "with menstrual blood, mouse or cat droppings," etc.

Be that as it may, we are informed at the conclusion of all this preparation, that this will afford a variety of malicious benefits in harmony with the malevolent intentions of its bearer. Yet, we are also informed that if you create this magic square "with Mars benefic, direct, and rising in Mercury and brightness, and with the Moon above," and then "suffumigate it with red silk" to which is added "1 dram of carnelian," and then carry the item on your person, "you will defeat your adversaries in court and battle, or they will fly from your face, or they will fear you. And if you put it on someone's shin, it will ease immoderate blood flow."[95]

Whilst most enthusiasts of "Magic Squares" would consider Agippa's version of the square in question to be the most authentic, there are again variants. In this regard, consider the following *Kamea* delineated in an anonymous 19th century North African Hebrew "*Book of Amulets*":

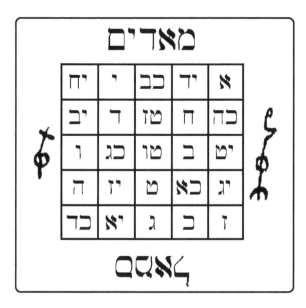

Incorporating the Hebrew appellative for the planet Mars (מאדים—*Madim*) as well as the name of the "venomous" angel סמאל (S*ama'el*), this *Kamea* is employed for the most poisonous intensions. In this regard, it is inscribed on a red copper plate on a Tuesday, i.e. the "Day of Mars," when the said planet is well aspected, and including certain rather unpleasant accompanying actions meant to trigger most nefarious results, i.e. hatred, sowing discord, cursing and the destruction of home and hide. This is definitely not the kind of thing I wish to share in this tome.

Notwithstanding this odious use of the fivefold (Mars) square, I have, as said, not encountered many references to the application of the "Magic Square of the Fifth Order" in Jewish magical traditions. However, I have chanced upon the following curious variant of this *chotam*:

14	10	1	22	18
20	11	7	3	24
21	17	13	9	5
2	23	19	15	6
8	4	25	16	12

יד	׳	א	כב	יח
כ	יא	ז	ג	כד
כא	יז	יג	ט	ה
ב	כג	יט	טו	ו
ח	ד	כה	טז	יב

This magic square appeared in the marginal notes of a 15th century Hebrew manuscript titled *"Liber Cabbalae Operativae"* in the Biblioteca Medicea Laurenziana.[96] In every instance the numerical values of the respective rows, as well as that of the square as a whole, remains exactly the same as the one published by Agrippa.

In addressing "Magic Squares" appearing on a variety of Hebrew amulets held in various German and Austrian libraries and other collections, W. Ahrens highlighted the following very interesting fivefold square:[97]

1	18	21	22	3
20	14	9	16	6
19	15	13	11	7
2	10	17	12	24
23	8	5	4	25

א	יח	כא	כב	ג
כ	יד	ט	טז	ו
יט	טו	יג	יא	ז
ב	י	יז	יב	כד
כג	ח	ה	ד	כה

The values of this square are equal to those of the other listed "Magic Squares" of the fifth order, but what makes this square particularly interesting are the central nine squares, i.e. the ones numbered from 9 to 17. Tracing those numbers in exact order on the square in question, affords the very same pattern of the "Magic Square of the Third Order," as shown below:

1	18	21	22	3
20	14	9	16	6
19	15	13	11	7
2	10	17	12	24
23	8	5	4	25

Be that as it may, we now come to the "Magic Square" of the sixth order, which is attributed to the "Sun." Cornelius Agrippa[98] as well as W. Ahrens in his "*Hebraeische Amulette mit Magischen Zahlenquadraten*"[99] agree on its format, which is as follows:

ו	לב	ג	לד	לה	א
ז	יא	כז	כח	ח	ל
יט	יד	טז	טו	כג	כד
יח	כ	כב	כא	יז	יג
כה	כט	י	ט	כו	יב
לו	ה	לג	ד	ב	אל

6	32	3	34	35	1
7	11	27	28	8	30
19	14	16	15	23	24
18	20	22	21	17	13
25	29	10	9	26	12
36	5	33	4	2	31

The numerical value of each row is 111, and the total value of the square is the ever so "ominous" 666 of "Apocalypse" infamy, which is also the *gematria* of the subservient spirit of the Sun, i.e. סורת (*Sorat* [ס = 60 + ו = 6 + ר = 200 + ת = 400 = 666]). Being attributed to the Sun, Agrippa indicated the main planetary serving spirit of the sixfold square to be נכיאל (*Nachi'el* [נ = 50 + כ = 20 + י = 10 + א = 1 + ל = 30 = 111]). In this instance, the *gematria* pertains to the total value of single rows, columns, and diagonals comprising the "magic square."[100]

Agrippa also attributed the letter ו (*Vav* = 6) and the combination הא (the spelling of the letter *Heh* with an *Alef* [ה = 5 + א = 1= 6]) to the "Magic Square of the Sixth Order." In both instances the numerical values are understood to reference the sixfold square. He further listed the term אלה [א = 1 + ל = 30 + ה = 5 = 36] to be associated with the "magic square" in question,[101] since it indicates the thirty-six sectors comprising the grid of the sixfold square. Be that as it may, Agrippa lists the pronunciation of the mentioned Hebrew term to be "*Eloh*," which might mean that he is either referring to the Divine Name *Eloah*, which in this instance would be wrongly spelled, or he might be referring to the term for a goddess or a terebinth. In the latter instance the pronunciation would be *Elah*, and the spelling would be correct.

However, besides the listed possible meanings, it should be noted that the אלה letter combination could be read "*Eleh*" ("these"); "*Alah*" (an "adjuration," "oath" or "imprecation"); "*Alah*" ("to swear or "curse") or "*Alah*" (to "lament"). Furthermore the same letter combination, also pronounced "*Alah*" refers to a "lance," "club," etc. So I suppose one might pick any of these, and wrench as much meaning as one possibly can out of the "magic square" of the Sun.

Now, the 6 x 6 square appears in a very different format in the earlier mentioned "*Esh M'tzaref*", as shown below:[102]

11	63	5	67	69	1
13	21	53	55	15	59
37	27	31	29	45	47
35	39	43	41	33	25
49	57	19	17	51	23
71	9	65	7	3	61

As you have probably noticed, this square comprises odd numbers only, i.e. 1, 3, 5, 7, 9, etc., and the total value of each row, column and diagonal is 216, which is the *gematria* (numerical value) of the word אריה (*Aryeh*—"lion" [א = 1 + ר = 200 + י = 10 + ה = 5 = 216]). In the mentioned alchemical text this square is attributed to gold and aligned with *Tiferet* on the sefirotic tree.[103]

Whilst I have not actually seen much use of the "Magic Square of the Sixth Order" in primary Jewish magical texts, Agrippa listed this square as pertaining to the Sun, and to which is assigned the following planetary seal, and sigils of the related serving spirit and subservient spirit:[104]

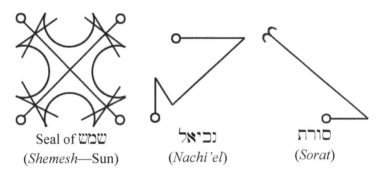

Seal of שמש
(*Shemesh*—Sun)

נכיאל
(*Nachi'el*)

סורת
(*Sorat*)

The Renaissance Magus maintained that when the "Magic Square of the Sixth Order" and its associated "Characters of the Sun," and "the spirits thereof" be "engraven on a Golden plate with the Sun being fortunate, renders him that wears it to be renowned, amiable, acceptable, potent in all his works, and equals a man to Kings, and Princes, elevating him to high fortunes, inabling to do whatsoever he pleaseth: but with an unfortunate Sun, it makes a tyrant, and a man to be proud, ambitious, unsatisfiable, and to have an ill ending."[105]

Expanding on Agrippa's basic exposition of the sixfold square, the author of the "*Liber de Angelis*" elaborates saying that when you wish to employ the "Sun Square" for magical purposes, you should "see when the sun is in its exaltation in its hour in the 5th degree of Aries, and take 6 drams of gold and make from them a round thin plate on the day and hour of the Sun. Suffumigate it with saffron, wash it with rose water in which is musk and ambrosia, and wrap it in saffron-coloured silk, and carry it with you. You will then always be continually happy and lucky in all, and you will prevail in whatever you seek."[106]

Again, I have not chanced upon anything in Practical Kabbalah relating to the "Magic Square of the Sixth Order" in any way similar to the curious notions of Agrippa and his successors. Admittedly I have certainly not perused the totality of the mass of manuscripts on Jewish Magic which have surfaced in recent years, and much of which remains in the hands of private collectors.

4. Magic Square of the Seventh Order

Since the "Magic Square" of the seventh order, the so-called "Venus square," is fairly extensively addressed in primary Jewish Magical literature, there are again a number of variants. The best known format is once again the one appearing in the writings of Cornelius Agrippa,[107] as shown below:

כב	מז	טז	מא	י	לה	ד
ה	כג	מח	יז	מב	יא	כט
ל	ו	כד	מט	יח	לו	יב
יג	לא	ז	כה	מג	יט	לז
לח	יד	לב	א	כו	מד	כ
כא	לט	ח	לג	ב	כז	מה
מו	טו	מ	ט	לד	ג	כח

22	47	16	41	10	35	4
5	23	48	17	42	11	29
30	6	24	49	18	36	12
13	31	7	25	43	19	37
38	14	32	1	26	44	20
21	39	8	33	2	27	45
46	15	40	9	34	3	28

In the case of this "Magic Square," each row, column and diagonal adds to 175, and its total value is 1225. The first number pertains to the *gematria* of the "Spirit of Venus," i.e. קדמאל (*Kedem'el*

[ק = 100 + ד = 4 + מ = 40 + א = 1 + ל = 30 = 175]). However, whilst the second number appears to indicate the so-called "Intelligencies of Venus," i.e. בני שרפים (*Bnei Serafim* [ב = 2 + נ = 50 + י = 10 + ש = 300 + ר = 200 + פ = 80 + י = 10 + ם final = 600 = 1252]), we notice that the *gematria* does not quite fit, despite Agrippa "wishing" it so.[108] There is also the main planetary "Intelligence of Venus," i.e. הגיאל (*Hagi'el* [ה = 5 + ג = 3 + י = 10 + א = 1 + ל = 30 = 49]). The *gematria* here indicates the forty-nine "chambers" of the grid comprising the sevenfold "magic square." Agrippa included a Hebrew letter combination, i.e. אהא [א = 1 + ה = 5 + א = 1 = 7] in his list of important "Venus square" name associations.[109] Whilst this letter combination is sometimes employed as an abbreviation, e.g. of אדני הוא אלהים (*Adonai hu Elohim*—"The Lord is God"); איש האלהים (*Ish ha-Elohim*—"Man of God"); etc.,[110] the listed letter combination is not a Hebrew term *per se*, and in this regard is meaningless.

Be that as it may, the following seals pertain to the planet, serving spirits and subservient spirit of the "Venus Square":[111]

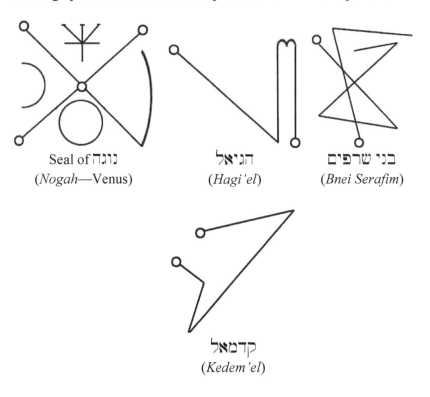

Seal of נוגה
(*Nogah*—Venus)

הגיאל
(*Hagi'el*)

בני שרפים
(*Bnei Serafim*)

קדמאל
(*Kedem'el*)

It should be noted that the format of the sevenfold square as delineated by Agrippa, also features in "*The Kabbala*" by Erich Bischoff,[112] as well as in "*Hebraeische Amulette mit Magischen Zahlenquadraten*" by W. Ahrens,[113] and the mirror image of this square appears in the marginal notes of the "*Liber Cabbalae Operativae.*"[114]

This is not the most popular format of this "Magic Square" in Jewish Magic. That honour belongs to the following square of the seventh order which is extensively addressed in primary Jewish Magical texts, amongst others in "*Toldot Adam*" by Elijah Baal Shem Tov,[115] "*Niflaim Ma'asecha*" by Avraham Chamui,[116] etc.:

כב	יט	ט	ו	מה	מב	לב
לג	כג	כ	י	ז	מו	לו
לז	לד	כד	כא	יא	א	מז
מח	לח	לה	כה	טו	יב	ב
ג	מט	לט	כט	כו	טז	יג
יד	ד	מג	מ	ל	כז	יז
יח	ח	ה	מד	מא	לא	כח

22	19	9	6	45	42	32
33	23	20	10	7	46	36
37	34	24	21	11	1	47
48	38	35	25	15	12	2
3	49	39	29	26	16	13
14	4	43	40	30	27	17
18	8	5	44	41	31	28

This specific version of "Magic Square" of the seventh order, being aligned with the planet Venus, is said to be a special *segulah* encouraging the generation and birth of sons.[117] In this instance an individual desiring male offspring, has to take sixteen pieces of silver which is handed to a woman who has children. She is then to deliver this hoard of silver to a silversmith or a jeweller, who in turn has to purify the silver and shape all of it into a large, clean silver disc. On concluding this task, the jeweller has to purify himself, e.g. take a ritual bath inside a *Mikveh*, and, only after such purification, to engrave on both sides of the disc the "magic square" under current discussion, including the earlier addressed phrase from *Genesis 47:23* reading הא לכם זרע (*Hei lachem zera*—"Here you have semen").

We are reminded that all the letters on this *Kamea* should be *ashurit*, i.e. the standard square Hebrew letters, and also that they should be spaced in such a manner on the construct that none are touching. On conclusion of this procedure, the silver amulet is placed inside three white bags which have been sewn with white cotton. First it is located in a white bag made from pure silk, which is in turn placed inside a bag made of garment quality linen. All of these are finally located inside another white silk bag of equally as good quality, and the procedure concluded with the individual requiring this magical service suspending the amulet on a Friday, the day of Venus, in a bedroom window of his residence, where it is left until the following Tuesday.

There is yet another interesting variant of the sevenfold number square addressed by W. Ahrens in his interesting book on "Magic Squares,"[118] as shown below:

ג	מב	לח	ד	מג	מ	ה
מד	יג	ל	לג	לד	טו	ו
א	לב	כו	כא	כח	יח	מט
לט	לא	כז	כה	כג	יט	יא
ב	יד	כב	כט	כד	לו	מח
מא	לה	כ	יז	טז	לז	ט
מה	ח	יב	מו	ז	י	מז

As in the case of the earlier mentioned unusual "Magic Square" of the fifth order addressed in "*Hebraeische Amulette mit Magischen Zahlenquadraten*," W. Ahrens focussed attention on this variant of the current "Magic Square" for the very same reasons, i.e. the central nine numbers are arranged in the same format as those comprising the "Magic Square" of the third order, as shown below:[119]

3	42	38	4	43	40	5
44	13	30	33	34	15	6
1	32	26	21	28	18	49
39	31	27	25	23	19	11
2	14	22	29	24	36	48
41	35	20	17	16	37	9
45	8	12	46	7	10	47

Now, according to Agrippa and his followers, the standard "Magic Square of the Seventh Order," when "engraved on a Silver plate, Venus being Fortunate, procureth concord, endeth strife, procureth the love of women." We are further informed that it "conduceth to conception, is good against barrenness, causeth ability for generation, dissolves enchantments, and causeth peace between man, and woman, and maketh all kind of Animals and Cattle fruitful; and being put into a Dove-house, causeth an increase of Pigeons." Moreover, "it conduceth to the cure of all melancholy distempers, and causeth joyfulness; and being carryed about travellers makes them fortunate. But if it be formed upon Brass with an unfortunate Venus, it causeth contrary things to all that hath bin above said."[120]

Expanding on this theme elsewhere, we are told that the "Venus Square" is "a figure of luck proper to woman's matters and all delights and sex," and that the item should be created when "Venus be in Pisces, for there is its exaltation, or in Taurus or in Libra, which are its houses, and that it be benefic and increasing in brightness, fast in its course and rising direct." We then have to acquire "7 drams of pure silver in its day (Friday) and hour," and from this "make a thin plate and write on it the figure." At the conclusion of its construction we have to "suffumigate it with aloe wood, ambrosia, and mastic; wrap it in white silk cloth; and then carry it with you." We are informed this will resulted in "all the women you see will love you, and you will behold miracles. And if a man or woman is slow to marry, let that person carry it and that person will soon marry. And if your wife or some other favourite hates you, wash the aforesaid plate with spring water or rose water and give it to her to drink, and she will love you and do as you wish. And if you boil camomile and wash the plate and sprinkle that water in places of discord or in any places of the world, all evil will cease. And if you sprinkle this water in business places or farms, they will prosper. And if you put this figure in your bed, you will abound in sex and your wife will love you very much."[121]

Whilst I recognise in Jewish magic the value of the "Magic Square of the Seventh Order" in terms of love, marriage and birth, I have once again not observed any application of the same dramatic intent as expressed in the previous paragraph.

5. Magic Squares of the Eighth & Ninth Order

As far as the "Magic Squares" of the eighth and ninth order are concerned, I have to date not seen any variants to the "standard" version. It would seem that beyond the cogitations of Cornelius Agrippa[122] and the "*Esh M'tzaref,*"[123] the deliberations of Rabbi Joseph Tzayach, the 16th century Kabbalist whose writing on magic squares and the planets[124] has been described as being "very similar to that of ancient astrology and alchemy";[125] the marginal notes in the "*Liber Cabbalae Operativae,*"[126] the brief references in "*The Kabbala*" by Erich Bischoff,[127] and the deliberations on these "Magic Squares" in "*Hebraeische Amulette mit Magischen Zahlenquadraten*" by W. Ahrens,[128] there is not much to be found in Jewish Magic on either the eight or the ninefold "magic squares."

Regarding the format of the "Magic Square of the Eighth Order," it appears Agrippa, the author of the alchemical "*Esh M'tzaref,*" as well as other primary sources I have consulted on "Magic Squares," concur that the layout of this "Magic Square" is as follows:

ח	נח	נט	ה	ד	סב	סג	א
מט	טו	יד	נב	נג	יא	י	נו
מא	כג	כב	מד	מה	יט	יח	מח
לב	לד	לה	כט	כח	לח	לט	כה
מ	כו	כז	לז	לו	ל	לא	לג
יז	מז	מו	כ	כא	מג	מב	כד
ט	נה	נד	יב	יג	נא	נ	טז
סד	ב	ג	סא	ס	ו	ז	נז

8	58	59	5	4	62	63	1
49	15	14	52	53	11	10	56
41	23	22	44	45	19	18	48
32	34	35	29	28	38	39	25
40	26	27	37	36	30	31	33
17	47	46	20	21	43	42	24
9	55	54	12	13	51	50	16
64	2	3	61	60	6	7	57

Agrippa again informed us regarding certain Divine and Angelic Names pertaining to the eightfold square, i.e. אזבוגה (*Azbogah* [א = 1 + ז = 7 + ב = 2 + ו = 6 + ג = 3 + ה = 5 = 24]). Referring to this Name as "eight extended,"[129] Agrippa is obviously referring to the fact that this Divine Name is called "The Name of the Eights," which, as noted earlier, refers to the *gematria* of the three component letter pairs comprising the Divine Name being respectively 8. He also included in his list of attributes the term דין (*Din*—"judgment" [ד = 4 + י = 10 + ן = 50 = 64]), the *gematria* here referring to the total number of numbers comprising the eightfold square.[130]

The "Magic Square of the Eighth Order" being attributed to the planet Mercury, Agrippa also lists its associated planetary spirit and serving spirit, respectively טיריאל (*Tiri'el* [ט = 9 + י = 10 + ר = 200 + י = 10 + א = 1 + ל = 30 = 260]), the *gematria* here referring to the total value of single lines, columns and diagonals, and תפתרתרת (*Taftartarat* [ת = 400 + פ = 80 + ת = 400 + ר = 200 + ת = 400 + ר = 200 + ת = 400 = 2080]).[131] The *gematria* of the name of the latter Spirit Intelligence indicates the total value of the "Mercury Square."

To these attributions must again be added the seal of the planet, as well as the "sigils" of the planetary spirits, these being portrayed in the following manner:

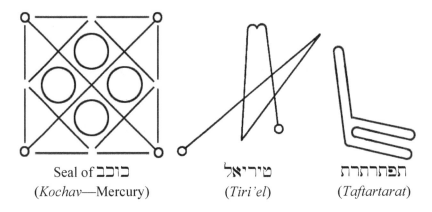

Seal of כוכב
(*Kochav*—Mercury)

טיריאל
(*Tiri'el*)

תפתרתרת
(*Taftartarat*)

Whilst there might be little reference to the "Magic Square of the Eighth Order" in the primary literature of Practical Kabbalah, we find some interesting instructions on its use in the magical writings of Christian Kabbalists, who tell us that if this "magic square" is "engraven upon Silver, or Tin, or yellow Brass, or be writ upon Virgin Parchment," when Mercury is well aspected, "it renders the bearer thereof gratefull, and fortunate to do what he pleaseth." It is further said "it bringeth, gain, and prevents poverty, conduceth to memory, understanding, and divination, and to the understanding of occult things by dreams: and if it be an unfortunate Mercury, doth all things contrary to these."[132]

There were once again further elaborations on this theme elsewhere in the writings of the followers of the great Magus, where we are informed that to Mercury "are attributed soul, virtue, knowledge, wisdom, philosophy.....and painting."[133] Regarding the construction of an amulet comprised of the eightfold square, we are instructed to "take 8 drams of pure silver and make a thin plate in the hour of Mercury on its day (Wednesday), when Mercury is powerful, direct, and fast on course, suffumigate it with aloe wood, cloves, and mastic, and carry it with you, you will then succeed in all you pursue. And if you cannot use silver, write on orange paper instead of silver and it will be good enough." It is also said that "if you put this figure in someone's seat, his rule will last. And if you carve this figure on a ring, or in glass, or in a basin, on the day of Mercury in the morning on the first 7 lunar days in the Moon's ascension, and if you wash this figure with clean water from some spring and drink that water, then after three days you will remember all you have utterly forgotten, and, further, you will easily learn all that you wish."[134]

There are further qualities and magical benefits assigned to the "Magic Square of the Eighth Order," i.e. dream questioning, etc. In fact, much of the magical work involving the eightfold square in Christian and Hermetic Magic aligns with similar practices found in Jewish Magic, albeit in the latter instance with the support of magical seals and symbols very different from the eightfold "Magic Square." However, whilst there is much information on the "Magic Square of the Ninth Order" in the writings of Christian magicians, related details are very sparse in Jewish magic and mysticism.

The ninefold square is attributed to the Moon in Jewish occult writings, i.e. the writings of Rabbi Tzayach, but he employed all the planetary squares for meditative purposes only.[135] In this regard, the esteemed Rabbi noted "I do not have the authority to explain the mystery of these luminaries,"[136] hence he left methods unexplained.

According to Cornelius Agrippa and his successors the format of the ninefold square is as follows:[137]

לז	עח	כט	ע	כא	סב	יג	נד	ה
ו	לה	עט	ל	עא	כב	סג	יד	מו
מז	ז	לט	פ	לא	עב	כג	נה	טו
טז	מח	ח	מ	פא	לב	סד	כד	נו
נז	יז	מט	ט	מא	עג	לג	סה	כה
כו	נח	יח	נ	א	מב	עד	לד	סו
סז	כז	נט	י	נא	ב	מג	עה	לה
לו	סח	יט	ס	יא	נב	ג	מד	עו
עז	כח	סט	כ	סא	יב	נג	ד	מה

37	78	29	70	21	62	13	54	5
6	38	79	30	71	22	63	14	46
47	7	39	80	31	72	23	55	15
16	48	8	40	81	32	64	24	56
57	17	49	9	41	73	33	65	25
26	58	18	50	1	42	74	34	66
67	27	59	10	51	2	43	75	35
36	68	19	60	11	52	3	44	76
77	28	69	20	61	12	53	4	45

In addition to the format of the "Square of the Ninth Order," Agrippa listed the following magical seals (sigils) of the Moon and associated planetary spirits:

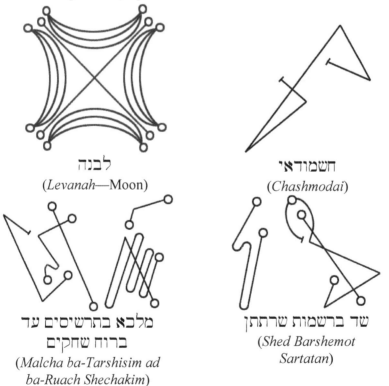

לבנה

(*Levanah—Moon*)

חשמודאי

(*Chashmodai*)

מלכא בתרשישים עד
ברוח שחקים

(*Malcha ba-Tarshisim ad
ba-Ruach Shechakim*)

שד ברשמות שרתתן

(*Shed Barshemot
Sartatan*)

Agrippa informs us that the Moon Square is comprised of "a square of nine multiplied into itself, having eighty one numbers, in every side and Diameter nine, producing 369, and the sum of all is 3321."[138] Paraphrasing Agrippa's writing on the ninefold square in clear terms, a successor of Cornelius Agrippa tells us in *"A Treatise on Angel Magic"* that "this table engraven in silver, the Moon fortunate, makes the bearer thereof, lovely, grateful, cheerful, honoured, taking away all malice and ill will; makes one secure in travelling and getting riches, sound in body. It expels enemies and other hurtful things from any place you desire." However, he further informs us that "if this table is made on a Lamen of Lead, wheresoever you shall bury it, that place shall be unfortunate,"[139] also listing other highly unpleasant inhumane actions to be worked on our fellow humankind by means of the "Magic Square of the Ninth Order."

There were again further elaborations on the construction and use of the ninefold square in the writings of Agrippa's followers. In one of these we are advised to "take a parchment and write on it this figure on the day of the Moon (Monday) and its hour, in its ascent; and write with ink of musk and saffron — both tempered with rose water." We are told to "suffumigate" this item with "cucumber and watermelon seeds," and then to "put it on a thin plate of silver made in the shape of a dog," and then to carry it on ones person. The item is then said to be "good for pursuing all noble affairs, and it diverts all evil. And whoever has this in his possession will fear neither a thief nor other evil."[140]

In this instance, the author likewise shares some baneful applications of the item, telling us that "when you wish to expel from town someone you hate, to write this figure on parchment from a virgin sheep, and on the other side draw a crab, using the blood of a black cock,"[141] and taking other deplorable measures which are by far much too vicious to be aligned with the material shared in this manual!

I wish to conclude this investigation into Hebrew magic squares with the following clear, direct, and fairly unambiguous account of the construction and magical employment of the seven planetary magic squares, which was published by a certain Octavius Morgan in the mid 19th century.[142] Whilst the essay is worth reading in full, I will share only the portion relevant to our current investigation. It reads:

"An extraordinary belief in astrology and amulets prevailed in Europe during the sixteenth and seventeenth centuries, but especially during the period from 1550 to 1650. The amulets of that time were usually made under the special influence either of the constellations, the fixed stars, or the planets. Those made under the influence and, as it was termed, in the Seal of the Planets (and they were sometimes called Seals of the Planets), were either made under the influence of them altogether, of one single planet, or of two or more combined. They were made of the metals, each of the seven planets having one peculiar to itself. The symbol, therefore, of the planet became also the symbol of the metal; thus there was a close connexion between astrology and alchemy. The metals employed were all purified and employed in a particular manner, and also at particular seasons. They were usually formed into circular or multangular plates or laminae, and were engraved with the necessary mystic characters.

For the preparation of an amulet in the seal of Saturn the metal employed was lead, and this is the direction for its purification given by Hiebner — 'Take pounded lead ore, let it run through a fine sieve, wash and press it, and then set it on a gentle charcoal fire — to one part of the ore take two parts of tartar, and of common salt half a part, put them into a crucible and melt them with a tolerably strong fire, and the lead (*Saturnus*) will fall to the bottom; let it become cold, then melt the lead again, and pour it into strong vinegar or cold water — so is it purified.'

On one side of the amulet when formed was to be engraved a table or magic square consisting of nine divisions or lesser squares, three on each side, and in these were engraved in Hebrew characters the numbers from 1 to 9, so arranged that on being added up, either vertically, horizontally, or diagonally, they should amount to the number 15. There were also engraved either Hebrew words denoting the name of the planet Saturn. It was to be worn suspended round the neck covered in black silk, and its virtue was to promote success in building and agriculture, the cure of saturnine diseases, and ease in childbirth.

For Jupiter the metal was tin, and it was to be thus prepared: 'Melt tin, and when it is well heated throw rosin upon it a little at a time for eight or nine times, and when it burns upon it pour it into water or juice of rue, and it is purified. This must be done under the influence of Jupiter.' On this was to be engraved a square of 16 divisions, four on each side, filled up with numbers from 1 to 16 in Hebrew characters which added up any way would make the sum of 34.

There was also engraved in Hebrew the name of the planet Jupiter. It was to be worn round the neck, wrapped in blue silk, and its virtues were efficacious in gaining the favour of ecclesiastics and lawyers, in curing such diseases as were under the influence of Jupiter, and in expelling demons and the plague.

For mars the metal was iron, and the following is the instruction for its preparation: 'Wash iron filings very clean, put them into human urine and distilled wine vinegar, let them lie nine or ten hours, then take them out and wash away the thick coating, put the same filings into solution of tartar, and they will become red as copper, then wash them again and they will be all right. This purgation must be done under the influence of Mars.'

The square engraved on this must consist of 25 small squares, five on a side, having engraved in them the numbers from 1 to 25 in Hebrew characters, so arranged that when any line is added up together the sum shall be 65; the name of the planet in Hebrew is also engraved on. It was to be worn enclosed in red silk, and its virtues procured success in war and contests, as also the cure of martial diseases. Annexed is the square containing the numbers for this amulet.

For Sol the metal was gold (the sun being considered a planet moving in an orbit round the earth when this science was arranged). It was to be thus prepared: 'Melt three parts of gold, and when it is in fusion add one part of antimony, and expose them to the action of the fire for the eighth part of an hour, then pour it into a greased melting pot, and knock it and the gold will fall to the bottom and part from all impurities; there will, however, still remain a little antimony with the gold. Put to it a little of the best lead and set it on a refining cupel, then put the refined gold into a new crucible with a little borax, and melt it; thus is the gold pure and fit for the work.'

The table was to consist of 36 squares, containing the numbers in Hebrew characters from 1 to 36, so arranged that each line shall count 111. It was to be inclosed in yellow silk and hung round the neck, and its virtues were to ensure the favour of princes and great personages, honour, power, and general prosperity.

For Venus the proper metal was copper, which was to be thus purified: 'Melt some copper and throw on it some powdered glass when in a state of fusion, and let it work for a good hour, then pour it into distilled vinegar and it will granulate; this must be done when a favourable time of the planet's influence begins.'

The square for Venus was to be divided into 49 compartments, seven on a side, filled with the numbers from 1 to 49, so arranged that each line when added up should make the sum of 175. It was to be worn in a bag of green silk, and the special virtues were power to conciliate the love of all mankind, especially that of the fair sex, and a hostile adversary might be recalled to former favour, if rain-water which had imbibed the power of the amulet on its being thrown into it were brought near him; it also gave an aptitude to learn and perform music, and was a preservative against gunshot and sabre wounds.

For Mercury the metal to be used was coagulated quicksilver, that is, solidified by being amalgamated with lead; the mode of its preparation was as follows: 'Press the mercury twenty or thirty times through a leather, afterwards rub or wash it with distilled vinegar, and it is purified. This must be done under a good Mercurial influence.' Paracelsus directs that the mercury should be thus coagulated: 'Take fine lead two ounces, let it melt at a low temperature in a crucible, when melted take it off the fire, let it cool, and when about to set firm add two ounces of mercury.'

The square was to consist of 64 compartments filled with the numbers from 1 to 64, arranged as above described, each line when added up was to make the number 260, and the name of the planet in Hebrew was also to be engraved on it. It was to be enveloped in purple silk, and it insured to the wearer the cure of certain diseases, safe journeys, and a wonderful aptitude for learning any art; water imbued with its properties gave strength of memory to those who drank it, and to those who slept with it under their heads, whatever they desired would appear to them in their sleep.

For the Moon silver was used, and it was thus purified: 'Put finely divided silver in a cupel with some lead, and if you intend that it should be quite free from other metals, put it into a crucible and melt it again, and when it begins to shine and glitter in the crucible like water or a mirror, throw in tartar at ten or twelve times; this purification must be made under a lunar influence.'

The virtues belonging to a lunar amulet depended on the house or sign of the zodiac, under the influence of which it was made, as well as on the relation she bore to the planets at the time of the operation. No colour is given, and it was probably only worn suspended round the neck."[143] This concludes our investigation into Hebrew magic squares.

. ...The frog took a piece of paper, wrote down several charms, and then told Haninah to swallow it. In this way, he promptly knew the entire Torah and the seventy languages... ... ...

.

Chapter 3
Nogah — Venus
SACRED WRIT & *KAMEOT*

A. A River went out of Eden

In this chapter we will investigate sections of the Hebrew Bible employed in magical practice. In ancient days two kinds of scriptural texts were chosen for practical or magical purposes, i.e. verses containing God-names, or referring to Divine power and deeds, and those verses which appear to be especially aligned with the specific condition necessitating their employment. It was believed that these portions of scripture were filled with a celestial power capable of affecting a definite result, when used with proper *Kavvanah*, i.e. appropriate attitude, mindset and focussed intention. It should be noted that the entire Hebrew Bible is considered to be comprised of "God-names," these being understood to be present in every single sentence of holy writ. Thus we often encounter magical instructions which are accompanied by the instruction to "recite this verse with its name....."

It has been written that "the entire Torah is composed of the names of God, and in consequence it has the property of saving and protecting man."[1] So, since the *Torah* is considered to be one, enormous Divine Name, we might as well commence at the very beginning— *Bereshit!* We are told that "a river went out of Eden to water the garden; and from thence it was parted, and became four heads" [*Genesis 2:10*]. Tradition would have it that the original river is the "River of Life," which is channelled by its four divisions into the whole of manifestation. These, named *Pishon*, *Gichon*, *Chedekel* and *Frat*, have a number of specialised functions in Jewish magical traditions, and, in the age old tradition of the "Doctrine of Signatures," are aligned with a set of unique correspondences. The 13th century Rabbi Isaac of Akko lists some of these in his "*Me'irat Einayim*,"[2] of which I think the following will be of great interest to readers interested in Jewish magic and the doctrines of the Western Mystery Tradition in general:

פרת	חדקל	גיחון	פישון
Frat	Chedekel	Gichon	Pishon
צפון	דרום	מערב	מיזרח
Tzafon–North	Darom–South	Ma'arav–West	Mizrach–East
אפר	רוח	אש	מים
Afar–Earth	Ruach–Air	Esh–Fire	Mayim–Water
רפאל	אוריאל	גבריאל	מיכאל
Rafael	Oriel	Gavriel	Michael
נשר	אדם	שור	אריה
Nesher–Eagle	Adam–Man	Shor–Bull	Aryeh–Lion
נחושת	ברזל	זהב	כסף
Nechoshet–Copper	Barzel–Iron	Zahav–Gold	Kesef–Silver

The addition of four associated *Sefirot* are also listed, these being respectively *Chesed* (Loving-kindness/Mercy) = *Pishon*, *Gevurah* (Strength/Severity) = *Gichon*, *Tiferet* (Beauty) = *Chedekel*, and *Malchut* (Kingdom) = *Frat*. I am sure some of these correspondences might be startling, and quite at odds with what some readers may have learned previously. However, I believe one should not be too concerned about the "rightness" or "wrongness" of any of these attributions, since there are many variances to be found in this regard, not only between mainstream Kabbalah and the Christian or Hermetic varieties, but even within the far too glibly considered "uniform doctrines" of "Jewish Kabbalah." A knowledge of affiliated traditions, i.e. traditional astrology, etc., and a good dose of common sense, will soon clarify matters.

Besides this, there are the "magical" applications of the names of the four "rivers" to consider. Since these streams are believed to be channeling the primordial "River of Life," it is thought one could, as it were, "invoke" their respective powers by means of their names, hence the appellatives *Pishon*, *Gichon*, *Chedekel* and *Frat* are considered "Names of Power," and as such are used in Hebrew amulets, incantations, and magical healing practices. I thought I might share some with you.

Amongst the more simple magical applications there is one delineated in the "*Sefer Rafael ha-Malach*,"[3] which pertains to the alleviation of all kinds of fever. In this regard an apple is selected on which is written with ink in simple graphics the names of the four Edenic rivers. The procedure necessitates that the apple is first divided into four parts, then the four names are respectively written on the four portions, i.e. one name for each part. The afflicted individual is then fed the four sections of the apple in the exact marching order of the listed names, i.e. the part with the name *Gichon* on it is consumed first, thereafter the *Pishon* portion, followed by the *Chedekel* one, and concluding with the *Frat* section. We are told that God willing, the fever will abate and the sufferer healed.[4]

Suspecting that there was a lot more to the four "Edenic Rivers" than meets the eye, Kabbalists closely scrutinised the names of the four streams. By means of somewhat complex application of *Temurot*, in this instance exchanges of Hebrew letters by means of six special ciphers, i.e. *Achas Beta*, *Atbach*, *Atbash*, *Albam*, *Avgad*, *Ayak Bachar*, they concluded that, with the exclusion of the final *Nun* (ן) of the names *PishoN* (פי"שון) and *GichoN* (ג'יחון), the first three names of the "Rivers of Eden" are hidden references to the three Divine Names which are vital for our continued well-being on this planet. It is also understood that the three letters derived from, or, as it were, "hidden" within the name of the last "river," indicate a very unique Hebrew abbreviation. The Divine Names and mentioned abbreviation are shown below [read from right to left]:

פרת (Frat) יבק (YBK)	חדקל (Chedekel) אדני (Adonai)	גיחו [ן] (Gichon) אהיה (Ehyeh)	פישו [ן] (Pishon) יהוה (YHVH)

Of course, the three Divine Names are immediately recognised, and, considering the Kabbalistic doctrine on the flow of the "river of *Shefa*" (Divine Abundance) into manifestation by means of *tzinorot* [spiritual channels] which are "controlled," so to speak, by these important Divine Names aligned with the *sefirot* of *Keter* [Crown—*Ehyeh*], *Tiferet* [Beauty—*YHVH*] and *Malchut* [Kingdom —*Adonai*], it is only natural that they should be included in amulets comprising the names of the four divisions of the Edenic "River of Life."

What remains to be considered is the unique transposition of the three letters of the "river" *Frat*, i.e. פרת = ק״בי. Since the three letters in question could be read *Yabok*, i.e. the river where the Patriarch Jacob wrestled "a man" (*Genesis 32:23–31 [24–32]*), and, as mentioned in my *"The Book of Sacred Names,"*[5] it was ascertained from this saga that Jacob wrestled with the angel *Pani'el*, and that his attacker was actually the Almighty virtually in person, so to speak, some curious deliberations could be derived from the *Frat/Yabok* affiliation. After all there are also very special "numerical" connections between the *YBK* letter combination and two Divine Names, i.e. the *gematria* of *Yabok* [י = 10 + ב = 2 + ק = 100] is 112 and so is the combined value of the Names *YHVH* [י = 10 + ה = 5 + ו = 6 + ה = 5 = 26] and *Elohim* [א = 1 + ל = 30 + ה = 5 + י = 10 + ם = 40 = 86]. However, in the current instance the *YB"K* letter combination is generally conceded to be an abbreviation. On the one hand it refers to the concluding portion of *Psalms 20:10* reading יעננו ביום קראנו (*ya'aneinu b'yom kar'einu*—"answer us in the day that we call"), the verse being uttered three times during morning prayers,[6] on the other hand it indicates יחוד ברכה קדושה (*yichud b'rachah k'dushah*—"Unification Blessedness Holiness").[7]

As it is, the three letters in question and the words comprising each of these Hebrew phrases, are themselves understood to be direct references to the three mentioned vital Divine Names. In fact, the "Divine Unification," "Blessedness" and "Holiness" of *YB"K* are said to indicate the union of *Keter* [*Ehyeh*], *Tiferet* [*YHVH*] and *Malchut* [*Adonai*], or the "unification" of the *Neshamah*, *Ru'ach* and *Nefesh*, the "Higher Self," "Middle Self" and "Lower Self" aspects of the human soul.[8]

With such profundity of meaning hidden in the names of the four "Rivers of Eden," it is no wonder the names *Pishon*, *Gichon*, *Chedekel* and *Frat*, as well as the affiliated Divine Names and that unique abbreviation, should be included in Hebrew amulets employed for a variety of "life supporting" reasons. In fact, amongst the most important uses of the names of the four "Edenic Rivers" in Hebrew amulets is the promotion of a long life.

In this regard, the standard arrangement of the names are permuted, written forwards and backwards, and the component letters of the names intertwined in special ways.[9] Whilst there are variations on these arrangements in Jewish magical tomes, I have consulted as many primary sources as I could find, and after due consideration settled on the following list:

B				A			
פנחפפ	יידר	שחקת	וולנן	פרת	חדקל	גיחון	פישון
תלנן	רקוו	פדחש	חייגפ	תרפ	לקדח	נוחיג	נושיפ
פחגפ	רדיי	תקחש	לוונן	פישון	גיחון	חדקל	פרת
ננלת	ווקר	שחדפ	ייחפג	נושיפ	נוחיג	לקדח	תרפ
חגפפ	דייר	קחשת	לוונן	פרת	פישון	גיחון	חדקל
תננל	רווק	פשחד	ייחפג	תרפ	נושיפ	נוחיג	לקדח
פחגפ	ידיר	שקחת	ולונן	פרת	גיחון	חדקל	פישון
תנלן	רוקו	פחדש	פחיגפ	תרפ	נוחיג	לקדח	נושיפ

A friend who is a Rabbi of Moroccan descent, insisted emphatically that this amulet is not only for "a long life," but for a "long SUCCESSFUL life." I have perused a number of amulets comprising these sets of names, and noted that it is usually customary to engrave section "A" on the front side of a metal disc [usually silver], with a header in certain instances comprising the earlier addressed יהוה אהיה אדני יבק (*YHVH Ehyeh Adonai YB"K*) combination of Divine Names.[10] However, this header is not standard throughout, since I have noted different headers accompanying the same, e.g. the fully spelled letters of the three associated Divine Names, the first two being written as a header, and the third as a footer as shown below:[11]

> [Header]
> יוד הה וו הה
> אלף הה יוד הה
> [Central Sector]
> River Names combination – Section A
> [Footer]
> אלף דלת נון יוד

In this instance the *YB"K* combination is omitted on the front of the amulet, but it does appear on the rear. More often than not the back of these specific amulets comprise the set of names derived from the intertwined component glyphs of the "River Names" as shown in section "B" above. This portion of the amulet is sometimes also accompanied by a header, e.g. the three associated Divine Names and the full spelling of the component letters of the first two Names, whilst the full spelling of the letters of the third Divine Name as well as the *YB"K* combination is added as a footer. In the same instance, the entire construct is completed with a repeat of the affiliated Divine Names. The rear of the amulet then appears like this:

[Header]

יהוה אהיה אדני

יוד הה וו הה

[Central Sector]
River Names Permutations – Section B
[Footer]

אלפ הה יוד הה יבק

יהוה אהיה אדני

Whilst the headers and footers of this specific amulet might appear quite complex, there are simpler presentations in which only the יהוה אהיה אדני יבק combination heads the entire construct. I have also perused an amulet in which the front of the same construct is headed by the Divine Name שדי (*Shadai*) only, whilst the rear is concluded with a footer comprising the name of the owner.[12]

Of course, the simplest format is to plainly engrave the names of the four "Edenic Rivers" without any of the complexities of permutations and conjoining of component letters. For example, I perused an amulet of this nature comprised of nothing more than the name of the bearer as a header, followed by the Divine Name טפטפיה (*Taftafyah*) and the names of the four "Rivers" written in the standard manner, with a single permutation of each name. In this instance the front and rear of the amulet are exact copies. Here is the complete construct:

> [Header]
> Name of the owner
> טפטפיה
> [Central Sector]
> גיחון יחגון פרת
> רפת חדקל דקלה
> פישון יפשון

I have chanced upon a number of very interesting reflections on the "Four Rivers" of Gan Eden. Amongst these, consider for example a unique Kabbalistic *tikkun*, a magical "mending rite," intended to "heal" the "breaches" within the Divine One, as depicted by Abraham Miguel Cardozo, the 17th century Shabbatean prophet and "magus."[13] Of course, the "broken deity" is understood to refer to the "lower aspects" of the "Divine in Manifestation," and not to the primordial oneness of the Eternal Living Spirit beyond time, space and events.

The rectification ritual requires one to select sets of five stones respectively representing five holy *sefirot* and five "demonic" counterparts, or perhaps the "demonic counterparts" of the five aspects of the human "Self," the latter being the *Nefesh*, *Ru'ach*, *Neshamah*, *Chiah* and *Yechidah*. The ritual procedure requires practitioners to alternatively position the stones inside streams of water, remove them, replace, remove and to scatter them, and so forth, whilst simultaneously reciting prayers and selected biblical verses. Cardozo informed us "the demonic powers are called 'stumbling stone' and 'obstacle stone' [*Isaiah 8:14*].....[while] the holy *sefirot* are called 'smooth stones.'....."[14]

Regarding Cardozo's mentioned magical "divine mending rite," he told us that "when you take up these stones, your purpose is not to separate or to distance them from the brook, to distance, that is, the Persons from the Primordial Adam. God forbid! These are our portion and our heritage; it is our task fully to mend the flaw inflicted upon them by our ancestor's sins and by our own, and it is for this purpose that you are taking them up. For it is he who has true knowledge of God who is able to do the 'Mending'." In delineating the rite in question, Cordozo instructed those intending to work this "mending" of the "disfigured deity," to recite *Genesis 2:10-14* whilst standing on the banks of a brook, stream or river. He explains "the 'river' is Primordial Adam.....He perpetually 'goes forth from Eden,' this being 'Adam of the World of Emanation.' The 'garden' is that vacant space, which, according to Rabbi Isaac Luria, was left when the Infinite initially contracted Itself into Itself.....This is, in the truest sense, that 'garden,' and it is for the purpose of watering it that the river — Primordial Adam — goes forth from the primordial Eden, which is 'Adam of the World of Emanation'....." Having completed the recitation of the mentioned verses, the practitioner is required to place "the five stones of the realms of holiness into the river's waters," which is followed by prayers and a variety of further actions.[15]

Regarding the division of the one Edenic river into four, Cardozo believed this to be a division of the "divine flow" commencing within the *sefirah Keter* (Crown), or in the *partzuf* (Countenance) of *Arich Anpin*, i.e. the "Long-suffering" or "Patient One." The "Four Rivers" are then understood to refer to the four divisions or "faces" as explicated in the Lurianic doctrine of the "*partzufim*," i.e. "Father," "Mother," "Son" and "Daughter" respectively indicating the four *sefirot* of *Chochmah* (Wisdom), *Binah* (Understanding), *Tiferet* (Beauty) and *Malchut* (Kingdom). The "four" are also considered to represent four "messianic figures": Messiah ben David, Messiah ben Ephraim, Moses, and the fourth, according to David Halperin, "is something of a mystery."[16]

Being a Shabbatean, Cardozo naturally included the failed Messiah Shabbetai Tzvi in his deliberations on the four "rivers" of Eden. Hence he informed us that "the name of the first [river] is *Pishon* [*Genesis 2:11*]. This is the *Sefirah Chochmah* [= Father].....The name of the second river is *Gichon*: This is *Binah* [= Mother].....[whose] role is to cover and to protect.....The roots of the two Messiah's souls derive from Father and Mother. This is why the numerical value of the words 'the name of the first is *Pishon*,' when the number of its letters are counted in, is equivalent to the value of 'Shabbetai Tzvi'."[17] Actually the *gematria* does not quite add up so nicely, but with some additional reasoning and a bit of manipulation here and there, anything is achievable.

Notwithstanding this, it would seem Abraham Miguel Cardozo assigned himself a special "messianic" mission, one perhaps a little greater than that of Shabbetai Tzvi. Continuing the theme of the "Four Rivers" and their "messianic" affiliations, he informed us that "at Messiah ben David's coming.....the *sefirah Chochmah* witdrew itself.....Messiah ben David was then left 'a waterless river, all dried up' [*Job 14:11*].....He was unable to reveal the Divinity in any explicit fashion, and he withdrew himself to the heights. Messiah ben Ephraim, by contrast, is the *Sefirah Yesod* (Foundation)."[18] In Lurianic doctrine the phrase "broad places of the river" is identified with *Yesod* as the sex organ of the "Son" *partzuf* in *Tiferet* (Beauty), the messianic figure of which Cardoza maintained derived "from the Mother's genital, which is called 'the broad places of the river.' He is thus able to spread doctrine throughout the world, and the divine effluence along with it, to make known the faith of the Cause Above All Causes, through the Blessed Holy One and His *Shechinah*. This is why the numerical value of 'the broad places of the river'," with again a little push and shove here and there to forcefit the issue nicely, is equivalent to that of the name of......"Abraham Miguel Cardozo" himself![19]

Regarding the remaining two Edenic rivers, Cardoza informed us that the third named "*Chedekel*" (Tigris) refers to the *partzuf* of *Ze'ir Anpin*, the "Impatient One" whose unique locale is *Tiferet* (Beauty) on the sefirotic tree. This Cardozo said corresponds to Moses whom he maintained incorporates "the roots of both Messiahs." In conclusion, he told us that the fourth river *Frat* (Euphrates) "is the *sefirah Malchut*, which is the source of all that is produced."[20] Regarding the latter "river," Cardoza noted that there is no special reference in the bible, which he understood to mean that *Malchut* (Kingdom), the associated *sefirah*, "takes on various names, in accord with whatever effluence this *sefirah* receives"[21] from the higher sefirot, and hence there is also some ambivalence regarding the affiliated messianic personage. On the one hand it is understood to indicate the prophet Elijah, said to be "the Man Who Brings Good News" [*ha-Mevaser*], but that "it remains unclear whether Elijah is really the one who will announce the Redemption." In this regard Cardozo conjectured that "it is possible also that this will be done by a woman," i.e. *Mavaseret Tziyon*, 'She Who Brings Good News to Zion'."[22]

In terms of the Lurianic doctrine of the "*partzufim*" (divine countenances) on the sefirotic tree, the *sefirah Malchut* is associated with *Nukva*, the divine feminine or "Daughter," manifested by and through all women on earth. This is the *Shechinah*, the female counterpart of the Divine One, regarding whom Cardozo implored the Infinite One: "O Master of all the worlds, You who necessarily exist! O God, above whom there is no God! O Lord over all the lords, King over all the Kings! Like the soul in the body and in its clothing, You shine within the ten *sefirot* of the World of Emanation, the ten *sefirot* of the World of Creation, the ten *sefirot* of the World of Fashioning, the ten *sefirot* of the World of Making. You join together all the worlds: the *Yod* to the *Heh*, the *Heh* to the *Vav*, and the *Vav* to the *Heh*. You give life to them all, and the host of heaven prostrates itself to You before Your honoured throne. You it is who unites the Blessed Holy One and His Shechinah. In the light of the manifest faces [is] Your face. May it be Your will to bring the *Shechinah* near, from You, to the Blessed Holy One. For, as seen from Your perspective, there is no separation or dissociation, no banishment or distancing."[23]

Several magical uses of the four Edenic rivers still remain to be addressed, amongst which the most generally employed is their inclusion in amulets intended to aid women suffering difficulties during childbirth. For example, there is a unique magical practice which is enacted on the seventh day of the festival of *Sukkot*, i.e. *Hoshana Rabbah* (Great *Hoshana*). On this day it is customary to make seven *hakafot* (sacred circumambulations) in the synagogue, whilst carrying the *Lulav* and chanting *Hoshanot* (supplications).

For those who do not know, the term *Lulav*, meaning a palm branch, is used in reference to the "four species" delineated in *Leviticus 23:40*, which are conjoined into a special construct during *Sukkot*, i.e. "branches of palm trees"—a single palm branch (*lulav*) which forms the backbone of the contraption; "boughs of leafy trees"—traditionally three myrtle branches (*hadasim*) located to the right of the assemblage; and "willows of the brook"—these comprising two willow branches (*aravot*) positioned to the left. It is customary to carry this palm/myrtle/willow construct in the right hand, whilst holding the remaining "species" which is a "fruit of

goodly trees," traditionally a citron (*etrog*), in the left hand. Since
the "four species" are meant to be conjoined, the two hands are
held together during the waving of the *lulav*.[24]

Regarding the relevant "magical practice" mentioned
above, one is instructed to remove five unimpaired leaves from the
willow branches after the completion the seven *hakafot*
(circumambulations) and the conclusion of the *Hoshana Rabbah*
prayers. One then has to write the names of the four "rivers" on
these leaves, afterwards offering them to a woman who is suffering
difficulties during labour, and who is said will then give birth
forthwith.[25]

Now, whilst this practice is all good and well for any
woman about to procreate in the immediate period following
Hoshana Rabbah, one might well wonder what "magical support"
could be employed for the same purpose at other times when there
are assuredly many women who would be enduring problematic
confinements. In this regard, there is, amongst others, the
following very famous "birth" *Kamea*:[26]

We are instructed that this amulet should be written on a deerskin parchment, however I can attest that it works just as well when written on a sheet of clean, white paper. Afterwards the amulet is tied to the navel of the pregnant woman, and one has to whisper in her ear the phrase from *Exodus 11:8* reading:

צא אתה וכל העם אשר ברגליך

Transliteration:
 Tze atah v'chol ha'am asher b'raglecha
Translation:
 Get thee out, and all the people that follow thee.

Beside the inclusion of the names of the four "Rivers of Eden" on its four corners, the outer circle of the *Kamea* comprises the names of our "primordial parents"; *Lilit*, the mother of all demons; the names of angelic entities directly affiliated with the matter in question; certain Divine Names; as well as *Psalm 91:11*, these being:

אדם וחוה חוץ לילות חוה ראשונה שמריאל חסדיאל
סנוי וסנסנוי וסמנגלף כוזו במוכסז כוזו
[*Psalm 91:11*] כי מלאכיו יצוה לך לשמרך בכל דרכיך
אמן סלה

Transliteration:
 Adam v'Chavah chutz Lilit [Lilot] chavah rishonah, Shamri'el, Chasdi'el, Sanoi, v'Sansanoi v'Semangelof, Kuzu B'mochsaz Kuzu
 [*Psalm 91:11*] *ki malachav yitzaveh lach lishmor'cha b'chol d'rachecha Omein, Selah.*
Translation:
 Adam and *Eve* away *Lilit* [*Lilot*] the first Eve, *Shamri'el, Chasdi'el, Sanoi, v'Sansanoi v'Semangelof, Kuzu B'mochsaz Kuzu,*
 [*Psalm 91:11*] For He will give His angels charge over thee, to keep thee in all thy ways *Amen, Selah.*

The biblical saga of *Adam* and *Eve* is well known, but the tale of *Lilit*, the first wife of *Adam*, whose remonstrations regarding her marital status which ultimately resulted in her becoming the "mother of all demons," is perhaps not so well known. We are told that she is not only a sexual temptress of the first order, who, according to the Talmudic legend, lurks around for shed seed, stealing it with the intention of creating demons in order to torture mankind, but that she is also a killer of infants. Regarding the latter behaviour, the three angels *Sanoi, Sansanoi* and *Semangelof* (or *Sana'ui, Sansina'ui* and *S'man'g'lof* according to the *Shorshei ha-Shemot*),²⁷ were sent to stop her in her tracks, and hence their names are included in amulets protecting women during childbirth, as well as in safeguarding those infants.

The peculiar term חוץ (*chutz*) preceding the name of *Lilit* in the *Kamea*, has been said to mean "away" or "outside," however it was also suggested that the final *tzadi* (ץ) is a transposition of the letter *heh* (ה) by means of the *Atbash* cipher. In this regard the word in question could then be perceived to be a hidden reference to חוה (*Chavah*—"Eve"), and hence it is claimed "the word itself is supposed to be protective for mother and child against *Lilith* herself."²⁸

Next we note the Divine Name כוזו במוכסז כוזו (*Kuzu B'mochsaz Kuzu*), which we addressed earlier, and which we noted is aligned with the sphere of Severity (*Gevurah*), hence its inclusion as a measure of powerful protection in the "birth" amulet under discussion.

Focussing attention on the central hexagram of the amulet in question, and starting top right and reading around from right to left, the outer borders and corners of the hexagram comprise the earlier addressed "Forty-two Letter Name." The centre of the hexagram is comprised of the earlier mentioned phrase from *Exodus 11:8*, concluding with בשם קוף קפו וקף ופק פקו פוק (*b'shem KVP KPV VKP VPK PKV PVK* — "In the name of *KVP KPV VKP VPK PKV PVK*").

We should pay some attention to the peculiar Divine Name קוף and its permutations. In Hebrew the word קוף (*Kof*) refers to an "ape," hence the inclusion of this term as a Divine Name in this amulet must appear most odd. An acquaintance made the tongue in cheek observation that the word in question might be referring to the "little monkey" about to issue from the womb of the sorely distressed woman, however, I believe there is a lot more hidden here than meets the eye of casual observation. For one thing, the *mispar katan* (small *gematria*) of קוף is 15 which is equal to that of י״ה, the "*Digrammaton*," an important and often employed abbreviation of the Ineffable Name. Furthermore, in perusing the six permutations of the Divine Name in question, it would seem that the central idea behind them is the principle of "opening."

In this regard we might note that the combination פוק, the concluding permutation in the set, which could be read *Puk* meaning "to totter" or "reel," also indicates ideas of "producing," as shown for example in the word הפיק (*heifik*) meaning "to bring out" or "produce." Furthermore, the פק letter combination also appears in words pertaining to the concept of "opening," e.g. פקח (*pakach*) meaning "to open," as in opening the eyes or ears.

In my estimation these ideas relate directly to the very fundamental purpose of this amulet which was constructed to "open the womb" so as to facilitate easy birth. Curiously enough, the six permutations of קוף are employed separately for the same purpose.[29] In this regard, we are informed that they are to be engraved on a silver coin which the pregnant woman has to put under her tongue, whilst one whispers ten times in her ear a larger portion of *Exodus 11:8* reading:

וירדו כל עבדיך אלה אלי והשתחוו לי לאמר צא אתה
וכל העם אשר ברגליך

Transliteration:
> *V'yardu chol avadecha eileh eilai v'hishtachavu li leimor tze atah v'chol ha'am asher b'raglecha*

Translation:
> And all these thy servants shall come down unto me, and bow down unto me, saying: "Get thee out, and all the people that follow thee."

This verse is said to comprise several hidden meanings. For example, the *gematria* of the initials of the words comprising the opening phrase are revealing associations with special Divine Names, e.g. the initials *Vav* and the *Kaf* of (כ)ל (וירדו) are said to pertain to the Ineffable Name, since the numerical value of these letters is 26, which is equal to that of יהוה.[30] The *gematria* of the initials of the succeeding three words, (ע)בדיך א(לה) א(לל)י, is 72, which is said to indicate the "Name of Seventy-two Names." In turn, the numerical value of the initials of the words ל(אמר) ו(השתחוו) ל(י) is 66, which is equal to that of אדני (*Adonai*) with the addition of the *kollel*, the extra count for the word itself, and the *gematria* of the word צא is 91, which is equal to the combined numerical value of the names יהוה אדני (*YHVH Adonai*). We are also reminded that the numerical value of פוק, the Divine Name employed in this instance, is 186 which is equal to that of the Divine Name מקום (*Makom*—"Place"), etc.[31]

Getting back to the magical technique in question, at the conclusion of working the ritual, the coin should be sold to an individual inside a synagogue or temple, and the money employed in the purchasing of olive oil which is to be donated to that specific place of worship. In a variant version of the foregoing techniques, we are instructed to write the six permutations of קוף on a cube of sugar, or on a piece of kosher candy, to be consumed by the afflicted woman, whom, we are told, will then give birth forthwith.[32]

Now, we are informed that through the Names of the four "Edenic Rivers" we can witness the wonders of *El Chai*, the Powerful Overlord of Life. As noted previously, the very Name of the Eternal One is in פישון (*Pishon*), the name of the first of the four "Rivers." In this regard we are told that there is no disease in the world which cannot be cured by the letters of this single Name, including the alleviation of conditions like infertility; the elimination of all plagues and epidemics, whether pertaining to man or beast; etc.[33]

Moses Zacutto advised us that there is nothing to compare with the power of the Name in question, which can be employed to control the injurious impact of crawling insects on our world and ourselves. As delineated earlier, the "secret" of פישון (*Pishon*) is in the first four letters of this name expressing the Ineffable Name. Just as *Pishon* includes the Name יהוה (*YHVH*), so is the name אהיה (*Ehyeh*) hidden in the first four letters of the Name גיחון (*Gichon*). In like manner the "secret" of the name חדקל (*Chedekel*) is the Name אדני (*Adonai*), and that of the fourth "Edenic River," פרת (*Frat*), is said to be its connection to the מרכבה (*Merkavah*), the divine "Chariot Throne," which we are told pertains to the Name יבק (*Yabok*).[34]

Be that as it may, considering the remarkable powers of the Names of the four "Edenic Rivers," we are informed that these pertain to a most potent *segulah*, the latter being delineated in "*The Book of Sacred Names*" to be "a unique action or an object, often comprised of Divine Names, special signs, words or phrases, which is considered to be a most precious 'spiritual treasure' to be employed in a unique manner, in order to affect a physical outcome in harmony with the intention of the one who employs the *segulah*."[35] In the current instance the *segulah* comprises the previously delineated Names of the "four Rivers," including their combinations and permutations, written in soluble ink on parchment (clean white paper will do nicely).

Following the writing of these combinations, the letters comprising the names are dissolved by soaking the parchment in *havdalah* wine, which is afterwards quaffed by the one requiring the *segulah*. In this regard, some stress that all the wine must be consumed to the very last drop, whilst others claim that a single drop of this wine is enough to work the full power of this *segulah* within ones body. Still others maintain that the Names of the four "Edenic Rivers," as well as their mentioned combinations and permutations, should be engraved on the inside of the silver cup, effectively turning the chalice into a *Kamea* or "power object." In this manner the wine, when poured into the cup, would be potently infused with the "forces" inherent in the Names. This is considered to be equally as powerful as writing the Names on parchment and then dissolving them in the wine. There is however some disagreement about this, which includes variant instructions regarding the exact amount of the "magically infused wine" one has to imbibe.[36]

Personally I could not care less about such disparities, and have no interest in any of the affiliated bickering, my only concern being the effectiveness of the "method" employed to work the "magic," i.e. whether it achieves the sought-after objective. However, in my estimation, I believe it would be much easier to write the Names, combinations and permutations on parchment, than it would be to find anybody who would be willing to work the arduous task of engraving that mass of peculiar writing faultlessly on the inside of a silver chalice!

Some might find even this task to be somewhat confusing, since written *Kameot* like the one we have been considering, could turn out to be quite complex in their construction. However, it should be noted that there are other, simpler amulets, which equally fulfil the function of protecting a pregnant woman and her offspring, i.e. against malevolent spirit forces, the evil eye, as well as counteracting evil magic. The following *Kamea* is employed for those very reasons.

First the following magical seal is written on one side of a small silver tablet:

לעם	אקפ	תרר
ההי	יבמ	האי
מרך	שצא	ככמ
לאל	התא	ומל

This word square was derived from *Exodus 23:26*:

לא תהיה משכלה ועקרה בארצך את מספר ימיך אמלא

Transliteration:

> *Lo tihyeh m'shakelah va'akarah b'artzecha et mispar yamecha amalei*

Translation:

> None shall miscarry, nor be barren, in thy land; the number of thy days I will fulfil.

On the opposite side of the platter write *Leviticus 1:1* first in the standard manner, then in reverse:

ויקרא אל משה וידבר יהוה אליו מאהל מועד לאמר

Transliteration:

Vayikra el Mosheh va'y'daber YHVH elav mei'ohel mo'ed leimor.

Translation:

And *YHVH* called unto Moses, and spoke unto him out of the tent of meeting.

The completed amulet should be worn by the pregnant woman from the first indication of a foetus is developing in her womb right up to the actual birth.[37]

Most of the Hebrew Bible has been employed in some or other way for magical purposes. As it is, this volume simply does not afford the scope for a complete investigation into this subject matter, however it certainly allows us to peruse at least some of the most important uses of sacred writ in Jewish Magic. In this regard the "*Book of Psalms*" holds prime position, and it is to the use of Psalms in Hebrew amulets that we now turn our attention.

B. Psalms.....Psalms.....Everywhere!

Some years ago I was queried as to whether it was appropriate for non-Jewish students of Kabbalah "to use the Jewish Prayer book and the *Tehillim* on a daily basis." As it is, I believe it absolutely appropriate for *anybody* to use the *Siddur* (Jewish Prayer Book)[38] and the Hebrew Bible. Why not? What is important is the intention of the one using these texts. If a person is inspired and moved by their use, I cannot see why that individual should not derive great benefit rather than otherwise. Naturally I cannot be sure that the whole of international Jewry would back me on this, but I certainly cannot see the Divine One imposing some sort of frightful reprisal on any individual using a *Siddur* and reciting *Tehillim* with proper *Kavvanah* (focussed intention). The reference in the query to "*Tehillim*" (Psalms) is of particular importance to those interested in the magical workings of *Kabbalah Ma'asit* (Practical Kabbalah). Recognising the power of the Hebrew psalms, an entire magical system was developed and published in a work titled the "*Sefer Shimmush Tehillim*" (*Book of the Magical Use of Psalms*).[39]

Though attributed to Rav Hai Gaon, this text was written by an anonymous author. It is a fairly small, anonymous, mediaeval compilation, existing in several Hebrew editions, as well as in an Aramaic manuscript, which was translated into several languages. Its popularity led to the Vatican ultimately placing it on the *"Index Librorum Prohibitum"* (*"Index of Forbidden Books"*).[40] An acquaintance and serious researcher of this text, referred to the *Shimmush Tehillim* as a "cookbook" since "it gives a list of recipes, each requiring the use of a chapter or verses from the book of Psalms, to solve various problems, but gives no rationale or explanation for them."[41]

This mysterious text pertains to the magical and theurgical use of Divine Names, which, as said, is based on the idea that the entirety of holy writ is comprised of the Names of God. In many instances in the *Shimmush Tehillim*, the special emphasis is on "Divine Names" which give the psalms their magical potencies. Individual verses and entire psalms are employed in a magical way for a wide range of physical and spiritual needs, like protection from demons, illness, or against an attack from man and beast, etc. Using several Kabbalistic methods, magical names were formed from letters derived from their respectively associated psalms. In most cases the methodology employed in the construction of these Names is lost, or at least very difficult to ascertain, since the possible combinations and permutations of the Hebrew letters are factually endless. Of course, the manner in which the Divine Names, employed in this enigmatic text, were composed, is really unimportant. What really matters is the effectiveness of the magical techniques shared in this remarkable little text.

The various psalms are considered extremely powerful, and their religious fervour and beauty are highly regarded. Psalms are recited during all critical situations in the public and private lives of people, and each week the entire book is completely read in certain communities, not only as part of religious ritual, but in the belief that this is the most powerful protection of the community against harm. It was often considered good enough to recite in alphabetical order the psalms which spell the name of a city in danger, as the most effective means of protection. In the *Shimmush Tehillim* psalms are employed in a magical sense for highly personal and quite mundane objectives, albeit very important ones in terms of human survival on this planet. In fact, the entire biblical *Book of Psalms* formed a major component of the "magical gear" of mediaeval magicians.

A popular English translation, available since 1788, was made of the *Sefer Shimmush Tehillim* by an anonymous translator in America from a certain Godfrey Selig's German version of this text. It was eventually incorporated in a spurious magical compilation titled "*The Sixth and Seventh Books of Moses.*"[42] A favourite of "Hoodoo" and those who have a predilection for American "folk magic," this translation was also published under the title "*Secrets of the Psalms.*"[43] Besides being extremely verbose, there are unfortunately many errors and corruptions of Hebrew words and Divine Names in this translation. One would have expected the translator to have cross-checked each magical prescription with its associated Psalm in the Bible, so as to ensure that the terms used were correct, especially in cases where a word clearly does not exist in Hebrew, and a quick perusal of the appropriate Psalm would have exposed it as a corruption of a well-known Hebrew term. In fact, the translator/publisher deemed it necessary to insert every now and again an "admonition from the translator" in the text, cautioning against the incorrect use of these magical techniques, which again leaves one quite perturbed as to why these only too obvious errors were allowed into the translation.

When it comes to the recitation of the Psalms for magical purposes, I personally prefer doing so in Hebrew, since I concur with those Kabbalists who believe every word of the Hebrew Psalms to be a "Holy Name," the utterance of which will invoke specific forces with very definite effects. For that reason it would be extremely important to pronounce the words correctly, and this is not as easy as it may seem. Besides, the inability of most readers to do so, being unfamiliar with Hebrew, would probably necessitate the psalms having to be learned "parrot fashion," thus allowing for mistakes to creep in, which might well invoke psycho-physical responses not quite bargained for. The pronunciation of Hebrew words is in itself a problem, as there are different ways of speaking Hebrew amongst different communities. Hence it is most important to know how to pronounce Hebrew terms properly, yet with some reservations, since the utterance of Hebrew Divine Names equally differs amongst the various factions.

Be that as it may, we certainly have Psalms everywhere, used for every imaginable "magical purpose." However, in this volume of the "Shadow Tree Series," we will pay attention to the employment of Psalms and other portions of the *Tanach* (Hebrew Bible) in Hebrew amulets only. It should also be kept in mind that the Psalms and their respective verses are presented in the order they appear in the Hebrew Bible, which is different from their format in the Protestant Christian Bible. Hence we will commence this investigation with the first Psalm employed for "amuletic" purposes.

PSALM 1 — The anonymous author of the *Sefer Shimmush Tehillim*[44] instructs us to write the first three verses of this Psalm on deer skin to be worn as a pendant, for the purposes of preventing a pregnant woman from premature delivery or from suffering a miscarriage. The mentioned verses read:

(Verse 1) אשרי האיש אשר לא הלך בעצת רשעים
ובדרך חטאים לא עמד ובמושב לצים לא ישב
(Verse 2) כי אם בתורת יהוה חבצו ובתורתו יהגה
יומם וליל
(Verse 3) והיה כעץ שתול על פלגי מים אשר פריו
יתן בעתו ועלהו לא יבול וכל אשר יעשה יצליח

Transliteration:

(Verse 1) *Ashrei ha-ish asher lo halach ba'atzat r'sha'im uv'derech chata'im lo amad uv'moshav leitzim lo yashav*
(Verse 2) *Ki im b'torat YHVH chef'tzo uv'torato yeh'geh yomam v'lailah*
(Verse 3) *V'hayah k'etz shatul al palgei mayim asher pir'yo yiten b'ito v'aleihu lo yibol v'chol asher ya'aseh yatzli'ach*

Translation:

(Verse 1) Happy is the man that hath not walked in the counsel of the wicked, nor stood in the way of sinners, nor sat in the seat of the scornful.

(Verse 2) But his delight is in the law of *YHVH*; and in His law doth he meditate day and night.

(Verse 3) And he shall be like a tree planted by streams of water, that bringeth forth its fruit in its season, and whose leaf doth not wither; and in whatsoever he doeth he shall prosper.

We are informed that the associated Divine Name is *El Chad* (חד אל), which Selig informs us signifies "great, strong, only God."[45] The term "*Chad*" in the Divine Name does not really mean "great," "strong" or "only." The Hebrew term means "sharp" or "acute." The translator may have derived the meaning of "only," by seeing a connection between the words "*Chad*" and "*Echad*," the latter meaning "one." As it is, the Divine Name, *El Chad*, was derived from the initial letters of first, second and fourth words, and the last letter of the second, i.e. א from אשרי (*Ashrei* — "Blessed" [verse 1]); ל from לא כן (*Lo chen*—"not so" [verse 4]); ח from יצליח (*Yatzliach*—"prosper" [verse 3]; and ד from דרך רשעים (*Derech R'sha'im*—"way of the ungodly" [verse 6]).

I cannot quite fathom why the author chose these specific words in the mentioned verses, as there are several others he might have chosen which would equally have sufficed. For example, the word *Derech* appears several times in the psalm, in fact in the very first verse. So why select the term from verse 6, when the latter is not employed in the amulet? I was also left somewhat stranded, when I thought that I might find any meaning by reading the four words as a sentence. This proved to be somewhat nonsensical. Of course, one could "force" a meaning out of it, but I prefer to leave this to the speculations of those more intrigued than I am by this peculiarity in the *Sefer Shimmush Tehillim*. Be that as it may, to complete the construction of the amulet in question, we are informed to include on it the following prayer:[46]

יהי רצון מלפניך אל חד שתעשה לאשה [פלונית בת
פלונית] שלא תפיל ותרפאנה רפואה שלימה מעתה
ועד עולם אמן אמן אמן סלה סלה סלה סלה

Transliteration:

> *Y'hi ratzon milfanecha El Chad sheta'aseh l'ishah [.....Plonit bat Plonit.....] shelo tapil v'tirpa'enah r'fu'ah shleimah me'atah va'ed olam Omein Omein Omein Selah Selah Selah*

Translation:

> May it be your will *El Chad* to protect this woman [.....insert the name of the woman.....] against miscarriage and to heal her completely from now unto eternity. *Amen Amen Amen, Selah Selah Selah.*

Curiously enough, the same three verses from the first Psalm are also recommended as an amulet to promote success in all ones endeavours. In this regard the specific reference is to the concluding phrase of verse 3 reading "and in whatsoever he doeth he shall prosper."

Whilst addressing the use of Psalms in Hebrew amulets, I keep wondering why the anonymous author of the *Sefer Shimmush Tehillim* chose those specific uses for each psalm, when there are several other listed applications. It is clear that he derived much of his suggestions from timeworn traditional sources pertaining to the "magical" uses of the *Book of Psalms*, some of which can be found in the *Talmud* and in various *Midrashim*. There are however many more magical uses of individual and groups of psalms, which did not find their way into the *Sefer Shimmush Tehillim*.

Besides, it is not only the first Psalm which is used to avoid miscarriage. In the *"Magical Use of Psalms"* it is suggested that four copies of an amulet comprising *Psalm 126*, employed in conjunction with the names of the angels סנוי, סנסנוי and סמנגלף (*Sanoi, Sansanoi* and *Semangelof*), be located on the four walls of a house, in order to change the fortune of a woman whose children are constantly dying.[47] These unique Spirit Intelligences are addressed in greater detail later in this work, but we might note that the *"Sefer Shimmush Tehillim"* also recommends *Psalm 128* written on a "kosher parchment" to be worn by women for a successful pregnancy.[48]

There is also related counsel found elsewhere, in which further portions of Holy Writ, e.g., amongst others, *Genesis 21:1* and *Exodus 11:8*, are used to lighten childbirth.[49] Furthermore, not only selected verses from the *Torah* were used to ease childbirth, but in this regard the entire *Sefer Torah* (the scroll of the Pentateuch or "Five Books of Moses") became a most venerated "amulet," so to speak. Many still believe that an exhortation in the name of the "*Torah*" is good enough to get a womb to respond in the required manner. For example, Joshua Trachtenberg relates a popular Ashkenazic incantation which reads: "*Baermutter* (womb) lie down! With these words I adjure thee with nine *Torahs*, with nine pure *Sefer Torahs*!"[50]

We might also recall that in Judaism there are stringent rules regarding personal behaviour towards a *Torah* scroll.[51] However, the very fact that it is considered an extraordinary special "sacred object," looked upon by many to be a manifested portion of the very "Being" of the Divine One, often encouraged the ordinary folk to use it as a most powerful talisman so to speak. Even though any act of impiety towards the *Torah* would be met with strong retribution, Trachtenberg tells us that some Jewish clergy actually allowed "such practices only in case a life was in danger."[52] For example, "when an infant was ill and could not sleep, or a woman was convulsed in labor pains, the Scroll was brought in and laid upon the sufferer to alleviate the pain."[53] The many voices objecting to this kind of practice, and the statement of a Rabbi in the *Talmud* that "it is forbidden to heal by words of *Torah*," whilst allowing their use for protection only, proved quite fruitless when we observe the magical and theurgical uses Scripture was put to down the ages to this day. "The Bible performed functions for which its inspired creators had never intended it," noted Trachtenberg laconically.[54]

We are reminded that the usual formula in the magical use of holy writ is: "Recite this verse with its name...," with the understanding of course, that the power of the verse derives from the Divine Name which is claimed to be hidden in certain words in the Biblical text. This is quite a standard pattern in magical texts of this nature, but I should add that the Bible is used in Jewish

Magic for both incantational and talismanic purposes.[55] For example, the verses from *Genesis* and *Exodus* referred to earlier were not only employed in magical incantations, but were equally used in Hebrew amulets, i.e. to be worn by the woman in labour.[56] Sometimes not even the entire verse was engraved on an amulet, but only the initial letters of each word were used to construct what was considered to be a most effective amulet which would successfully work the purpose of its design.[57]

PSALM 2 — The second Psalm is also employed for "health purposes."[58] It reads:

(Verse 1) למה רגשו גוים ולאמים יהגו ריק

(Verse 2) יתיצבו מלכי ארץ ורוזנים נסדו יחד
על יהוה ועל משיחו

(Verse 3) ננתקה את מוסרותימו ונשליכה ממנו
עבתימו

(Verse 4) יושב בשמים ישחק אדני ילאג למו

(Verse 5) אז ידבר אלימו באפו ובחרונו יבהלמו

(Verse 6) ואני נסכתי מלכי על ציון הר קדשי

(Verse 7) אספרה אל חק יהוה אמר אלי בני אתה
אני היום ילדתיך

(Verse 8) שאל ממני ואתנה גוים נחלתך ואחזתך
אפסי ארץ

(Verse 9) תרעם בשבט ברזל ככלי יוצר תנפצם

(Verse 10) ועתה מלכים השכילו הוסרו שפטי
ארץ

(Verse 11) עבדו את יהוה ביראה וגילו ברעדה

(Verse 12) נשקו בר פן יאנף ותאבדו דרך כי יבער
כמעט אפו אשרי כל חוסי בו

Transliteration:

(Verse 1) *Lama rag'shu goyim ul'umim yeh'gu rik*

(Verse 2) *Yit'yatz'vu malchei eretz v'roznim nosdu yachad al YHVH v'al m'shichu*

(Verse 3) *N'nat'kah et mos'roteimo v'naslichah mimenu avoteimo*

(Verse 4) *Yoshev bashamayim yis'chak adonai yil'ag lamo*

(Verse 5) *Az y'daber eleimo v'apo uvacharono y'vahaleimo*

(Verse 6) *Va'ani nasach'ti malki al tzion har kad'shi*

(Verse 7) *Asap'ra el chok YHVH amar eilai b'ni atah ani hayom y'lid'ticha*

(Verse 8) *Sh'al mimeni v'et'na goyim nachalatecha va'achuzat'cha af'sei aretz*

(Verse 9) *T'ro eim b'shevet bar'zel kich'li yotzer t'nap'tzeim*

(Verse 10) *V'atah m'lachim haskilu hivasru shof'tei aretz*

(Verse 11) *Iv'du et YHVH b'yir'ah v'gilu bir'adah*

(Verse 12) *Nash'ku var pen ye'enaf v'tov'du derech ki yiv'ar kim'at apo ashrei kol chosei vo*

Translation:

(Verse 1) Why are the nations in an uproar? And why do the peoples mutter in vain?

(Verse 2) The kings of the earth stand up, and the rulers take counsel together against *YHVH*, and against His anointed:

(Verse 3) 'Let us break their bands asunder, and cast away their cords from us.'

(Verse 4) 'He that sitteth in heaven laugheth, *Adonai* hath them in derision.

(Verse 5) Then will He speak unto them in His wrath, and affright them in His sore displeasure:

(Verse 6) 'Truly it is I that have established My king upon Zion, My holy mountain.'

(Verse 7) I will tell of the decree: *YHVH* said unto me: 'Thou are My son, this day have I begotten thee.

(Verse 8) Ask of Me, and I will give the nations for thine inheritance, and the end of the earth for thy possession.

(Verse 9) Thou shalt break them with a rod of iron; thou shalt dash them in pieces like a potter's vessel.'

(Verse 10) Now therefore, O ye kings, be wise; be admonished, ye judges of the earth.

(Verse 11) Serve *YHVH* with fear, and rejoice with trembling.

(Verse 12) Do homage in purity, lest he be angry, and ye perish in the way, when suddenly His wrath is kindled. Happy are all they that take refuge in Him.

Regarding the earlier mentioned "health" application, write down the first nine verses of this Psalm up to the phrase "Thou shalt break them with a rod of iron" on clean parchment. This is to be worn like a pendant on ones person in order to alleviate headaches.[59] Be that as it may, the *Sefer Shimmush Tehillim* lists a further application of the second Psalm. In this instance it refers to occassions when one might find oneself caught in a violent storm at sea. In order to be saved from the deluge it is suggested that one should first recite *Psalm 2* in its entirety, then write it on a potsherd, and afterwards cast the latter into the raging waves.

PSALM 67 — Not many Psalms are listed in the *Sefer Shimmush Tehillim* as far as "amuletic uses" are concerned. Furthermore, scant attention is paid to *Psalm 67*, i.e. references being made only to its magical uses by prisoners and the mitigation of unrelenting fevers,[60] whereas this Psalm is extensively employed in Hebrew amulets. It has been suggested that this Psalm is based on the earlier mentioned Priestly Blessing in *Numbers 6:24-26*,[61] and the eight verses of the Psalm are often arranged in the shape of a *menorah* (seven-branched candelabrum). We are reminded that the "word" of the Almighty "often took the shape of light. So frequent was the writing of *Psalm 67* in candelabrum design that it was called the *menorah psalm*. Letters of the words shaped the branches of the light holders: 'God bless us, be merciful to us, and cause the light of his face to shine upon us'."[62]

The 15th century kabbalist Isaac Arama maintained in his "*Akedat Yitzchak*" that this Psalm was engraved in the image of the *Menorah* on the shield of the biblical King David.[63] In terms of this conjecture that *Psalm 67*, rather than the hexagram, comprised the original "*Magen David*," there is a statement in a tractate titled "*The Golden Menorah*," published around 1580 in Prague, that "this psalm together with the *menorah* alludes to great things.....When King David went out to war, he used to carry on his shield this psalm in the form of a *menorah* engraved on a golden tablet and he used to meditate on its secret. Thus he was victorious,"[64] and hence it is no wonder that the psalm in question has been accredited enormous powers of healing and protection. It is mainly in terms of the latter magical quality that *Psalm 67* is employed in a variety of Hebrew amulets.

We might note that *Psalm 67* is also closely associated with the "period of introspection and purification" titled the "Counting of the *Omer*" (Counting of the Sheaves [of wheat]). The latter comprises the period of 49 days between *Pesach* (Passover) and *Shavuot* (Festival of Weeks), which is divided into 7 groups of 7 days each, these being assigned to the seven lower *Sefirot*, i.e. from *Chesed* (Loving-kindness) to *Malchut* (Kingdom) on the sefirotic tree. Regarding the 49 days of *Omer*, it should be noted that seven verses of *Psalm 67* (verses 2[1] to 8[7]) comprise 49 words.[65]

Be that as it may, as far as its employment in Hebrew amulets is concerned, this Psalm features particularly prominently in protection amulets, and amongst the most important uses of the "*Menorah*" Psalm, is its inclusion in the earlier mentioned *Shiviti* meditational plaques and amulets of which there are numerous examples, including the following one created by the 19th century Rabbi Abraham Chamui,[66] who not only expressed a particularly keen interest in "Practical Kabbalah," but also freely shared his great knowledge of Jewish magical practices in his extensive writings devoted to this topic:[67]

כי עמך מקור חיים באורך נראה אור

שויתי יְהוָה לנגדי

ברכות   תמיד   קדישים

יְאַהדֹונְהֵי   אֵידְהנֵוְיַה

אגלא פאי חתך

מהש   הקם

							שיר:		

יאי
אבג
קרע
נגד
בטר
חקב
יגל
שקו

אלי   יתץ
יתץ   שטן
שטן   יכש
יכש   צתג
צתג   טנע
טנע   פזק
פזק   צית
צית

צום   הכם

קול ממון   אדני הללו

תנחם יה סלה:

This *Shiviti* amulet commences with an opening phrase comprising *Psalm 36: 9 (10)*:

כי עמך מקור חיים באורך נראה אור

Transliteration:
>*Ki imcha mekor chayim b'orcha nir'eh or*

Translation:
>For with Thee is the fountain of life; in Thy light do we see light.

The standard header accompanying all *Shiviti* plaques and amulets is located directly below this phrase, and underneath it in two rows we read:

[left]	[right]
Kadishim (Sanctifications)	*B'rachot* (Blessings)
אידהנויה	יאהדונהי

These are again the earlier addressed two Divine Name constructs derived from the conjunction of the Ineffable Name and *Adonai*, which in this instance include specific vocalisations, i.e. [right] *Y'ahodovanaheiyo* and [left] *Ay'dohonavayohei*. As noted, these Divine Name combinations are respectively aligned with *B'rachot* (Blessings) and *Kadishim* (Sanctifications), these being references to the actual applications of the associated Divine Name constructs in the Hebrew blessings and prayers for the deceased (*Kadish*). In this instance, the reference is to the visualisation and mental expression of the יאהדונהי combination when giving the *Omein* (*Amen*) response after a blessing, and doing the same with the אידהנויה construct every time the *Omein* answer is given during the *Kadish* prayer.[68]

There are several reasons for doing this practice. As indicated earlier, in the case of the practice of mentally tracing and expressing the first Divine Name combination, the intention is to direct the flow of "Light" from the higher (*Tiferet*) to the lower (*Malchut*), which is the "sequence of the Sun," whilst in the instance of following the same procedure with the second Divine Name construct during *Kadish*, the intention is to reflect "Light" from the lower (*Malchut*) back to the higher (*Tiferet*), this being the "sequence of the Moon."

The basic difference between the two formats of the *YHVH/Adonai* Divine Name combination is the order of the letters. The "direct light" combination commences and ends with the letter *Yod* (י), indicating the יחודא עלאה (*Yichuda Ila'ah*—"Higher Union") in which the whole of creation is united with the Eternal One beyond all manifestation. On the other hand, the "returning light" Divine Name construct begins with *Alef* (א), the "Life-death Principle of all that Is and all that Is-not,"[69] and ends with *Heh* (ה), the concluding letter of the Ineffable Name, in this instance indicating the return of the life-force into the higher "realms of spirit," this being יחודא תתאה (*Yichuda T'ta'ah*—"Lower Union"). In this regard, it is worth noting that the collective *gematria* of the Ineffable Name and *Adonai* [י = 10 + ה = 5 + ו = 6 + ה = 5 + א = 1 + ד = 4 + נ = 50 + י = 10 = 91] is equal to that of the word אמן [א = 1 + מ = 40 + ן = 50 = 91], hence the association of the two Divine Name constructs under discussion with the word *Omein*.[70]

Now, centrally below the אידהנויה/יאהדונהי portion, the upper section of the *Shiviti* construct is completed with a set of Divine Names written in two rows, specifically:

אגלא פאי חתך

הקם   מהש

On the upper right we read the earlier addressed Divine Name אגלא (*Agala'a*), and the upper centre and left Divine Name constructs reading פאי חתך respectively comprise the initials and concluding letters of the first three words of Psalm *145:16* reading פותח את ידך (*Poteach et yadecha*—"Thou openest Thy hand"). These Divine Names are included in *Kameot* for purposes of benefaction and the generation of a good income.[71]

The lower row comprises two Divine Names selected from the seventy-two tri-letter portions of the "Name of Seventy-two Names," i.e. מהש (*Mahash*) and הקם (*Hakem*). The combination to the right, מהש, is employed in amulets as a protection against death and destruction, i.e. as a safeguard against all manner of danger, whilst the one on the the left, הקם, is utilised to raise onself and to establish a strong personal status.[72]

Now, the central and major portion of the *Shiviti* comprises the *Menorah Psalm*. The full Psalm reads:

(Verse 1) למנצח בנגינ[נ]ת מזמור שיר
(Verse 2 [1]) אלהים יחננו ויברכנו יאר פניו אתנו סלה
(Verse 3 [2]) לדעת בארץ דרכך בכל גוים ישועתך
(Verse 4 [3]) יודוך עמים אלהים יודוך עמים כלם
(Verse 5 [4]) ישמחו וירננו לאמים כי תשפט עמים מיש[נ]ר
ולאמים בארץ תנחם סלה
(Verse 6 [5]) יודוך עמים אלהים יודוך עמים כלם
(Verse 7 [6]) ארץ נתנה יבולה יברכנו אלהים אלהינו
(Verse 8 [7]) יברכנו אלהים וייראו אותו כל אפסי ארץ

Transliteration:

(Verse 1) *Lamnatze'ach binginot mizmor shir*

(Verse 2 [1]) *Elohim yechoneinu vivar'cheinu ya'eir panav itanu Selah*

(Verse 3 [2]) *lada'at ba'aretz darkecha b'chol goyim y'shu'atecha*

(Verse 4 [3]) *yoducha amim Elohim yoducha amim kulam*

(Verse 5 [4]) *yishm'chu viran'nu l'umim ki tishpot amim mishor ul'umim ba'aretz tanchem Selah*

(Verse 6 [5]) *yoducha amim Elohim yoducha amim kulam*

(Verse 7 [6]) *eretz nat'nah y'vulah y'var'cheinu Elohim eloheinu*

(Verse 8 [7]) *y'var'cheinu Elohim v'yir'u oto kol afsei aretz*

Translation:

(Verse 1) For the Leader; with string-music. A Psalm, a Song.

(Verse 2 [1]) God be gracious unto us, and bless us; may He cause His face to shine toward us; *Selah*

(Verse 3 [2]) That Thy way may be known upon earth, Thy salvation among all nations.

(Verse 4 [3]) Let the peoples give thanks unto Thee, O God; let the peoples give thanks unto Thee, all of them.

(Verse 5 [4]) O let the nations be glad and sing for joy; for Thou wilt judge the peoples with equity, and lead the nations upon earth. *Selah*

(Verse 6 [5]) Let the peoples give thanks unto Thee, O God; let the peoples give thanks unto Thee, all of them.

(Verse 7 [6]) The earth hath yielded her increase; may God, our own God, bless us.

(Verse 8 [7]) May God bless us; and let all the ends of the earth fear Him.

In the *Shiviti* the superscript of the *menorah* construct is made up of the twenty letters of the introductory verse of *Psalm 67* divided into six groups of three letters each, i.e. three to the right and three to the left, with the centre column headed by the two middle letters of the verse. In turn, the seven branches of the construct comprise the remaining seven verses, with verse 5[4] forming both the central branch and the base of the *menorah*.

Heading the two columns of tri-letter combinations we trace to the right יא׳ and left אל׳. As noted earlier, the combination יא׳ is comprised of the initials of the expression יהוה אלהי ישראל (*YHVH Elohei Yisra'el*),[73] however, since the major portion of the *Shiviti* amulet incorporates *Psalm 67*, I am inclined to align with the author of the *Shorshei ha-Shemot* who maintained יא׳ to be a Divine Name constructed from the initials of the opening words of verses 5 [4] ישמחו (*yishm'chu*—"be glad"); 6 [5] יודוך (*yoducha*—"thanks unto Thee"); and 7 [6] ארץ (*aretz*—"earth").[74] On the opposite side the combination אל׳ is said to be comprised of the initials of the words in *Psalm 116:9* reading אתהלך לפני יהוה (*Et'halech lifnei YHVH*—"I shall walk before *YHVH*").[75] Next, tracing the remaining tri-letter combinations of the two columns conjointly from top to bottom, e.g. אבג יתץ; קרע שטן; etc., we trace the complete "Forty-two Letter Name of God."

Finally, the bottom portion of the amulet is headed by the words צוה הכם located on either side of the bottom stem of the *menorah*. These two tri-letter combinations are comprised of the concluding letters of verses comprising the very bottom glyphs of the outer six branches of the *Menorah* Psalm, i.e. the three letters of צוֹם being derived from the concluding letters of *Psalm 67:5–7* [6–8] listed in reverse order, and הכם from the concluding letters of verses 1–3 [2-4] equally represented in reverse order.[76] In this regard, the two combinations הכם צוֹם represent respectively the three arms to the right and the same on the left, all of which are facing inwards towards the central arm of the *Menorah Psalm*, thus symbolising the Divine Abundance (*Shefah*) which descends from the Almighty and nurtures all.

Besides their association with *Psalm 67*, the importance of these two tri-letter combinations, as indicated in the illustration, is their respective numerical values. The *gematria* of צוֹם [צ = 90 + וֹ = 6 + ם = 40 = 136] is indicated to be equal to those of the words קוֹל (*kol*—"voice" or "sound" [ק = 100 + וֹ = 6 + ל = 30 = 136]) and מָמוֹן (*mamon*—"money" [מ = 40 + מ = 40 + וֹ = 6 + ן = 50 = 136]). On the other hand the *gematria* of הכם [ה = 5 + כ = 20 + ם = 40 = 65] is equivalent to those of the Divine Name אֲדֹנָי (*Adonai* [א = 1 + ד = 4 + נ = 50 + י = 10 = 65]) and הלל (*halel*—"praise" [ה = 5 + ל = 30 + ל = 30 = 65]). Reading the word pairs conjointly presents us respectively with the phrases קוֹל מָמוֹן (*Kol mamon*—"the sound of money [wealth]," and הלל אֲדֹנָי (*Adonai halel*—"praise Adonai").

Be that as it may, the *Shiviti* amulet is concluded with the final two words of *Psalm 67:5* [4], תַנְחֵם סֶלָה (*Tanchem Selah*—"will lead"; "shall guide"; "will comfort"), the two words being interspersed by an emboldened *Digrammaton*, יָּה. Collectively the three terms could be read "*Yah* will guide *Selah*." This *Shiviti Kamea* is clearly a most valuable power object, not only in terms of its properties to guard and protect its bearer, but also to generate wealth and general well being.

Whilst we have thus far looked at complete Psalms or large sections comprising several verses being used in *Kameot*, entire Psalms or verses therefrom are, as already indicated, often employed in abbreviated formats in Hebrew amulets. Such condensations are considered equally as effective as the Psalm it represents. Taking *Psalm 67*, the "*Menorah Psalm*," as a case in point, the entire Psalm was abbreviated with its traditional *menorah* format maintained, in order to fit on fairly small metal amulets. In this regard, the method of abbreviation employed here is "*Serugin*" or "trellis writing,"[77] which is affiliated to the Kabbalistic system of *Notarikon*. I previously defined this specific Kabbalistic method of reading the Hebrew Bible to be "a sort of short-hand, or system of acronyms. *Notarikon* is therefore a method in which the single letters of a word become a word themselves."[78]

Employing the *Serugin* method, an entire biblical chapter can be condensed by employing the initials or the first two letters of a word. In the case of the *Menorah Psalm*, it is engraved in abbreviated format on relatively small metal amulets as a protective measure for women in childbirth, against the "evil eye" and the demoness *Lilit*.[79] However, it should be noted that the "*Menorah Psalm*" is also abbreviated on Hebrew amulets as a protection against troublesome situations, and as a call for help by individuals who find themselves in grievous circumstances.

In this regard, there are *Kameot* constructed from only the initials of the words comprising this psalm, all of which are configured into a set of seventeen tri-letter combinations and a concluding combination comprising two letters,[80] as shown below:

לבמ שאי ויפ אסל בדב גיי עאי עכי ולב
תעמ ובת סיע איע כאנ ייא איא ואכ אא

Whilst this presentation is quite simple, others seeking an even quicker and somewhat easier "call for spiritual help" when they find themselves in dire need, have noted that single verses from the same Psalm can equally be employed in Hebrew amulets in the same abbreviated manner, e.g. verse 2 is abbreviated אייפאס; verse 1 and 2 reduced to לבמשאי ויפאס; and verse 2 and 3 to ויפאסל.[81] It is understood that any of these abbreviations could be applied for the very same purpose assigned to the entire Psalm.

PSALM 91 — Known as the "Psalm of Protection," it is amongst the most popular Psalms in Jewish Magic, of which several portions are liberally employed in Hebrew amulets. Verses 10 and 11 are particularly popular, as you have probably ascertained from the many references in this tome. Of course, other verses from this

Psalm are also employed in *Kameot*. In this regard, it should be noted that the first four words of the fifth verse of this psalm, reading לא תירא מפחד לילה (*lo tira mipachad lailah*—"Thou shalt not be afraid of the terror by night"), are sometimes employed by parents in a tried and tested *Kamea*. It is suspended around the necks of youngsters who may have to travel around at night, and might require a reinforcement of special protection, and also to ward off bad dreams.[82]

The front of the *Kamea* comprises the following letter square, constructed from the initials of the listed words of the said verse:

ל	מ	ח	ל
ל	ל	מ	ח
ח	ל	ל	מ
מ	ח	ל	ל

The rear portion of the amulet comprises the initials of all the words from verse 5 to the very end of the psalm, all arranged in twenty sets of four letters each and one concluding set of three letters, as shown below:

לתמל מיימ בימי צימא ומאל ירבת ורתכ אימע שמלת
ארול יבכמ יללב דעכי פתבר עשות תכוכ בחוא כישי
ועאב אואי אוב

As might be expected, *Psalm 91* features, either in full or in an abbreviated format, prominently in Hebrew amulets, as indicated in the following representation of a Moroccan amulet created to protect the home.[83] In this instance the full abbreviation of the sixteen verses of *Psalm 91* and the eight verses of *Psalm 121* are employed conjointly in this unique amulet:

Here is the complete abbreviation of both psalms for easy reference:

(*Psalm 91*) יבע בשי אלמ ואא בכה ימי מהב ילו כתצ ואל
תמל מיי מבי מיצ ימא ומא ליר בתו רתב אימ עשמ לתא
רול יבכ מיל לבד עבי פתב רעש ותת כוכ בחו אבי שיו
עאב אוא יאוב
(*Psalm 121*) שלא עאה מיע עמי עשו איל ראי שהל יוי שיי
שיצ עיי יהל יוב יימ ריא ניי צומ ועע
אנס״ל

The concluding four letter combination comprises the abbreviation of the standard formula [ועד] אמן נצח סלה לעולם (*Omein Netzach Selah l'olam* [*Va'ed*]—*Amen*, Enduring [Victory], *Selah*, throughout Eternity [Forever]).

I have addressed *Psalm 91* as well as *Psalm 121* earlier in this tome. However, as far as the remainder of this "Home Protection" is concerned, the header comprises the interesting construct וֹנ"י אע"ו יכ"ע וי"כ רדפמיאל. The four tri-letter combinations were composed from the initials of the twelve words comprising *Psalm 90:17*, reading:

ויהי נעם אדני אלהינו עלינו ומעשה ידינו כוננה עלינו
ומעשה ידינו כוננהו

Transliteration:

Vi'hi no'am adonai eloheinu aleinu uma'aseh yadeinu kon'nah aleinu uma'aseh yadeinu kon'neihu

Translation:

And let the graciousness of the Lord our God be upon us; establish Thou also upon us the work of our hands; yea, the work of our hands establish Thou it.

As far as רדפמיאל (*Radafmi'el*) or רד פמיאל (*Rad Pami'el*) is concerned, we are told that this particular Spirit Intelligence protects women in confinement.[84]

Be that as it may, the central portion of the *Kamea* is comprised of a large hexagram, external to which we trace the six letters comprising the earlier addressed Divine Name טפטפיה (*Taftafyah*). In the upper portion of the upper triangle we note the *Digrammaton* י"ה (*Yah*), and located diagonally below this Name, both to the right and left, we trace the Ineffable Name. In turn, located in the lower horizontal corners of the hexagram, we read right to left the expression מגן דוד (*Magen David*—"Shield of David").

As expected, certain Divine Names are also included in a somewhat obscure phrase located in the centre of the hexagram, the whole reading:

באב קבול כסן כסאן כסאבן שמו שדי צורי אליהו[ן]

Transliteration:

Ba'ava Kabul Kesen Kesan Kesaban sh'mo Shadai tzuri Eliyahu

Translation:

Ba'ava (*Bab* according to Rafael Patai) *Kabul Kesen Kesan Kesaban Shadai* is his name, my rock Elijah.[85]

Whilst I am reading the opening term as a Divine Name, i.e. באב (*Ba'ava*), it could be understood to be a common expression meaning "through father." However, this three letter combination is comprised of the initials of the phrase ברוך אתה בבאך (*Baruch atah b'vo'echa*—"Blessed shalt thou be when thou comest in") derived from the opening words of *Deuteronomy 28:6*. This would be entirely appropriate to the meaning and purpose of the amulet in question. Furthermore, באב (*Ba'ava*) is said to have the power to bring success, i.e. make the occupants of the home successful as per the meaning of the listed verse from whence the Divine Name was derived.[86]

PSALM 106 — Whilst this psalm is not listed in the *Shimmush Tehillim* ("Magical Use of Psalms") in terms of talismans, the thirtieth verse of this Psalm is employed in the form of "word square," as an amulet for a variety of important purposes as far as basic human survival on this planet is concerned. In this regard, there are two formats, as shown below:[87]

ד	מה	עו	יה	וי
ס	חה	נו	יה	פי
ל	לה	פו	יה	וי
ר	צה	עו	תה	וי
ה	פה	גו	מה	חי

ה	וה	וו	פה	וי
ם	תי	יה	יו	יה
ג	עה	פי	נה	עו
פ	צו	לה	חי	מה
ה	רה	לו	סה	די

Moses Zacutto included a variant of the latter square in his mammoth tome on the magical uses of Divine Names:[88]

ודהה	וו	פה	וי
תים	יה	יו	יה
עהג	פי	נה	עו
צופ	לה	חי	מה
רהה	לו	סה	די

This amulet is constructed from the five words comprising *Psalm 106:30*. The verse reads:

ויעמד פינחס ויפלל ותעצר המגפה

Transliteration:
va-ya'amod Pinchas va-y'falel va-te'atzar ha-magefah
Translated:
Then stood up Phinehas, and wrought judgment, and so the plague was stayed.

This verse comprises five words, each of which consists of exactly five letters. Each of these letters are individually aligned with a single letter of the Ineffable Name, and, as indicated, this is done in two ways. In the first version the letter י (*Yod*) is aligned with the initials of the five words comprising the said verse; the first ה (*Heh*) of the Explicit Name with the second letter of each word; the letter ו (*Vav*) with the third; and the concluding ה (*Heh*) with the fourth letter of each word. The concluding letter of the five words is left "unsupported" by the Ineffable Name. In the second version, the four glyphs comprising the *Tetragrammaton* are simply added in exact marching order to the first twenty letters of the verse.

To compose this *Kamea*, one has to construct a five by five grid, i.e. a square comprised of 25 little blocks. The letters of the five verses are then written either horizontally along the five rows, or vertically along the five columns, in both instances commencing top right with the first word, and ensuring that the letters are aligned to the right of each block. When all the rows or columns are completed, we are instructed to complete the letter grid of the "horizontal version" of the construct by adding the letter ׳ (*Yod*) adjacent the first letters of the five words comprising the enigmatic verse from the "*Book of Psalms*," then similarly conjoining the letter ה (*Heh*) to the second letters; the letter ו (*Vav*) to the third letters; and finally the concluding letter of the Ineffable Name, i.e. ה (*Heh*), is added to the concluding letters of the five words.

The "vertical version" of the word square amulet is constructed by conjoining the four letters of the Ineffable Name sequentially with the first twenty letters of the verse:

ס	ח	נ	י	פ	ד	מ	ע	י	ו
ה	י	ה	ו	ה	י	ה	ו	ה	י

ר	צ	ע	ת	ו	ל	ל	פ	י	ו
ה	ו	ה	י	ה	ו	ה	י	ה	ו

As might be expected, these versions are by no means "standard," since variants do surface from time to time. In this regard, there is a version of this *Kamea* included in a manuscript of magical recipes in the Wellcome Collection,[89] in which the conjoined letter attributions are decidedly odd, as shown below:

ד	מה	עו	יה	וי
ס	חה	נֹה	יה	פ״י
ל	הל	פֻו	יה	וי
ר	צה	עו	תה	וי
ה	פה	ג״י	מא	הי

As in the case of the first version of the word square in question, the four letters of the Ineffable Name are respectively assigned to each of the initial letters of the first four words of the verse we are addressing, with the concluding letters of the five words being left "unsupported" by the component letters of the *Tetragrammaton*. However, as indicated, there are certain inexplicable anomalies in the arrangement.

In the second row comprising the word פינחס (*Pinchas*), the third letter (נ–*Nun*) is accompanied by a ה (*Heh*) instead of the expected letter ו (*Vav*). Likewise the second and third letters of the fifth word המגפה (*ha-magefah*—"the plague"), i.e. מ–*Mem* and ג–*Gimel*, are respectively coordinated with an א (*Alef*) and a י (*Yod*) instead of the letters ה (*Heh*) and ו (*Vav*). I have been unable to ascertain whether these oddities were intentional, or merely errors on the part of the anonymous author of the manuscript, who might have been copying the letter square from some or other primary magical source text.

Now, I have observed a variety of uses of this *Kamea* ranging from the most simple to quite complex.[90] Amongst the former are certain Hebrew amulets found in the Wellcome Collection.[91] As indicated in the following illustration, the format of the amulet is comprised of nothing more than the first version of the word square, as well as a brief subscript delineating its protective purposes and the name of the owner. In this regard, you could employ the exact inscription, and simply insert your own name, or that of the intended bearer of the amulet, in the space marked פב״פ [*Ploni ben Ploni*—"So and So"). This is the standard manner in Jewish magical texts of saying "so and so," in order to indicate where you should insert your own name, or that of the individual for whom the amulet is intended.

וי	פה	וו	וה	הה
יה	יו	יה	תי	מ
עו	נה	פי	עה	ג
מה	חי	לה	צו	פ
די	סה	לו	רה	ה

שמירה והגנה ל[.....פב״פ.....] מדבר
וממגפה ומאבן נגף מו״ע א״ס

The Hebrew abbreviations at the end of the phrase, refer to a standard expression often employed in protection *Kameot* reading מעתה ועד עולם אמן סלה. In transliteration, the inscription below the word square reads:

> *Shmirah v'haganah l'[.....Ploni ben Ploni.....] mideber u'mimagefah u'mi'aven negef me'atah va'ed olam Omein Selah.*

Translation:

> Protection and safety for [.....insert the name of the recipient.....] from pestilence and from plagues, and from being stoned, from now unto eternity *Amen Selah.*

As far as the referenced version in the Wellcome Collection is concerned, the *Kamea* was drawn on the upper portion of a suitably sized fragment of deerskin parchment, and since the construct was meant to be carried on the person of the individual for whom it was created, it was located in a slightly larger square leather envelope.

As can be expected, there are yet more complex presentations of this amulet, as can be seen in the following *Kamea* listed amongst a variety of magical recipes appearing in the earlier mentioned anonymous magical manuscript in the Wellcome Collection:[92]

In the current instance the five concluding letters of the words employed in the formatting of the *Kamea*, are located external to the actual word square. We further note that the entire construct is encircled with Divine and Angelic Names, specifically:

(Top) *Agala'a Ehyeh Yelel* [אגלא אהיה ילאל]

(Bottom) *Avgitatz Kra Satan Shadai* [אבגיתץ קרע שטן שדי]

(Right) *Ori'el Ehyeh* [אוריאל אהיה]

(Left) *Nuri'el Ehyeh* [נוריאל אהיה]

Transliterated the incantation below the word square construct reads:

> *Achatri'el Shamri'el yishmor ha-nose kamia zo mimagefah u'mideber u'mikol choli u'mi'ayin ha'ra u'miruach ra me'atah va'ed olam omein v'chen y'hi ratzon*

Translated:

> *Achatri'el Shamri'el* protect the carrier of this amulet from plagues and pestilence, and from all disease, and from the evil eye, and from evil spirits, from now unto eternity *Amen* and thus be it so willed.

Whilst we saw the "word square" under consideration being employed to keep one from all the baneful forces one may encounter in ones life, i.e. diseases, the evil eye, evil spirits, and even from being stoned to death, the construct in question mainly features in amulets pertaining to protection against plagues and epidemics.

It should also be noted that the two listed formats of this *Kamea* can be employed singly or conjointly. In this regard, we might consider the following amulet delineated in *Sefer Rafael ha-Malach*:[93]

שׂטן				קרע			שׂדי
מהד	עו	יה	וי	והה	וו	פה	וי
חהס	נו	יה	פי	תים	יה	יו	יה
להל	פו	יה	וי	עהג	פי	נה	עו
צהר	עו	תה	וי	צופ	לה	חי	מה
פהה	נו	מה	הי	רהה	לו	סה	די

As said, this *Kamea* is employed against plagues and epidemics. Similarly to instructions mentioned earlier in this tome, the one creating the amulet has to cut sprigs of "rue" prior to sunrise on a Wednesday during the period close to the Full Moon. We are told the leaves must be cut with a golden coin or disc. As it is, we are informed in Jewish magical writings that rue has wondrous healing and protective powers. Hence it is suggested that it is good to inhale its smoke when the dried herb is burned,[94] and it is equally good when employed as a fumigation in a residence.

It has been suggested that *Psalm 90:17* should be recited seven times prior to cutting the rue. Still others maintain this recitation should include the entire *Psalm 90*, reading:

(Verse 1) תפלה למשה איש האלהים אדני מעון אתה
היית לנו בדר ודר

(Verse 2) בטרם הרים ילדו ותחולל ארץ ותבל ומעולם
עד עולם אתה אל

(Verse 3) תשב אנוש עד דכא ותאמר שובו בני אדם

(Verse 4) כי אלף שנים בעיניך כיום אתמול כי יעבר
ואשמורה בלילה

(Verse 5) זרמתם שנה יהיו בבקר כחציר יחלף

(Verse 6) בבקר יציץ וחלף לערב ימולל ויבש

(Verse 7) כי כלינו באפך ובחמתך נבהלנו

(Verse 8) שת עונתינו לנגדך עלמנו למאור פניך

(Verse 9) כי כל ימינו פנו בעברתך כלינו שנינו כמו
הגה

(Verse 10) ימי שנותינו בהם שבעים שנה ואם בגבורת
שמונים שנה ורהבם עמל ואון כי גז חיש ונעפה

(Verse 11) מי יודע עז אפך וכיראתך עברתך

(Verse 12) למנות ימינו כן הודע ונבא לבב חכמה

(Verse 13) שובה יהוה עד מתי והנחם על עבדיך

(Verse 14) שבענו בבקר חסדך ונרננה ונשמחה בכל ימינו

(Verse 15) שמחנו כימות עניתנו שנות ראינו רעה

(Verse 16) יראה אל עבדיך פעלך והדרך על בניהם

(Verse 17) ויהי נעם אדני אלהינו עלינו ומעשה ידינו
כוננה עלינו ומעשה ידינו כוננהו

Transliteration:

(Verse 1) *Tefila l'Mosheh ish ha-elohim adonai ma'on atah hayita lanu b'dor vador*

(Verse 2) *b'terem harim yuladu vat'cholel eretz v'teivel umei'olam ad olam atah el*

(Verse 3) *tasheiv enosh ad daka va'tomer shuvu v'nei adam*

(Verse 4) *ki elef shanim b'einecha k'yom etmol ki ya'avor v'ashmurah valaila*

(Verse 5) *z'ramtam sheina yih'yu baboker kechatzir yachalof*

(Verse 6) *baboker yatzitz v'chalaf la'erev y'moleil v'yavesh*

(Verse 7) *ki chalinu v'apecha uvachamat'cha niv'halnu*

(Verse 8) *shata avonoteinu l'negdecha alumeinu lim'or panecha*

(Verse 9) *ki chol yameinu panu v'evratecha kilinu shaneinu ch'mo hegeh*

(Verse 10) *y'mei sh'noteinu vahem shiv'im shanah v'im big'vurot sh'monim shanah v'rahbam amal va'aven ki gaz chish vana'ufah*

(Verse 11) *mi yodei'a oz apecha uch'yir'atcha evratecha*

(Verse 12) *limnot yameinu kein hoda v'navi l'vav chochmah*

(Verse 13) *shuvah YHVH ad matai v'hinacheim al avadecha*

(Verse 14) *sab'einu vaboker chasdecha unran'nah v'nism'cha b'chol yameinu*

(Verse 15) *sam'cheinu kimot initanu sh'not ra'inu ra'ah*

(Verse 16) *yeira'eh el avadecha fa'olecha vahadar'cha al b'neihem*

(Verse 17) *vi'hi no'am adonai eloheinu aleinu uma'aseh yadeinu kon'nah aleinu uma'aseh yadeinu kon'neihu*

Translation:

(Verse 1) A Prayer of Moses the man of God. Lord, Thou hast been our dwelling-place in all generations.

(Verse 2) Before the mountains were brought forth, or ever Thou hadst formed the earth and the world, even from everlasting to everlasting, Thou art God.

(Verse 3) Thou turnest man to contrition; and sayest: 'Return, ye children of men.'

(Verse 4) For a thousand years in Thy sight are but as yesterday when it is past, and as a watch in the night.

(Verse 5) Thou carriest them away as with a flood; they are as a sleep; in the morning they are like grass which groweth up.

(Verse 6) In the morning it flourisheth, and groweth up; in the evening it is cut down, and withereth.

(Verse 7) For we are consumed in Thine anger, and by Thy wrath are we hurried away.

(Verse 8) Thou hast set our iniquities before Thee, our secret sins in the light of Thy countenance.

(Verse 9) For all our days are passed away in Thy wrath; we bring our years to an end as a tale that is told.

(Verse 10) The days of our years are threescore years and ten, or even by reason of strength fourscore years; yet is their pride but travail and vanity; for it is speedily gone, and we fly away.

(Verse 11) Who knoweth the power of Thine anger, and Thy wrath according to the fear that is due unto Thee?

(Verse 12) So teach us to number our days, that we may get us a heart of wisdom.

(Verse 13) Return, *YHVH*; how long? And let it repent Thee concerning Thy servants.

(Verse 14) O satisfy us in the morning with Thy mercy; that we may rejoice and be glad all our days.

(Verse 15) Make us glad according to the days wherein Thou hast afflicted us, according to the years wherein we have seen evil.

(Verse 16) Let Thy work appear unto Thy servants, and Thy glory upon their children.

(Verse 17) And let the graciousness of the Lord our God be upon us; establish Thou also upon us the work of our hands; yea, the work of our hands establish Thou it.

Whilst cutting the herb in question, the individual has to vocalise his or her intentions, i.e. "I am collecting this herb in honour of 'so and so'." Again whilst we are told on the one hand that this statement should be uttered in his or her mother tongue, on the other hand some maintain this action necessitates the following statement which must be uttered in Hebrew:[95]

אנכי לוקט עלי רוטא האלה בשם יהוה אלהי
ישראל לאסותא מן שמיא ולשמירה עבור
[.....פלוני בן פלוני....] מן כל פגעים רעים
ומרעין בישין

Transliteration:

> *Anochi loket alei ruta ha-eleh b'shem YHVH Elohei Yisra'el l'asuta min shmaya ulishmirah avur [.....Ploni ben Ploni.....] min kol p'ga'im ra'im umar'in bishin*

Translation:

> I am collecting this rue in the name *YHVH*, God of Israel, for health from heaven and the protection of [.....insert the name of the recipient.....] from all bad mishaps and evil doing spirits.

Prior to writing the amulet in question, the individual set with this task, who must be a man, has to fast and be purified by performing the ritual submersion in the waters of a *Mikveh* (Ritual Bath).[96] It might be conjectured that the instruction that only a man should write the amulet in question, pertains to prevailing sexism when these instructions were first written down. However, it should be noted that in all major religious traditions of the world, Judaism included, women are considered to be "ritually impure" during *Niddah* (term of menstruation),[97] a period when many women experience great hormonal variations and equally great energy fluctuations physically, emotionally and mentally, quite out of sync with their natural disposition. Some might indeed consider such imbalances to have a disadvantageous impact on the flow of "subtle forces" channelled by an amulet.

Be that as it may, when all ritual purity requirements are fulfilled, the amulet is written in *ashurit* on a pure scroll, i.e. a good, clean sheet of quality paper. On completion, the rue is rolled into the *Kamea* and the whole carried on the person for the entire period of an epidemic in an appropriately sized, thin leather envelope-like pouch, to be worn around the neck of the person for whom the amulet was intended. No harm will befall this individual, and, God willing, he or she will be spared the disastrous effects of the epidemic.[98]

The following more complex amulet, derived from a *Kamea* published in the 18th century Polish edition of Chaim Vital's "*Shaar ha-Yichudim*," is constructed and prepared in exactly the same manner as the previously addressed amulet, and is employed for the very same purpose:[99]

Beside the word square we are currently considering being located in the palm of the central hand illustration, this *Kamea* is comprised of further biblical verses and Divine Names. The amulet commences with two sets of tri-letter arrangements [upper two lines], these being abbreviations comprised of mainly the initials of *Exodus 12:27* [upper] and *Exodus 12:23* [lower]. These read:

[*Exodus 12:27*] ואמרתם זבח פסח הוא ליהוה אשר פסח
על בתי בני ישראל במצרים בנגפו את מצרים ואת בתינו
הציל ויקד העם וישתחוו

[*Exodus 12:23*] וְעָבַר יהוה לִנְגֹּף אֶת מִצְרַיִם וְרָאָה אֶת הַדָּם
עַל הַמַּשְׁקוֹף וְעַל שְׁתֵּי הַמְּזוּזֹת וּפָסַח יהוה עַל הַפֶּתַח וְלֹא
יִתֵּן הַמַּשְׁחִית לָבֹא אֶל בָּתֵּיכֶם לִנְגֹּף

Transliteration:

> [*Exodus 12:27*] *va-amartem zevach pesach hu la-YHVH asher pasach al batei v'nei Yisra'el b'mitzrayim b'nog'po et mitzrayim v'et bateinu hitzil va-yikod ha-am va-yishtachavu*

> [*Exodus 12:23*] *v'avar YHVH lingof et mitzrayim v'ra'ah et ha-dam al ha-mashkof v'al sh'tei ha-m'zuzot ufasach YHVH al ha-petach v'lo yiten ha-mash'chit lavo el bateichem lingof*

Translation:

> [*Exodus 12:27*] That ye shall say: It is the sacrifice of *YHVH*'s passover, for that He passed over the houses of the children of Israel in Egypt, when He smote the Egyptians, and delivered our houses.' And the people bowed the head and worshipped.

> [*Exodus 12:23*] For *YHVH* will pass through to smite the Egyptians; and when He seeth the blood upon the lintel, and on the two side-posts, *YHVH* will pass over the door, and will not suffer the destroyer to come in unto your houses to smite you.

As said, in the centre of the *Kamea* is a large hand on the palm of which is displayed the *Psalm 106:30* word square. This verse conjoined with the expression *b'ma'amar El Shadai* ("in the saying *El Shadai*"), constitute the right border of amulet. The tips of the ring and little fingers also comprise an abbreviation of the same verse, whilst the tips of the thumb, forefinger and middle finger, comprise an abbreviation of *Psalm 32:7*, this verse being the one which forms the left border of the amulet, reading:

אַתָּה סֵתֶר לִי מִצַּר תִּצְּרֵנִי רָנֵּי פַלֵּט תְּסוֹבְבֵנִי סֶלָה

Transliteration:

> *Atah seter li mitzar titz'reini ranei falet t'sov'veini Selah*

Translation:

> Thou art my hiding-place; Thou wilt preserve me from the adversary; with songs of deliverance Thou wilt compass me about *Selah.*

The verse comprising the bottom border, and which does not appear in any abbreviated format in the *Kamea*, is *Numbers 25:12* reading:

לכן אמר הנני נו]נ[תן לו את בריתי שלום

Transliteration:
> *Lachen emor hin'ni noten lo et b'riti shalom*

Translation:
> Wherefore say: Behold, I give unto him My covenant of peace.

Next, we need to peruse the extraordinary Divine and Angelic Names included in the amulet. Whilst we are considering the image of the hand, we next note the strange double tri-letter combinations written along each of the fingers from the little to the forefinger. The first three letter combinations comprise the Divine Names said to be "great in holiness,"[100] these being:

צָדְנִלְבָשׁ קָהְסְמֹגָת פָּגְמְכֹאָר
(*Tzod'n'lobosh Koh's'mogot Pogm'ko'or*)

We are informed that the power of this Divine Name combination also pertains to protection against plagues and epidemics, and the first of the three Names was constructed from the initials of the names of the six "choice fruits of the land" listed in *Genesis 43:11*, i.e. צרי (*Tzori*—"Balm"); דבש (*D'vash*—"Honey"); נכאת (*N'chot*—"Spicery"); לט (*Lot*—"Ladanum"); בטנים (*Botnim*—"Nuts"); and שקדים (*Sh'kedim*—"Almonds"). The central Name was composed from the letters succeeding the six letters of the first Name in the Hebrew alphabet, i.e. ק (*Kof*) succeeding צ (*Tzadi*); ה (*Heh*) succeeding ד (*Dalet*); etc., and the concluding Name was similarly derived from the letters preceding those comprising the first Name, i.e. the letter פ (*Peh*) preceding צ (*Tzadi*); ג (*Gimel*) preceding ד (*Dalet*); etc.[101]

Now, in addition to the listed three Divine Names, we note the combination נָשְׁחֶסָלְזָ (*Nash'chesal'za*) which is written along the length of the forefinger. I have not found any extensive elucidation on the meaning or uses of this Divine Name. All I could find is the combination נשחסל ז was constructed from the initials of the precious substances referred to in *Exodus 30:34*, which were used in the mixing of the *Ketoret* (Sacred Incense) employed in the Tabernacle and later the Temple in Jerusalem.[102] The said substances are נטף (*Nataf*—"Stacte" [gum resin from the balsam tree]); שחלת (*Sh'cheilet*—"Onycha" [Labdanum]); חלבנה (*Chelb'nah*—"Galbanum"); סמים (*Samim*—"Sweet Spices"); and לבנה זכה (*L'vonah Zakah*—"Pure Frankincense").

These substances would both fumigate and purify sacred spaces, and keep all evil and infectious diseases at bay. Since Kabbalistic tradition has it that the "quality" of anything can be found in its Hebrew name, it is clear that the capitals of the appellatives of the listed items were combined into a Divine Name to be employed against epidemics.

Sometimes the combination נעוירירון (pronounced *N'oriyiro'un, Nei'a'ureiri'un*, etc.)[103] is added to the listed four plague combating Divine Name constructs, and this one equally appears at the very base of the thumb.[104] It is said this Name was derived from certain letters in *Genesis 43:11*,[105] as indicated by the emboldened letters in the phrase from this verse reading:

כן אפוא זאת עשו קחו מזמרת הארץ בכליכם והורידו
לאיש מנחה

Transliterated:
> *Ken eifo zot asu k'chu mizimrat ha-aretz bich'leichem v'horiru la'ish minchah*

Translated:
> [thus] do this: take of the choice fruits of the land in your vessels, and carry down the man a present.

Whilst there is no indication as to why those specific letters in the said verse were specifically selected, it would certainly link this Divine Name with the four listed earlier. However, we are told that this Divine Name construct is directly related to the concluding letters of three word pairs in *Exodus 14:30*. The full verse reads:

ויושע יהוה ביום ההוא את ישראל מיד מצרים וירא
ישראל את מצרים מת על שפת הים

Transliterated:

> *Vayosha YHVH bayom ha-hu et Yisra'el miyad Mitzrayim vayar Yisra'el et Mitzrayim met al sh'fat ha-yam*

Translated:

> Thus *YHVH* saved Israel that day out of the hand of the Egyptians; and Israel saw the Egyptians dead upon the seashore.

The mentioned letters are ע in ויושע (*vayosha*) and ה in יהוה (*YHVH*); ת in את (*et*) and ל in ישראל (*Yisra'el*); as well as ד in מיד (*miyad*) and the concluding ם in מצרים (*Mitzrayim*). Beyond hints in terms of *gematria* affiliations, it is not clear why these letters should be aligned with the Divine Name in question.[106] However, the stated association of נעורירון (*N'oriyiro'un*) with the said biblical verse, affords us the reason why this Divine Name construct is said to be the appellative of the "Prince who governs Fear,"[107] who is in charge of all weaponry,[108] and who not only benefits individuals from all dangers in the waters of the seas and rivers,[109] but who will actually save those who mention his Name from drowning.[110] In fact, we are informed that someone in danger of drowning, should raise his or her unto the heavens and say:

הושיעני אלהים כי באו מים עד נפש ועזרני בכח השם
הקדוש נעורירון שאנצל מטביעת מים ברב רחמיך
וחסדיך הרבים אמן סלה נצח

Transliteration:

> *Hoshi'eini Elohim ki ba'u mayim ad nafesh az'reini b'koach ha-shem ha-kadosh N'oriyiro'un she'enatzel mit'vi'at mayim b'rov rachamecha v'chasdecha ha-rabim Omein Selah Netzach*

Translation:

> Rescue me *Elohim*, for the water is overwhelming my soul, help me with the power of the Holy Name *N'oriyiro'un* to be rescued from drowning waters, in your mercy and great kindness. *Amen, Selah*, Enduring [Victory].[111]

It should be noted that the Name נעורירון (*N'oriyiro'un*) is also said to have the power to control epidemics, and to solve problems.[112] We noted this Divine Name located at the bass of the thumb in the amulet we are addressing. Imprinted above it, along the main length of the thumb, we note the name of the angel קסטיאל (*Kasti'el*). This is the Angel in charge of the sword, whose name is often employed conjointly with the Divine Name מצמצית (*M'tzamtzit*) as a defense against sword or knife attacks.

As an aside, *Tzod'n'lobosh* (צָדְנִלָבָשׁ), the primary of this set of Divine Names, is sometimes employed separately in amulets, as shown in the following *Kamea* against miscarriages:[113]

There are six Spirit Intelligences associated with the Divine Name in question, one for each letter of the Name. These are:

צוריאל דודיאל נוריאל להביאל ברוכיאל שמריאל
(*Tzuri'el Dodi'el Nuri'el Lehavi'el Baruchi'el Shamri'el*)

As indicated, the initials of these Angelic Names spell the Name צדנלבש, and they are arranged in a "word square" located on the left of the *chotam* (magical seal). The two hexagrams at the bottom of the construct, comprise respectively the Names שמרירון (*Shamriron*) and עזרירון (*Azriron*). We have encountered these Divine Names earlier in conjunction with an amulet which is likewise employed to counteract spontaneous abortion.

The current *Kamea* is likewise written on a scroll and accompanied by a similar incantation to the one employed with the earlier mentioned amulet. It should be written in the name of the individual requiring its support. The adjuration reads:

יהי רצון מלפניך שומר ונפשות חסידיו שתשמור פרי
בטנה של נושאת קמיע זה עליה מכל מיני נזקי שידין
ולילין ורוחין בישין מעתה ועד עולם בכח שמותיך
אלה צדנלבש קהסמגת צמרכד לתא רול יבכ מיל
לבד עכי פתב רעש ותת כוכ בחו אכי שיו עאב אוא
בישו עתי

Transliteration:

> *Y'hi ratzon milfanecha shomer nefashot chasidav shetishmor pri bitnah shel noset kamea zeh aleah m'kol minei nez'kei shedin v'lilin v'ruchin b'ishin me'atah va'ed olam b'koach shmotecha eileh Tzod'n'lobosh Koh's'mogot Tzamarchad (Psalm 91:10) LTA RVL YBK MYL LBD AKY PTB RASh VTT KVK BchV AKY ShYV AAB AVA BYShV ATY*

Translation:

> May it be your will, He who protects the souls of His devotees, to safeguard the fruit of her belly with this amulet she is carrying on her, from all kind of harmful *shedin* (demonic fiends), and *lilin* (night demons), and *ruchin* (ghosts), and *ishin* (evil spirits) from now unto eternity in the power of these Your Names *Tzod'n'lobosh Koh's'mogot Tzamarchad* [abbreviation of *Psalm 91:10*] *LTA RVL YBK MYL LBD AKY PTB RASh VTT KVK BchV AKY ShYV AAB AVA BYShV ATY*

Returning to the employment of *Psalm 106:30* in a word square as special protection during epidemics, the following somewhat more complex *Kamea* is constructed to guard residences against invasion of infectious diseases. In this regard, it is located on the left side of a doorframe, directly opposite the *Mezuzah*, which is traditionally affixed to the right side of all the entrances to a Jewish residence, or to all the rooms thereof:

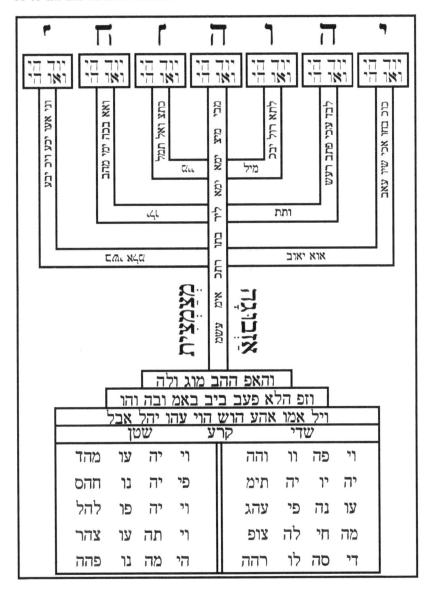

In the current instance, we notice the two mentioned word squares of *Psalm 106:30* positioned as the pedestal, so to speak, of a unique "*Menorah*."[114] Above the seven-branched candelabrum we trace the Ineffable Name written in two directions, in a manner which allows both readings of to conjoin in the central concluding letter ה (*Heh*). In this way the Ineffable Name is written with seven letters, one each for every branch of the *Menorah*. The seven capitals of its arms are also comprised of the earlier mentioned "*Sag*"-expansion of the *Tetragrammaton*, i.e. יוד הי ואו הי (*Yod-vav-dalet Heh-yod Vav-alef-vav Heh-yod*), also called the "Sixty-three Letter Name of God." This "expansion" of the Ineffable Name corresponds to the first ה (*Heh*) of the Ineffable Name; the "World of *Bri'ah*" (Creation); the *sefirah Binah* (Understanding) on the sefirotic tree, as well as its related "mother" (*Ima*) concept.

The seven-branched candelabrum itself comprises a set of Divine Names constructed with slight variations from the initials of the words of the earlier mentioned *Vihi No'am* prayer. Commencing with the leftmost arm, the construct reads:

[Left] וני אעו יכע ויכ יבע בשי אלם
[Left centre] ואא בכה ימי מהב ילו
[Centre Left] כתצ ואל תמל מיי
[Centre] מבי מיצ ימא ימא ליר בתו רתכ אים עשם
[Centre Right] לתא רול יבכ מיל
[Right Centre] לבד עכי פתב רעש ותת
[Right] כוכ בחו אכי שיו עאב אוא יאוב

Transliteration:
[Left] *VNY AAV YKA VYK YBA BshY ALM*
[Left centre] *VAA BKH YMY MHB YLV*
[Centre Left] *KTTz VAL TML MYY*
[Centre] *MBY MYC YMA YMA LYR BTV RTK AYM AShM*
[Centre Right] *LTA RVL YBK MYL*
[Right Centre] *LBD AYK PTB RASh VTT*
[Right] *KVK BHV AKY ShYR AAB AVA YAVB*

Located along the sides of the lower portion of the central stem of the *Menorah*, we trace the earlier addressed Divine Names אזבוגה (*Azbugah*) and מצמצית (*M'tzamtzit*). The base of the *Menorah* comprises the Divine Name combination והאפ ההב מוג ולה (*VHAP HHB MVG VLH*), which was formulated from the initials of the words comprising *Genesis 19:11*. The original verse reads:

ואת האנשים אשר פתח הבית הכו בסנורים מקטן ועד
גדול וילאו למצא הפתח

Transliteration:

*V'et ha-nashim asher petach ha-bayit hiku ba-sanveirim
mikaton v'ad gadol va'yil'u limtzo ha-patach*

Translation:

And they smote the men that were at the door of the house
with blindness, both small and great; so that they wearied
themselves to find the door.

Interestingly enough, the abbreviation of *Genesis 19:11* is also said
to be good in amulets for eye diseases,[115] and to achieve
invisibility.[116]

Be that as it may, the two "steps" below the base of the
Menorah respectively comprise the tri-letter arrangements of
Exodus 12:27 and *Exodus 12:23*, which we have already addressed
in terms of the complex hand amulet. In turn, we notice below the
mentioned "steps," i.e. heading the "word squares" of *Psalm
106:30*, the expression שדי קרע שטן (*Shadai K'ra Satan* —
"*Shadai* rend (rip) Satan"), which is very popular in protection
amulets.

Now, we are informed that for the amulet to be effective,
it must be placed full length with the writing visible, rolled up but
not folded, inside a glass tube to be suspended on the doorframe in
the manner mentioned. We are told that a small test tube acquired
from a chemist, will facilitate this task.[117]

Probably the most complex *Kamea* of this "plague
combating" genre, is the one found in the Polish edition of Chaim
Vital's "*Shaar ha-Yichudim,*" which was edited by Meir Poppers
and published in 1783 in Koretz.[118] The claim that this amulet
originated from the pen of Rabbi Isaac Luria, is not only
unsubstantiated but highly unlikely, since the Ari was against all
forms of Jewish magic. It should also be noted that this amulet
does not appear in any of the earlier editions of the text in question.
However, notwithstanding this, it is a very interesting and, I dare
say, most useful amulet.

We are told that besides the fundamental purpose of this *Kamea*, which is to protect its bearer against epidemics, the item comprises the Divine Names explicated by Eleazer m'Garmiza (Eleazer of Worms), the great 13th century German Pietist, who was certainly well acquainted with Jewish magical doctrines. We are further informed that Rabbi Israel Baal Shem Tov, the founder of current *Chasidism*, was equally informed on the Divine Names employed in this amulet. After all, he was a "Baal Shem," a term referring to East European Jewish "Masters of the Name" or Jewish "folk magicians," who were well-versed in writing amulets.

As might be expected, the popularity of the *Kamea* in question, ensured its inclusion with slight variations, into much larger amulets, which were printed in Jewish centres in North Africa and in Jerusalem. Whilst I am addressing such printed amulets later in this tome, I thought we might consider this extended *Kamea* here, since it is relevant to the present study.

As its popularity spread throughout the Jewish diaspora, this impressive *Kamea* was reprinted many times during the 19th and 20th century, especially in North African cities with a large *Sefardi* populace, e.g. Casablanca in Morocco. It is worth noting that numerous amulets derived from the Jewish populace residing in North Africa. In this regard, André Chouraqui, the acclaimed Algerian author, mentioned that these *Kameot* were "inspired by the Cabala," and that they "contained Hebrew prayers or cabalistic texts in Aramaic that had been composed by Cabalists of renown, sometimes those who had died in Morocco, preferably those who had come from Palestine."[119] He also informs us that whilst it is difficult to ascertain "the extent of cabalistic knowledge in North Africa in recent years," because "the adepts of the Cabala understandably talked little about it," the amulets deriving from this area were "inspired by the Cabala."[120]

Chouraqui succinctly delineated the function of these amulets, stating that they were meant "to protect the wearer against the influences of the demons which surrounded him on all sides and to turn away the dangers of the *ayin ha'ra*, the evil eye." He continued saying "the amulets frequently referred to the beneficial influence of the prophet Elijah who had struggled and triumphed against all the demonic spirits. The better to reduce them to impotence, the names of all the demons were listed on the amulet. It was enough to inscribe the names of the spirits near an infant in order to unmask them and thus chase them away."[121]

He made especial reference to amulets protecting mothers and infants, saying "the entire spirit was given over to the mystic combat which was required to break the devastating hold of Lilith, Queen of the Demons, whose demonic influences were the source of the worst evils. The fear of Lilith, so it was believed in North Africa, was part of the beginning of the acquisition of wisdom."[122] So, keeping this in mind, we can now take a closer look at the mentioned expanded version of the amulet we are currently addressing. Whilst the format of this *Kamea* varied slightly from one locale to the next, its contents remained mainly the same.

Scrutinising this *Kamea*, we note it opens with a framed statement of purpose located top-centre reading:

שמירה לילד וליולדת

Transliteration:

Shmirah l'yeled ul'yoledet

Translation:

Protection for a child and for women in confinement.

To the right and left of this opening phrase, we read:

בסימן טוב ובמזל טוב

Transliteration:

b'siman tov u'b'mazel tov

Translation:

in a good sign (omen) and in good fortune (luck)

Located to the right, directly beneath the wish for a "good omen" is the Divine Name שדי (*Shadai*), and similarly to the left, immediately below the expression "good fortune," is located the expression קרע שטן, the second six-letter portion of the "Forty-two Letter Name," which we noted is extensively employed in Hebrew amulets to banish baneful forces. Reading the two Divine Names conjointly, we note the formulae שדי קרע שטן (*Shadai K'ra Satan* — "*Shadai* rend (rip) Satan*").

Next we notice *Psalm 121* printed in full with vowels, obviously to make it easy to read for anyone perusing the amulet. The magical use of this Psalm is addressed more fully in the very next section.

To the right of the hand located centrally in the upper portion of the amulet, we note the header לחש לעין הרע (*Lachash l'ayin ha-ra*). This is an announcement of the extensive "Incantation (spell) against the Evil Eye" located below a claim regarding the origins of the incantation reading:

מהרב חיד"א ז"ל [זכרונו לברכה]

Transliteration:

m'harav Chida [Chayim Josef David Azulai] [*zichrono livracha*]

Translation:

From the Rav *Chida*, may his memory be blessed.

The "spell" in question, which is probably the largest adjuration of "eyes" to be found in Jewish Magic, is written mainly in Aramaic and appears somewhat modified from one *Kamea* to the next. In the current instance it reads:

משביע אני עליכם כל מין עינא בישא עינא אוכמא עינא
צרובא עינא תכלתא עינא ירוקה עינא ארוכה עינא
קצרה עינא רחבא עינא צרה עינא ישרה עינא עקומה
עינא עגולה עינא שוקעת עינא בולטת עינא רואה עינא
מבטת עינא בוקעת עינא שואבת עינא דדכורא עינא
דנוקבא עינא דאיש ואשתו עינא דאשה ובתה עינא דאשה
ובתה עינא דאשה וקרובותיה עין דבחור עין דזקן עין
דזקנה עין דבתולה עין דבעולה עין דאלמנה עין דנשואה
עין דגרושה כל מין עינא בישא שיש בעולם שראתה
והביטה ודברה בעין הרע על פב״פ [פלונית בתה פלוניתן
גזרנא ואשבענא לכון בההוא עינא עילאה עינא קדישא
עינא חדא עינא חיורא עינא דאיהי חיור גו חיור עינא
דכליל כל חיור עינא דבלא ימנא עינא פקיחא עינא
דאשגחותא תדירא עינא דכלא רחמי עינא דלית עלה
גבניני עינא דלא אדמיך ולא נאים עינא דכל עייניין
בישין אתכפיין ואיטמרן גו כיפין מן קדמוהי עינא
דנטיר לישראל דכתיב הנה לא ינום ולא יישן שומר
ישראל [*Psalm 121:4*] וכתיב הנה עין ה׳ [יהוה] אל יראיו
למיחלים לחסדו [*Psalm 33:18*] בההיא עינא עילאה גזרית
ואשבעית עליכון כל מין עינא בישא שתסורו ותערקו
ותברחו ותרחיקו מעל (פב״פ) ומעל כל ב״ב ולא יהיה
בכם שום כה לשלוט (בפב״פ) וכל ב״ב לא ביום ולא
בלילה לא בהקיץ ולאבחלום לא בשום אבר מרמ״ח
אבריו ולא בשום גיד משס״ח גידיו מהיום ולעולם
אמן נצח

Translation:

> I adjure you all sorts of Evil Eye, a black eye, yellow eye, blue eye, green eye, a long eye, short eye, broad eye, straight eye, crooked eye, round eye, sunken eye, bulging eye, a seeing eye, a blocked eye, cracked eye, absorbing eye, penetrating eye, eye of a woman, eye of a man and his wife, eye of a woman and her daughter, eye of a woman and her family, eye of a young man, eye of an old man, eye of an old woman, eye of a virgin, eye of one who is not a virgin, eye of a widow, eye of a married woman, eye of a divorced woman, all kinds of evil eye in the world which stared and spoke with a malevolent glance against [.....so and so (the bearer of this amulet).....], I command and adjure you by the Most Holy and Mighty and Exalted Eye, the Only Eye, the White Eye, the Right Eye, the Compassionate, the Ever Watchful and Open Eye, the Eye that never slumber or sleep, the Eye to Which all eyes are subject, the Wakeful Eye that preserves Israel, as it is written "Behold, He that keepeth Israel doth neither slumber nor sleep" [*Psalm 121:4*], as it is written "Behold, the eye of *YHVH* is toward them that fear Him, toward them that wait for His mercy" [*Psalm 33:18*]. By this Most High Eye, I adjure you all evil eyes to depart and be eradicated and to flee away to a distance from the bearer of this amulet, and that you are to have no power whatever over her who carries this amulet. And by the power of this most Holy Seal, you shall have no authority to hurt either by day or by night, when asleep or when awake; nor over any of her two hundred and forty-eight limbs, nor over any of her three hundred and sixty-five veins henceforth and forever *Amen*, Enduring (Victory)

I have not included a transliteration of this Aramaic incantation, and the translation is a slightly modified version of the one by J.E. Hanauer.[123] As it is, this adjuration appears in a number of formats, and there is also an extended, very convoluted version.[124]

Be that as it may, to the left of the hand, there is the famous saga regarding the Prophet Elijah's encounter with, and fateful restraining of, the demoness *Lilit*, which is preceded by two opening phrases:

מס״ [מספר] עבוה״ק [עבודת הקודש] הרב חס״ל ז״ל
[זכרונו לברכה] בשם ה׳ [יהוה] אלקי [אלהי] ישראל
ששמו גדול ונורא

Transliteration:

> *m'sefer avodat ha-kodesh ha-rav Chayim [zichrono
> livrachah] b'shem YHVH Elokei [Elohei] Yisra'el sheshmo
> gadol v'nora*

Translation:

> From the book *Avodat ha-Kodesh* of Rabbi Chayim
> [Azulai], may his memory be blessed. In the Name of
> *YHVH*, God of Israel, whose Name is great and awesome.

The mentioned *Elijah/Lilit* saga, which is regularly employed in
printed *Shmirah Kameot*, often comprises a few spelling and
grammatical errors. In the current instance it reads:

אליהו ז״ל [זכרונו לברכה] היה מהלך בדרך ופגע
בלילית ואמר לה טמאה אנה תלכי אמרה לו אני
הולכת לבית היולדת פב״פ [פלונית בת פלונית]
לתת לה שנת המות ולקחת את בנה לאכלו אמר לה
תהיה בחרם עצורה מאת השי״ת [השם יתברך] אבן
דומם תהיה ענתה ואמרה לו אדוני התירני ואני
נשבעתי בשם ה׳ [יהוה] לעזוב דרכי זה וכל זמן שאני
רואה או שומעת את שמותי מיד אברח ועתה אודיע
לך שמותי וכל זמן שיזכירו שמותי לא יהיה לי כח
להרע או להזיק ונשבעתי אני לגלות את שמותי לך
ותתנם לכתוב ולתלותם בבית הילד או היולדת ומיד
אני בורחת
ואלו הם שמותי שטרונא לילית אביטו אמיזרפו אמיזו
קקש אודם איק פודו איילו פטרוטא אברו קטא קלי
בטנה תלתו פרטשה
וכל מי שיודע שמותי מיד אני בורחת מן התינוק ותלה
בבית היולדת או הילד זאת הקמיע והילד וגם אמו לא
ינזקו ממני לעולם

Transliteration:

> *Eliyahu [zichrono livracha] haya m'halech ba'derech*
> *v'paga b'lilit v'amar lah t'meah anah telchi amrah lo ani*
> *holechet la'beit ha-yoledet [.....Plonit bat Plonit.....] latet*
> *lah shnat ha-mavet v'lakachat et b'nah le'achlo amar lah*
> *tihyeh b'cherem atzurah m'et ha-shem yit'barach even*
> *domem tihyeh antah v'am'rah lo adoni hatireni v'ani*
> *nish'bati b'shem YHVH la'azov darki zeh v'kol z'man*
> *sh'ani ro'ah o shoma'at et sh'motai miyad evrach v'atah*
> *odeia l'cha sh'motai v'kol z'man sh'yazkiru sh'motai lo*
> *yihyeh li koach l'hara o l'hazik v'nishbati ani l'galot et*
> *sh'motai l'cha v'tit'nem lich'tov v'litlotam ba-bayit ha-*
> *yeled o ha-yoledet v'miyad ani borachat*
>
> *V'elu hem sh'motai Shatruna Lilit Abitu Amizrafu,*
> *Amizu Kakash [Chakash] Odem Iyak Pud [Pudu] Iyilo*
> *Petrota Avru Kata K'li Bitnah Talto Paritashah*
>
> *V'kol mi sheyodea sh'motai miyad ani borachat*
> *min ha-tinok v'taleh b'beit ha-yoledet o ha-yeled zot ha-*
> *kamia v'ha-yeled v'gam imo lo yinaz'ku mimeni l'olam*

Translation:

> Elijah, may his memory be blessed, was walking on the
> road when he encountered *Lilit*, and said to her "Impure
> one, where are you off to?" She said to him "I am going to
> the house of [.....so and so.....] who gave birth, to give her
> the sleep of death and to take her son and devour him." He
> told her "Be banished and imprisoned by the Name of the
> Holy One. You will be a silent stone." She responded and
> said him, "Master grant me indulgence, and I vow in the
> Name of *YHVH* to forsake this my way, and that every time
> I will see or hear my names, I will flee forthwith, and now
> I will tell you my names, and whenever my names are
> mentioned, I will not have the power to do evil or hurt, and
> I vow to reveal my names to you, and if they are written
> and suspended in the home of mother, or the child, or this
> amulet placed on the child as well as his mother, I will flee
> immediately.
>
> These are my names *Shatruna, Lilit, Abitu,*
> *Amizrafu, Amizu, Kakash [Chakash], Odem, Iyak, Pud*
> *[Pudu], Iyilo, Petrota, Avru, Kata, K'li, Bitnah, Talto,*
> *Paritashah.*

And whoever knows my names, I shall forthwith flee from the baby, and when this amulet is suspended in the home of the mother or the child, and no harm will befall the child or his mother from me forever."

A further brief "kabbalistic instruction" is presented in a section directly below and separate from the *Lilit* legend. It reads:

קבלה מר״ [מרבין] אליעזר מגרמיזא בעל התוספות
ז״ל [זכרונו לברכה] שמירה למגפה ושרפה ה״ [יהוה]
ישמרנו לתלות זאת נגד החלון או נגד הפתח ובדוק
ומנוסה וגם האר״י הק״ [הקדוש] הבי״א בכתב ידו כל
זאת נפלא וגם מר״ אליהו בעל שם טוב זלה״ה [זכרונו
לברכה לחיי העולם הבא]

Transliteration:

> *Kabbalah m'rabbi Eleazer mi'Garmiza ba'al ha-tosfot [zichrono livrachah] sh'mirah l'magefah v's'refah YHVH yishmareinu litlot zot neged ha-chalon o neged ha-petach v'baduk v'minoseh v'gam ha-Ari ha-kadosh havi b'k'tav yado kol zot nifla v'gam mi'rebbe Eliyahu Ba'al Shem Tov, [zichrono livrachah l'chayei ha-olam ha-ba]*

Translation:

> Kabbalistic Instruction — Rabbi Eleazar of Garmiza, the master of the *Tosefta*, may his memory be blessed, said for protection against plagues and fire, *YHVH* protect us, hang this against the window or the entrance door, and it is tried and tested, and also the Holy Ari in his writings mentioned the wonders of this, and also by Rabbi Elijah Baal Shem Tov, may his memory be blessed for life in the World to Come.

Be that as it may, the *Kamea* also includes the names of our primordial parents, as well as those of the patriarchs and matriarchs, located to the sides of the bird-like depiction of the "evil eye" in the lower portion of the amulet. These should be read in pairs, i.e. the names of the males to the right conjointly with those of the females on the left, as shown below:

Left	Right
וחוה (*v'Chavah*—and Eve)	אדם (*Adam*—Adam)
ושרה (*v'Sarah*—and Sarah)	אברהם (Avraham—Abraham)
ורבקה (*v'Rivkah*—and Rebecca)	יצחק (*Yitz'chak*—Isaac)
ולאה (*v'Leah*—and Leah)	יעקב (*Ya'akov*—Jacob)

Below the male ancestors listed to the right, there is an inscription regarding the three angels protecting infants against *Lilit*, reading סנוי וסנסנוי וסמנלגף פנימה (*Sanoi v'Sansanoi v'Semangelof p'nimah*—*Sanoi* and *Sansanoi* and *Semangelof* present!). On the left side, located similarly below the names of the female ancestors, is a phrase reading לילית וכל כת דילה חוצה (*Lilit v'kol kat dilah chutzah*—*Lilit* and all of her kind [sect] out!)

Next, directly below the personal names of our primordial ancestors on both sides, we trace the following protection incantation constructed from the three words מכשפה לא תחיה (*m'chashefah lo t'chayeh*—"Thou shalt not suffer a sorceress to live") (*Exodus 22:17 [16]*). This verse is specifically employed in amulets to counteract evil spells. The mentioned incantation is effectuated by permuting the three words comprising the verse six times, these being:

Left	Right
לא תחיה מכשפה	מכשפה לא תחיה
תחיה מכשפה לא	מכשפה תחיה לא
תחיה לא מכשפה	לא מכשפה תחיה

Now we need to peruse the centre portion of the *Kamea* which is comprised of the two constructs derived from the listed edition of Rabbi Chaim Vital's *Shaar ha-Yichudim*.[125] In the current amulet the upper portion comprises the following hand image, which in the original *Kamea* is located in the lower portion of the construct.

This portion of the *Kamea* we are addressing, though somewhat more elaborate, comprises most of the details listed in the earlier addressed hand-shaped *Shmirah Kamea*. The fingertips comprise the exact same letter combinations, these being the abbreviation of *Psalm 32:7*. Likewise the fingers and the palm of the hand comprise mostly the same Divine Name combinations, with some variation as far as their location on the construct is concerned.

What is different in this instance, is the addition of the earlier addressed six permutations of the Name שדי (*Shadai*) located below the four fingers and to the side of the thumb; the peculiar הימל and חמיסלו written along the thumb; the combination מהש (*Mahash*), i.e. the earlier addressed fifth tri-letter portion of the "*Shem Vayisa Vayet*" written along the lower portion of the index finger; the inclusion of the Divine Names אדני (*Adonai*); אראריתא (*Ar'arita*); אהיה (*Ehyeh*); a *chotam* (magical seal/script) in the centre of the palm; and the combination מצמצית ביט (*Matzmatzit BYT*) on the wrist.

Having already paid attention earlier to the majority of the Divine Names appearing in this amulet, I need only explain the Divine Names אראריתא (*Ar'arita*), הימל and חמיסלו written along the thumb. As mentioned in *"The Book of Sacred Names,"* *Ar'arita* is employed "to empower prayers," and that it is believed to bring "illumination."[126]

The Divine Name construct הימל was derived from the capitals of the words in *Genesis 24:7* reading:

הוא ישלח מלאכו לפניך

Transliteration:
hu yislach mal'acho l'fanecha
Translation:
"He will send His angel before thee"

Being considered the "Name of Success,"[127] this Divine Name is employed in *Kameot* to generate prosperity for those bearing the said amulets.

The combination חמיסלו comprises the first two tri-letter portions of the following Divine Name:

חמי סלו טוב טיא היב

This Divine Name combination was derived from the initials of the words comprising *Psalm 34:8-9 [7-8]* reading:

(Verse 8 [7]) חנה מלאך יהוה סביב ליראיו ויחלצם
(Verse 9 [8]) טעמו וראו כי טוב יהוה אשרי הגבר יחסה בו

Transliteration:
(Verse 8 [7]) *Choneh mal'ach YHVH saviv lirei'av vai'chaltzem*
(Verse 9 [8]) *Ta'amu ur'u ki tov YHVH ashrei ha-gever yecheseh bo*
Translation:
(Verse 8 [7]) The angel of *YHVH* encampeth round about them that fear Him, and delivereth them.
(Verse 9 [8]) O consider and see that *YHVH* is good; happy is the man that taketh refuge in Him.

This set of Divine Names is sometimes employed in amulets in conjunction with *Psalm 121* in support of infants who cry incessantly.[128] We will address the latter Psalm in greater detail shortly. Let us next consider the following birdlike image of the "Evil Eye" located in the central lower portion of the *Kamea*:

In the corners there are images of sacred ancestral locations, i.e. the Cave of *Machpelah*, the Wailing Wall, the Tomb of Rachel and the Holy City. Next, the outer circle comprises four Divine Name constructs respectively located directly adjacent the mentioned four sacred locations:

Top Right: כעבי״צ
Top Left: כיקעני
Bottom Right: והאפה הב
Bottom Left: מוג ולה זיו

The combination located top right should read בעבי״צו. This is an abbreviation of a phrase, the last four words of which comprise the opening portion of *Psalm 121:8*:[129]

ברוך עושה בראשית יהוה ישמר צאתך ובואך

Transliteration:

> *Baruch oseh b'reishit YHVH yishmor tzeit'cha uvo'echa*

Translation:

> Blessed be Maker of Creation, *YHVH* will guard your going and your coming.

We are told the combination top left should spell ביקעני.[130] We are not told why this specific entry in the *Kamea* in question should appear in the latter format, and we are not informed regarding its origin, hence this combination remains obscure. The concluding Divine Name constructs bottom right and left comprise the earlier mentioned abbreviation of *Genesis 19:11*, which we noted is employed in Hebrew amulets to counter eye diseases and to become invisible.

The circular border surrounding the illustration of the bird-like "Evil Eye," comprises four sets of Divine Names combinations constructed from the initials of the words comprising *Exodus 12:27, Psalm 91:10, Numbers 17:13 [16:48], Psalm 106:30*, as well as portions of the "Forty-two Letter Name" and other standard Divine Names:

(Upper Left) וזפ הלא פעב ביב באמ ובה והו

(Lower Left) ילש תבא שרבו ליב

(Lower Right) ובהווהוה קרע שטנ יוהך כלך אגף סגף נגף

(Upper Right) ופווה רוטא נעוריררון יגל פזק

We have earlier addressed the abbreviations of *Exodus 12:27* and *Psalm 91:10* employed in Hebrew amulets. Hence we will peruse the abbreviation of *Numbers 17:13 [16:48]* located lower right, and which is employed conjointly with the Divine Names קרע שטנ (*K'ra Satan*), יוהך כלך (*Yohach Kalach*), as well as the peculiar אגף סגף נגף. We will address the latter Divine Name construct in greater detail in the following chapter. For now let us consider *Numbers 17:13 [16:48]*, which is employed in *Kameot* as a protection against plagues.[131] The verse reads:

ויעמד בין המתים ובין החיים ותעצר המגפה

Transliteration:

*Vaya'amod bein ha-meitim u'vein ha-chayim va'tei'atzar
ha-magefah*

Translation:

And he stood between the dead and the living; and the
plague was stayed.

The "secret," and perforce the "power," of ובהוהוה (vocalised
Vabei'uhavaha), is said to be its *gematria* [ו = 6 + ב = 2 + ה = 5
+ ו = 6 + ה = 5 + ו = 6 + ה = 5 = 35] which is equivalent to those
of the Names אגלא (*Agala'a* [א = 1 + ג = 3 + ל = 30 + א = 1 =
35]) and אלד (*Elad* [א = 1 + ל = 30 + ד = 4 = 35]).[132] As noted
elsewhere, אלד, the tenth tri-letter portion of the "Name of
Seventy-two Names," "is understood to be 'a branch of the branch
of Mercy' (*Rachamim*)," and regarding which "we are told that the
Divine One, in 'His Mercy,' abolishes everything which impacts
negatively on us."[133] The Name אגלא (*Agala'a*) is likewise
employed in banishing evil, and this Divine Name features very
prominently in, as it were, the "impalement" of the "Evil Eye" in
the current amulet.

Be that as it may, the upper right segment of the four listed
Divine Name constructs comprises an abbreviation of *Psalm
106:30*, the word רוטא (*Ruta*—"Rue"), the Name נעורירון
(*N'oriyiro'un*), and the portion of the "Forty-two Letter Name"
reading יגלפזק (*Yaglefzok*). We have earlier encountered the
employment of these Divine Names in Hebrew amulets, and we
have likewise investigated the appearance of *Psalm 106:30* in
magical "word squares." However, in this instance the initials of
the words comprising this verse, were arranged into the construct
ופווה, which is likewise employed in the control of epidemics.[134]

Next, we need to focus on the central portrayal of the "Evil
Eye" as a bird-like creature with a wicked beak, and whose body,
wings and nasty claws are restrained by a number of Divine
Names. This segment of the *Kamea* opens with a header comprised
of the phrase from *Psalm 91:7* reading אליך לא יגש (*elecha lo
yigash*—"it shall not come nigh thee"). Below it we see the
impaled depiction of the "Evil Eye," with its claws, wing feathers

and the lower feathers respectively transfixed by אגלא (*Agala'a*), אזבוגה (*Azbogah*), and צמרכד (*Tzamarchad*). The body of the malevolent creature is likewise held in check by the following set of Divine and Angelic Names:

אל שדי אנקתם טפטפיה על צבא סנוי בטר מזריה שמור

Transliteration:

El Shadai Anaktam Taftafyah al Tz'va Sanoi Bitaro Mazriyah ("Scatter") *Shamor* ("Preserve")

As you have probably noticed, this set of Names incorporates only the opening sections of Divine Name constructs, i.e. the first of portion of the "Twenty-two Letter Name"; the Name of the first of the three Angels guarding infants; the בטר (*Bitaro*) segment of the "Forty-two Letter Name"; etc. These are considered good enough to hold the "Evil Eye" in check.

That concludes our investigation into this curious amulet. In case you were wondering, the writing at the very bottom of the amulet comprises the publishers imprint.

Psalm 121 — This Psalm is employed in Hebrew amulets, both in full and in an abbreviated format, as a call for help and protection.[135] We have earlier listed the abbreviation of *Psalm 121*, however the standard order of abbreviation with vowels is as follows:

שְׁלָא עָאֶה מֵיְעַ עָמְיַ עֹשָׁוַ אַיְלַ רַאָיַ שֹׁהֲלֹ יְוִי
שַׁיְּיִ שֹׁיְּיִ שֹׁיְּתְצִי אַיַּיְ יֹהֲלֹ יַוְבַ יְיְמַ רְיָא נַיְּיִ צֵוּמֵ עָוְעֹ

Transliteration:

Shila'e Ei'ehe Mei'a'e Emiy' Oshava Ayila Ra'aya Shohilo Yav'yi Shoyiy' Shoy'tzi Ayay' Yohalo Yav'va Yiyimi Rayi'e Nay'yi Tzei'umei Av'o

We are told that individuals who wake at night in states of fear and trembling with their imagination running wild, should write the full abbreviation of *Psalm 121* on parchment. The Hebrew letters should be written with great care, as if every letter is a garment of some special being, at the same time imagining them streaming with Divine Light. Afterwards the writing should be rubbed off with rose petals and seven pepper corns inside water. Then the individuals must consume some of this liquid, and rub the remainder on their bodies.[136]

We are also told that if one is obliged to travel around alone at night, reciting *Psalm 121* seven times will afford one complete protection.[137] Written on paper, this Psalm is hung near or on the bed of a mother and the unborn.[138] We are further told that "metallic amulets, inscribed with this psalm were worn by men as well as women at all times and became an article of decoration."[139] It is also said that this Psalm is good for protection against and alleviating sun stroke.[140] This was obviously deduced from the portion of the sixth verse reading "By day the sun shall not smite."

Be that as it may, *Psalm 121* is considered one of the most important defense mechanisms against the evil eye and the demoness *Lilit*, hence, the eight verses of this Psalm are often inscribed in full on amulets protecting the home, as well as mothers, the unborn and infants, as shown in the following amulet:

We already noted the very important Divine Name derived from this Psalm, i.e. עשצי—*Ashtzei*, which was constructed from the five letters immediately succeeding the five appearances of the Ineffable Name in this Psalm. It should also be noted, that similarly to the "*Menorah Psalm*," *Psalm 121* is sometimes presented on *Shiviti* plaques and *Kameot* in the format of the seven-branched candelabrum:

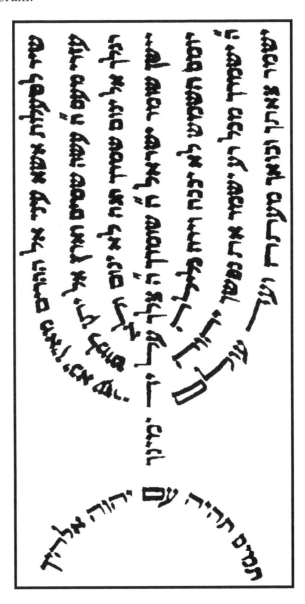

The base of this *menorah* is comprised of *Deuteronomy 18:13* reading:

תמים תהיה עם יהוה אלהיך

Transliteration:
> *Tamim Tih'yeh im YHVH elohecha*

Translation:
> Thou shalt be whole-hearted with *YHVH* thy God.

Whilst I have attempted to share the uses of certain biblical psalms in Hebrew amulets, it should be noted that this investigation is by no means exhaustive. Several Psalms remain which are employed either singly or conjointly for amuletic purposes. In this regard, it is worth noting that a *Kamea* comprised of the whole of *Psalm 127* is recommended to be worn by children as a protective measure immediately following their birth.[141]

As indicated throughout this work, selected verses from various Psalms are equally frequently employed in *Kameot*. The same applies to the whole of the Hebrew Bible, in which an extensive array of Hebrew amulets are comprised of verses carefully selected for their inherent "magical propensities." These verses are then applied in a number of specialised magical ways.

. ...Next the frog turned to Haninah's wife and said: '.....I would like you to accompany me as far as the Forest of Trees.' And so they went into the woods with him and, upon arriving, the frog emitted a loud croak, calling together all the beasts in the forest... ... .

Chapter 4
Shemesh — Sun
SECRET ALPHABETS
&
MAGICAL SEALS

A. Celestial Alphabets

W hen I was a little boy I overheard a conversation between a burly Jewish biker, and my paternal grandfather who was trying to convince the biker of the "error of his ways." The gentleman in question used to go on, what appeared to be, long journeys at night on his bike, traversing for no apparent reason the extensive flat-lands of the Free State province of South Africa. When my grandfather advised him to rather stay at home, say his bedtime prayers and retire to bed, the biker said that he was communicating every night with the Almighty. In fact, he maintained that he knew the "secret language" by which creation is being manifested, and that he could read its "unfoldment" in the night sky whilst crossing the open spaces of the Free State.

As my grandfather shook his head in disbelief, and waved the "heathen" away most indignantly, I ran after the biker and asked him if he could teach me how to read the "secret messages" in the sky. He gently informed me that the stars are part of the very big saga of the beginning and end of everything happening at once in an enormous, most holy "talisman." He told me that the universe changes all the time in accordance with this ongoing "telling of life in the sky," and that, when I was a little older, he would teach me the very "Holy Alphabet of Creation." Then I too may read the "Word of God" at night in the stars. Being at the time unacquainted with the term "talisman," I wanted to know what it was. In very simple language, he called it a deliberately constructed "spiritual channel" through which Divine Power can be transmitted for our benefit.

To say that I was deeply impressed by this individual would be an understatement. I imagined a diversity of huge invisible pipes reaching down from the stars, through which the "Holy Power" of the Divine One flowed down into our world, in order to affect our lives for the better. Alas, that was the only conversation my biker friend and I would ever have, since he died a short while afterwards in an automobile accident.....during the hours of daylight, when he was not being "distracted" by divine messages in the night sky!

Around twelve years later, when I chanced upon the conception of Guillaume Postel that the will of the Eternal One appears in the vault of the heavens in the form of special Hebrew glyphs,[1] I surmised my biker friend gained his notion of reading the "Word of God in the night sky" either from Postel, or from his admirer Jacques Gaffarel, a 17th century French Kabbalist and librarian to the famous Richelieu, who adopted Postel's cosmic writing notions, and created the following illustration of the "celestial alphabet" in the ever changing "talisman of the heavens."[2]

The endings of each letter comprise little circles. Each of these represents a star, sets of which are joined by lines to form the "magical language" of the "celestial alphabet." These constructs are based on the Hebrew alphabet, and Gaffarel derived his version of this alphabet from the "occult" writings of Cornelius Agrippa,[3] as shown in the following table indicating the formats of the "Celestial Alphabet" from Agrippa to our own time:

	Agrippa[4]	Gaffarel[5]	Barrett[6]	Modern
א				
ב				
ג				
ד				
ה				
ו				
ז				
ח				
ט				
י				
כ				

ל				
מ				
נ				
ס				
ע				
פ				
צ				
ק				
ר				
ש				
ת				

The "Celestial Alphabet" is probably the most well known of all the angelic scripts. As indicated, it appears in a miscellany of calligraphical configurations ranging from simple lines to the following emboldened and outlined format:[7]

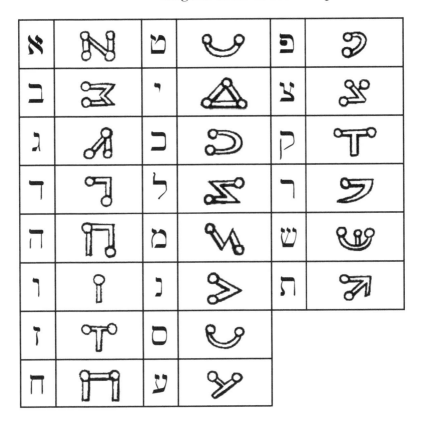

An entire magical system was built around a magical alphabet comprised of glyphs emboldened in this manner.[8] Such "fattened" glyphs are at times employed in Hebrew amulets, as indicated in the following *Kamea* created for the purpose of finding an answer to a vexing question, or a beneficial response to a special request:[9]

In standard Hebrew script the magical inscription reads:

ועד מאב

מאטמב

These three names, which we are informed should be drawn in the format of the magical seals listed above, are in fact acronyms of the following angelic names:

וְדָאֵל עָאמָאֵל דְעַבִיאֵל מִיכָאֵל [מִבָאֵל] אַבְמִיאֵל בַּבְדָאֵל מַמַוְאֵל אַאַבְאֵל טַטְבַעִיאֵל מַטְרִיאֵל בְּמָטִיאֵל

Transliteration:
> *Vad'el A'ma'el D'avi'el Micha'il [Miva'el] Av'mi'el Vav'da'el Mamav'el A'av'el Tat'va'i'el Mat'ri'el B'mati'el*

The magical inscription, the associated angelic names, as well as five concluding Divine Names should be written on deerskin parchment, or a sheet of clean, good quality paper. The mentioned five concluding Names are:

אֲגַף נְגַף שְׁגַף תְּגַף רְגַף

Transliteration:
> *'gaf n'gaf sh'gaf t'gaf r'gaf*

Thereafter the writing is dissolved in a glass of water, which is then ingested by the one seeking the spiritual response. This is followed by spontaneous prayer which does not include any form of adjuration. We are told that without a doubt, the query will be answered in dream during sleep, and that this is a tried and tested technique.[10]

It should be noted that the first three of the odd sounding concluding Divine Names, i.e. אֲגַף נְגַף שְׁגַף, are also employed in a somewhat more complex "Dream Question" procedure.[11] In this regard, one is instructed to carefully wash the body from the hips downwards. Afterwards the "*Hashkiveinu*" prayer is said. It reads:

השכיבנו יהוה אלהינו לשלום והעמידנו מלכנו לחיים ופרוש עלינו סכת שלומך ותקננו בעצה טובה מלפניך והושיענו למען שמך והגן בעדנג והסר מעלינו אויב דבר וחרב ורעב ויגון והסר שטן מלפנינו ומאחרינו ובצל

כנפיך תסתירנו כי אל שומרנו ומצילנו אתה כי אל מלך
חנון ורחום אתה ושמור צאתנו ובואנו לחיים ולשלום
מעתה ועד עולם ופרש עלינו סכת שלומך ברוך אתה
יהוה שומר עמו ישראל לעד

Transliteration:

> *Hash'kiveinu YHVH Eloheinu l'shalom v'ha-amideinu malkeinu l'chayim ufros aleinu sukat sh'lomecha v'tak'neinu b'eitzah tovah milfanecha v'hoshi'einu l'ma'an sh'mecha v'hagen ba'adeinu v'haser me'aleinu oyev dever v'cherev v'ra'av v'yagon v'haser satan milfanenu u'mei'achareinu uv'tzel knafecha tastireinu ki El shomreinu u'matzileinu atah ki El melech chanun v'rachum atah ush'mor tzeiteinu uvo'einu l'chayim ul'shalom mei'atah v'ad olam uf'ros aleinu sukat shlomecha baruch atah YHVH shomer amo Yisra'el la'ad*

Translation:

> Help us *YHVH* to lie down in peace, and raise us up, our King, to life. Spread over us the shelter of Your peace; guide us with Your good counsel, and save us for the sake of Your Name, and shield us from foe, pestilence, and from starvation, sword and anguish. Remove the evil forces that surround us, and shelter us in the shadow of Your wings, *El* who watches over us and delivers us, and *El* our gracious and merciful King. Guard our coming and our going, to life and to peace from now unto eternity. Blessed are You *YHVH*, Guardian of Your people Israel forever.

Next, after donning clean clothes and prior to falling asleep, one has to address the listed Divine Names with strongly focussed intention (*Kavvanah*) and in great purity, extend the query to which one is seeking an answer in sleep and dream, saying:

בבקשה מכם שמות הקדושים והטהורים שתראוני
בחלום בלילה הזה שהנחתי את שמותיכם מראשותי
תשובת שאלתי שהיא [.....state the question.....] ולא אירא
ולא אפחד ולא ישכח ממני כלום בשם אַרְגִי נַרְגִי
סַרְגִי אֲגַף נְגַף שְׁגַף

Transliteration:

> *b'vakashah mikem shemot ha-kadoshim v'ha-tehorim shetar'uni b'chalom ba'lailah ha-zeh shehenachti et shmoteichem m'rashoti tshuvat she'elati shehi* [.....state the question.....] *v'lo ira v'lo afached v'lo yishachach mimeni klum b'shem Argi Nargi Sargi 'gaf N'gaf S'gaf*

Translation:

> Please I request from you pure and Holy Names, to receive in dream this night, in which I put your names under my head, an answer to my question which is [.....state the question.....] I will have no fear and I will not be scared, and I will not forget anything, in the name *Argi Nargi Sargi 'gaf N'gaf S'gaf*

Afterwards write the Divine Names on a kosher scroll, and place it under your pillow, then go to sleep.

Curiously enough, the earlier listed three Divine Names, vocalised שַׁגַף נַגַף אַגַף (*Agaf Nagaf Shagaf*), are employed in protection *Kameot* by both the healthy and the sick during an epidemic.[12] These are also used to halt the spontaneous flow of semen, i.e. "wet dreams," however, in the latter instance the two vowels employed in sounding these names are the same as in the earlier addressed amulet.

Elsewhere these three Names, employed without vowels and conjoined with a fourth Divine, i.e. אגף נגף סגף שגף, are employed to halt a hemorrhage and the likely death of an individual, who has suffered a serious injury which has resulted in excessive and dangerous bleeding.[13] In this instance the blood of the sufferer is used to write the four Divine Names on his or her forehead, after which the injured individual's head is turned to face the northern quarter.

Be that as it may, let us now investigate certain Hebrew based "magical alphabets." It is worth considering that there are several such scripts, called *Kolmosin* (lit. "angelic pens") or "*ketav einayim*" ("eye writing"), believed to be angelic alphabets. These are addressed in certain primary Hebrew magical manuscripts,[14] as well as in a number of Latin texts, in which it was surmised these scripts were derived from the Samaritan alphabet.[15] This claim is debatable, and the origins of these magical alphabets still remain obscure. It has been noted that whilst "in many discussions of Jewish magic these signs are often referred to as 'Kabbalistic signs'," "they are mostly non-Jewish in origins, and predate the rise of Kabbalah."[16]

1. *KOLMOSIN MICHA'EL*:
Alphabets of *Michael*

Magical alphabets and seals are extensively employed in Jewish magic for a variety of special purposes. It is in this regard that we commence our investigation into *kolmosin* or "angelic alphabets" with the "Alphabet of *Michael*."

A set of divergent magical alphabets are titled "*Kolmos Micha'el*" or "*K'tav Micha'el*" in Jewish magical literature.[17] In order to afford greater insight into these curious "Alphabets of *Michael*," I have included three of the relevant alphabets in the following table, since I believe these will offer a broader insight into this curious angelic alphabet:

	Version 1[18]	Variant[19]	Version 2[20]	Version 3[21]
א				
ב				
ג				
ד				
ה				

ו				
ז				
ח				
ט				
י				
כ				
ד				
ל				
מ				
ם				
נ				
ן				
ס				

ע				
פ				
ר				
צ				
ז				
ק				
ר				
ש				
ת				

Perusing the glyphs comprising the various versions of the "Alphabet of *Michael*," it is clear that in several instances the differences between letters are so slight that one might easily mistake one for the other. Consider for example the magical glyphs of the letters ו and ז, which in the first version of the *Micha'el* alphabet appear to be virtually the same. A minor adjustment was employed in the later variant version in order to show a difference between the glyphs in question.

Consider also the magical glyphs of the letters צ compared with the magical ק in the first version. The only difference appears to be the horizontal line which in the case of the letter *tzadi* is in the centre of the glyph, whilst in the second glyph it is located more towards the top. As it is, similar problems occur in all versions of the "*Kolmosin Micha'el*."

Another point we should keep in mind is the fact that as far as "Magical Alphabets" are concerned, there are so many variants of versions that it is virtually impossible to ascertain the "originals." In this regard the glyphs employed in the first version and its variant do equate in most instances. Consider for example the following alternative to the first version of the "Alphabet of *Michael*":[22]

א	[glyph]	י	[glyph]	ע	[glyph]
ב	[glyph]	כ	[glyph]	פ	[glyph]
ג	[glyph]	ך	[glyph]	ף	[glyph]
ד	[glyph]	ל	[glyph]	צ	[glyph]
ה	[glyph]	מ	[glyph]	ץ	[glyph]
ו	[glyph]	ם	[glyph]	ק	[glyph]
ז	[glyph]	נ	[glyph]	ר	[glyph]
ח	[glyph]	ן	[glyph]	ש	[glyph]
ט	[glyph]	ס	[glyph]	ת	[glyph]

In the current instance the magical glyphs of the letters ג, כ, מ, ס, ם, פ, ף, צ, ק and ר are quite different from the listed first version of the "Alphabet of *Michael*." However, despite the calligraphical differences in the presentation of several glyphs, it is obvious that both versions of this magical alphabet were derived from the same source. In this regard, the variant listed adjacent the first version is, despite minor differences, only a seventeenth century "update." In that instance the glyphs representing the letters *Lamed* and *Mem* should be switched to align with primary Hebrew sources.

As far as the second listed version of the "Alphabet of *Michael*" is concerned, the situation is, as it were, somewhat more quirky. It is entirely different from the first listed version, and we are confronted with certain anomalies arising from the following incomplete variant of this version:[23]

א	[glyph]	ט	[glyph]	פ	[glyph]
ב	[glyph]	י		צ	[glyph]
ג	[glyph]	כ	[glyph]	ק	[glyph]
ד	[glyph]	ל	[glyph]	ר	[glyph]
ה	[glyph]	מ	[glyph]	ש	[glyph]
ו	[glyph]	נ	[glyph]	ת	[glyph]
ז	[glyph]	ס	[glyph]		
ח	[glyph]	ע	[glyph]		

Whatever the case may be, the second version of the "Alphabet of *Michael*" and the above variant are respectively employed in their entirety as protection against the wiles of the demoness *Lilit* and other spirit adversaries; the evil machinations of our fellow humankind; and to acquire loving-kindness and grace.[24]

The third version of the "Alphabet of *Michael*" equally appears in a number of formats in different manuscripts, and sometimes as such even in the same manuscript.[25] The following is a version of the same alphabet found in a 17th century Latin text:[26]

There are some differences between the current version of this alphabet and the one listed in the earlier *Shoshan Yesod Olam*.[27] The most problematic is the similarity of the glyphs representing the letters ה and ו, which are clearly different in the version listed earlier.

Now, readers would naturally presume that magical alphabets such as these are employed to present special incantations in a written manner. Whilst this has been the case especially amongst modern magical practitioners, it should be noted that the set of glyphs comprising a magical alphabet are also utilised collectively in exact letter order for special purposes. Consider for example the listed "first version" of the "*Kolmosin Micha'el*," which is employed in amulets to heal and sooth the throat. In this regard, the instruction is to write the set of glyphs comprising the said alphabet on clean parchment, or to engrave it on a little golden platter or disk, and afterwards to tie it directly to the throat.[28]

2. *KOLMOSIN GAVRI'EL*:
Alphabets of *Gabriel*

I have investigated a number of presentations of the "Alphabet of *Gabriel*," and so as to indicate again a number of variant formats of this "magical alphabet," I have included three complete versions in the following table:

	Version 1[29]	Version 2[30]	Version 3[31]
א			
ב			
ג			
ד			
ה			
ו			

ז			
ח			
ט			
י			
כ			
ד			
ל			
מ			
ם			
נ			
ו			

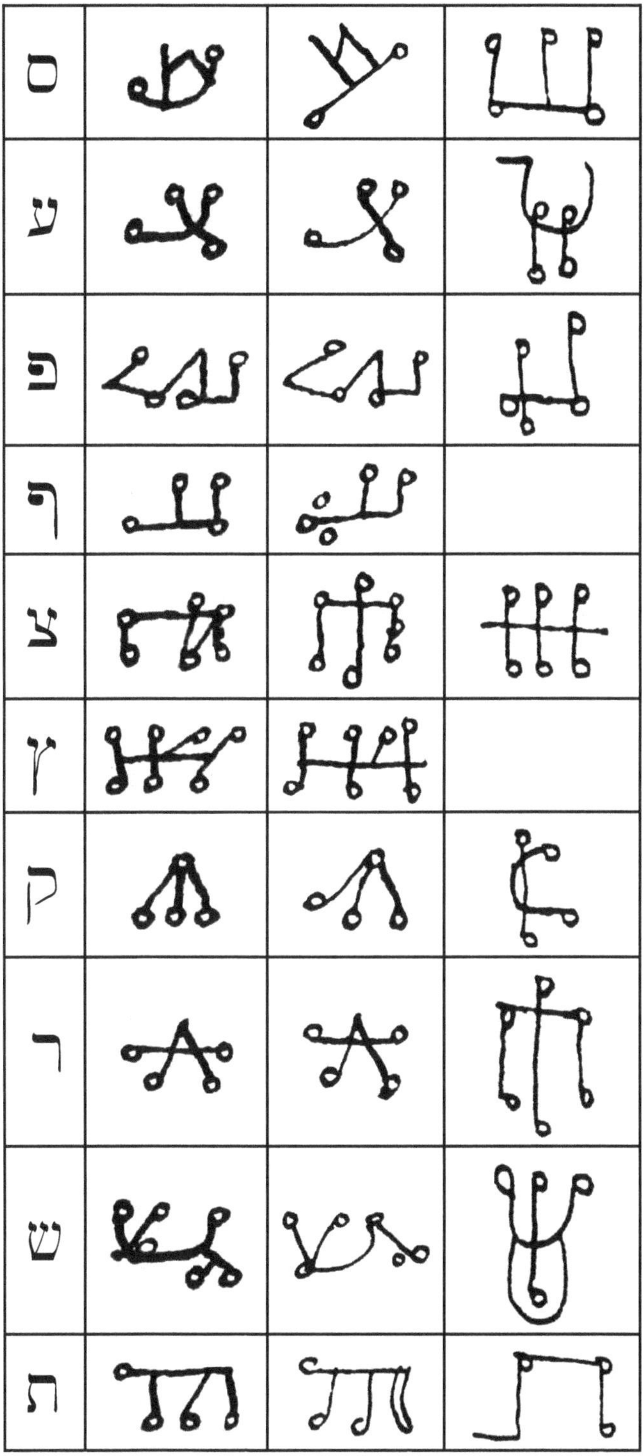
ס
ע
פ
ף
צ
ץ
ק
ר
ש
ת

Regarding the first two versions of the "*Kolmos Gavri'el*," we are informed that the entire alphabet should be written on deerskin parchment or a kosher scroll, i.e. a clean sheet of good quality paper, to be carried on the person of a woman who requires support in halting the loss of her offspring.[32] Be that as it may, Moses Zacutto presented us with the following incomplete version of this alphabet in his *Shorshei ha-Shemot*.[33]

א	[symbol]	י	[symbol]	פ	[symbol]
ב	[symbol]	כ	[symbol]	ף	[symbol]
ג	[symbol]	ל	[symbol]	ץ	[symbol]
ד		מ	[symbol]	ז	[symbol]
ה	[symbol]	ם	[symbol]	ק	[symbol]
ו		נ	[symbol]	ר	[symbol]
ז	[symbol]	ן	[symbol]	ש	[symbol]
ח	[symbol]	ס	[symbol]	ת	[symbol]
ט	[symbol]	ע	[symbol]		

The "Alphabet of *Gavri'el*" is employed in support of a woman who suffers the demise of her offspring in infancy. The instruction is to write the magical glyphs in alphabetical order on a scroll, and for the individual in question to wear it on her person.[34]

3. *KOLMOSIN ORI'EL* (*NURI'EL*):
Alphabets of *Oriel*

Version 1[35]   Version 2[36]

The "Alphabet of *Ori'el* [*Nuri'el*]" is employed as an aid to the fulfilment of whatsoever required purpose. As in the case of most *Kameot*, this alphabet is written on clean parchment, and carried on the person of the one requiring this spiritual support.[37] A similar use is made of the "Alphabet of the Heavenly Hosts" of which more *anon*.

4. *K'TAV AVAR HA-NEHAR*:
Passing the River Alphabet

Version 1[38]	Version 2[39]	Version 3[40]	Version 4[41]

ך	◻	◻	◻	◻
ל	◻	◻	◻	◻
ם	◻	◻	◻	◻
ן	◻	◻	◻	◻
ס	◻	◻	◻	◻
ע	◻	◻	◻	◻
ף	◻	◻	◻	◻
ץ	◻	◻	◻	◻
ק	◻	◻	◻	◻
ר	◻	◻	◻	◻
ש	◻	◻	◻	◻
ת	◻	◻	◻	◻

In the current instance, the variations between the first three versions of the "Passing the River" alphabet are fairly minor. The most prominent variances appear to be between the different representations of the *Shin* symbols. It is quite clearly related to the Hebrew letter, with minor differences of presentation at the hands of different scribes. The same can be said of the *Alef* symbol which is clearly a recognisable representation of the glyph it is meant to represent.

It would seem that over time magical glyphs representing Hebrew letters became more fanciful. In this regard, the fourth version of the current alphabet is very ornate. Whilst this version of the "Passing the River" alphabet appeared in a much later text than the first three listed versions, there is a curious factor regarding the title of the alphabet in question. In this instance the author titled it the "Alphabet of *Abraham*."[42] I perused a primary Hebrew manuscript in which the same alphabet is named "*ha-Kolmos Avraham ha-Ivri*" (Alphabet of Abraham the Hebrew):[43]

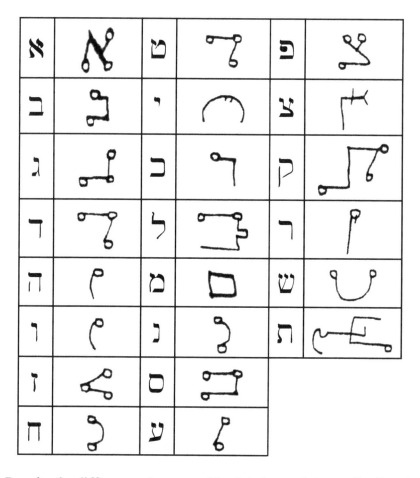

Despite the differences between this alphabet and the earlier listed "Passing the River" alphabets, as well as the practical difficulties arising therefrom, e.g. the use of the same signs to represent more than one Hebrew glyph, it is obvious that all of these alphabets were derived from the same basic source.

5. *K'TAV HA-MALACHIM*:
Alphabet of the Angelic Messengers

	Format 1[44]	Format 2[45]	Format 3[46]	Format 4[47]
א				
ב				
ג				
ד				
ה				
ו				
ז				
ח				

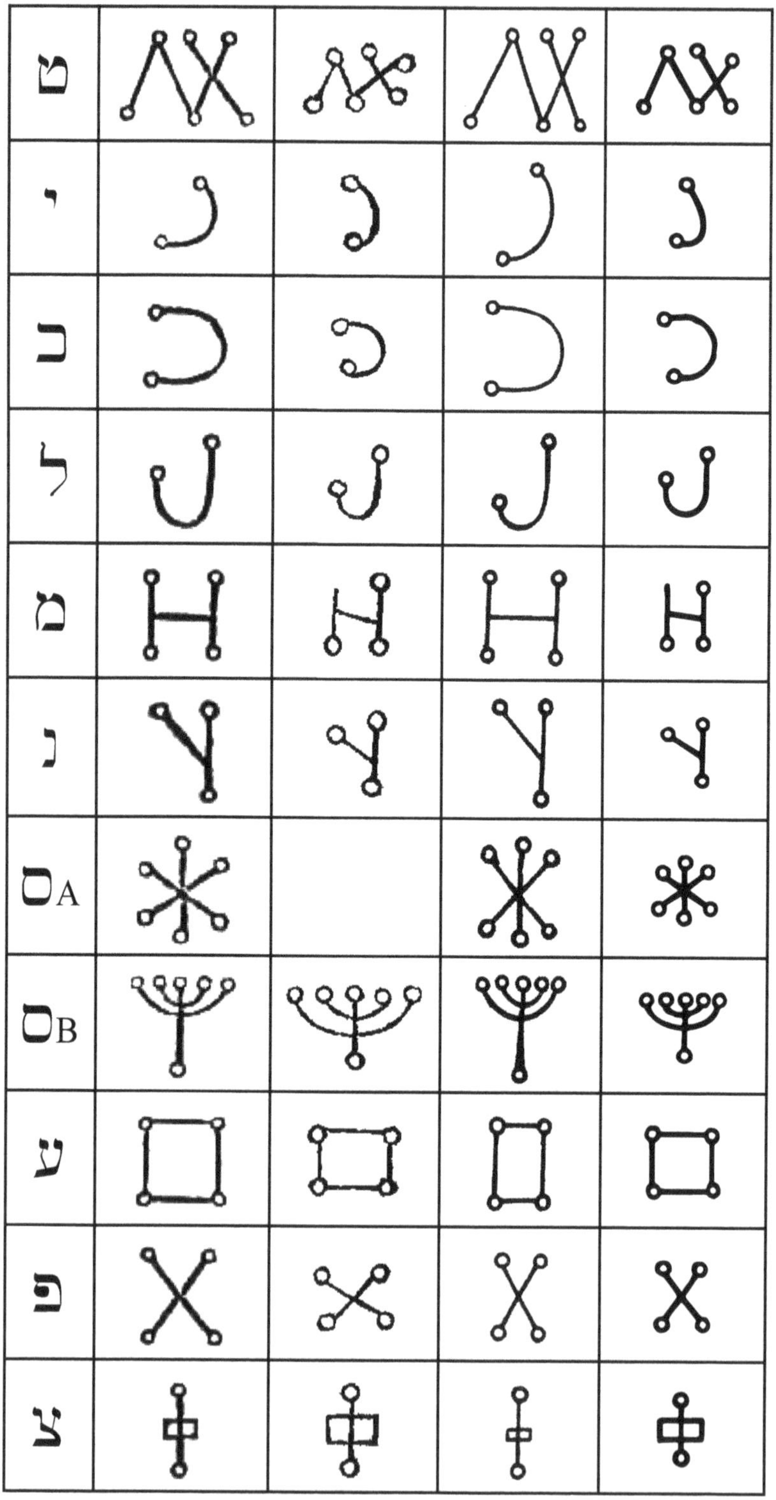
ט
י
כ
ל
מ
נ
ס A
ס B
ע
פ
צ

ק	(glyph)	(glyph)	(glyph)	(glyph)
ר	(glyph)	(glyph)	(glyph)	(glyph)
שׁ	(glyph)	(glyph)	(glyph)	(glyph)
ת	(glyph)	(glyph)	(glyph)	(glyph)

It would seem that several of the magical glyphs comprising the *Malachim* alphabet, closely resemble the same found in the *Kolmosin Micha'el* and the *Alpha-Beta shel Metatron*. Also, comparing the four formats of the alphabet in question, it is clear that, despite the very minor difference in the presentation of the magical glyph representing כ in the second (Bartolocci) and fourth (contemporary) formats, as well as the absence of the first magical glyph for the letter ם in the second list, all four presentations are identical and were again derived from the same source, i.e. Cornelius Agrippa.[48] Regarding the latter author, there have been several suggestions as to whence he derived the versions of the magical alphabets appearing in his writings, some claiming the *Picatrix*[49] to be the original source.

Whilst the latter text comprises delineations of amulets and talismans, and references to certain magical glyphs of similar format to some of those appearing in the "Heavenly Alphabets," I have not found direct reference to any of the complete magical alphabets listed by Agrippa, most of these appearing in the oft mentioned *Shoshan Yesod Olam*.[50]

It is however clear, as Moshe Idel and other scholars noted, that the *Picatrix* had a "profound influence" on "Renaissance magic,"[51] and there are indeed direct correlations between certain magical glyphs appearing in both the *Picatrix* and Jewish magical literature. After all, the *Picatrix* was translated into Hebrew in an abbreviated format under the title "*Tachlit he-Chacham*" ("Aim of the Wise"),[52] which is said to have "significantly influenced Jewish circles in the 14th and 15th centuries."[53] This certainly suggests the *Picatrix* as a primary source in certain Jewish magical traditions.

Be that as it may, the following magical alphabet is equally assigned to celestial messengers:[54]

6. *K'TAV TZ'VA HA-SHAMAYIM*:
Alphabet of the Heavenly Hosts

א	[symbol]	ט	[symbol]	פ	[symbol]
ב	[symbol]	י	[symbol]	צ	[symbol]
ג	[symbol]	כ	[symbol]	ק	[symbol]
ד	[symbol]	ל	[symbol]	ר	[symbol]
ה	[symbol]	מ	[symbol]	ש	[symbol]
ו	[symbol]	נ	[symbol]	ת	[symbol]
ז	[symbol]	ס	[symbol]		
ח	[symbol]	ע	[symbol]		

As suggested by its title, the "Alphabet of the Heavenly Hosts" is said to be good for invoking the "Angelic Hosts" in support of all purposes. In this regard, those intending to employ this alphabet are required to fast and be purified, while also covering their skin with a pure virgin body wax. Following this purification, the magical alphabet is inscribed on a deerskin scroll, and thereafter worn on their person.[55]

7. *ALFA BETA SHEL METATRON*:
Alphabet of *Metatron*[56]

Gershom Scholem, the late great scholar of Jewish Mysticism, maintained the "Alphabet of Metatron, the celestial scribe," to be the oldest of these angelic alphabets, which he mentioned "is preserved in many manuscripts and came to the German Hasidim with the Babylonian Merkabah material."[57]

Now, whilst the *"Alphabet of Metatron"* is perhaps more employed for mystical/contemplative rather than magical/talismanic purposes, I believe a closer investigation of the form of its component glyphs indicates that these magical alphabets are not composed of randomly chosen signs. In fact, judging the detailed analysis of this alphabet in a commentary which Scholem thought might have "derived from the pen of Eleazar of Worms,"[58] it appears that each glyph is loaded with meaning.

Unfortunately detailed delineations of Hebrew based magical alphabets are rare, and since we have really only one such analysis of a magical alphabet, i.e. the *"Alphabet of Metatron,"*[59] which was written by an anonymous author some centuries back, we are still in the dark as to the primary reasoning behind the construction of most of these magical alphabets. Notwithstanding this, we can get greater clarity from a closer perusal of the *"Alpha Beta shel Metatron,"* regarding which we find the following details.[60] The information shared here does not comprise a full translation of the text in question, but merely a description of some of the relevant material:

(*Alef*) We are reminded that the "Ten Commandments" commence with א (*Alef*), i.e. אנכי יהוה אלהיך (*Anochi YHVH Elohecha* —"I am the Lord thy God") (*Exodus 20:2*). We are also told that those who fulfil this and every other letter of the law, will after their demise be led into paradise by the archangel *Metatron*. It is said this awesome Spirit Intelligence will clothe those who are worthy, with eight raiments of the *Shechinah*, i.e. the feminine aspect of Divinity.

Curiously enough, in the *"Alphabet of Metatron"* the glyph for the letter *Alef* comprises eight endings, six of which are said to represent the six directions, three opposite three, i.e. East—West, North—South, Above—Below, plus a further two said to indicate the Unique Holy One beyond time, space and events, the "One" who encompasses everything above and all below.

We are also told that the four groupings and eight endings of the lines comprising the current magical glyph for *Alef*, denote the "Throne of Glory" resting on the four *Chayot ha-Kodesh* (Holy Living Creatures), each of which has four faces and four wings. In this regard we read in *Ezekiel 1:6*:

וארבעה פנים לאחת וארבע כנפים לאחת להם

Transliteration:

v'arba'ah fanim l'echat v'arba k'nafayim l'achat lahem

Translation:

And every one had four faces, and every one of them had four wings.

The four "faces" and four "wings" are said to be represented by the eight endings of the magical glyph for the letter *Alef*. However, this very letter indicates the absolute oneness of the Eternal One, as expressed in the *Shema* (*Deuteronomy 6:4*) reading:

שמע ישראל יהוה אלהינו יהוה אחד

Transliteration:

Shmah Yisra'el, YHVH Eloheinu, YHVH Echad

Translation:

Hear, O Israel, *YHVH* our Lord, *YHVH* is One.

(*Bet*) The magical glyph for the letter ‏ב‎ (*Bet*) comprises four endings, three reaching upwards and the fourth downwards. In this regard, we are informed that the Divine One established three of the four borders of the manifested universe, i.e. East, West and South, and that he kept the North unbounded in order to instruct an arrogant monarch, who might consider himself to be a god, that the Divine Creator (‏בורא‎—*Borei*) set bounds for the three listed quarters, and that the insolent human ruler should validate his power by wrapping up the fourth.

We are informed that the four endings have a further significance. In this regard, we are told that after we utter the *Shema* (*Shmah Yisra'el, YHVH Eloheinu, YHVH Echad* —"Hear, O Godwrestler, *YHVH* Our God, *YHVH* is One") (*Deuteronomy*

6:4), and formulate Divine Sovereignty over all four *ruchot* (winds/directions) of the earth, i.e. North, South, East and West, we bless the handiwork of the Almighty One. Starting with the letter *Bet*, we verbalise the phrase *Baruch shem k'vod malchuto l'olam va'ed* (ברוך שם כבוד מלכותו לעולם ועד—"Blessed be the Name of His glorious Kingdom throughout eternity"). This is said to affirm the Talmudic statement (*Berachot 13b*) that "once you have declared Him king over all that is above and below and over the four quarters of heaven, no more is required."

(*Gimel*) We are told that the letter ג (*Gimel*) refers to גדול (*Gadol*—"greatness"), regarding which it is written (*Psalm 147:5*):

גדול אדונינו ורב כח לתבונתו אין מספר

Transliteration:
> *Gadol adoneinu v'rav koach lit'vonato ein mispar*

Translation:
> Great is our Lord, and mighty in power; His understanding is infinite.

The three-pronged shape of the current magical glyph for the letter *Gimel* is said to represent a bow and arrow, and we are reminded that a bow comprises three forms, i.e. the bow, the string and the arrow. Hence, the letter *Gimel* also stands for גיבור (*Gibor*—"Mighty"). In this regard, the "*Pirkei Avot*" (4:1) informs us that individuals who are truly "mighty" are those who can control their personal impulses.[61]

(*Dalet*) The magical glyph for the letter ד (*Dalet*) comprises four corners, each crowned with a circlet. The number aligns with the *gematria* of *Dalet* which is four. In delineating the magical glyph, we are told that it comprises four extensions, a descending line extending from top right to bottom left, and two "openings" respectively at the top and bottom of the image. The latter reminds us that the residence of the rich man should have a minimum of two entrances to allow easy thoroughfare for the poor דל (*Dal*—"poor"). It is understood that our very success in life depends on our kindness to the lowly. In fact, the diagonal line extending from upper right corner to the bottom left of the magical glyph, indicates the blessings and abundance the Divine One extends to those who support the poor. In this regard we are told אשרי משכיל אל דל (*ashrei maskil el dal*—"Happy is he that considereth the poor") (*Psalm 41:1* [2]).

The two openings in the magical glyph, and the foursquare form of the design, are said to refer to the openings and measure of ones house, of which any floorspace of 4 (*Dalet*) by 4 (*Dalet*) or more cubits necessitates a *Mezuzah*. I have addressed the amuletic virtues of the latter item in a previous volume.[62] In this regard, Joshua Trachtenberg noted that the *Mezuzah* "retained its original significance as an amulet despite rabbinic efforts to make it an exclusively religious symbol."[63] As it is, we are informed that all homes with *Mezuzot* are filled with the Presence of the Divine One, protecting it against dangers of all kind.

(*Heh*) Regarding the current magical glyph for the letter ה (*Heh*), we are told its shape pertains to the world having been created out of this letter. This statement is substantiated by a special interpretation of *Genesis 2:4* reading:

אלה תולדות השמים והארץ בהבראם

Transliteration:
> *Eleh toldot ha-shamayim v'ha-aretz b'hibar'am*

Translation:
> These are the generations of the heaven and of the earth when they were created.

In the current instance the concluding fifth term in the phrase, i.e. בהבראם [*b'hibar'am*], is interpreted בה" בראם (*b'Heh baram*) which translates "they created with *Heh*." Similarly to the magical glyph for the previous letter, the current glyph has two openings, i.e. upper and lower, and four corners, the latter said to indicate the four *ruchot* (directions), i.e. East, West, North and South. In this instance we are informed regarding the two openings, that after death the worthy individual is directed into *Gan Eden* (Garden of Eden) via the narrow upper opening. However, undeserving individuals are directed via the wide lower opening into *Gehinom* (a locale of rectification). This is said to be reflected in *Isaiah 5:14* reading:

לכן הרחיבה שאול נפשה ופערה פיה לבלי חק

Transliteration:
> *La-chen hir'chivah sh'ol naf'shah u'fa'arah fiha livli chok*

Translation:
> Therefore the nether-world (*She'ol*) hath enlarged her desire, and opened her mouth without measure.

Be that as it may, we are told that the magical glyph for *Heh* is open above and below in order to show that everything in manifestation is changeable, and that a man granted with dignity and wealth, could lose everything when in his pride he raises himself above his fellow humankind. In this regard we are reminded in *Proverbs 16:5*

תועבת יהוה כל גבה לב

Transliteration:
> *To'avat YHVH kol g'vah lev*

Translation:
> Every one that is proud in heart is an abomination to *YHVH*.

Thus the Divine One brings the haughty down, and raises up the lowly as said in *Psalms 75:7 [8]*:

כי אלהים שפט זה ישפיל וזה ירים

Transliteration:
> *Ki Elohim shofet zeh yashpil v'zeh yarim*

Translation:
> For *Elohim* is judge; He putteth down one, and lifteth up another.

(*Vav*) The current magical glyph for ו (*Vav*) is said to be comprised of two horizontal "sticks," which, with a link from one to the other, indicate steps ascending a lofty mountain. Regarding the latter, we are informed that the Israelites received the *Torah* on the sixth day of the month *Sivan*, six being the numerical value of *Vav*, and legend further has it that the Holy One held Mount Sinai over their heads and told them to either accept the *Torah* or have the mountain burying them. After all, tradition informs us that the Almighty created the world in six days for the sake of the *Torah* alone.

Whatever you may believe, or not believe, regarding the biblical saga of creation, the four endings of the magical glyph for the letter *Vav* are said to refer the vastness of the *Torah* which transcends that of the four directions of space, i.e. East, West, North and South, as emphasised in *Job 11:9* reading:

ארכה מארץ מדה ורחבה מני ים

Transliteration:
    Arukah mei-eretz midah ur'chavah mini yam
Translation:
    The measure thereof is longer than the earth, and broader than the sea.

(*Zayin*) We are told the magical glyph for the letter ז (*Zayin*) reflects in some manner a foetus inside the womb, and similarly to a mother consuming foodstuffs in order to feed the unborn. The Divine One supplies the whole of creation, from the smallest to the greatest, with all kind (זן—*zan*) of nourishment.

Otherwise, the meaning of the name for the current letter is a "weapon" (זיין—*Zayin*). The three upper endings of the current magical glyph are said to protect the lower ending, like a man who is armed (מזויין—*m'zuyan*). In this regard, studious study of the *Torah* is said to be a safeguard against all manner of evil, and we are told in *Psalm 149:6*:

רוממות אל בגרונם וחרב פיפיות בידם

Transliteration:
    Rom'mot El big'ronam v'cherev pifiyot b'yadam
Translation:
    Let the high praises of *El* [God] be in their mouth, and a two-edged sword in their hand.

(*Chet*) We are given the simplest delineation of the magical glyph for the letter ח (*Chet*). It is said to comprise surrounding "walls," these indicating those who are pious, who shut themselves off from the affairs of the world, and who are humble and maintain silence in the face of all humiliation and persecution. We are informed that to be truly worthy, such individuals are to maintain a simple lifestyle in a simple dwelling ("tent"), avoiding all the worldly temptations of the חצוף (*Chatzuf*—"insolent").

Whilst I have no issue with being humble in ones person, I do not buy any of this stern, pietistic, and overtly patronizing rhetoric employed in the current interpretations of this and other glyphs of the *"Alpha Beta shel Metatron."* As far as I am concerned, the words of the unknown author in this instance comprise a lot of fundamentalist presumption and prejudiced innuendo regarding anyone not "officially" deemed "pious." In this regard I have time and again observed the so called "pious" employing "humility" to intimidate and manipulate all and sundry in their vicinity into eating "humble pie." Sadly adopting a humble stance is in many instances itself a form of self-aggrandisement, e.g. "there are none as humble [and as intolerant] as *we* are."

This being said, I am a believer in simplicity, i.e. to live sparingly in a chaste manner. However, even the term "chaste" in its purity is a dirty word these days, because people see the unpollutedness and cleanliness of the term to be without any form of happiness, but since when does happiness and joviality make a "chaste" person dirty? The interesting thing here is that most people see the word "chaste" to mean total abstinence from sex and other things called "impurities." This is totally the wrong idea. Firstly sexuality, eating and drinking are not in themselves steering towards impurities. The "impurities" are in the intentions of the user. Thus, as far as I am concerned, the term "chaste" means purity of intent and not abstinence. There is certainly a measure of restraint in being chaste, but there is nothing wrong in being restrained, since moderation ensures greater appreciation, greater enjoyment, and an understanding that life is not to be taken for granted.

As I noted elsewhere, "the 'Law' (*Torah*) which orthodox Judaism and *Kabbalah* keep harping on about so much, *was* and *is* in fact God. All the scriptures, writings, concepts, and so forth called *Torah* are only symbols for God, and intellectual symbols at that."[64] I have no doubt there are many remarkable "mystical mysteries" to be found in the Pentateuch, and, for that matter, in the whole of the Hebrew Bible. However, it is absolutely clear to me that "God indeed '*the Law of Life*,' and all the writings are only human opinions and beliefs about that Power, Energy, Control, or whatever you like to call *IT*."[65] I am again reminded of Edmond Fleg writing regarding the moment when the Divine One gave the *Torah* to the world, and then granted Moses a vision of distant future teachers. Moses queried "Lord, how is this thing possible? I do not recognise the *Torah* thou gavest me. Is that new *Torah* thy *Torah*?" He received the response, "There are fifty gateways of Understanding: I have opened for thee forty-nine, but the last is closed, for no man, even though he be Moses, can know everything. The *Torah* thou understandest hath a thousand senses which thou understandest not, and which others in the course of the ages will come to know: for in each century it will speak the language of that century; but what each century will find is already there, and each new *Torah* will still be my *Torah*."[66]

In this regard, I have written that "'studying Torah' did not necessarily mean pouring over ancient scrolls, but *Living the Law of Life*. In other words just living according to ones beliefs that God is living through you, and respecting God in the way you lived; but with typical literalness, many spend wasted time with their eyes glued to papyrus and parchment scrolls in the honest belief that they are 'studying *Torah*' as an ideal way of spending a whole lifetime."[67]

(*Tet*) Elucidation is somewhat obscure as far as the symbolical significance of the present magical glyph for the letter ט (*Tet*) is concerned. The indication is that it might refer to the toothed edge of a wall. However, we are informed that the shape comprises two hidden letters *Tet* at the top and three at the bottom. In this regard, it is said that the intimation is that the one who walks in humbleness and avoids all contention, will receive a threefold measure of goodness. This pertains to the injunction in *Proverbs 17:14* reading:

פוטר מים ראשית מדון ולפני התגלע הריב נטוש

Transliteration:

Poter mayim reishit madon v'lifnei hit'gala hariv netosh

Translation:

The beginning of strife is as when one letteth out water;
therefore leave off contention, before the quarrel break out.

As it is, the letter *Tet* is the initial of the word טוב (*Tov*—"good").
In this regard, we are again sternly admonished that at the end of
time the whole world will be judged, and whilst Israel will be
granted the blessing of goodness, all who are found to have acted
for personal benefit alone will suffer dire consequences for having
sinned in this manner.

In this regard, I have noted previously that "the old idea of
a touchy, ill-tempered God raging away at human antics because
those 'offended' His ideas of propriety, does not 'go over' any
more," and that "sin," as seen by modern eyes, refers to "wrongful
behaviour which damages us by the doing in such a way, that we
fail to achieve anything like the 'Intention of God' in ourselves for
our period of incarnation. Therefore, in 'falling short' of the mark
by so far, we hinder our progression toward 'Perfection' by that
much. In sinning against ourselves, we sin against the 'God-in-
us'."[68]

I also maintained "the old-time concepts of 'sin' as
intentional offenses against a God, who laid down arbitrary
dictates of behaviour, did not stand up very well in the light of
experience," and in this regard listed two axioms which I thought
were very revelatory.[69] The first is that "a thing is not just because
God wills it, but God wills it because it is just,"[70] and the second
is that "we are punished *by* our sins, not *for* them."[71] In fact, human
behaviour has become so complex that definite pronouncements no
longer apply to a great deal of it. All we can do is accept certain
overall codes of conduct as being best to observe amongst us for
the sake of general welfare. We might try our best to keep to those
codes, i.e. strike an average, and let individuals sort out their own
affairs, providing they do not hurt those who are undeserving of it.

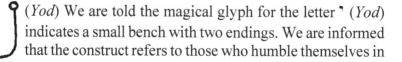 (*Yod*) We are told the magical glyph for the letter י (*Yod*)
indicates a small bench with two endings. We are informed
that the construct refers to those who humble themselves in

the physical world, and who deserve to inherit a lofty throne in the world to come. Regarding the biblical King David we are told ודוד הוא הקטן (*v'David hu ha-katan*—"And David was the youngest [literally 'smallest']") (*I Samuel 17:14*), and that this humbleness of the king earned him the most exalted status in the hereafter, regarding which it is related in *Psalm 89:36 [37]*:

וכסאו כשמש נגדי

Transliteration:
   v'chis'o kashemesh neg'di
Translation:
   and his throne as the sun before Me.

We are also reminded that even the Divine One selected from the entire Hebrew alphabet the smallest letter, i.e. י (*Yod*), to be the initial of the Ineffable Name, i.e. יהוה (*YHVH*).

(*Kaf*) The magical glyph for the letter כ (*Kaf*) is said to stand upright, and, like a monarch, it is wearing a crown. The *gematria* of *Kaf* is twenty. In this regard, we are told that there were twenty generations between our primal ancestor Adam and the patriarch Abraham, and that in this period there was no acknowledgment nor sanctification of the Divine Creator, that is until Abraham honoured and recognised the holiness of the Divine One. Hence he established the Covenant of Circumcision, and we are informed that he was granted the knowledge and wisdom of creation (*Yetzirah*). Tradition has it that the *Sefer Yetzirah*, the mystico-magical "Book of Creation," derived from Abraham.[72]

   Now, the rest of the jargon on the magical glyph for the letter *Kaf* pertains to the amount of lashes to be dished out in the afterlife to the wicked for their transgressions. In this regard, I refer to my earlier remarks regarding "sin" and "divine" punishment. Besides, I would think the worst pain of "hell" is, as a theological saying puts it, feeling ones own unworthiness of Heaven, i.e. the realisation that one has excluded oneself deliberately from the Divine Presence. In this regard, I do acknowledge the validity of the Kabbalistic teaching of "*Chibut ha-Kever*" (חבוט הקבר—"torment of the grave"),[73] but not in any way of it being understood as punishment inflicted upon us by the Divine One in person.

We are told that "The body begins to decompose soon after it is buried. The effect of watching this must be both frightening and painful. The Talmud teaches us, 'Worms are as painful to the dead as needles in the flesh of the living, as it is written, "his flesh grieves for him" (*Job 14:22*).' Most commentaries write that this refers to the psychological anguish of the soul in seeing its earthly habitation in a state of decay.

The Kabbalists call this '*Chibut ha-Kever*,' the punishment of the grave. We are taught that what happens to the body in the grave can be an even worse experience than *Gehenom*.

This varies among individuals. The more one is obsessed with one's body and the material world in general during his lifetime, the more he will be obsessed with it after death. For the person to whom the material was everything, this deterioration of the body is most painful.

On the other extreme, the person who was immersed in the spiritual may not care very much about the fate of his body at all. He finds himself very much at home in the spiritual realm and might quickly forget about his body entirely.....

Many of us think of death as a most frightening experience. *Tzaddikim*, on the other hand, have looked forward to it. Shortly before his death, Rabbi Nachman of Breslav said, 'I very much want to divest myself of this garment that is my body.'

If we truly believe and trust in a merciful God, then death has no terror for us....."[74]

Whilst our bodies are animals, it does not mean that we should be unkind to them. You should no more ill treat your own body, than you would beat any animal to death. Yet people persist in ill treating their bodies, bashing them about and scourging them. This is just sheer cruelty and abuse of a harmless, innocent creature, which does not help their evolution in the least. If we really befriend our bodies, we might well be freed eventually from the confinements of three dimensional existence. Some might think they are occupying a lump of meat, however one should at least try to befriend the "poor brute" and guide it along its path of progress on this planet. We certainly do not have to treat our bodies as gods, but at least we *should* treat them as friends.

From what I understand, ones actions sometimes result in "*klipot*" (demonic shards) attaching themselves to ones being, hence a "purification" process is required after death, in order to prepare the "Self" for "life to come" or rebirth. We should always keep in mind that distress leads to release. This is the penalty we have to bear in life and death, if "*Chibut ha-Kever*" is to be believed, and we should realise that there is only compensation in the "Divine Judgment" which we carry within ourselves.

Now, when it comes to dealing with those mentioned "demonic shards" which may have become attached to ones being, the traditional "beating" of the willow branches during *Rosh Hashanah* is, as it were, a kind of "sympathetic magic," the action being to drive away and untie oneself from *klipot*. I have observed this procedure being delineated a "lightening of *Chibut ha-Kever*." In this regard, it appears the "beating of the willows" to be somewhat akin to the practice of *Tashlich*, the latter referring to "casting" ones "sins" upon the waters of a running stream. Collectively these actions pertain to breaking the "ties that bind." A similar intention is behind the Kabbalistic *Agala'a* fire ritual enacted on *Erev Rosh Hashanah*.[75]

A related and somewhat easier practice in terms of execution, is the very assertive chanting of the "*Shem Vayisa Vayet*" conjoined with the Name *Agala'a*, e.g. *Agala'a Vehu Yeli Sit Elem Mahash Lelah Agala'a; Agala'a Achah Kahet Hezi Elad Lav Hahah Agala'a; Agala'a Yezel Mebah Hari Hakem Lav Keli Agala'a; etc*. However, I am not informed regarding the employment of any amulets one might carry on ones person as a protection against "*Chibut ha-Kever*." However, I do know that there was (and perhaps still is) a custom in which the Name קרע (*KaRo'*), the third three-letter portion of the "Forty-Two Letter Name," was written on a piece of parchment, which was afterwards stuck up the nose of a corpse so as to protect the deceased individual from the afflictions of "*Chibut ha-Kever*" and from going to "hell." As mentioned elsewhere, this practice is somewhat meaningless to me, since "I do not buy into the idea of 'hell' *per se*."[76] However, as indicated, I do believe in a posthumous purification process as far as the "Self" is concerned, and also concede "that there may indeed be parties interested in saving family and friends from a presumed infernal destiny in the hereafter" by sticking amulets up the nostrils of their cadavers![77]

(*Lamed*) The magical glyph for the letter ל (*Lamed*) is said to represent the crown of a king. In this regard, we are informed that those who are studying (למד—*Lamed*) *Torah*, and who are controlling their darker passions, so to speak, will be granted an exalted status befitting a king as well as a crown in the world to come, similarly to the biblical Joseph who, by controlling his emotional self, was granted rulership and a crown by the Pharaoh of Egypt.

We are reminded that the letter *Lamed* is located in the Hebrew alphabet between כ (*Kaf*) and מ (*Mem*). When read in reverse, the combination spells מלך (*Melech*—King).

(*Mem*) We are told that the magical glyph for the letter מ (*Mem*) represents an empty womb. We are also reminded that the numerical value of this letter is forty since the womb remains empty after conception for around forty days when the foetus starts to take on a definite shape. We are further informed that this magical glyph indicates an empty stomach, referring to Moses having maintained a fast for forty days during the period he remained in the celestial realms during his reception of the *Torah*.

On the other hand, the meaning of the letter *Mem* is "water" (מים—*Mayim*), and it is said that the current magical glyph symbolizes a pool which requires the exact amount of forty "*seahs*" (measures) to qualify as a *Mikveh* (ritual bath).

(*Nun*) The magical glyph for the letter נ (*Nun*) is said to symbolize a shield. In this regard, we are enjoined יתהלל הגבור בגבורתו (*yit'halel ha-gibor big'vurato* —"Let not the mighty man glory in his might") (*Jeremiah 9:22* [*23*]), and that he should rather trust in the One who is Awesome (נורא—*Nora*), Almighty God.

In the current instance the magical glyph is said to be a "shield" with three endings, i.e. two on top and one below. "shield." The upper two endings are said to refer respectively to two biblical figures, i.e. the Patriarch Abraham and King David, who were granted Divine protection. In this regard, the Eternal

One told our father Abraham אנכי מגן לך (*Anochi magen lach*—"I am thy shield") (*Genesis 15:1*), and King David exclaimed מגני וקרן ישעי (*magini v'keren yish'i*—"my shield and my horn of salvation") (*Psalm 18:2* [3]).

On the other hand, we are informed that the three endings of the current magical glyph refer to the first three letters of the Ineffable Name, i.e. יהו (*YHV*), which were engraved on the impregnable shield of King David conjointly with the opening phrase of *Exodus 15:11* reading מי כמכה באלם יהוה (*Mi chamochah ba'elim YHVH*—"Who is like unto Thee *YHVH* among the mighty?"). The initial letters of the four words comprising this phrase form the acronym מכבי (*Makabi*). In this regard, we are told that the last recipient of King David's shield was the great Judas Maccabeus (*Yehudah ha-Makabi*).

(*Samech*) The letter combination סמך (*Samech*) refers to the concept of sustaining or supporting. This is said to pertain to the statement סומך יהוה לכל הנפלים (*Somech YHVH l'chol ha-noflim*—"*YHVH* upholdeth all that fall") (*Psalm 145:14*). In this regard, we are told that the magical glyph for the letter *Samech* represents a tree extending its fresh green leafy branches.

We are also told that whilst the magical symbol for the letter *Samech* is upright, it appears to be pierced by an arrow. In this regard, we are informed that Pharaoh pursued the Israelites after they departed Egypt, and that he fired arrows at them, but that the latter were swallowed up by the clouds protecting the Israelites all round (סביב סביב—*Saviv saviv*).

(*Ayin*) The magical glyph for the letter ע (*Ayin*) is said to comprise two parallel horizontal bars. These, we are told, pertain to Moses and Aaron who confronted the Egyptian sorcerers whose magical activities were illusions meant to deceive the eye (עין—*Ayin*). In this regard, we are told (*Exodus 7:12*):

וישליכו איש מטהו ויהיו לתנינם ויבלע מטה
אהרן את מטתם

Transliteration:

va-yashlichu ish matechu va-yih'yu l'taninim va-yivla mateh Aharon et matotam

Translation:

For they cast down every man his rod, and they became serpents; but Aaron's rod swallowed up their rods.

We are informed that in the Hebrew alphabet the letter order נ (*Nun*), ס (*Samech*), ע (*Ayin*) reminds us of this miracle (סנ—*Nes*), by means of which the trickery worked on the eye (ע—*Ayin*) is exposed.

(*Peh*) We are told the magical glyph for the letter פ (*Peh*) represents an open bucket, representing something like a divine cornucopia by means of which the Eternal One provides (פרנס—*Pirnes*), an infinite flow of abundance to the whole of manifestation, like the miracle foodstuffs, i.e. the daily manna, quails, and a wellspring afforded the Israelites during their long sojourn in the desert. In fact, these miraculous substances are said to be represented by the three endings of the magical glyph.

As it is, the word פה (*Peh*), the name of the letter in question, means a "mouth," the organ of eating but also of speaking. Regarding the latter ability, we are informed that a real savant is a wellspring of wisdom, whose *Torah* elucidations motivate a descent of the *Shechinah*, i.e. the Divine Presence and "face" of the Almighty to descend on his or her person. This is because a Spirit Messenger (angel) affords the wise one endless insights.

(*Tzadi*) The magical glyph for the letter צ (*Tzadi*) is said to be a kind of walled stronghold which could be accessed via a side entrance (*Petach*—"opening"). In this regard a *Tzadik*, i.e. a righteous individual, is said to constantly alternate between two entrances, i.e. the one to the synagogue and the other to the "House of Study." Considering some of the sentiments I expressed earlier, that "*Torah* Study" means "living the law of life," I "naturally" think it quite "unnatural" and even "ungodly" to cut oneself off from the natural world. After all, the very beauty which we see in this world *is* in fact God, and acknowledging beauty is a most sacred act.[78]

In this regard, we are told that "when you desire to eat or drink, or to fulfill other worldly desires, and you focus your awareness on the love of God, then you elevate that physical desire to spiritual desire. Thereby you draw out the holy spark that dwells within. You bring forth holy sparks from the material world. There is no path greater than this. For wherever you go and whatever you do—even mundane activities—you serve God."[79] We are further reminded to "use the things of the world to recognize No-thing. By this I mean, approach everyday life as an ongoing opportunity for raising the sparks. Take a micro-moment for establishing a meditative attitude, whether that moment be painful or joyous or neutral. Practice *hitbodedut* (meditation/all-one-ness) everywhere, at all times. When tempted away from righteousness by idleness, anger, or greed, let yourself listen to the sounds of that moment until you are all ear, nothing but listening. Wrap yourself in listening until even the still, small voice of the moment has vanished and there is No-thing there at all."[80]

 (*Kof*) It is said the magical glyph for the letter ק (*Kof*) represents a tree, and the *gematria* of this Hebrew letter is one hundred. Regarding the latter we are reminded that Abraham fathered Isaac at the ripe old age of 100, and as far as the "tree" symbol of the magical glyph is concerned, we are informed that this refers to the thicket (tree) in which a ram was caught, and which was substituted as sacrifice in the place of his son. We are also told that the main portion of the magical glyph in question portrays a *shofar* (ram's horn), whilst the two side extensions refer to the two days when the *shofar* is sounded during *Rosh Hashanah* (New Year), for all to hear its קול (*Kol* —"voice").

(*Resh*) The magical image for the letter ר (*Resh*) is said to represent a boat with a mast. In this regard, we encounter the only magical instruction listed in the dissertation on the magical "*Alpha Beta shel Metatron*."[81]

We are told that in summer *Rahav* (רהב), who is the angel of the sea, would allow foul smells to surface the waters — methane perhaps! Seeping into boats this would kill all and sundry on them. However, we are instructed that invoking the Divine Name אדירירון (*Adiriron*) would forthwith dispel the nasty odour. We are also informed that invocation of this Divine Name calms the violent storms of winter.

Regarding the Divine Name אדירירון (*Adiriron*), I noted previously that this is an ancient Divine Name the meaning of which is said to be "The Mighty One sings," and that this Name is called the "Name of Joy" or the "Name of glad song" (רנה—*rinah*).[82] *Adiriron* is associated with the word אדיר (*adir*—"mighty").

I also noted that the Name "*Adiriron* is utilised both in Hebrew amulets and magical incantations, and is considered particularly efficacious as a protection against demonic forces." Hence we are informed that "whosoever builds a new house and yard, lest he come to any bodily harm he must write the great name *Adiriron Adiron* (אדירירון אדירון) on deerskin parchment and place it on the door of each and every room. And it is best to write this on a Sunday, Thursday or a Friday. And he must drill a hole and place the same in the doorway both from above and from the side."[83]

(*Shin*) The magical glyph for the letter ש (*Shin*) is said to indicate a very deep wellspring gushing forth an abundance of water which spills over its edges. In this regard, there is the saga of King David digging pits on the side of the Holy Altar, and in the process unleashing subterranean waters which were surfacing and which might inundate the world. We are told that the King wrote the Divine Name on a shard which he cast into the depths in order to halt the threat and seal the opening of the depths.

Be that as it may, we are told that the letter *Shin* is the initial of the Divine Name שדי (*Shadai*), and that the five endings of the magical glyph representing this letter, refer to the five cubicles of the *Tefilin* (phylacteries). Regarding the latter we are reminded that there are four in the phylactery tied to the forehead, and only one in the phylactery tied to the left forearm.

(*Tav*) The magical glyph for the letter ת (*Tav*) comprises three vertical bars crossing a horizontal line, and there are altogether eight endings in the glyph. In this regard we are informed that the two outer verticle lines represent the two handles of a *Torah* scroll, and the centre line the reader. At the conclusion of perusing its contents, the scroll is wound and enclosed in a beautiful mantle-cover. The latter is symbolized by the horizontal bar in the current magical glyph.

We are also instructed that the three vertical lines represent the threefold division of the *Tanach* (Sacred Scriptures): תורה (*Torah*—Pentateuch), נביאים (*N'vi'im*—Prophets) and כתובים (*Ketuvim*—Writings). The "Prophets" section of the Hebrew Bible comprises eight books, which are said to be symbolized by the eight endings of the magical glyph of the letter *Tav*. We are informed that the Divine One autographs his name with this Hebrew letter, since it stands for אמת (*Emet*—"Truth").

In conclusion, I should make it clear that the investigation into certain Magical Alphabets based on the Hebrew alphabet which I have shared in this tome, does not comprise a complete study. I have not listed all such alphabets, but merely shared what I thought might be useful to anyone interested in a more detailed delineation of this topic than what is generally available to date. I have also addressed only some of the practical applications of these alphabets for the betterment of day to day existence on this planet.

B. *Chotamot* (Magical Seals)

As seen in the many *Kameot* as well as other related written incantations which have survived the travails of time, there have been over the centuries numerous amulets constructed, in which glyphs from the magical alphabets feature prominently.[84] In certain instances we might recognise some of the "magical letters" employed, but, as said, it is generally quite difficult to ascertain their exact meaning, or, for that matter, the reasoning behind the employment of such signs in a particular amulet.

That being said, it is absolutely clear that there always was, and still is, a fundamental reason for the employment of any "magical glyph" in Hebrew amulets, and whilst in many instances we may not be able to ascertain the exact meaning of these signs, they are located in an amulet to trigger spiritual potencies in alignment with the fundamental purpose of the amulet, i.e. protection, healing, success, etc. Here are a set of amulets comprised of glyphs derived from the "Angelic Alphabets."

The first one appears in the "*Sefer Raziel.*"[85] It has been reproduced in a number of tomes dealing with Hebrew amulets, and I have elected to include it here as well because it pertains to a fundamental factor of human existence, i.e. finding love, grace, loving-kindness and mercy. *Kameot* dealing with such matters obviously rank amongst the most popular, hence the inclusion of this amulet for finding favour. In this regard, the instruction is to write an adjuration and a set of magical seals on a kosher deerskin scroll. As mentioned elsewhere, a clean sheet of parchment or good quality paper will suffice. The adjuration reads:

בשמך דחנינא וחסד יהוה בעולם יהיה חסדך יהו על
[פלוני בן פלוני] כשם שהיה עם יוסף הצדיק שנעמר
ויהי יהוה את יוסף ויט עליו חסד ויתן את חנו בעיני
כל רואיו בשם מיכאל גבריאל רפאל אוריאל כבשיאל
יה יה יה יה יה יה יה אהיה אהה אהה אהה יהו יהו יהו
יהו יהו יהו יהו יהו יה

Transliteration:

> *b'shimcha d'chanina v'chesed YHVH b'olam yiyeh chasdecha YHV al [.....Ploni ben Ploni.....] keshem shehayah im Josef ha-tzadik shene'emar va-y'hi YHVH et Josef (Genesis 39:2) vayet alaiv chesed v'yiten et chono b'enei kol ro'av b'shem Micha'el Gavri'el Rafa'el Ori'el Kavshi'el YH YH YH YH YH YH YH Ehyeh AHH AHH AHH YHV YHV YHV YHV YHV YHV YHV YHV YH*

Translation:

> In your name of grace and loving-kindness *YHVH* of the universe, bestow your kindness *YHV* upon [.....fill in the name of the recipient.....] in the same way it was with Joseph the righteous, as it is said 'and *YHVH* was with Joseph' (*Genesis 39:2*), and bestowed mercy on him and

granted him to find favour in the eyes of all who saw him. In the name of *Micha'el Gavri'el Rafa'el Ori'el Kavshi'el YH YH YH YH YH YH YH Ehyeh AHH AHH AHH AHH YHV YHV YHV YHV YHV YHV YHV YHV YH.*[86]

The mentioned set of magical glyphs are included below the adjuration, these being:

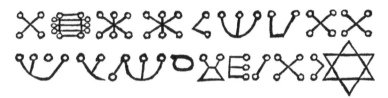

Whilst it appears the magical signs in this *Kamea* were derived from "magical alphabets," in the main they are very difficult to decipher. Be that as it may, the reference to "grace" in this amulet is an important one in Hebrew amulets, in which the Hebrew word חן (*chen*— "gracefulness") features very prominently and is often conjoined with the word חסד (*chesed*—"loving-kindness"). Both these terms are linked to the "heart" in *Kabbalah*, hence a number of *Kameot* said to affect this specific organ of the human anatomy, pertain to being granted "grace and loving-kindness." This is the fundamental objective of the earlier addressed *Machshavah* amulets the fundamental intention of which is "opening the heart."

This is equally the purpose of the following "magical seals" said to be good for matters of the "heart," and there are certainly many *Kameot* composed to engender "love." In this regard, it is understood that "love" equally equates with "grace" and "kindness," hence *Kameot* meant to effectuate love also incorporate references to gracefulness and loving-kindness, as indicated in the next set of amulets. As it is, the following amulet is for love, grace and loving-kindness,[87] and all seeking to increase these qualities in their lives should simply write the following seals on parchment, or a clean sheet of paper, and carry it on their person:

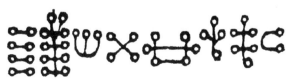

In the next amulet for finding favour and love in the eyes of specific individuals, the magical procedure is somewhat more intricate. In this instance you are required to write the following magical seals on the palm of your right hand:

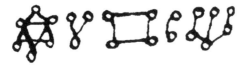

Afterwards the hand with the writing is wiped on your face as you simultaneously say ten times ונח מצא חן בעיני יהוה (*v'noach matza chen b'enei YHVH*—"and Noah found grace in the eyes of *YHVH*") [*Genesis 6:8*]. Continue the procedure by uttering the following adjuration:

יהי רצון מלפניך שתתנני לחן ולחסד בעיני [פלוני בן
פלוני]

Transliteration:
> *Y'hi ratzon milfanecha shetitneni l'chen v'l'chesed b'enei [.....Ploni ben Ploni.....]*

Translation:
> May it be your will that I will find grace and loving-kindness in the eyes of [.....fill in the Name.....]

Conclude the action by rinsing your hand in a bowl of water, and then imbibe this infused liquid. One final instruction remains. We are told that each time you should find yourself in the presence of the individual whose name you mentioned in your adjuration, i.e. the one from whom you are seeking favour and kindness, look at the palm of your right hand and say זמן פרעון אוריאל (*Z'man peira'on Ori'el*—"Payback time *Ori'el*").[88]

The next amulet pertains to restoring affection between two friends. In this regard, we are told that when a conflict ensues between yourself and a friend, that you should write the following *chotamot* (magical seals) on a piece of parchment, which is afterwards tied to your arm:

We are told that the friend will neither have peace nor find rest, until the matter is resolved and the friendship restored.[89]

Now, the following seal pertains to being "in love," or to affection of the "mating" kind. In this instance, when a woman openly expresses her desire for a man, he could affirm and, as it were, "seal" that attraction by first writing the following seals on his hand:

This is followed by placing the hand comprising the writing on her head. We are told that "then she will have you."[90] I would say if both parties wanted each other that badly, they could certainly "have" each other without any further ado! I suppose one might say these seals and actions set the right mood and energy like a spiritual aphrodisiac.....so to speak!

On the other hand, we are informed that when a husband suspects his wife of infidelity and desires her to "tell all," he should write the following *chotamot* on his left hand, afterwards placing it on her heart:[91]

We are told the lady in question will pour out her heart, revealing her every action. It is said the situation may be resolved, by her submitting to a period of around ten days of deliberate fasting and purification with fully focussed intent. Obviously this entire action pertains to a very forgiving husband.

Regarding magical seals the fundamental purpose of which pertains to the generation of love of the more emotional/physical kind, a fair number can be traced in primary Jewish magical texts, amongst others the following famous one of which various versions can be found in primary Jewish magical literature:[92]

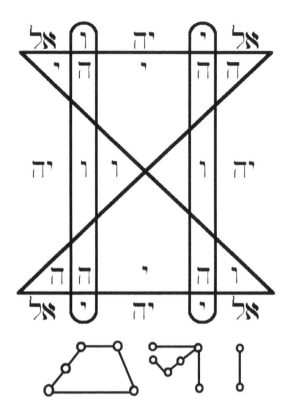

These "magical seals" are employed to kindle or rekindle love between a husband and wife, or between one individual and another. We are instructed to write *Deuteronomy 6:5* at the very top of the amulet:

ואהבת את יהוה אלהיך בכל לבבך ובכל נפשך ובכל
מאדך

Transliteration:
> *v'ahavta et YHVH eloheicha b'chol l'vav'cha uv'chol nafsh'cha u'v'chol m'odecha*

Translation:
> And thou shalt love *YHVH* thy God with all thy heart, and with all thy soul, and with all thy might.

Below this is written the following adjuration, which includes the names of a set of Spirit Intelligences in charge of Love, of which the following arrangement is said to be correct:[93]

יהי רצון מלפניך יהוה אלהי ואלהי אבותי שתשלח
מלאכיך הקדושים הממונים על אהבה פתצשא תא
הוהי כיהלא שלך כששל פשלך טובל שישימו אהבה
ואחוה בין [פלוני בן פלוני] ובין [פלוני בן פלוני]
ולא תהיה להם שנאה ולא קנאה ולא תחרות ולא
קטטה ולא דבר רע ולא לב רע אלא לב שלם ולב
טוב ואהבה ואחוה שלום וריעות מעתה ועד עולם
אמן נצח סלה ועד

Transliteration:

> *Y'hi ratzon milfanecha YHVH Elohai v'Elohei avotai
> shetishlach malachecha ha-kadoshim ha-memonim al
> ahavah PTTzShA TA HVHY KYHLA ShLCh KShShL
> PShLCh TVBL shiyasimu ahavah v'achvah bein [.....Ploni
> ben Ploni.....] u'vein [.....Ploni ben Ploni.....] v'lo tihyeh
> l'hem sin'ah v'lo kin'ah v'lo tacharut v'lo k'tatah v'lo
> davar ra v'lo lev ra ela lev shalem v'lev tov v'ahavah
> v'achvah shalom v'rei'ut mei'atah v'ad olam Omein
> Netzach Selah Va'ed*

Translation:

> May it be your will *YHVH* my God, and God of my fathers,
> to send your Holy Angels in charge of love *PTTzShA TA
> HVHY KYHLA ShLCh KShShL PShLCh TVBL* to establish
> love and unity between [.....fill in the name of the first
> individual.....] and [.....fill in the name of the second
> individual.....], and they will not have hatred, and no
> jealousy, and no rivalry, and no quarrels, and no bad thing,
> and no bad heart, only a complete heart and a good heart,
> and love and unity and peace and friendship, from now
> unto eternity *Amen*, Enduring (Victory), *Selah*, Forever.

In conclusion, the "Magical Seal" is located on the reverse side of
the amulet.

Whilst this amulet may be somewhat complex in its
construction, the following three sets of "magical seals" are also
employed in *Kameot* to encourage physical love, and are easily
constructed. The first set is utilised in the strengthening of love
between married partners, or between a woman and a man. To
achieve this aim, the following *chotamot* (magical seals) should be
written by each one of the partners on sheets of clean, good quality

paper, which is afterwards exchanged between them, and respectively carried on their persons:[94]

The second set of magical seals is employed to engender a bond of love between one individual and another. In this regard, the instruction is for the individual seeking to engender love, to write on the second day of the week (Monday – Day of the Moon), his personal name and the name of his mother on the palm of his hand, i.e. "so and so son of so and so." Next, the name of the one in whom the fire of love is to be awakened, as well as the name of her mother, is likewise written on the palm of the same hand. This is concluded by adding the following magical seals to the writing. It is said that if the individual seeking love should afterwards put his hand on the one he desires, "he will be blessed" with affection.[95]

The third set is for a young lady seeking to be married. In this regard, the instruction is for her to write the following *chotamot*, which should be hung on the door of her residence or bedroom:[96]

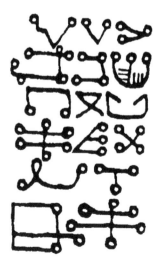

Now, I think most "believers" in the power of amulets would like to own one which can be employed, as it were, universally. In the following construct, the magical seals and letter combinations are said to pertain directly to the "Explicit Name" (*Shem ha-Meforash*), i.e. יהוה (*YHVH*). We are informed that this combination of magical glyphs and Hebrew letters will serve any purpose of whatsoever kind. The intention here is to write the complete square with the magical seals bottom left on a piece of clean parchment or paper, which is then carried on ones person:[97]

בההביה	ההוריה	הדייה
יההניה	מדיבניה	הנניה
בניהניה	הגמיהנה	רישערטיה

יה	נהבני	עה

Whilst many "magical seals" comprise glyphs from the "magical alphabets," most are quite unique and inexplicable. As already indicated, not all "magical seals" are presented in unadorned ways. In fact, many are quite embellished, and, in this regard, the following seal can be considered amongst the most ornate magical seals employed in Hebrew amulets.[98]

הוא היא

שי שפיפיאל כשך
שומיאל

On perusing a variety of written contemporary amulets being sold on the internet, I have noticed this seal being included in a great mishmash of differing amulets, all conjoined in a single *Kamea* and sold at hefty prices as an item which would bring the bearer "great fortune." In this regard, it should be noted that in several instances, the variety of Divine and Angelic Names, including magical seals, merged in such a willy-nilly manner, are respectively applied for a number of quite divergent purposes, hence they should not be intermingled in a single amulet.

Of course, it is perfectly clear that there are "*soferim*" (scribes) who are not only keen to devote themselves to writing and selling amulets, but are all too eager to impact the minds of potential clients with impressive seals and signs. It would seem that they think this approach would generate the best possible prices for their fanciful talismanic constructs, and they appear to be wholly indifferent to the fundamental influences of the active "psycho-spiritual potencies" triggered and channeled by the amulets in question. It is also worth noting that much of this amalgamated material was derived directly from the "*Shorshei ha-Shemot.*"[99] As it is, the author of this seminal text on Jewish Magic, delineated in the greatest detail the construction and employment of each of its listed amulets, hence there is nothing to be said in mitigation of a mindless approach to Hebrew amulets.

In fact, I recently perused a very decorative contemporary amulet comprised of Hebrew words and angelic names aligned with magical seals. For anyone with a knowing eye it was abundantly clear that the item combined several divergent magical signs and seals in a most complex amulet which was said to bring "good luck," etc. The *Kamea* included the ornate seal listed earlier. In this specific regard, perusing the magical seal in question, it would seem the Hebrew terms הוא ("he") and היא ("she") respectively refer to the magical seals directly below and to the left of the writing. I was told these indicate, as it were, the "male" and "female" expressions of the same magical glyph. The phrase at the bottom of the amulet reads שי שפיפיאל כשך שומיאל. This could be translated "a gift from *S'fifi'el, Shumi'el* splattered."

This amulet is basically recommended to individuals desiring an increase in personal prominence.[100] So if anyone wishes to increase his or her social status, etc., they could create this amulet by tracing the magical seals and writing the words and names on a piece of deerskin parchment. Regarding the latter, which may be hard to acquire today, I have noted that a clean sheet of high quality paper will do nicely. The amulet is then worn on the person of the individual requiring this support, and we are informed that the said individual will be perceived by all and sundry with great love and affection.

We are further told that if anyone should desire to grow and succeed in all his or her endeavours, that individual should draw the seals and write the Divine Names pertaining to this amulet on the lines of the palm of his or her hand.[101] In this instance the procedure is concluded by uttering the following incantation:

יהי רצון מלפניך יהוה אלהי ואלהי אבותי
אלהי הצבאות בכח אלו השמות והחותמות
שתצליחוני בכל מה שארצה

Transliteration:
> *Y'hi ratzon milfanecha YHVH Elohai v'Elohei avotai Elohei ha-tzva'ot b'koach eilu ha-shemot v'ha-chotamot sh'tatzlichuni b'chol mah she'ertzeh*

Translation:
> May it be your will *YHVH* my God, and God of my fathers, God of the Hosts, in the power deriving from the names and the seals for me to have success in all that I want to.

As said, there are Hebrew amulets doing the rounds in which this *Kamea* is combined with unrelated material, in fact, conjoined with certain seals and signs which many might loathe wearing on their persons. Maybe I am just overly fussy, but I personally prefer to be informed regarding the methods of construction and actual meanings of amulets I select to wear on my person, or carry in my wallet!

. ...The frog ordered each of them to bring
as many jewels and pearls as he could carry. In
addition, they were to bring all kinds of herbs
and roots to cure the ill... ... .

Chapter 5
Madim — Mars
ANGELS, DEMONS
&
AMULETS FOR PROTECTION

A. Angelic Hosts

It has been said that "the religious fancy and speculation of almost all nations has endeavored to fill a wide gap which separates man from the lowest animals on the one hand and from the highest divinity on the other, by imagining the existence of a host of spirits, good or evil."[1] Now, whilst folklorists and a host of other "learned-ists" may dismiss "spirit forces" as mere fantasies of superstitious religionists, I am fully aware of the enormous mass of evidence to the existence of Spirit Intelligences which has impacted humans in both benevolent and malevolent ways. Hence my query in the "*Book of Self Creation*" whether "the scientist's non-belief in 'Spirits' preclude the intrusion of such beings in their activities," and concluded "that humans are far more influenced by so-called 'spirits' than they know about."[2]

Be that as it may, the names of angelic messengers and infernal forces appear prolifically in *Kameot*. In this regard, we are reminded that "within the name, that which bears the name is present,"[3] hence the first names of angelic agencies are employed in Hebrew amulets as virtual "conduits of power," each granting a specific kind of spiritual support towards an appropriately related physical, mental, emotional or spiritual purpose, the latter being always in harmony with the fundamental nature of one or more of these "Celestial Intelligences." Thus it has been written "There is not a thing in the world, not even a little herb, over which there is not an angel set, and everything happens according to the command of these appointed angels."[4]

We are informed that the "elements and all the phenomena of nature are controlled and produced by the agency of angels,"[5] hence there are thousands of celestial hosts, i.e. *Erelim*, *Galgalim*, *Serafim*, etc., ruling over the heights and the depths. Individual Spirit Intelligences are also assigned the task of overseeing specific factors of physical existence, i.e. *Uri'el* governs thunder and earthquakes; *Yehu'el* is in charge of fire; *Ruchi'el* rules the winds, etc.[6] However, sources do not always agree on the exact task of each Spirit Intelligence, hence אוריאל (*Uri'el/Ori'el*), גבריאל (*Gavri'el*), רעמיאל (*Rami'el*), and others are assigned rulership over thunder. Thus, when it comes to "Angels" in Judaism, not to mention Jewish mysticism, there are enough discrepancies and inconsistencies to confuse even *the* most hardnosed scholar.

Yet, whilst there are disagreements galore regarding the exact designation of an angel, some of the most heated arguments are reserved for the actual "nature" of angels, i.e. whether they are all "spirit" or sometimes "embodied," etc., and consensus is yet to be reached. For example, consider the famous dispute between Maimonides and Nachmanides, which so divided the Jewish world. Some agreed with the "rationalist" *Rambam* (Maimonides), whilst others "rationally" dismissed him like a spent penny in favour of the insights of the *Ramban* (Nachmanides). Regarding the "nature of angels," the *Rambam* maintained angels are incorporeal, and that they cannot be perceived in our ordinary awake state. He claimed the angelic visions of the prophets occurred during sleep.[7] On the other hand, Nachmanides quoted several examples from the Hebrew Bible where angels appeared in human form and even pretended to eat. Hence the *Ramban* insisted that angels can be perceived via our ordinary senses, and that they do take on human form.[8]

As far as depicting celestial beings is concerned, I noted that humanoid depictions of angels, "comprise a relatively late phenomenon in Jewish writings," and that despite the "thou shalt not" statements regarding "graven images," there are depictions of angels in Jewish literature, e.g. Jewish illuminated manuscripts.[9] I also mentioned that "those very vivid descriptions of angels in human and other forms in the holy books of Judaism, have powerfully impacted on the imagination of the ordinary worshipper, the indulgence of whose fantasising skills were being limited only by personal mindsets" and " many centuries of careful cultivation and control."[10]

As indicated, it is understood that every single thing in existence has a Spirit Intelligence overseeing its existence. In this regard, it is believed that there are also "Guardian Angels" overseeing human existence. In fact, each of us is understood to have two such guardian spirits. As it is, we often see portrayals of such beings in humanoid form with long hair draping gracefully, the extended wings of a dove, robed in flowing, mainly white garments, and gracefully extending a protective hand.

Whilst many would happily acknowledge these sentimental images, it might come as a surprise to learn that in primary Jewish magical literature there are also descriptions of very large, heavy muscled, naked "guardian angels," whose appearance is probably more akin to the "Incredible Hulk" rather than "Superman" without his leotard and fancy cape! For example, one set of instructions involving the use of Divine Names, amulets, etc., for protection, also includes the visualisation of two angelic beings accompanying one like two body guards. To ones right is a naked spirit being who is riding a white horse and brandishing an unsheathed sword, whilst to the left there is another, equally naked spirit entity on foot, who is carrying a spear in readiness to defend against the onslaught from any would be attacker(s). Elsewhere we find delineations of equally naked angelic beings, whose bodies are bristling with all sorts of weaponry.[11]

Be that as it may, the names of literally hundreds of angels can be traced in Hebrew amulets, and it is certainly not my intention to turn this tome into a "Dictionary of Angels," or "demons" for that matter. However, we might investigate the primordial powers of some of the most important Spirit Entities listed in this tome, and also recognise their purpose within the scheme of creation. In some instances this could be quite a complex matter, especially when primary sources are not as comprehensive as one would like them to be, and when there are differences regarding the basic functions of Spirit Intelligences.

For example, in the *"Key of Solomon"* we are informed that בריאל (*Bari'el*) is the angel of the "fourth pentacle" of the planet Jupiter, the one which we are told "serveth to acquire riches and honor, and to possess much wealth."[12] However, this Spirit Intelligence is another amongst the angels said to be in charge of thunder,[13] and, as noted elsewhere, is associated with the set of five tri-letter portions of the "Name of Seventy-two Names" employed to "open the heart" to "spiritual teachings."[14] Of course it could be said that all of these aspects are in harmony with the "expansive" qualities of Jupiter (Jovial) as reflected in the said Spirit Intelligence.

The same angel is listed amongst a set of Spirit Forces aligned with the earlier mentioned *Sanoi, Sansanoi* and *Semangelof* in the following most acclaimed amulet from the *Sefer Raziel*.[15] We are told this is a tried and tested *Kamea* for the protection of pregnant women and infants. It is also meant to protect a mother during birth against bad magical spells and the Evil Eye, so that no evil or injury may befall her or her baby.

אשבעית ,עליך חוה ראשונה בשם שהוא יוצרך
ובשם שלשת מלאכים ששלח יוצרך בשבילך
ומלאך באיי הים ונשבעת להם במקום שתמצא
שמותם שלא תזיקו אתה ולא אחת ,ממחנותך
ומשרתיך ליכל מי שישא שמותם לכן בשמותם
ובחתומים הכתובים פה אני משביעך ואר‏ ‏ ת
מחנותיך משרתיך שלא תזיקו את יולד‏ ‏ ת

ולהילד שנולד, לא ביום ולא ,בלילה לא במאכלם
ולא במשתם לא בראשם ולא בלבם לא ברמח
איבריהם ולא בשס"ה ,גידיהם בכח השמ‏ ‏ ת
והחתימות האלה אלי אני משביעך ואר‏ ‏
מר‏מו‏ ‏ ניך ומש‏ ‏ ניך‏

אדם וחוה חוץ לילית   אדם וחוה חוץ לילית
סנוי וסנסנוי וסמנגלף

בשם אהיה והא ההא אא בב או מאב אאא

Besides the central images of the three famous Angels of
protection, the upper portion of the amulet incorporates a written
adjuration aimed at *Lilit*, the "first Eve." According to Moses
Zacutto the adjuration should read:[16]

אשבעית עליך חוה ראשונה בשם יוצרך ובשם שלשת
מלאכים ששלח יוצרך בשבילך ומצאוך באיי הים
ונשבעת להם במקום שתמצא שמותם שלא תזיקו אתה
ולא אחת ממחנותיך ומשרתיך ולא לכל מי שישא
שמותם לכן בשמותם ובחותמם הכתובים פה אני
משבעך ואת מחנותיך ומשרתיך שלא תזיקו את יולדת
[פלונית בת פלונית] ולהילד שנולד לה לא ביום ולא
בלילה לא במאכלם ולא במשתם לא בראשם ולא בלבם
ולא בשני מאות וארבעים ושמונה איבריהם ולא בשלש
מאות וששים וחמשה גידיהם בכח השמות והחותמות
האלה אני משביעך ואת מחנותיך ומשרתיך

Transliteration:

> *Ashbe'it alecha Chavah rishonah beshem yotzrecha
> v'b'shem shloshet malachim sheshalach yotz'recha
> bish'vilcha v'matz'ucha b'iyei ha-yam v'nishbata la'hem
> b'makom shetimtza shmotam shelo taziku otah v'lo achat
> mimachanotecha v'meshartecha v'lo l'kol mi shisa
> shmotam lachen b'shmotam v'b'chotamam ha'k'tuvim poh
> ani mashbi'acha v'et machanotecha v'meshartecha shelo
> taziku et ha-yoledet [.....Plonit bat Plonit.....] v'l'ha-yeled
> shenolad lah lo b'yom v'lo b'lailah lo b'ma'achalam v'lo
> b'mishtam lo b'rosham v'lo b'libam v'lo b'shnei m'ot
> v'arba'im v'shmoneh evreihem v'lo b'shlosh m'ot
> v'shishim v'chamishah gideihem b'koach ha-shemot v'ha-
> chotamot ha-eleh ani mashbi'acha v'et machanotecha
> v'meshartecha*

Translation:

> I adjure you First Eve in the Name of your Creator and in
> the name of the three Angels your Creator sent to you, and
> they found you on the islands of the sea, and you vowed to
> them, that in a locale where their names are found, there
> will be no harm from you and neither from anyone of your

faction, and your servants, not to any who carry their Names. Therefore in their Names and seals written here, I adjure you and your faction and your servants, not to bring harm to the pregnant woman [.....fill in the Name.....] and the child which will be born to her, not by day and not by night; not when eating and not when drinking; not in the head and not in the heart; and not in the 248 organs and 365 tendons, in the power of these Names and seals I adjure you and your faction and your servants.

There is also a list of seventy angelic Names at the bottom of the *Kamea*. These Names are listed in the amulet, with slight variation from their appearance in the *Sefer Raziel*.[17] However, once again the following version is said to be correct:[18]

מיכאל גבריאל רפאל נוריאל קדומיאל מלכיאל
צדקיאל פדיאל תומיאל חסדיאל צוריאל רמאל
יופיאל סתורי גזריאל ודריאל להריאל חזקיאל
רחמיאל קדשיאל שבעאל ברקיאל אקיאל חניאל
לאהאל מלכיאל שבניאל רהסיאל רומיאל קדמיאל
קדאל חכמיאל רמאל קדשיאל מניאל עזריאל
חכמאל מחניאל קניאל גדיאל צורטק עופפיאל
רחמיאל סנסניה ודרגזיה רססיאל רומיאל סניאל
טהריאל עזריאל נריה סמבאל עינאל תסיריה
רנאל צוריה פסיסיה עוריאל סמביא מחניה
קנוניה ירואל מטרוסיה חוניאל זכריאל ועריאל
דניאל גדיאל בריאל אהניאל

Transliteration:
> *Micha'el, Gavri'el, Rafa'el, Nuri'el, Kedumi'el, Malchi'el,*
> *Tzadki'el, Pedei'el [Padi'el], Tumi'el, Chasdi'el, Tzuri'el,*
> *Rema'el, Yofi'el, Saturi, Gazri'el, Vadri'el [Udri'el],*
> *Lehari'el [Lahari'el], Chazki'el, Rachmi'el, Kadshi'el,*
> *Shva'el, Barki'el, Aki'el, Chani'el, L'aha'el, Malchi'el,*
> *Shebni'el, R'hasi'el, Rumi'el, Kadmi'el, Kad'el,*
> *Chochmi'el, Ram'el, Kadshi'el, M'ni'el, Azri'el,*
> *Chacham'el, Machni'el, K'nei'el, Gadi'el, Tzurtak,*
> *Ofifi'el, Rachmi'el, Sansinyah, Udragziyah, Rasasi'el,*

Rumi'el, Snei'el, Tohari'el, Azri'el, Neryah, S'mach'el, Ayin'el, Tasiryah, Ron'el, Tzuryah, Pesis'yah, Iveri'el, Smachia, Machneyah, Kinunyah, Yeru'el, Tutrusyah, Choni'el, Zachri'el, Va'ari'el, Dani'el, Gedi'el, Bari'el, Ahani'el

The central portion of the amulet comprises graphic presentations of the angels *Sanoi, Sansanoi* and *Semangelof,* accompanied as usual by the earlier mentioned phrase *Adam v'Chavah chutz Lilit* (*Adam* and *Eve* away *Lilit*). The following is another stylised graphic portrayal of the said celestial entities.

We are told the name of the first Angel, סנוי (*Sanoi* [*Sana'ui* according to Moses Zacutto]), was derived from the initials of three words in *Exodus 30:34* reading סמים נתף ושחלת (*samim nataf ush'chelet*—"sweet spices, stacte, and onycha"). In turn the appellative of the second Spirit Intelligence, סנסנוי (*Sansanoi* [*Sansina'ui* according to Moses Zacutto]), is a variant of the word בסנסיניו (*b'sansinav*—"of the boughs thereof") in *Song of Songs 7:9* [8]. The third name, סמנגלף (*Semangelof*) is said to have originated from the words סמים ולבנה זכה (*samim ul'vonah zakah*—"sweet spices with pure frankincense"), also found in *Exodus 30:34.*[19]

As stated earlier, the three mentioned Angels were sent to restrain and return the demoness *Lilit.* We are informed that she requested to be left alone, and pledged that wherever she would encounter the listed names and images of the three Spirit Intelligences, she would refrain from working her wicked ways. However, whilst the presence of these three Spirit Intelligences are considered vital in the protection of would-be mothers and their offspring against demonic forces, an inordinate number of angelic names were, as it were, roped in for additional support.

Amongst the latter the first four listed in the current amulet, i.e. מיכאל (*Micha'el*), גבריאל (*Gavri'el*), רפאל (*Rafa'el*), נוריאל (*Nuri'el*), as well as the angel אוריאל (*Ori'el* [*Auriel*]), should be acknowledged as the "Supreme Five." Collectively termed ארגמן (*Argaman*), an acronym constructed from the initials of the names of these five angels, the unique status of these Spirit Intelligences is highlighted in the teaching regarding the time of the "Redemption," when it is said the five angels of *Malchut* (Kingdom) will connect the head—יהוה (*YHVH*) and *Malchut*—אדני (*ADNY* [*Adonai*]) as יאהדונהי (*Yahadonahi*).[20]

We are further reminded the *gematria* of יאהדונהי (*Yahadonahi* [י = 10 + א = 1 + ה = 5 + ד = 4 + ו = 6 + נ = 50 + ה = 5 + י = 10 = 91]), is equal to that of the word אמן (*Amen* [א = 1 + מ = 40 + נ = 50 = 91]). The "secret" of *Amen* is said to be its spelling, i.e. comprising the initials of the first and last two of the *Argaman* angels.[21] Considering the great importance of the "Supreme Five," it is no wonder the said acronym should feature so prominently in *Kameot*, as shown in the following representation of a 19th century *Shadai* amulet in which the five platelets dangling below the fish ornament collectively spells the *Argaman* acronym.

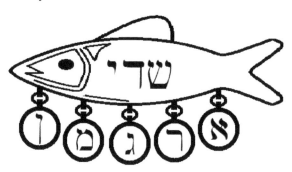

Curiously enough, fish are directly associated with one of the "*Argaman*" angels, i.e. *Rafa'el*. The *Book of Tobit* relates how this Spirit Intelligence instructed a young man on how to exorcise demons by fumigating those afflicted with the heart and bladder of a fish.[22] Be that as it may, we will peruse the symbol of the fish in *Kameot* later in this text.

We are informed that the mentioned five Angels, "together with the mnemonic ארגמן (*Argaman*) are by far the commonest found in the metallic amulets from the Oriental Hasidic diaspora."[23] However, it is worth noting that the first (אוריאל—*Ori'el*) and the last (נוריאל—*Nuri'el*) of the five angels, were understood to be different appellatives, each perhaps referring to a different aspect, of the same Spirit Intelligence.[24] Hence there are really four Angelic Princes said to be "the honoured ones, who are appointed over the four camps of the Shekina."[25] Considering the services rendered by these four great angelic "Presences," it is only natural that their names should feature in Hebrew amulets ranging from those affording good fortune to those engendering health, wealth and protection.

Ancient sources tell us that the angel רפאל (*Rafa'el*) "is set over all the diseases and all the wounds of the children of men,"[26] whilst מיכאל (*Micha'el*), "the merciful and long-suffering," is "set over the best part of mankind and over chaos."[27] He is the champion of Israel, and slayer of evil. We are told the archangel גבריאל (*Gavri'el*) "is set over all the powers,"[28] hence it is maintained that this Spirit Intelligence grants one the power to break down walls.[29] Regarding אוריאל (*Ori'el* [*Uri'el*]), we are informed that this angel "is over the world and over Tartarus."[30] It is said the name of this archangel pertains directly to the phrase in *Exodus 33:23* reading ופני לא יראו (*Ufanai lo yera'u*—"but My face shall not be seen").[31]

Now, the mentioned "five angels of *Malchut*" are sometimes associated with the earlier mentioned שמעיאל (*Shmai'el*) in Jewish Magical literature. The name of this אופן (*Ofan*) is said to be related to ישמע אל (*Yishma El*—"*El* shall hear"), and we are told he is in charge of all waking "dream question" procedures.[32] As I noted elsewhere, this Spirit Intelligence is aligned with the fourth tri-letter portion of the "Forty-two Letter Name," as well as the thirty-sixth portion of the "Name of Seventy-two Names."[33]

Talking of dreams, another Spirit Intelligence often employed in conjunction with the "Supreme Five," is שמריאל (*Shamri'el*). I previously noted that this angel is "Ruling Prince" of the nineteenth tri-letter portion of the "Name of Seventy-two Names," and that he is "in charge of protection."[34] *Shamri'el* also "has the power to fulfil dreams," however he is equally empowered "to instill trepidation."[35]

As you would have noticed by now, the greatest tendency by far is the conjoint employment of several Angelic names in Hebrew amulets. It should be kept in mind that Angelic Names are not always employed in a strictly "benevolent" manner in Practical Kabbalah, and neither are the appellatives of Demonic Entities exclusively employed for "malevolent" purposes. The current tome does not afford us the space to discuss this in any great detail, but as a case in point consider the following procedure in which a known thief is, as it were, "psychically boiled" in order to coerce the said individual to reveal his or her identity. Of course, it might be argued that the final result is "benevolent" for all.

Be that as it may, in the mentioned magical practice the names of the archangels מיכאל (*Micha'el*), גבריאל (*Gavri'el*) and the angel שרפיאל (*Sarfi'el*) are employed to expose and, as it were, "draw out" someone known to be a thief. In this regard, the instruction is to write the name of thief and that of his mother, as well as the names of the mentioned angelic beings on a palm frond taken from a *lulav*. The leaf is then submerged in boiling water, which is said will "draw out" the thief who will then come forth, i.e. out of hiding.[36] I bet he will when he finds himself in such "hot water"!!

B. Fiendish Hordes

Whilst the patronage of higher spiritual forces are enlisted by means of their names, malevolent powers are equally identified in *Kameot* in order to, as it were, bind them and weaken their impact on the living. Restraining demonic entities is particularly necessary, since it is said that "if the eye had the power to see them, no creature could endure the demons." Furthermore, "they are more numerous than we are and they surround us like the ridge round a field," and it is claimed "every one among us has a thousand on his left hand and ten thousand on his right hand." [*Talmud Bavli, Berachot 6a*]

It is said demonic entities are "living souls without bodies,"[37] and it is believed they resemble humans in three ways, "they eat and drink like human beings; they propagate like human beings; and they die like human beings" [*Talmud Bavli Chagigah 16a*].[38] We are informed that "the injury of the human race in every possible way was believed to be the chief delight of evil spirits,"[39] which is another "quality" they share with so many of the human race who "delight" in doing just that to their fellow human kind. The earlier mentioned primordial demoness *Lilit* certainly ranks amongst the most dangerous of those spirit forces who take pleasure in killing humans.

The saga surrounding the person and career of this demonic dame reads like a popular soap opera. She "was a failure as Adam's intended wife, became the paramour of lascivious spirits, rose to be the bride of Samael the demon King, ruled as the Queen of Zemargad and Sheba, and finally ended up as the consort of God himself."[40] Her incredible career in evil and depravity spanning more than four millennia, rivals that of any other career criminal, whether human or demonic. At least there is some protection against the killer instincts of this lady. We are told she informed the Propher Elijah "whenever I shall see or hear any of my names I shall straightway flee.... And whenever my names shall be mentioned I shall have no power to do evil or to injure."[41]

It would seem the history of *Lilit* can be traced back to the *Lillu*, who "was one of four demons belonging to a vampire or incubi-succubae class" mentioned in a Sumerian King list.[42] Thus it has been suggested that the traditions regarding "*Lilit*" were derived by Jews from Sumerian and Gnostic lore, and it is further alleged that much of Sumerian folklore was absorbed into Judaism by the patriarch Abraham, and the fact that he hailed from Chaldean Ur was cited in support of this claim.[43]

There is certainly no evidence that Abraham received the *Lilit* mythology from the Sumerians, or that it was from thence that it found its way into kabbalistic lore. There is also no reference to *Lilit* in the Pentateuch, and all evidence points to it having been extracted from Babylonian-Assyrian sources. After all, Jews lived in exile in Babylonia for centuries, and even after the "return" and Nehemiah's rebuilding of the Temple and the walls of Jerusalem, many preferred to remain in the settled comfort of Babylonia, where the great Jewish academies continued to thrive well into the early centuries of the common era.

We know for certain that *Lilit* is part of Babylonian demonology, and that there are some Sumerian antecedents.[44] In fact, *Lilit* was one of a demonic couple, *Lilu* the male and *Lilitu* the female, both of which were associated with a whole set of "harmful spirits" called *mazikim*.[45] Now, whilst *Lilit* in "Jewish lore" is particularly associated with endangering the life of the newly born infant, the Babylonian equivalents of this spirit fulfilled various nefarious functions. For example, there is an incantation in an Assyrian ritual text against an *Ardat-Lili* who preys on males.[46] Others would strangle infants and threaten pregnant women.

There is only one reference to *Lilit* in the Bible (*Isaiah 34:14*), hence it is understood that most of what we know of the early Jewish traditions regarding *Lilit*, derives mainly from the Babylonian *Talmud*.[47] Amongst the early "Jewish" references to *Lilit* we should include one from the Qumran community (Dead Sea Scrolls),[48] whilst aspects of this tradition were also absorbed into "*The Testament of Solomon*," a third century Greek work.[49] More details on *Lilit* as the first wife of Adam were also included in the "*Alphabet of Ben Sira*."[50]

Now, just because *Lilit* is called the "mother of demons," does not mean that she does not have enemies amongst her own kind. In this regard, the demoness מחלת (*Machalat*), the "Dancer," and her daughter אגרת בת מחלת (*Agrat bat Machalat*), the latter noted earlier to be the consort of *Ashmodai* and queen of the demons, are said to live "in strife with Lilith." The hostility of these female demons towards *Lilit* is no simple matter. *Agrat bat Machalat* is not only the consort of *Ashmodai* and ranking "queen of the demons," she is said to have "a retinue of one hundred and eighty thousand evil spirits."[51]

Be that as it may, there are many references to all manner of demonic forces in Hebrew amulets, usually in terms of kin type and, except for a very few like the demoness *Lilit*, are rarely named individually. Even when it comes to referencing a single "malevolent spirit," it is often in the third person. For example, mention is made of the collective רוחין בישין (*Ruchin b'ishin*) or to רוחות רעות (*Ruchot ra'ot*), all of which have been translated "evil spirits" (some say "ghosts"), and they are considered to be of both the feminine and masculine kind.[52] We also find references to a singular רוח רעה (*Ruach ra'ah*—"evil spirit"), i.e. one from amongst the "*Ruchin*" or "*Ruchot ra'ot*."

As it is, Hebrew amulets include references to several classes from amongst the demonic legions. Amongst those mentioned in *Kameot* listed in this tome, are the מזיקים (*Mazikim*) or מזיקין (*Mazikin*), i.e. injurers (harmful spirits), who have been described "imps."[53] It has been claimed that the *mazikim* are the offspring of Adam and Eve having had liaisons with demonic entities. It is said they "and their demonic consorts account for the proliferation of demons."[54] However, there appears to be some confusion as far as these claims are concerned. Elsewhere it is indicated that the *mazikim*, "beings who injure (נזק [*nezek*]),"[55] are comprised of a number of demonic classes.

Past research referenced two main factions amongst the *mazikim*, the first is comprised of "fallen angels who are wholly supernatural,"[56] and the second of beings who are "half supernatural and half human."[57] Amongst the latter group there are two demonic classes which are of interest to us, since they are often referred to in protection amulets. First there is the ליליין (*Lilin*) faction of demons, which were "begotten of Adam on the one side, and Lilith and other female spirits on the other,"[58] rather than from Eve, the primordial human mother, and we are told that "Lilith reigns over these as queen."[59]

Next there are the שדים (*Shedim*) or שידין (*Shedin*), the most cited of the demonic types listed in Hebrew amulets. We find references in the Hebrew Bible to these "demonic fiends," i.e. in *Deuteronomy 32:17* in which we are told regarding those who forsook the good ways of the Almighty One, יזבחו לשדים (*yizb'chu la-shedim*—"they sacrificed unto demons"). This accusation is emphasised and expanded upon in *Psalm 106:37* where we read ויזבחו את בניהם ואת בנותיהם לשדים (*v'yizb'chu et b'neihem v'et b'noteihem l'shedim*—"Yea, they sacrificed their sons and their daughters unto demons").

The *Shedim* are said to be of the mischievous or "hobgoblin type,"[60] and we are informed that their king, *Ashmedai*, "resembles the merry if also mischief-making hobgoblins of fairy tales."[61] It is said the *Shedim* were born from the sexual relations of two angels, i.e. *Aza* and *Azael*, with *Na'amah*, the daughter of *Lamech* who was the great-great grandson of the Biblical *Enoch*. All of this supposedly happened prior to the biblical "great flood."[62] However, the *Shedim* may "assume any shape and form they like," and are "able to see without being seen themselves."[63] If you should find this disconcerting, especially as far as your personal safety against these malevolent forces is concerned, it is worth noting that all demonic forces are said to be subordinate to the four great Archangels of the Divine Throne, i.e. *Micha'el, Gavri'el, Rafa'el* and *Ori'el*.[64] In this regard, the 14th century Kabbalist Menachem ben Meir Tziyoni tells us "And know, that each party (of demons) is (subordinated) to certain archons and divine angels, as it is known among men of understanding."[65]

C. Amulets for Protection

I noted elsewhere that "Magic" is "a hand-down of early 'spiritual survival' systems, which enabled our forefathers to find souls of their own amongst all kinds of hostile conditions and circumstances."[66] Consensus all round might be that our ancestors coped with hostilities which no longer impact us, however today living conditions, whether in the average city or in yet untamed rural areas, are no less hostile. The sum-total of human suffering all round is incredible, yet it seems to be considered quite a normal condition.....as long as it is happening to somebody else!

Be that as it may, it certainly does not take a stretch of the imagination to comprehend that we live in a world in which violence and violent crimes proliferate. Some of us might have elected not to "buy" into that "reality," but for the average citizen this is indeed a most dangerous world, one in which protection is sought not only against malevolent powers of the spirit kind, but also against the malice, enmity, hostility, cruelty and murderous intentions of the human kind.

Now, it is popularly believed that amulets will protect wearers against foes, whether these be of the physical or spirit kind. The powers of a great variety of Divine Names, some quite standard and others specially constructed from biblical verses, were called on to guard the vulnerable. Hence it should come as no surprise that there should be a Hebrew amulet the intention of which is protection against all kinds of weaponry, i.e. knives, guns, etc.[67]

In this regard, those who should find themselves in circumstances which necessitate this form of safeguard, are advised to write the following *Kamea*, commencing with the following adjuration, comprised of a set of Divine and Angelic Names (which I have been assured are correct), at the top of deerskin parchment:

עתיאל וריאל הוריאל המרריאל שובריאל עורריאל
שוריאל מיכאל גבריאל הגריאל הגדהדאל שובראל
צבחר עתניק צורטק אנקתם פסתם פספסים דיונסים
ליש ועת בכן יתי יהוה אבג יתץ קרע שתן נגד יכש
בטר צתג חקב טנע יגל פזק שקן צית קבצאל
אהמנוניאל ומסתיה הירשיתאל עאנה פיה אלעה
אבג יתץ ענעה עה עזור [לפלוני בן פלונית]

Whilst several of the Divine Names addressed in this tome can be recognised in this adjuration, some of the Angelic and Divine Names are most obscure. Transliterated the adjuration might read:

Oti'el Vari'el Hori'el Hamariri'el Shov'ri'el Ovrari'el Shuri'el Micha'el Gavri'el Hagri'el Hag'dahad'el Shuvar'el Tzavchar Atneik Tzurtak Anaktam Pastam Paspasim Dionsim LYSh VAT KKV YTY YHVH AViGe YaToTzi KaRo' SaTaN' NaGiDa YeiCheiSha BiTaRo TzaTaG' CheKeVa Tin'I YaGaLi P'Z'Kei ShuKoVa TzoYaT' Kivetz'el Ahamnoni'el Vamsatyah Hairoshit'el O'anah Peyah Ala'ah AViGe YaToTzi Ona'ah Ah azor l' [.....Ploni ben Plonit.....]

Translation:

Oti'el Vari'el Hori'el Hamariri'el Shov'ri'el Ovrari'el Shuri'el Micha'el Gavri'el Hagri'el Hag'dahad'el Shuvar'el Tzavchar Atneik Tzurtak Anaktam Pastam Paspasim Dionsim LYSh VAT KKV YTY YHVH AViGe YaToTzi KaRo' SaTaN' NaGiDa YeiCheiSha BiTaRo TzaTaG' CheKeVa Tin'I YaGaLi P'Z'Kei ShuKoVa

TzoYaT' Kivetz'el Ahamnoni'el Vamsatyah Hairoshit'el O'anah Peyah Ala'ah AViGe YaToTzi Ona'ah Ah extend help to [.....fill in the name of the recipient.....]

The amulet is completed with "magical seals" located below the adjuration. Thereafter the *Kamea* is worn like a pendant around the neck of the individual requiring this support.

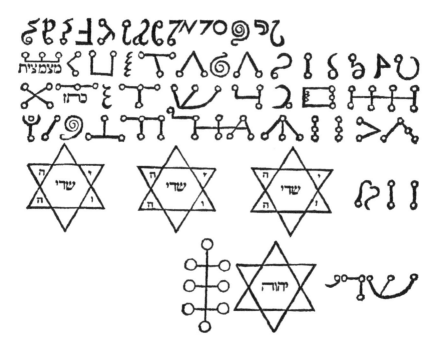

Whilst it is difficult to ascertain the meaning of most of the magical glyphs employed, the three signs bottom right, clearly represent a stylized version of the Divine Name שׁדי. As mentioned earlier, this Divine Name features on the front of every *Mezuzah*, which I noted is popularly recognised "as an effective shield for one's home against demons and evil spirits."[68] In fact, the *Talmud* maintains *Mezuzot* protect homes against harm [*Menachot 33b; Bereshit Rabba 35*]. Thus it is believed *Mezuzot* keep *Mazikin* away from ones home. In this regard Rabbi Menachem Recanati commented, "when confronted by the name of God, which is on the exterior of the *mezuzah*, these messengers of harm realize that God is watching over this domicile." He also suggested the word to be "a combination of the words '*zaz*' and '*mavet*' which means literally '*Death: Remove thyself*'."[69]

A *Mezuzah* usually contains a simple scroll. However, in acknowledging the talismanic qualities of the item, the parchment is sometimes expanded to include further biblical verses, Angelic and Divine Names, as well as magical glyphs and seals. It is believed these will enhance the magical efficacy of a *Mezuzah* as a protection amulet. This is very well illustrated in the following *Mezuzah* which was published by Joshua Trachtenberg:[70]

As in the case of all *Mezuzot*, the major portion of this item is comprised of *Deuteronomy 6:4—9* [line 1–6] and *Deuteronomy*

11:13—21 [line 7–22]. These verses were written over twenty-two lines, so as to align with the twenty-two letters of the Hebrew alphabet. To the left of the scroll we trace the Divine Names יה (*Yah*) listed twice; the names of seven Spirit Intelligences, i.e. מיכאל (*Micha'el*), גבריאל (*Gavri'el*), עזריאל (*Azri'el*), צדקיאל (*Tzadki'el*), שרפיאל (*Sarfi'el*), רפאל (*Rafa'el*) and ענאל (*An'el*). These seven angels are said to indicate the seven Planets as well as the seven days of the week.[71]

There are three additional angelic names at the bottom of the amulet, i.e. אוריאל (*Ori'el*), יופיאל (*Yofi'el*) and חסדיאל (*Chasdi'el*). Thus there are in fact ten listed Spirit Intelligences in this *Mezuzah*. There are also ten Pentagrams which, we are told, represent the "Ten Commandments," whilst the fifty endings of the Pentagrams (five per Pentagram) reference the "Fifty Gates of Understanding" as well as the fifty "days of the giving of the Law" between the Festivals of Passover and Pentecost.[72]

I would like to think that this scroll was written by a Kabbalist who intended the ten pentagrams to reference the ten *sefirot*. There are also ten little circles interspersed throughout the main text of this *Mezuzah* scroll. These, we are told represent "the ten elements of the human body." Five of them are said to refer to "the five names of the soul," whilst the concluding three at the bottom indicate the "three faculties" of "hearing, sight and speech," etc.[73]

Be that as it may, interspersing the seven angelic names to the left, are the seven words comprising *Psalm 121 :5* reading:

יהוה שמרך יהוה צלך על יד ימינך

Transliteration:
> *YHVH shomrecha YHVH tzil'cha al yad yeminecha*

Translation:
> *YHVH* is thy keeper; *YHVH* is thy shade upon thy right hand.

There are also a number of obscure magical seals, some on the front and others on the rear of the scroll. Those located on the back of the scroll are carefully positioned so as to align with certain words on the front. In this regard, the Name/Seal שׁדי is located directly behind the opening word of *Deuteronomy 11:13* in line 7, i.e. והיה (*v'hayah*—"and it will be"); and the magical seal is positioned directly behind the words כימי השמים (*kimei ha-shamayim*—"as the days of heaven") in line 21. The combination כוזו במוכסז כוזו is located at the bottom of the rear portion of the scroll, and two further magical seals, i.e. and , are likewise added to the back in unspecified locations.[74]

In conclusion we are told all of "these features make it sufficiently evident that during the Middle Ages the *mezuzah* acquired all the trappings of the legitimate amulet, becoming one in actuality as well as by reputation."[75]

When it comes to Divine Names being employed as safeguards against the onslaughts of infernal forces, the "Forty-two Letter Name" certainly ranks amongst the most important. It should be remembered that this unique Divine Name is aligned with *Gevurah* (Might/Severity) on the sefirotic tree, hence even the smallest portion of this Divine Name is employed for some or other, as it were, "power purpose." For example, regarding the biblical saga on the "splitting of the sea," we are told that the Divine One accomplished this miraculous deed by means of the expression קרע.

This tri-letter construct comprises the first portion of the combination קרע שטן (*Kra Satan*—"Tear Satan"). In turn, the latter expression is the second of the seven divisions of the "Forty-two Letter Name," and is often employed in conjunction with the Name שׁדי (*Shadai*) for purposes of protection. In this regard, we are told that those who are afflicted by an evil spirit should acquire an amulet comprised of the Divine Name קרע שטן written with "*tagin*" on deerskin parchment, i.e. קְרַע שׁיטָן. As said before, a clean sheet of good quality paper will serve very well in the writing of such amulets. On completion, the amulet should be carried on the person of the afflicted individual.[76]

Another talismanic use of the "Forty-two Letter Name" pertains to the Divine Name אקנב (*Akanav*), which is an acronym of both the biblical phrase את קשתי נתתי באנן (*et kashti natati be'anan*—"I have set My bow in the cloud") (*Genesis 9:13*), and the first four six-letter sets of the "Forty-Two Letter Name, i.e. אבגיתץ קרעשטן נגדיכש בטרצתג (*Avgitatz Karastan Nagdichesh Batratztag*). Regarding the latter affiliation, it should be noted that, like the "Forty-two Letter Name," the Name אקנב pertains to the sphere of *Gevurah* on the sefirotic tree. [77]

As mentioned elsewhere, "this Name has the power to make you brave and strong, so as to survive in a place of danger. It further has the power to chase away demons."[78] In this regard, one has to engrave the Name אקנב (*Akanav*) on a silver disc to be worn as a *Kamea* on one's person. Then, whenever one finds oneself in circumstances requiring its power, one simply visualises אקנב as one's *Kavvanah*, one's fully focussed attention, is brought to bear on the situation at hand, whilst at the same time reciting mentally the mentioned four sets of the "Forty-two Letter Name."[79]

We are informed that there are numerous *Shedim* (demons) who are inclined to hunt and attack humans. Amongst this group of malevolent forces, there is apparently a silent faction named תורפן (*Torfan*). Whilst this lot appears to not speak and to maintain a gloomy disposition, they do tend to use a kind of sign language, i.e. hinting their intentions with their hands in a morose manner. We are told that they especially attack the human heart, but they can be resisted during daylight hours. Hence, when an individual is experiencing some form of physical stress or pain around the heart, an individual bringing health should whisper the following words in the ear of the sufferer:

מעיד אני עלי טורפאן בשם בשר שרה ובשם הגדול
סאל שהוא שם הכח של השם הגדול של ע״ב שתניחו
את [....פלוני בן פלוני.....] עד שיעשה מלאכתו

Transliteration:

> *Mei'id ani elai torfan b'shem basar Sarah ub'shem ha-gadol Se'al shehu shem ha-koach shel ha-shem ha-gadol shel ayin-bet, shetanichu et [.....Ploni ben Ploni.....] ad she'aseh m'lachto*

Translation:

> I bear witness to *Torfan* in the name "Flesh of *Sarah*," and in the great name *Se'al*, which is the name of power from the Name of Seventy-two, to leave [.....insert the name of the sufferer.....] alone till he completed his lifework.

Next, the following Names should be written on the right hand of the afflicted individual: אמתלאי בת כרנבו and אהדי (*Amtalai bat Karnavu* and *Ahadi*). The individual in question should verbally utter the Names written on his hand, then rinse his mouth with a bit of water. It is said this will ease the harmful condition.

However, we are informed that if the demonic assault has not subsided, and no relief is experienced by the following day, the earlier addressed "Magic Square of the Third Order" should be inscribed on parchment conjointly with the "Fourteen Letter Name of God," i.e. כוזו במוכסז כוזו (*Kuzu B'mochsaz Kuzu*), the latter being written along the four borders of the magic square in the following manner:[80]

This magic seal is to be inscribed three times, and additionally the following pterygoma and adjuration should accompany the construct:

יהא רעוא מן קדמך אלהי הצבאות שתרפא את [....פלוני
בן פלוני.....] מכל מיחוש וכאב וחולי שיש לו ברמ״ח
איבריו ושס״ה גידיו בכח זה השם אבגיתץ קרעשטן
אמן אמן

Transliteration:

> *Y'hei ra'ava min kadamach Elohei ha-tzva'ot sheterape et
> [.....Ploni ben Ploni.....] mikol michush v'ke'ev v'choli
> shiyesh lo b'ramach evarav v'shasah gidav b'ko'ach zeh
> ha-shem Avgitatz Karastan Omein Omein*

Translation:

> May your Will extend *Elohei Tzva'ot* [*Elohei of Hosts*] to
> heal [.....fill in name of afflicted.....] from all aches and
> pains, and sickness he has in all his 248 organs and 365
> tendons, in the power of this Name *Avgitatz Karastan
> Amen Amen*

Regarding the listed Divine Names, the expression בשר שרה
(*Basar Sarah*) correctly translates "flesh of *Sarah*," and this is the
only instance in which I have seen this combination employed as
a "name of power." The tri-letter combination סאל (*Se'al*) is the
forty-fifth portion of the "Name of Seventy-two Names." The
appellative "*Amtalai bat Karnavu*," sometimes employed in some
Hebrew amulets, is the proper name of the mother of the Patriarch
Abraham, and we are informed the great Holy Name *Ahadi* is
derived from *Numbers 14: 21* reading:

ואולם חי אני וימלא כבוד יהוה את כל הארץ

Transliteration:

v'ulam chai ani v'yimalei ch'vod YHVH et kol ha-aretz

Translation:

But in very deed, as I live—and all the earth shall be filled with the glory of *YHVH*.

Interestingly enough, the following variant of the *Ehyeh*/Ineffable Name square is equally employed for the very same purposes in a Hebrew amulet:[81]

ה	י	ה	א
י	ה	ו	ה
ה	ו	ה	י
י	ה	י	ה

In the current instance one has to first prepare oneself to be in a condition of purity and holiness, and then to write the earlier addressed "Twenty-two Letter Name" on a kosher scroll, i.e. אנקתם פסתם פספסים דיונסים (*Anaktam Pastam Paspasim Dionsim*). Next, as in the previous *Kamea*, a written incantation is included. It reads:

יהי רצון מלפניך שבם הגדול והקדוש של כ"ב אותיות
שתרפא את [.....פלוני בן פלוני.....] מכל שידין ושידתין
ולילין ולילתין ומכל כאני ומיחוש וחולי שיש לו ברמ"ח
איבריו ושס"ה גידיו ובכח שם הגדול והקדוש אהיה אשר
אהיה

Transliteration:

Y'hi ratzon milfanecha b'shem ha-gadol v'ha-kadosh shel K"B otiot sheterafe et [.....Ploni ben Ploni.....] mikol Shedin v'Shedatin v'Lilin v'Lilatin umikol kani v'michush v'choli shiyesh lo b'ramach evarav v'shasah gidav v'b'ko'ach shem ha-gadol v'ha-kadosh Ehyeh asher Ehyeh.

Translation:

> May it be your will in the great and holy Name of Twenty-two Letters to heal [.....insert the name of the afflicted.....] from male and female *Shedin*, and male and female *Lilin*, and from all pains and aches, and sickness he has in all his 248 organs and 365 tendons, and in the power of the great and holy Name *Ehyeh asher Ehyeh*.

Thereafter the mentioned *Ehyeh*/Ineffable Name seal is likewise written three times, and the entire construct hung on the person of the afflicted individual.

Whilst most of the protection *Kameot* we are perusing in this volume are fairly straight forward and their purpose self-evident, this is not always the case. Keep in mind that in "Practical Kabbalah" there are literally thousands of Divine Names, many of which were derived from biblical verses, etc., by means of highly specialised techniques. Hence, in numerous Hebrew amulets we are faced with sets of Divine Names the origins of which are lost in the mists of time. Often these Names are presented in variant ways, as shown in the following set of amulets.

Take the following set of amulets as a case in point. All comprise variant formats of the same set of Divine Names, and are employed with slight variation for virtually the same purposes. Another common factor amongst all of them is the fact that one has to literally "drink the amulet." In this instance the procedure requires one to dissolve the "Divine Names" in water, which is then imbibed by the individual requiring this unique support. As it is, the latter action is not altogether unique, since it is recommended not too infrequently in a number of primary Jewish magical writings dealing with *Kameot*, *Segulot*, *Refuot*, etc.

Now, the first set of the mentioned mysterious Divine Names, was created to defend an individual against the offensives of injurious spirits, e.g. those who strangle humans, or of any malevolent force for that matter. Here the instruction is for one to write the following set of Divine Names in ink on a piece of paper with the right hand:[82]

אנפרוש אווליש אנפרופיש אית אדיש

The writing is then, as mentioned, dissolved in a glass of water, which is afterwards consumed by the one who is afflicted. Next, in order to prevent these malevolent forces from returning, one has to write the following seals with ink on a clean piece of paper to be carried on the victim's person:

I was informed the letters י״ in the top right and bottom left triangles of the large *Magen David*, are abbreviations of the Ineffable Name (יהוה) which, in combination with the expression ולך below, reading *v'lech* ("and go"), are meant to "inhibit" the power of the baneful spirit forces, and direct the "goodness" of the Eternal Living Spirit to the one carrying the amulet.

As indicated, the peculiar set of Divine Names listed above are employed in variant formats, all for purposes of protection against man, spirits, etc. In the next instance it is recommended the following version of the Divine Names in question being employed as a safeguard against negative thoughts and fantasies, especially those acting in a most powerful corrupting manner on ones personal being.[83] These are said to be particularly powerful on a Tuesday (the day of Mars pertaining to fury) and a Saturday (the day of Saturn pertaining to melancholy and despondency). Here the format of the said Divine Names is:

אנפרוש אופילש אנטרופיש אות אוריאש

The instruction is for a man to write this particular set of Divine Names on a piece of paper with his left hand, and for a woman to do the same with her right hand. The writing is again dissolved in a glass of clean, fresh water, which is afterwards consumed by the individual requiring the special support rendered by this activity. It is said, that with the help of the Divine One, the action will be effective, especially if one drinks the infused water from a *kosher* glass.

Elsewhere again, the set of Divine Names is listed as:[84]

אנפירוש אפילוש אנטפרוס אית אורי יאש

In this instance the application pertains to special protection when one is being threatened by humans intent on taking ones life. We are informed to write the listed set of Divine Names in *ashurit*, on a sheet of paper with the right hand. The writing is again dissolved in a glass of water, to be consumed by those whose lives are being threatened. Afterwards the set of Divine Names is rewritten and carried on the person of those requiring this unique protection. Considering the three variant formats of the Divine Names in question, I have been told that all of them could be and were successfully employed interchangeably for exactly the same listed purposes.

In Jewish mystical circles *Kameot* were not only employed to halt the deleterious designs of man, beast and spirit, but were equally employed to cure demonic possession. In this regard, it is worth considering the famous pterygoma based on the word "*Shebriri,*" this being the appellative of the "demon of blindness." The malevolent entity in question is listed in the *Talmud* [*Pesachim 112a*], and its name is traditionally arranged in the following format:[85]

שברירי
ברירי
רירי
ירי
רי
י

Transliteration:

ShBRYRY
BRYRY
RYRY
YRY
RY
Y

This pterygoma is written on a piece of kosher parchment or engraved on a metal disk, usually for the purpose of expelling the power of the "demon of blindness," and to encourage the curing of eye diseases. However, in recognising the power of the pterygoma to expel a demon from the human body, it is employed for this very purpose in the following manner. We are told to take earth from an anthill (wet I presume), and to write with it the *Shabriri* pterygoma on the trunk of a sour pomegranate tree. Afterwards take a length of string from the loom of a weaver, and cut it to the measurement of the afflicted individual. The string is then wrapped three times around the said tree three and tied. Next the string is removed and buried in a spot where it is highly unlikely that the sufferer will pass.[86] In a much simpler method employing the *Shabriri* construct for the same purpose, the said names are written horizontally, i.e. שברירי ברירי רירי ירי רי י, over the mouth of the afflicted individual, whom we are told "will be cured forthwith God willing!"[87]

Now, whilst we might in this manner have rid individuals from demonic possession, it is perhaps also necessary to take additional precautions to protect those who were at one time afflicted with demon possession from possible reentry of these malevolent forces. In this regard there is however a snag which has to be kept in mind. An amulet will not protect a wearer against "demon possession," when the malefic force is still present within the very being of the one seeking protection. Whilst, there are on this specific issue a number of reports to be found in primary literature dealing with this topic,[88] we will consider the following procedure and amulet employed not only to counter demonic possession, but to also preclude the demon from reentry in its erstwhile host body.

We are also told that when an individual should become possessed by a class of demon whose behaviour is to sulk and tear clothing, that one should take a new linen cloth and write on it the Names אוה בנינבי. Afterwards the cloth is shaped into a wick and burned under the nose of the afflicted individual. Should the malevolent spirit refuse to depart, address the spirit saying:

הנני משביעיך בשם בסך שכך שתצא ולא מעינו
ולא מפיו אלא מאצבע קטנה ולא תזיקנו

Transliteration:

> *Hineini mashbiacha b'shem Besach Shechach shetitze v'lo
> mi'eino v'lo mi'piv ela mi'etzba k'tana v'lo tazikenu*

Translation:

> Here I adjure you in the name *Besach Shechach* to depart
> not via his eye and not via his mouth, but via the little
> finger and without harming him.

Afterwards write the following *chotam* (magic seal), and hang it
around the neck of the erstwhile afflicted individual:[89]

אדי	רי	רון
סמ	רי	רון
סנ	רי	רון

Whilst I have not found any elucidation as to the meaning of the
curious Divine Name combination בסך שכך (*Besach Shechach*),
it is exclusively employed in adjurations the intention of which is
the exorcism of שדים (*Shedim*), who are instructed to depart via
the little finger without harming the afflicted individual in any
way.

Now, I have previously voiced my misgivings about
"demon possession" and "exorcisms."[90] I stated that I do not
believe people are possessed very often, that they are more likely
to be "*ob*sessed," hence they are, demonically speaking, rarely
"*po*ssessed." As noted, most of "our obsessions are products of our
own personalities, and while some of these are harmless enough,
others might turn out to be extremely dangerous and injurious,"[91]
but these are not necessarily "demonic." It is only too easy to
invent demons where none exist in order to blame some external
agency for ones own peculiarities.

It is also worth noting that whilst there are indeed "malevolent forces" which humans are at times coerced to deal with, many "demons" were invented to account for most of the natural ills of mankind. Yet, providing we know that we are personifying such factors for the convenience of our consciousness to deal with directly, there is no reason why we should not do this. That is the idea of acquiring a "demon-name" in terms of words with which our consciousness can cope with and to which our intentions can be applied. So *that* is not so ridiculous as one might suppose.

For example, people have a horrible fear of unnamed diseases. Identify what it is they have, and that removes much of the fear. Think of "rheumatism." There never was such a thing, even though we still go on using the word aimlessly. It was invented purely by doctors who then believed in a "fluid" theory of health, and rheumatism was supposed to be a condition of excess "*rheum*" which caused pains all over the body, especially in the joints. We still go on calling it that to this day for purely psychological reasons, in order to have a word as a label for pains we cannot account for. It is the *word* we need. So, we accept it as valid even though doctors know perfectly well it is not. I suppose in a way you could call "*rheumatism*" a magic word, because that was the reason all those "Names of Power" were invented. To name anything gave you some power over it, because you could then apply your consciousness intentionally to whatever it was. Without a name you could not very well focus on it, but with a name, you could.

Be that as it may, I certainly see no harm in having special protection against "evil forces," whether, as said earlier, these be of the physical or spirit kind. Regarding the latter, writing *Psalm 101* conjointly with *Psalm 68* on a scroll, which is afterwards carried on ones person, is said to be a most powerful defense against evil spirits.[92] However, it is one thing contending with the attacks of the denizens of the evil realms of spirit, yet it is quite another dealing with the evil intentions of humans. In fact, it is actually quite difficult to ascertain which is worse. Be that as it may, the following amulet was originally constructed to counteract the "evil spells" of our fellow humankind:

This curious amulet, employed to cancel all magical spells of both the written and spoken varieties, is constructed from the three words of *Exodus 22:17* [*16*] reading:

מכשפה לא תחיה

Transliteration:
> *m'chashefah lo t'chayeh*

Translation:
> Thou shalt not suffer a sorceress to live.

Note there is an additional י (*yod*) in the amulet, this being included in the word תחיייה. The reason for this appears to be the "harmonising," as it were, of the "incantational order" of the letters, hence the opening line comprises four tri-letter combinations. Furthermore, the יי abbreviation of the Ineffable Name is frequently employed in Hebrew amulets. The current amulet comprises:

Line 1 — Four sets of letter combinations incorporating three letters each formed from the said biblical verse;
Line 2 — The reverse of line 1;
Line 3 — Six two letter combinations, arranged in the following manner:

> a. the initial of the first word of the verse in question conjoined with the concluding letter of the third word;
> b. the second letter of the first word coalesced with the penultimate letter of the third word;

c. the third letter of the first word combined with the additional ' (*yod*) in the amulet;

d. the fourth letter of the first word correlated with the second letter of the third word;

e. the concluding letter of the first word coupled with the first letter of the third word;

f. the interchange of the two letters comprising the second word.

Line 4 — The reverse of line 3.

In conclusion, the entire construct is hedged in by the well-known conjugation of the Divine Names יהוה (*YHVH*) and אדני (*Adonai*), i.e. יאהדונהי (*YAHDVNHY*—"*Yahadonahi*"), the component letters of which having been divided into four groups of two letters respectively located in the four corners of the *Kamea*. Commencing top right, the entire word can be traced, *right-left-down-right*, around the construct.[93]

On sharing this amulet on a public internet forum, I was queried as to whether the fact that the term *m' chashefa* (sorceress) in the Biblical verse employed in this *Kamea*, would pertain to a man casting the "evil spell." In this regard, we might recall that in the overtly "sexist times" when that portion of the Bible was written, it was generally believed that sorcery was mainly practiced by women. However, in Practical Kabbalah there is no particular interest in whether the verse in question refers to a male or a female, since the actual Hebrew text is considered a powerful incantation against *ALL* magical spells of the evil kind, whether perpetrated by men or women.

The fundamental reasoning here is that the Hebrew letters comprising the verse in question, are basically the "bodies," so to speak, of powerful Spirit Intelligences, these being "channeled" in the mentioned manner in order to obliterate all "baneful psychic influences." Curiously enough, the amulet in question was tried and tested successfully by a woman who was impacted malevolently by a male "*sangoma*" (African medicine man). According to the lady in question "the *Kamea* worked like a dream!"

When it comes to amulets protecting pregnant women against the baneful spells of witches (female) and sorcerers (male), as well as the wiles of the evil *Lilit*, the following *Kamea*, comprised of seven magical constructs, should be ranked amongst the most important.[94] We are informed the seven sectors of this amulet must be inscribed on parchment in the exact order delineated below:

1.   The following image, comprised of the Names יּה (*Yah*), יהוה (*YHVH*), אהיה (*Ehyeh*), and טפטפיה (*Taftafyah*), is inscribed at the top of the amulet:

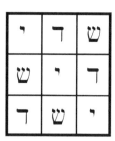

2.   Below this magic seal, to the right of the page, is copied the following שדי (*Shadai*) letter square:

3.   Beneath this letter square is located the framed name of the angel גבריאל (*Gavri'el*):

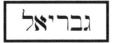

4. Directly below the Name of the said angel, are written the names of the angels מיכאל (*Micha'el*) and זבדיאל (*Zavdi'el*), both located within the same frame:

5. Next, a hexagram comprising the Divine Names יהוה אל (*YHVH El*) is located to the left, adjacent the *Shadai* letter square. As shown below, the Hebrew letters spelling שדי are located in the six corners of the hexagram:

6. Continue by adding the following framed section comprising the Divine Name construct כוזו במוכסז כוזו (*Kuzu B'mochsaz Kuzu*) underneath the hexagram:

7. Conclude by placing the following אהיה (*Ehyeh*) letter square centrally at the very bottom of the amulet:

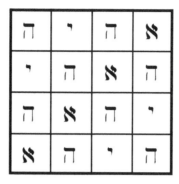

On completion the *Kamea* is suspended on a window, or at the entrance of a passage, and it should remain in place until the individual for whom it was created has given birth, and then for a further thirty days following the delivery of the infant. We are informed that the amulet may not be removed from the individual in question, since it is entirely her decision as to whether the *Kamea* should remain or be taken down. In fact, the amulet may remain in place for life, if that be her wish.[95]

Now, the following magic square is assuredly one of the most important in terms of protecting the body, mind, soul and spirit with the aid of a Hebrew amulet. I have addressed it in fair detail in *"The Book of Sacred Names,"*[96] but since it is ranked amongst the very best, I thought it needs to be dealt with here as well.

הַחֲרֹר	יְלָמָם	הֻשַׁשַׁשׁ	אִיִּי
הֲכַלְכַּב	וְרַכַת	הֲזָמָא	יְעַכֶּץ
יְשַׁשֶׁב	נְדִיָא	דְּקְעַב	אֲמָרוּ

As said previously, this word square "comprises a combination of Divine Names and Hebrew phrases, all of which were carefully intertwined into a powerful magical unit."[97] We are informed that, employed in *Kameot*, it will protect you against:

a.   abduction and attack from man or beast; and
b.   all diseases and assault from all kinds of malevolent forces.

The amulet comprises the three most important Divine Names conjoined with four biblical phrases. To read these, one has to trace the first letter in each box (starting with the right letter in the top right box), then all the second letters, followed by the third letters, and concluding by tracing all the fourth letters. The full meaning of the *Kamea* will then become apparent, the hidden phrase of which reads:

a.   Reading the first letter in each box:
Upper Row: אהיה—*EHYeH*
Middle Row: יהוה—*YHVH*
Lower Row: אדני—*AdoNaY*
b.   Reading the second letter in each box:
ישלח עזרך מקדש
Yislach Ezrecha Mikodesh (Psalm 20:3 [4])
c.   Reading the third letter in each box:
ישמרך מכל רע י"ש
Yishmar'cha mikol ra Y"Sh (Psalm 121:7)
d.   Reading the fourth letter in each box:
ישמר צאתך ובאך
Yishmor Tzet'cha Uvo'echa (Psalm 121:8)
Translation:
Ehyeh YHVH Adonai, may he send you help from (his) holiness, may he guard you from all evil (Blessed be His Name), may He guard your going forth and coming in.

This amulet can be written on deer skin, paper, or engraved on a metal disk, which can be worn as a pendant around the neck, or affixed by a chain around the upper arm. If written on parchment, it might be carried rolled up inside a special amulet holder, which is similarly carried on ones person.[98]

We should consider one of the most powerful magical actions employed to banish baneful forces, whether these be of the deceased human kind or of more demonic kind, e.g. *Klipot* (demonic shards). In this instance, a *Kamea* comprising the following "word square" is created:

$$
\begin{array}{|c|}
\hline
\text{לישועתך קויתי יהוה} \\
\text{לישועתך יהוה קויתי} \\
\text{קויתי לישועתך יהוה} \\
\text{קויתי יהוה לישועתך} \\
\text{יהוה לישועתך קויתי} \\
\text{יהוה קויתי לישועתך} \\
\hline
\end{array}
$$

As indicated, the phrase לישועתך קויתי יהוה (*Lishu'atcha kiviti YHVH*) (*Genesis 49:18*) is employed by permuting the words in every possible manner. Such formulas are often employed in Hebrew incantations and amulets, to "empower"a magical object or action in the most dynamic manner possible.

To employ the amulet for the mentioned purpose, one has to write it on clean parchment, which is tied to the left forearm and worn during periods when one appears most vulnerable, i.e. when a malevolent spirit is most likely to affect one directly, which may be at night during sleep. Immediately following the binding of the *Kamea* to the said limb, one has to verbally recite *Genesis 28:12* seven times. The verse reads:

ויחלם והנה סלם מצב ארצה וראשו מגיע השמימה
והנה מלאכי אלהים עלים וירדים בו

Transliteration:

Va'yachalom v'hineih sulam mutzav artzah v'rosho magi'a ha-shamaimah v'hineih mal'achei Elohim olim v'yordim bo.

Translation:

And he dreamed, and behold a ladder set up on the earth, and the top of it reached to heaven; and behold the angels of God ascending and descending on it.

Next, one has to utter the six permutations of the phrase listed on the amulet in the exact order,[99] and if one should suspect that the spirit onslaught is particularly severe, and that it is impacting ones life not only in a direct personal manner, but in a much more expanded way, i.e. affecting ones business, loved ones, etc., the *Kamea* should be worn at all times, and additional spiritual protection measures adopted.

In the case of current amulet, it has been suggested that, besides vocalising the listed six permutations, one should recite *Exodus 33:21* twenty-six times. The verse reads:

ויאמר יהוה הנה מקום אתי ונצבת על הצור

Transliteration:

Va'yomer YHVH hineih makom iti v'nitzavta al ha-tzur

Translation:

And *YHVH* said: 'Behold, there is a place by Me, and thou shalt stand upon the rock.'

The twenty-six utterances of this verse equate with the *gematria* of the Ineffable Name [י = 10 + ה = 5 + ו = 6 + ה = 5 = 26]. It should be noted, the same technique is delineated in the *Shorshei ha-Shemot*, where it is employed in conjunction with other Divine Names and additional spiritual cleansing activities, for the purpose of "Dream Questioning."[100]

Activities such as these may appear somewhat difficult to execute. In fact, I am quite sure the average English reader of this material would be a lot more comfortable procuring an amulet comprised of powerful Divine and/or Angelic Names; magic seals; perhaps including a potent written adjuration; etc., which could be carried on ones person as an effective amulet, not only against all manner of threats, i.e. psychic assault; the onslaught of infernal forces; illness; etc., but also in the promotion of personal well being in the broadest sense of the word. In this regard, the following *Kamea* fits the bill exactly.

Inscribed on clean parchment, it opens with the following "very potent adjuration" written at the very top of the scroll:

שישמרו וירפאו ויצילו ל"נ"ק"ז"ע]לנושא קמיע זה עליו[
מכל מיני חולאים רעים שיש בעולם ומכל מיני עין
הרע ומכל פחד ואימה ויראה וחרדה ורעה ובהלה

וחלחלה וזיע ורתת ומכל כאב ראש וכאב לב ונזילה
ותמהון לב ודפיקת לב ועילוף לב ורפיון מוח ומשדין
ושדתין ולילין ולילתין טהרירין צפרירין רמשיין
ארציים רוחניים אשים מימים ההולכים בסתר ובגלוי
ומכל קשור וכשוף שיש בעולם עבר הווה ועתיד בכח
מלאך הזה

Transliteration:

> *Sheyishmeru v'yirap'u v'yatzilu l'nose kamea zeh alav*
> *mikol minei chola'im ra'im shiyesh ba'olam v'mikol minei*
> *ayin ha-ra v'mikol pachad v'eimah v'yir'ah v'charadah*
> *v'ra'ah v'behalah v'chal'chalah v'zei'a v'retet v'mikol*
> *k'ev rosh v'k'ev lev v'nezilah v'timahon lev v'd'fikat lev*
> *v'iluf lev v'rifion moach v'mi-Shedin v'Shedatin v'Lilin*
> *v'Lilatin Tahoririn Tziporirin Remeshin Eretzim Ruchanim*
> *Eshim Mayimim ha-holchim b'seter v'b'galui v'mikol*
> *kashur v'kishuf shiyesh ba'olam avar hoveh v'atid b'koach*
> *mal'ach ha-zeh*

Translation:

> Protect and heal and rescue the bearer of this amulet from
> all kinds of bad diseases existing in the universe, and from
> all kinds of Evil Eye, and from all fear and terror and dread
> and anxiety, and wrong and panic and horror, and sweating
> and trembling, and from all headache and heart ache and
> leaks, and shock and heart palpitations and a faint heart and
> mental inertia, and from male and female *Shedin*, and male
> and female *Lilin*, and *Tahoririn* [spirits of impurity] and
> *Tziporirin* [birdlike (taloned) spirits] and *Remeshin*
> [Crawling Spirits]; and *Eretzim* [earth spirits] *Ruchanim*
> [air spirits] *Eshim* [fire spirits] *Mayimim* [water spirits],
> those who march in secret and openly, and from all related
> spirit forces and sorcery existing in the universe, past,
> present and future, in the power of this Spirit Messenger
> [Angel].

The "Angel" referred to is מכשפיאל (*M'chashpi'el*), a Spirit
Intelligence whose Name appears at the very top of the rightmost
portion of the following image, which is to be located below the
adjuration. As indicated below, the entire construct is comprised
of a set of Divine and Angelic Names, as well as magical seals:

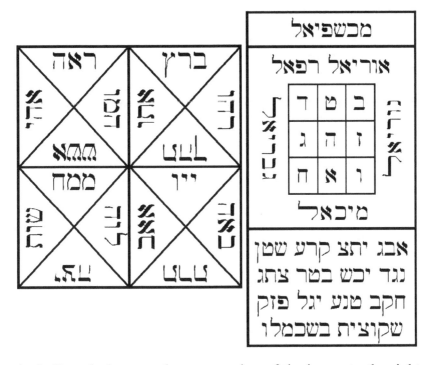

As indicated, the central upper portion of the image to the right contains the "Magic Square of the Third Order," which is, as it were, braced by the earlier mentioned "Supreme Five," i.e. Top—אוריאל (*Ori'el*) and רפאל (*Rafa'el*); Left—גבריאל (*Gavri'el*); Bottom—מיכאל (*Micha'el*); and Right—נוריאל (*Nuri'el*). In turn, the bottom portion of the image is comprised of the entire "Forty-Two Letter Name of God," concluding with the standard abbreviation of ברוך שם כבוד מלכותו לעולם ועד (*Baruch shem k'vod malchuto l'olam va'ed*—"Blessed be the Name of His glorious Kingdom throughout eternity").

Regarding the earlier referenced name מכשפיאל (*M'chashpi'el*), this is the appellative of a most unusual Spirit Intelligence who is one of three angels whose names are employed in an amulet to counteract and cancel evil spells. In this regard, there are instructions to write an amulet with ink composed of almond shell, quicksilver and wax on a parchment made from the skin of a fish.[101] The *Kamea* comprises a written incantation comprised of the mentioned three angelic names as well as Divine Names, as shown below:

משביע אני אליכם מכשפיאל סנדריאל הדרניאל
בשם יהוה צבאות שדי אלהים שתבטלו כל מיני
כישוף מי[נפלוני בן פלוני] אשר נעשה לו מעולם
אנסו

Transliteration:

> *Mashbi'a ani aleichem M'chashpi'el Sandri'el Hadarni'el*
> *b'shem YHVH Tzva'ot Shadai Elohim sh'tevatlu kol minei*
> *kishuf m'[.....Ploni ben Ploni.....] asher na'asah lo m'olam*
> *ANSV [Omein Netzach Selah Va'ed]*

Translation:

> I adjure you *M'chashpi'el Sandri'el Hadarni'el* in the name *YHVH Tzva'ot Shadai Elohim* to cancel all manner of spells from [.....fill in name of victim.....] which was done to him in the universe. *Amen*, Enduring (Victory), *Selah*, Forever.

Be that as it may, returning to the large *Kamea* under discussion, the peculiar image on the left comprises the following sixteen Divine Names:

ברץ ראה אהי שות יצה תרת באה רהו
אתו אאב לוה המו ייו ממח אשש תהך

This set of sixteen tri-letter combinations were constructed from the first forty-eight letters of *Genesis 1:1–2*, reading:

[Verse 1] בראשית ברא אלהים את השמים ואת הארץ
[Verse 2] והארץ היתה תהו ובהו וחשך

Transliteration:

> [Verse 1] *Bereishit bara Elohim et ha-shamayim v'et ha-aretz*
> [Verse 2] *v'ha-aretz haitah tohu va-vohu v'choshech*

Translation:

> [Verse 1] In the beginning *Elohim* created the heaven and the earth
> [Verse 2] and the earth was unformed and void, and darkness

Reading the first letters of each combination in exact order, then repeating the process by commencing with the second letter of the last tri-letter combination and reading backwards to the first combination, then continuing reading the third letters of each combination in the normal fashion, concluding with the third letter of the last combination, the full phrase is revealed.

We are told that the power of this Divine Name is "great," and the forty eight letters comprising this Name are sometimes employed with vowels, as a *Kamea* the intention of which is to banish demons. With vowels the Divine Name reads:

בְּרֵין רְאָה אֱהִי שׁוֹתְ יְצָה תְּרֵת בָּאֹה רְהָוּ
אָתֵוּ אֱאֵב לְוֹה הִמוּ יְיִן מְמַח אֱשָׁשׁ תֵּהַךְ

We are informed that if you should pronounce this Divine Name over a raging ocean, the stormy waters will calm down. Furthermore, it is used in support of any purpose whatsoever, and it is said that uttering it in stressful circumstances will get you out of any difficult situation, and solve all personal problems.[102]

Now, the peculiar presentation of this Divine Name in the earlier mentioned *Kamea*, also appears in the following *Kamea* for the protection of a woman during child birth:[103]

This *Kamea* should be written on a Kosher scroll, and as in the case of an earlier addressed "birth protection" amulet, it is suspended above a window or at the entrance of the room in which the woman in labour is to give birth. In the current instance she is afforded the choice as to where she would like the amulet to be located. However, it is important that the *Kamea* is fully exposed, and not placed inside a bag or envelope.

The Divine Names אתמפ לאדם לתארוליב אאדהצצפס, located in the centre of the amulet, were derived from the following sources:[104]

1. אתמפ from the initials and לאדם from the concluding letters of the first four words in *Proverbs 3:25* reading:

אל תירא מפחד פתום

Transliteration:
Al tira mipachad pit'om

Translation:
Be not afraid of sudden terror

2. לתארוליב from the initials of the words comprising *Psalm 91:10* reading:

לא תאנה אליך רעה ונגע לא יקרב באהלך

Transliteration:

> *lo t'uneh alecha ra'ah v'nega lo yikrav b'oholecha*

Translation:

> There shall no evil befall thee, neither shall any plague come nigh thy tent

3. אאדהצפס from the initials of the words comprising *Psalm 91:5* reading:

$$\text{לא תירא מפחד לילה מחץ יעוף יומם}$$

Transliteration:

> *lo tira mipachad lailah mechetz ya'uf yomam*

Translation:

> Thou shalt not be afraid of the terror by night, nor of the arrow that flieth by day.

We are told these four Divine Names have the power to save a woman from evil witchcraft. However, whilst these Divine Name constructs feature prominently in the *Kamea* we are addressing, it is the Divine/Angelic Name יואאהצצביירון, located in the block at the very bottom of the amulet, which is of particular significance both in Jewish Mysticism and Hebrew amulets.[105] In its original format this Divine Name construct reads יוחצצבירון, which is said to have been derived from *Exodus 33:21* by some or other inexplicable method. This Divine Name construct appears in a number of variant formats, יואהצצבירון (pronounced either *Yova'acheitzatzabeiyoreivanu* or *Yova'acheitzatzabeiyoreivan*); the incredible fifteen letter combination ייוהאאחוצצהבירון (*Y'yovaho'acheiveitzatzah'beiyoreivanu*); ייואהצצובירהון (*Yayova'ahachatzatzavebeiyoreihivanu*); etc.[106] It is clear that the latter two incorporate the strategic interspersing of the four letters of the Ineffable Name. Excluding these four letters from the Name in question leaves us with יואהצצבירון, the first listed variant, and there is an interesting study on the various ways in which this Divine Name construct is affiliated with the Ineffable Name.[107]

Be that as it may, we are told that the original Name and all its variants are the appellatives of a great and joyous Angelic Prince. This Spirit Intelligence is said to have a thousand mouths.

Each mouth has a thousand tongues, and every tongue is offering glad song and praise unto the Creator. He ranks amongst the Angels who are said to be in charge of song.[108] In this regard, I would say that the joyous event in the whole world, one worthy of gladsome song, is perhaps the birth of a child, hence the most joyous angel of song and praise, יואאהצצבבירון, features in amulets aiding women in childbirth. However, the power of the same Spirit Intelligence is enlisted in a "*House Kamea*," i.e. an amulet meant to guard a home and its occupants, as indicated in the following amulet:

וזפ הלא פעב ביב באמ ובה והו
והאפה הבמוג ולה

ילשת באשר בוליב
יואאחצצבבירון

This amulet is meant to protect a new house erected on previously unoccupied land. In this regard, we are told that the building might be obstructing "pathways" along which spirit beings travelled previously. Thus, to protect a new house and its occupants against possible attack by harmful Spirit Intelligences, the owner should request a *sofer* (scribe) to write the two portions of the listed *Kamea* on two separate kosher scrolls, i.e. clean sheets of good quality paper. The top portion is suspended above doors and the bottom one above windows.[109]

It is with regard to its "home protection" qualities that the Name יואאצצבבירון played a role in what has perhaps become somewhat "notorious" practice. This pertains directly to the person of Reb Yeshaya Steiner, who lived in the small town of Bodrogkeresztúr, Hungary. In fact, near the town on the crest of Dereszla hill and overlooking a sea of vineyards, stands a small building housing the gravesite of the good Rabbi. Founder of the Kerestir Chassidic dynasty, Reb Steiner is also acknowledged as a "wonder worker," i.e. a "practical kabbalist."

This very humble Hungarian Rabbi was born in Zbarav in 1851, and always referred to himself as "*Shayale*." The appellative stuck and to this day the good Rabbi is similarly referred to by those who remember him with great affection. Yet, whilst he may have considered himself in the diminutive, Reb Shayale was a very remarkable individual who was gifted with great "wonder working" skills. One report has it that a certain Yechezkel Taub consulted the Rebbe about the scarcity of fish in the nearby River Bodrog, especially since this was negatively impacting the lives of those who were making a living from fishing. We are told that the good Rabbi informed his visitor not to fear, and that there would be lots of fish the following day. The next day there were indeed lots of fish in the nets. We shall never know whether the Rabbi personally affected the sudden increase of fish, or merely displayed remarkable oracular skills.

However, Reb Shayale's current fame is not based on perceived "paranormal skills," or on the fact that he is the founder of an important Chassidic dynasty, but rather on a single photo of himself which is currently popularly hung on the walls of private homes as an amulet against vermin, i.e. mice and rats. Called the "mousser rebbe," it is reported that an individual who earned his living supplying food to his local community, was seeking the urgent advice of the Rabbi regarding an infestation of mice wreaking havoc in his granary, and destroying other foodstuffs in his warehouse.

There is a "twist" in the tale, which, according to some reports, pertains to the local pastor of the town, or, according to others, a local nobleman. Apparently this individual was particularly harsh and unkind to the local Jewish community, hence it is said Rabbi Steiner told his visitor to return to his warehouse where he was to order the vermin in the name of Reb Shayale to depart to the estate of the pastor/nobleman. The saga concludes with the mice racing away, and the Jewish businessman being spared further destruction of food commodities by vermin.

It is said that since this episode people have employed the photo of the Rabbi as an amulet to ward off mice and rats. However, this seems to work for some and not for others, and in this regard there have been a number of interesting, some quite amusing, reports doing the rounds on the world wide web. One individual mentioned that a friend had difficulties with rats on a boat, which ceased after he displayed on board a photo of Reb Steiner. Another tells of how he tried to rid his apartment of a pesky mouse, by running after it with the picture of Reb Shayale. In this instance the mouse won the day and stayed put.

Now, I believe everybody missed the boat as far as their faith in the Kerestirer Rabbi's photo is concerned. In fact, the good Rabbi wrote amulets to rid a residence/warehouse of vermin. A pair of *Kameot* composed by Reb Steiner for this very purpose was displayed in an exhibition held in the Bible Lands Museum, Jerusalem,[110] and, as shown in the reproduction below, these amulets are simply variants of the earlier addressed "house *Kamea*":

$$\boxed{\begin{array}{r} \text{ילשת באשר בוליב} \\ \text{והאפה הב מוגלה} \end{array}}$$

$$\boxed{\text{יואאחצצבבירון}}$$

. ...Meanwhile, he taught Haninah and his wife the virtues of each specific, and then ordered the animals to bring everything back to Haninah's house... ... .

Chapter 6
Tzedek — Jupiter
KAMEOT FOR
HEALTH, WEALTH
&
HAPPINESS

A. Health & Healing

Maintaining good health throughout ones natural life is a major issue for all of us. We appear to be extremely vulnerable, and the onset of sudden sickness and disabilities are constant reminders of just how vulnerable we mortals are. Come to think of it, the sum-total of human suffering all round must be incredible, and yet it seems to be considered quite a normal condition in this world, as long as it is happening to somebody else. It should therefore come as no surprise that next to "protection amulets," those promoting health must be ranked amongst the most popular.

I have broached the topic of magical healing elsewhere,[1] and will in the current instance focus on the use of *Kameot* in the promotion of healing and good health. In this regard we might commence with a careful investigation of pterygomas. Etymologically the term "pterygoma" refers to something "wing shaped." In the current instance, this term is employed in reference to the reduction of words, phrases, the names of demonic entities, etc., employed in magical amulets, this being done one letter at a time in order to sympathetically diminish and annihilate their impact in the lives of those impacted by malevolent forces.

The most famous pterygoma must assuredly be the אברא כדברא (*Abracadabra*) formula.[2] It was often used in the form of a pterygoma to dispel inflamation and fever, and for this purpose it was usually written in the following manner on a piece

347

of pure sheepskin parchment. The belief is that the word being reduced to nothing, would take the fever with it and likewise dwindle it to zero:

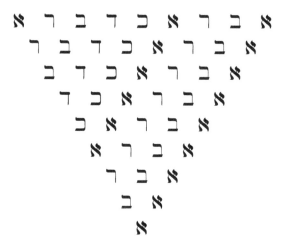

Having addressed the term *Abracadabra* and some related magical expressions to some extent in *"The Book of Sacred Names,"*[3] I will add here further clarification and talismanic uses which are not addressed in the mentioned tome. In this regard, a most important amulet comprises the אברקלוס/אברקלון (*Abrakolos/ Abrakolon*) pterygomas which are closely related to the *Abracadabra* pterygoma, and are likewise meant to reduce a raging fever, and to invoke healing for all kinds of contagious diseases. In fact, the term אברקלוס (*Abrakolos*) is said to be the name of the "Prince of Fever."[4]

    We are instructed to engrave the אברקלוס/אברקלון (*Abrakolos/Abrakolon*) *Kamea* on a small square plate made of lead, and to do so in the name of the individual requiring healing. Furthermore, this action should be executed with new knife comprising a black handle. The amulet is comprised of two virtually identical formats, these being respectively inscribed on the front and the rear of the amulet. As shown in the following illustration, the אברקלוס (*Abrakolos*) pterygoma is employed on the front of the leaden square, and the אברקלון (*Abrakolon*) one on the rear:[5]

Front

בשם יהוה אלהי ישראל אל נא רפא נא לפב״פ
רפואה שלימה מחולי קדחת

אברקלוס	כשם שמתמעט והולך זה	אברקלוס
אברקלו	השם של שר הקדחת כך	ברקלוס
אברקל	יתמעט חולי הקדחת מפב״פ	רקלוס
אברק	ויסתלק ממנו וילך לנוקבא דתהומא	קלוס
אבר	רבא וייצלל כעופרת במים אדירים	לוס
אב	במקום אשר לא יזכרו ולא יפקדו ולא	וס
א	יעלה על לב פב״פ ולא באבר אחד	ס

שבאבריו שבכל גופו של פב״פ אס״נ וכן יהי רצון
תהום תהו תהום תהו תהום תהו

Rear

בשם יהוה אלהי ישראל אל נא רפא נא לפב״פ
רפואה שלימה מחולי קדחת

אברקלון	כשם שמתמעט והולך זה	אברקלון
אברקלו	השם של שר הקדחת כך	ברקלון
אברקל	יתמעט חולי הקדחת מפב״פ	רקלון
אברק	ויסתלק ממנו וילך לנוקבא דתהומא	קלון
אבר	רבא וייצלל כעופרת במים אדירים	לון
אב	במקום אשר לא יזכרו ולא יפקדו ולא	ון
א	יעלה על לב פב״פ ולא באבר אחד	ן

שבאבריו שבכל גופו של פב״פ אס״נ וכן יהי רצון
תהום תהו תהום תהו תהום תהו

Beside the mentioned pterygomas, both sides of the *Kamea* comprise the same header and central incantation. The header reads:

בשם יהוה אלהי ישראל אל נא רפא נא לן[פלוני בן פלוני]
רפועה שלימה מחולי קדחת

Transliteration:

> *B'shem YHVH Elohei Yisra'el El na r'fa na l'[.....Ploni ben*
> *Ploni.....] r'fua Shleimah m'cholei kadachat*

Translation:

> In the Name *YHVH*, God of Israel, please *El* bring healing
> to [.....name of afflicted individual....], complete recovery
> from the raging fever sickness.

Next the central written adjuration reads:

כשם שמתמעט והולך זה השם של שר הקדחת כך
יתמעט חולי הקדחת מן פלוני בן פלונין ויסתלק ממנו
וילך לנוקבא דתהומא רבא וייוצלל כעופרת במים
אדירים במקום אשר לא יזכרו ולא יפקדו ולא יעלה
על לב]פלוני בן פלונין[ולא באבר אחד שבאבריו
שבכל גופו של]פלוני בן פלונין[אס"ן]אמן סלה נצח[
וכן יהי רצון

Transliteration:

> *K'shem shemitma'et v'holech zeh ha-shem shel sar ha-*
> *kadachat kach yitma'et cholei ha-kadachat mi[.....Ploni*
> *ben Ploni.....] v'yistalek mimeno v'yelech l'nukva d't'homa*
> *raba v'yotzlal ke'oferet b'mayim adirim b'makom asher lo*
> *yizkeru v'lo yipakdu v'lo ya'aleh al lev [.....Ploni ben*
> *Ploni.....] v'lo b'evar echad sh'v'evarav sh'b'kol gufo shel*
> *[.....Ploni ben Ploni.....] omein selah netzach v'ken y'hi*
> *ratzon*

Translation:

> Like this name dwindles down, this name of the prince of
> fever, so shall the fever sickness dwindle from [.....name of
> afflicted individual....], and depart from him and go to a
> great desolate abyss and sink like lead in mighty waters in
> a place where it will not be remembered, and not be
> missed, and not rest on the heart of [.....name of afflicted
> individual....], and not in a single organ of all the parts of
> the entire body of [.....name of afflicted individual.....]
> *Amen Selah* and thus be it so willed.

We are instructed to draw a line below this written incantation, and to write the words תהו תהום (*t'hom tohu*—"the depths of desolation") three times below it.

As you might imagine, the earlier mentioned *Abracadabra* and associated pterygomas are not the only ones employed in the reduction of fevers. The following pterygoma is utilised for the very same purpose:[6]

אוכנוטינוס
וכנוטינוס
כנוטינוס
נוטינוס
וטינוס
טינוס
ינוס
נוס
וס
ס

Transliteration:

OChNOTINOS
ChNOTINOS
NOTINOS
OTINOS
TINOS
INOS
NOS
OS
S

Derived from the writings of Eleazer of Worms,[7] or Yehudah ben Attar according to others,[8] there are additional practical complexities in the employment of this formula. We are instructed to write it on the shell of an unboiled egg. This is followed by roasting the egg in an open fire, after which its contents are consumed by the one suffering from fever. The remaining shell fragments are further incinerated, during which process the smoke produced by the eggshells is inhaled by the sufferer.

I am sure many readers would greatly appreciate a remedy which could be considered an effective "cure all." In this regard the following, as it were, "double pterygoma" is considered good for the curing of all ailments:[9]

רומילוס   רומילוס

ומילוס   ומילוס

מילוס   מילוס

ילוס   ילוס

לוס   לוס

וס   וס

ס   ס

Transliteration:

RVMYLVS   RVMYLVS

VMYLVS   VMYLVS

MYLVS   MYLVS

YLVS   YLVS

LVS   LVS

VS   VS

S   S

The magical word here is clearly *"Romilus"* or *"Romilos,"* which appears suspiciously to be a reference to the legendary founder of the City of Rome. Considering the rather displeasing power wielded over ancient Judea after the Roman invasion, and the equally unpleasant Jewish sentiments regarding the invader, I would not be in the least surprised if the pterygoma in question indeed pertains to a diminishing of the power of the "demon of Rome."

Whatever the case may be, I have certainly not found any clear indication regarding the origins, nor the meaning, of the peculiar magical term in question. Besides, the important factor is that this pterygoma is written conjointly with a special adjuration on parchment, in order to cure any illness. The adjuration reads:

יהי רצון מלפניך יהוה אלהי ואלהי אבותי כשם שזה השם
מתמעט עד תומו כן יתמעט החולי מי[ן\פלוני בן פלונין\ עד
תומו

Transliteration:

> *Y'hi ratzon milfanecha YHVH elohai v'elohei avotai
> k'shem shezeh ha-shem mitma'et ad tumo ken yitma'et ha-
> choli m'[.....Ploni ben Ploni.....] ad tumo*

Translation:

> May it be your will *YHVH* my God and God of my father,
> that in the same way this name is reduced to a finish, so the
> illness of [.....name of afflicted individual.....] is likewise
> reduced to a finish.

Sometimes a set of magical glyphs accompany a pterygoma. In this
regard, the following *chotamot* are employed conjointly with a
very large pterygoma to cure headaches:[10]

The first four magical seals in this set, reading right to left, are
included in that exact order in an amulet which is employed as a
pain killer, and also against all kinds of sickness. In this regard,
inscribe the following magical seals on a small metal plate to be
carried on the person of the one requiring this support:[11]

Regarding "Health & Healing," I have earlier shared magical
practices for the alleviation of headaches, and I have equally
addressed certain magical techniques for the curing of a few
common ailments, e.g. an incantation for headaches, a *Kamea* for
toothache, etc., in the previous volume of this series .[12] Hence I
thought that we might in the current instance, consider a further set
of Divine Names and magical seals which are employed to
alleviate a number of ailments, ranging from toothache to life
threatening conditions. In this regard, we might as well start with
one for problems with teeth:[13]

We are instructed to write these five magical seals on a fragment of parchment, and then to place these in the roof of the mouth adjacent the painful teeth. However, it should be noted that this set of magical seals are employed for teeth specifically, whilst the following are similarly employed to alleviate diseases of the gums:[14]

In this instance, the magical seals are located inside the mouth behind the lips, or against the cheek close to the infected portion of the gums.

Considering other common ailments, it is worth noting that the following *Kamea* comprises a set of Divine Names employed, in conjunction with magical seals, for the purpose of curing illnesses of the hands, feet, heart[15] and, I have been told, bad blood circulation:

לושין לושין מושין מושין קושין קושין
עוטיריש עוטוש

The basic instruction is to write the Names and the magical seals on a new, plain porcelain plate. Thereafter the writing is dissolved by dipping the plate in a bowl of clean water. Part of the water is then consumed, and a portion of it kept to be rubbed on the afflicted part of the anatomy. The very last portion of the action is repeated over a period of three days, hence enough infused water should be kept back to achieve this end.

Another common health matter which has afflicted numerous individuals down the ages pertains to the eyes. Hence, the next *Kamea* was constructed to cure maladies of the eyes:[16]

The instruction is to write these seals, e.g. on a small disc or a piece of parchment, and then suspend it on the indisposed eye. As far as painful and serious conditions of the eyes are concerned, the following *Kamea* was created to alleviate pain in the eyes.[17] For this purpose one has to write the following set of Divine and Angelic Names at the top of a clean sheet of paper or parchment:

פניאל פניאל עליון צבאות צבאות צבאות שדי
שדי שדי שדי שדי שדי צבאות

Transliteration:

> *Pani'el Pani'el Elyon Tzva'ot Tzva'ot Tzva'ot Shadai Shadai Shadai Shadai Shadai Tzva'ot*

Translation:

> *Pani'el Pani'el* lofty Hosts Hosts Hosts *Shadai Shadai Shadai Shadai Shadai* of Hosts

Conclude by writing the following Aramaic adjuration below the set of Divine/Angelic Names:

אתון שמהתא קדישייא וכל קטביגא תקיפו געורו בכל
מיחוש דאית בעינייא דנפלוני בן פלוני א״א נ״נ ס״ס ו״ו

Whilst it is difficult to present a transliteration of this adjuration, I believe it is meant to face all "forces" attacking the eyes to the protective and healing powers of the Divine Names. Hence a translation of the adjuration might read "You Holy Names drive away all pestilent affliction of blindness, every ache and problem in the eye(s) of [.....name of afflicted individual.....], *Amen Amen*, Victory Victory [Endurance], *Selah Selah*, Forever Forever.

Now, as far as some of the more life threatening conditions are concerned, there are equally a number of amulets for these. In this regard, consider the following *Kamea* created to alleviate disorders of the spleen:[18]

In this regard, we are told to engrave the magical seals on a plate made of tin, which is to be worn on ones person against the spleen, or the liver, or the head, or any painful area. However, these bodily areas should be cleansed of all dirt and impurities prior to locating the amuletic construct on it. Furthermore, when not in use, the amulet should be stored in a clean locale or container, as should all amulets comprising great and holy magical seals and Divine Names.

As an aside, I encountered this specific *Kamea* several decades ago, when I was a very young man having had a bit of a bother with what I thought was an overactive gallbladder. At the time I found it very difficult to eat or drink anything, every consumable substance giving me instant indigestion. A very dear Israeli friend, whom I greatly admired for being "in the know about these things," engraved these seals on a tin sheet, which he placed in a glass of cold water every night for the period of around a week. He had me drinking this infused substance every morning, and.....*voila!*.....indigestion cured, and, according to my general health to date, equally no more gallbladder issues.

Considering the amount of *Kameot* dealing with illnesses, it is clear that the frailty of our physical bodies is well attested to in Jewish magic. Obviously there were certain conditions which our ancestors found difficult to deal with, seizures and epilepsy being amongst these. However, there is a magical prescription which is said to alleviate seizures. In this regard, to aid an individual who is suffering a fit and who cannot communicate, whose body has gone rigid and lost all feeling, one has to write the following Divine Name construct, comprised of the conjunction of the Ineffable Name and אלוה (*Eloha*), on a piece of parchment which is placed under the head of the sufferer:

יֶאֱהֶלֲוָוָהֶהֶ

Transliteration:
>
> *Yo'aheilavavaheihei*

Following this action, one has to write a further set of Divine Names on a fragment of parchment and the writing dissolved in a bowl of water. Some suggest the writing should be done directly on the inside surface of the bowl. The mentioned set of Divine Names comprises:

המנל אשבי צכתע

The individual in question is afterwards encouraged to imbibe the Divine Name infused liquid, which is said will halt the seizure.[19]

As stated earlier, many would settle for a universal "medical panacea," so to speak, which can be used as a cure all. In this regard, *Deuteronomy 7:15* is extensively employed in amulets for healing purposes in general. The verse reads:

והסיר יהוה ממך כל חלי וכל מדוי מצרים הרעים
אשר ידעת לא ישימם בך ונתנם בכל שנאיך

Transliteration:
>
> *v'hesir YHVH mimcha kol choli v'chol mad'vei mitzrayim ha-ra'im asher yada'ta lo y'simam bach un'tamam b'chol shon'echa*

Translation:
>
> And *YHVH* will take away from thee all sickness; and He will put none of the evil diseases of Egypt, which thou knowest, upon thee, but will lay them upon all them that hate thee.

In some instances the letters comprising the verse are simply rearranged in direct order, into twenty-one groups comprised of three letters each, as shown below:[20]

והס ירי הוה ממך כלח ליו כלמ
דוי מצר יסה רעי סאש ריד עתל
איש יםם בדו נתן סבב לשן איך

These tri-letter groups are written on parchment and carried by an individual seeking healing from some or other illness. Elsewhere the same verse is arranged in a special manner into thirty-one letter pairs, as shown below:[21]

וך הא סנ יש רל יכ הב וֹם הנ מת
מֹנ דֹו כֹך לב חֹם לֹמ יי וש כי לא
מֹל דֹת וֹע יֹד מי צֹר רש יא סֹם הי רע

In this instance, the two glyphs of the letter pairs respectively comprise the first letter of the verse conjoined with the last letter; the second letter with the second last letter; the third letter with the fourth last letter; the fourth letter with the fifth last letter, etc. You may well wonder why the third letter should not be conjoined with the third last letter, and why the latter letter is excluded altogether. The main reason is that the resulting combination would be the reverse of the Divine Name יה (*YH*), hence being a baneful combination which would detract from the fundamental purpose of the amulet.

It is worth noting that the first portion of *Deuteronomy 7:15* is also employed in a *chotam* for the curing all kinds of illness:[22]

חִי	כָּל	מִךְ	יְהַ	וּרְ
וּרְ	חִי	כָּל	מָךְ	יְהַ
יְהַ	וּרְ	חִי	כָּל	מִךְ
מִךְ	יְהַ	וּרְ	חִי	כָּל
כָּל	מִךְ	יְהַ	וּרְ	חִי

This letter square is derived from the initials and concluding letters of the first five words of the verse. In this regard, an individual requiring healing need only write this amulet on clean parchment, and carry it on his or her person. There are variants of this magical seal which are equally employed in *Kameot* for the purpose of curing any kind of sickness. These are a lot more complex, requiring additional magic squares and adjurations to be included in the amulet, etc.[23]

As it is, most of the listed *Kameot* for healing, may appear somewhat complex to construct, however it is worth noting that sometimes the most basic combination of Divine Names is used for healing purposes. In this regard, the construct אאדדהיניה, which is a combination of אדני and אהיה, is employed in a *Kamea* to aid the healing of a gravely ill individual.[24]

The employment of Hebrew amulets for health and healing necessitates a much more detailed investigation than the current study can allow. However, let us conclude this brief study by considering one of the biggest health hazzards, one which particularly emphasises the frailty of our flesh, i.e. poisoning. In this regard, we are told that should someone have consumed a deadly poison, or have contracted a deadly condition brought on by a pandemic, then that individual should forthwith write the following *Kamea* in *ashurit* script on paper. Thereafter the amulet is rolled into a small ball, without anyone other than the writer seeing the writing on the amulet, which is then placed in the mouth of the individual in question who has to swallow it with hot water.[25] It is said he/she will promptly disgorge all of the poison.[26] The following format of the *Kamea* is said to be correct:

פרעון	קרון	האן	פינר
קרון	האן	פרעון	פינר
האן	פרעון	קרון	פינר
חנני	צירה	חנני	צידה

This amulet is said to be a tried, tested and verified method of clearing poison from the bowels of one who ingested it. Elsewhere we are told that if someone should contract a plague, these Divine Names should be placed in the mouth of the said individual the instant he/she starts vomiting or suffers diarrhea. In this regard, the Divine Names should again be ingested with hot water.[27]

We are informed that in the past this Divine Name construct was successfully employed by communities who were hit by the plague. We are told that many people rolled and drank these Divine Names.[28] It is also said that the great Rabbi Shalom Sharabi employed these Divine Names during *Shabat* (the Sabbath) to aid a girl who consumed poison. The Rabbi simply wrote these Divine Names on a piece of paper which she swallowed, and we are informed that the next morning her health was fully restored.[29]

I have not seen any description regarding the origins of this *Kamea*. However, I have seen this Divine Name construct depicted "The incantation of the Kabbalist the pious Rav Baal Shem Tov of Jerusalem,"[30] and elsewhere I perused what appears to be a kind of incantation comprised of a variation of these Divine Names, which are vocalised in the following manner:[31]

חָנֵנִי צֵידְהָ גֵידָה פָּרְעִיּוֹן קָרוֹן
חַאֵן פֵּיגָה פֵּינָר הָנֵנִי צֵידָה

Regarding the *Kamea* in question, it was suggested that three copies should be made of the amulet, which should then be ingested over a three day period. In this regard, there is a related amulet, the format of which is similar to the one we have been addressing, and which includes two of the Divine Names listed in the previous amulet:

גאהנמא פרעון קרעון	פרעון קרעון גאהנמא	קרעון גאהנמא פרעון

In this instance the amulet is used to halt a raging fever, and the instruction is to write the three rows of Divine Names respectively on three separate sheets of paper. Each of these are then burned over a three day period, one per day, allowing the smoke to rise in front of the fever struck individual.[32]

As indicated earlier, the correct manner of writing the Divine Names in the main *Kamea* is over four lines. However, one commentator insists it should be written over two lines in *ashurit* on a thin piece of paper.[33] As shown below, each row would comprise seven terms:

פרעון קרון האן פינר קרון קרון האן פרעון
פינר האן פרעון קרון קרון פינר חנני צורה

Be that as it may, this *Kamea* is addressed in a variety of primary Hebrew sources, all of which are extensive compendiums of Jewish magical practices, i.e. *Segulot*, *Refuot* and *Kameot*. However, the listed works and many others of the same kind, are still only available in their Hebrew original.[34]

B. Wealth & Success

There are many interesting *Segulot* (magical actions or "remedies") employed for the "invocation," as it were, of "abundance." These range from the simplest requirements as far as livelihood is concerned, to "incantations" in which the invocant is literally seeking cartloads of superabundant rewards for personal benefit and enjoyment. "And why not?" My late friend Nechamah Schiff would have said, "you only get what you *think* you deserve!"

Be that as it may, magical procedures sometimes include the permutation of Divine Names in a manner similar to the arrangement of letters and words in some of the "magic squares" and amulets shared in this tome. The idea is that one should utter the words in a great variety of combinations, as shown in the following amulet, which I am told, is used for the creation of abundance. Whilst this one is in English, I have been informed there are Hebrew, German and Yiddish versions. I have not actually seen any of the latter, however the one shared could easily be adapted into other tongues, provided one keeps the simple rhyming and rhythmic quality of the words. In English the "incantation" reads "Please Sire, Grant Desire, Forgive Error, Banish Terror."[35] These words are arranged in a "magic square" which forms the very basis of its subsequent use as a magical procedure, like this:

Please	Sire	Grant	Desire	Forgive	Error	Banish	Terror
Sire	Please	Desire	Grant	Error	Forgive	Terror	Banish
Grant	Desire	Forgive	Error	Banish	Terror	Please	Sire
Desire	Grant	Error	Forgive	Terror	Banish	Sire	Please
Forgive	Error	Banish	Terror	Please	Sire	Grant	Desire
Error	Forgive	Terror	Banish	Sire	Please	Desire	Grant
Banish	Terror	Please	Sire	Grant	Desire	Forgive	Error
Terror	Banish	Sire	Please	Desire	Grant	Error	Forgive

First one has to memorize the initial phrase, which is not a difficult matter. Next, one has to slowly visualize and construct the entire "code," i.e. the entire "magic square" in ones mind. When I did this some years back, it appeared quite a daunting task, but it was actually quite easily mastered. For example, start by reading the top line over and over for a few minutes. Affirm the position of each word. Then close your eyes, and visualize the same whilst uttering the words. Open your eyes, and scrutinize the next line comprising permutations of each word pair, i.e. (upper line) "Please Sire" — (next line) Sire Please"; (upper line) "Grant Desire"—— (next line) "Desire Grant"; etc. Read each upper pair followed by the permutation for a couple of minutes, and then close your eyes again and visualize the entire pattern mentally whilst uttering the words. This might require a little practice for say about fifteen minutes.

If you are able to execute this part of the pattern with some ease, you have more or less mastered the basics of the procedure. Then you can continue assembling the construct by reading the same pattern down the two left side columns of the "magic square." Slowly study the pattern until you can recognize its patterns and are able to conjure it in its entirety in your mind. At this stage you would be ready to use it as a most potent invocation, comprising both the visualization and verbalization. The words are then expressed rhythmically, permuted and read in as many ways and directions as one can — the more complex the better.

It is said, that the procedure is completed when, during the procedure, one begins to loose the desire for the end result, and when the words as well as their component letters are beginning to be but sounds without specific meanings, i.e, one is no longer, as it were, "forcing" the words into the fixed meanings set by ones desire. It is said that the action is halted when this stage is reached, and then one has to forget the entire action so as to allow the *real* "forces" behind the words to get on with the job, or, as my late mentor William Gray used to say, *"Now Leave well alone!!"*

There are many amulets pertaining to acquiring wealth and encouraging success in ones monetary affairs, of which we are able to share only a few in this already overly large tome on Hebrew magical seals and amulets. In this regard, the following "letter square" comprises the simplest amulet employed for success in business:

ד	ט	א
ז	ה	ת
ד	ה	ד

To date I have not found information regarding the origins of this amulet, or any details as to the meaning of its content. However, in this instance the only requirement is to inscribe the image, i.e. lines and letters, on a small leaden or pewter disc or square, and then to carry it on your person in all circumstances, whether these be social or business.[36]

As far as improving financial earnings is concerned, we are informed that the following "*Kamea* for success" from the *Book of Raziel*,[37] is employed to expedite this very purpose, and, with Divine support, to also have great success in all manner of negotiations:

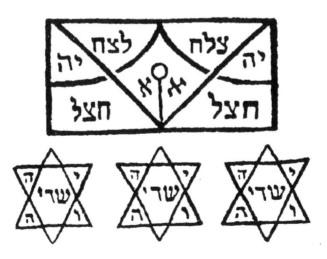

The biblical phrase associated with this *Kamea* is *Psalms 45:4* [5] reading:

והדרך צלח רכב על דבר אמת וענוה צדק ותורך
נוראות ימינך

Transliteration:

va-hadarcha tz'lach r'chav al d'var emet va-an'vah tzedek
v'torcha nora'ot y'minecha

Translation:

And in thy majesty prosper, ride on, in behalf of truth and
meekness and righteousness; and let thy right hand teach
thee tremendous things.

It is worth noting that *Psalm 45:4* [5], the verse associated with the
amulet in question, was itself sometimes reconstituted into a sct of
ten Divine Names employed to enhance or expand, as it were, the
"powers of success" in amulets constructed for financial matters,
or as an additional aid to furthering success in business. The
Names are:

ווֹעמי התנין דמותך ראהו דראצא צבדר לדקו חלונ
רעתך כבור

As you have probably noticed, the first letters of the ten Divine
Names, read in the normative manner, incorporate the first two
words of the verse and the first two letters of the third word. Next,
reversing the flow, i.e. commencing with the second letter of the
tenth Name, then reading backwards the second letters of the other
Names and working upwards towards the first Name, will offer us
the concluding letter of the third word, the fourth, fifth and sixth
words of the verse in question, as well as the first letter of the
seventh word. Continuing the flow by reversing direction again
and reading the third letter of each Name back down to that of the
tenth Name, will in turn provide the remainder of the seventh
word, the eighth word, and the first three letters of ninth word.
Finally, reversing the flow once again and reading the fourth letters
of the ten Divine Names backwards and upwards, we are presented
with the last two letters as well as the concluding two words of
Psalm 45:4 [5].

This is certainly one of the most interesting ways, amongst the many employed in the construction of highly specialised Divine Names from unique Biblical verses. However, as far as the use of this verse in the current amulet is concerned, the appropriate word to keep in mind is צלח (*Tzelach*), translated "prosper" in the English Bible. However, it also means "succeed" which is the fundamental intention behind this amulet. In fact, the *Kamea* construct comprises mainly the word צלח (*Tzelach*) and some permutations of the same, e.g. לצח top left and twice חצל located bottom right and left. In this regard it should be noted that writing permutations of words representing vital components of the basic intention of the individual requiring an amulet, is fairly common in Hebrew amulets.

Beside the term *Tzelach* and its permutations, we note the combination י"ה (*Yah*) which is an acknowledged abbreviation of the Ineffable Name, and a Divine Name in itself. The double *YH* appearing in the amulet could be read conjointly, i.e. *Yiyeh* meaning "will be." As you probably noticed, there are also two adjacent letters א (*Alef*) positioned centrally, and separated by a short vertical line with a circle on top which divides the amulet in half. I do not recall these two letters *Alef* in the amulet being always read conjointly. However, I was informed that they are in fact abbreviations of Hebrew words. As it is, there are literally thousands of abbreviations in the Hebrew language, especially in Rabbinical and Hebrew spiritual literature. In fact, there are so many, that the average individual who speaks Hebrew as his or her mother tongue, is unfamiliar with most of them.

If we read the double אא combination as a Hebrew abbreviation, it could have a number of meanings, depending on context, e.g. *Amen Amen*; *Adonai Elohecha* (Lord your God); *Ani Omer* (I say); etc. In the current instance the abbreviation could well mean *Amen Amen*, but I have also been told that each of these letters in combination with the first two letters of the Ineffable Name repeated in the amulet, are hidden references to the Sacred Name אהי"ה (*Ehyeh*).

The bottom portion of the Amulet comprises three images of the "Shield of David," on each of which are superimposed the four letters comprising the Ineffable Name, as well as שד"י

(*Shadai*), the great Name of Protection. It should be noted, there is also a set of Divine Names affiliated with this "Amulet for Success" we are addressing, the one given in the printed text of the *Sefer Raziel* being:

סנמכבד טנף כרב זג מכביתם עזך סג טמי סמסכרך
הכיסס קתקדר

A very different version appears in the *Sefer Rafael ha-Malach*,[38] and I am informed that there are also variations to be found in the various manuscripts of the *Sefer Razi'el*. Moses Zacutto, who examined all sources of this amulet, maintained in the *Sefer Shorshei ha-Shemot*[39] the correct Names to be:

סנמבר טגף כרר זג מכב ידד סזהסן טתא סדסבר
הסבקסד אדאהב

According to Moses Zacutto these Names should be vocalised:

Sanamav'ra t'gaf b'rar zag m'chav y'ded s'zah'san tete s'dos'v'ra hosvakos'd' idi'heva

A most pleasing incantation is included with the amulet. It reads:

יהי רצון מלפניך יהוה אלהי ישראל שתצוה
למלאכיך אלו לבא אל בית]פלוני בן פלוני[
וללכת עמו ויצליחו אותו בסחורתו ובכל מעשה
ידיו בהצלחה ובהרוחה גדולה בין ביום בין
בלילה בין בבית בין בחוץ לבית בין בעיר בין
בחוץ לעיר ושמך וחותמך הקדוש ירחיבו במעשיו
ובביתו והצליחו לי]פלוני בן פלוני[אמן סלה

Transliteration:

Y'hi ratzon milfanecha YHVH Elohei Yisra'el shet'tzaveh l'mal'achecha elu lavo el bet [.....Ploni ben Ploni.....] v'lalechet imo v'yatzlichu oto bis'chorato uv'chol ma'aseh yadav b'hatzlachah uv'har'vachah g'dolah bein ba-yom

bein ba-lailah bein ba-bayit bein b'chutz la-bayit bein ba-
ir bein b'chutz la-ir v'shimcha v'chotamcha ha-kadosh
yar'chivu b'ma'asav uv'veito v'hatzlichu li-[.....Ploni ben
Ploni.....] Omein Selah

Translation:

May it be your will *YHVH*, God of the God-wrestler, to
command your angels to visit the house of [.....insert the
name of individual], to accompany him, to make him
successful with all his endeavours, and bring success in all
his actions [works of his hands], and great expansion,
whether in the day, whether in the night; whether at home,
whether outside the house; whether in the city, whether
outside the city; and in Your Name and with Your Holy
Seal magnify his actions, and expand his house, and bring
success to [.....insert the name of individual.....] *Amen
Selah.*

I was informed that the entire construct, i.e. the biblical verse, the
set of Divine Names, the magical seals, as well as the incantation,
should be written on a "kosher parchment," traditionally deerskin.
It works equally well when written on a clean sheet of good quality
white paper. Thereafter the completed *Kamea* is carried on the left
side of the individual for whom the amulet was written.

Now, amongst the easiest ways in which an amulet is
employed to achieve success must be the one recommended in the
oft mentioned *Sefer Shimmush Tehillim* ("Magical Use of
Psalms"), in which we are instructed to write *Psalm 108*, e.g. on a
clean sheet of paper or parchment, and then to bury it at the
entrance of ones residence. In this instance, it is said success in all
ones business endeavours is assured.[40]

C. Amulets & Elements

A while back an unique *Kamea* was constructed for a very special
purpose. Named "*Tagiom*," the construct was meant to encourage
and facilitate good living. As it is, the amulet was inspired by the
idea that out of the worst possible situation must come the best
possible good. In fact, the intention was to find a way in which the

intensity of "malevolence" is compensated with double the amount of the same degree of "benevolence." In this regard, a decision was made to fashion a kind of "spirit force-form" which could be perceived to be an "artificial elemental" or a "spirit *golem*," so to speak, to achieve the hoped-for objective.

Method being very important, a way had to be found to conjoin "subtle forces" in a unique manner. However, these "spirit powers" first had to be identified, and then amalgamated to form, as it were, a single "entity." Considering the notion that "every letter of the Hebrew alphabet was, and still is, considered to be the 'embodiment' of a Spirit Intelligence, each being an 'Angel'," and that it is understood that Divine Names "actually are the respective qualities or aspects of Divinity hidden within their inner meanings,"[41] it was decided to employ certain Hebrew glyphs in a special "Magic Square"which would function as a kind of spirit "circuit-board," so to speak, through which, the required spirit forces could be, as it were, "triggered" and "enhanced" for the proposed purpose.

Of course, there has to be a method of ascertaining the exact quality of the "spirit force" which each Hebrew glyph is manifesting or, perhaps better, "channeling." In this regard, it was decided to employ what is sometimes termed the "Yetziratic Incantation Wheel." This comprises a circular diagram comprising three layers of Hebrew glyphs respectively indicating their Elemental, Planetary and Zodiacal attributions as delineated in the *Sefer Yetzirah*.[42] A number of versions of this diagram have been in circulation for some time, as shown in the following examples:

Sefer Yetzirah
Hebrew Glyphs
Arrangement 1

Sefer Yetzirah
Hebrew Glyphs
Arrangement 2

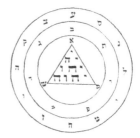

Sefer Yetzirah
Hebrew Glyphs
Arrangement 3

The image to the left is of course the central "Rose" of the much vaunted Golden Dawn "Rose Cross Lamen."[43] Its component twenty-two "petals," without the central crucifix, is derived directly from the three divisions of the Hebrew alphabet in the "*Sefer Yetzirah*,"three "Mother Letters" — א (*Alef*), מ (*Mem*), ש (*Shin*); Seven "Double Letters" — ב (*Bet/Vet*), ג (*Gimel/Djimel*), ד (*Dalet/Thalet*), כ (*Kaf/Chaf*), פ (*Peh/Feh*), ר (*Resh/Resh*), ת (*Tav/Thav*); and twelve "Single Letters" — ה (*Heh*), ו (*Vav*), ז (*Zayin*), ח (*Chet*), ט (*Tet*), י (*Yod*), ל (*Lamed*), נ (*Nun*), ס (*Samech*), ע (*Ayin*), צ (*Tzadi*), ק (*Kof*). In fact, the lay-out of the image of the "rose" was simply "lifted" from one of the "mainstream" kabbalistic commentaries on the *Sefer Yetzirah*, and "redecorated" in a "roseate" pattern in harmony with personal perspectives.

The same details are displayed in the centre, less decorative illustration,[44] as well as in the right image derived from traditional Kabbalistic sources.[45] Hence, beyond the Ineffable Name "*Tetractys*" in the centre of the "mainstream" Kabbalistic version and the crucifix in the centre of the Golden Dawn version, there is in fact not much difference amongst them. Regarding the image from "traditional" kabbalistic sources, in which this image is titled "God and the Universe," we are informed that "the letters and corresponding numbers of the Hebrew alphabet make up the entire model of the Name of God and the principles that govern the universe."[46]

Be that as it may, it should also be perfectly clear that there is nothing particularly remarkable, mysterious, or specifically oriental, etc. about this specific portion of the Golden Dawn "Rose Cross Lamen," and whilst claims have been made that this image is a product of "Hermetic Kabbalah" and not of the "Jewish" variety (which is obviously not factual), it is a plain fact that whilst exegesis may differ from one kabbalistic school of thought to the next, the fundamental principles and doctrines of Kabbalah are the same (or should be the same) throughout its different branches.

It should be noted that in none of the listed diagrams are there any indication of the "Elemental" or astrological attributions assigned to the Hebrew alphabet as portrayed in Latin letters in the following illustration:

Sefer Yetzirah
Hebrew Glyphs transliterated
Arrangement 4

This "Incantation Wheel" is described by William G. Gray in a work titled *"Magical Ritual Methods."*[47] He wrote regarding the three-fold division of the Hebrew glyphs and the accompanying design, saying: "It will be noticed that only the three 'active' Elements are used. These were thought to act upon Earth and produce whatever results were wanted. To make Magic Words from this design, it is necessary to think in the Magical terms of Element-Planet-Sign, then utter these according to their associated sonics. This would not necessarily spell a word of any known human language, but it would make a word intelligible to those accepting its Inner Meaning. If we see the Mothers as the 'soul' of a word, the doubles as the 'mind', and the singles as the 'body', this will provide a plan of construction..... All kinds of Magic Words can be made up by using this, or some similar system. Provided each sonic is properly linked to some comprehensible Inner meaning, the co-ordination of the letters is largely a matter of preference. One advantage of the Element-Planet-Sign system, is that it is generally understood regardless of national languages. If any Magic Words formed by these ideo-sonic codes are to be used in ritual practice, it is essential that participants should be aware of their individual significance."

Considering the fact that there are several versions of the enigmatic "*Book of Creation*," in which all the listed diagrams find their fundamental basis, one might well wonder which should be regarded as definitive. In this regard, reference to contemporary research comprising detailed analysis and translation of those early manuscripts of the "*Sefer Yetzirah*" which have survived the ravages of time,[48] would indicate the following Hebrew version of the "Yetziratic Incantation Wheel" to be more correct:

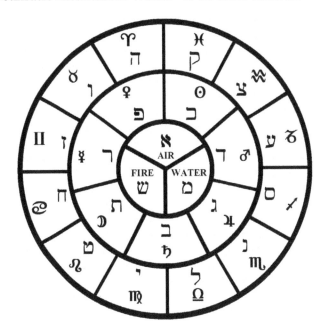

Now, employing the method regarding the construction of Divine Names by means of the "Yetziratic Incantation Wheel," and considering all relevant Elemental, Planetary and Zodiacal requirements, it was agreed that the following "force alignments" would be necessary in the creation of the "*Tagiom Kamea*" and for the ultimate achievement of the magical purpose:

Hebrew Letter Attributes

ט — *Aryeh* [Leo] — Fire

ג — *Tzedek* [Jupiter] — Air

א — *Ruach* — Air

מ — *Mayim* — Water

Vowel Attributes
A [*Ah*] — *Esh* — Fire
I [*Ee*] — *Ruach* — Air
O [*Oh*] — *Mayim* — Water

Here choices pertain to the two Elements of Fire [*Leo*] and Water [*Mem*] being respectively balanced by the Element of Air related to the planet Jupiter and the letter *Alef*. Firstly, the Hebrew glyph related to the Zodiacal sign *Leo*, the latter revealing the fiery splendour of the Sun and midsummer in the Northern Hemisphere, is ט (*Tet*), which is in this instance aligned with the splendour and strength of *Chesed* (Loving-kindness), the latter sphere on the sefirotic tree being associated with Jupiter, the power of which is "embodied" in the letter ג (*Gimel*). Secondly, the Element of Air [א] is conjoined with that of Water [מ], which occurs naturally in the actual substance of water, and the entire complex was arranged in such a manner, that Fire and Water are located opposite each other, with Air "tipping the scale between them."[49]

Next three vowels were chosen to aid articulation of the full Name comprised of the Elemental, Planetary and Zodiacal attributes. As explained elsewhere,[50] the vowels themselves are aligned with Elemental attributions, and in the current instance choice pertained to the order Fire/Air/Water, which in terms of vowels is *Ah* [Fire], *Ee* [Air], and *Oh* [Water]. Curiously enough, this arrangement aligns with one of the six three-letter permutations with which we are told the Divine One sealed the six extremities of the Universe.[51] In this instance, the concord referred to is יוה (*Yod/Vav/Heh*), the permutation with which the Eternal One sealed the depths below.

Be that as it may, a selection having been made in terms of relevant Elemental, Planetary and Zodiacal potencies aligned with a set of Hebrew consonants and vowels, the full name of the proposed "magical entity" could be traced to read as follows:

"TAH–GEE–OHM"

Considering the four component letters of the construct in question, it became clear that there would be much ambiguity regarding its pronunciation since Hebrew is customarily written without vowels. The letter combination טאם is likely to be read *Tag'am*, *Tag'em*, etc., rather than *Tagi'om*. Keeping this in mind, and considering the fact that the sound "*OH*" is often indicated in Hebrew by means of the letter ו (*Vav*) employed as a vowel, it was decided that this glyph should be included in the Name, which would now appear טגאום and which could be pronounced *Tagiom*. As it is, it was felt that since the letter ו is associated with the Zodiacal sign of *Taurus*, and the latter affiliated to the planet Venus, all of which are aligned with the Element of Earth, the inclusion of this Hebrew glyph was understood to introduce a measure of this specific "elemental force" in the task at hand.

The next stage in the process of creating a "spirit force-form" in concord with the mentioned magical intention, required the construction of a single *Chotam* (sigil or seal) to represent the entire Name טגאום. In this regard, a procedure was utilised based on what is called *AYaK BaChaR* or *AIK BeKaR*,[52] a kabbalistic system popularly termed "Qabalah of the Nine Chambers."[53] As explained elsewhere,[54] this system is comprised of a square of nine boxes ("chambers"), each of which contains three letters and the numerical value of each being reducible to the same single digit, e.g. א [1] – י [10] – ק [100] = 1; ב [2] – כ [20] – ר [200] = 2; etc, as shown in the following illustration:

The fundamental components of the mentioned magical sigil are acquired by tracing, in exact order, the angles of the boxes containing the component letters of the four primary Hebrew letters selected, i.e. ט (*Leo*), ג (Jupiter), א (Air), מ (Water):

Combining all four angles in their exact order will present a number of potential shapes, of which the following simple pattern was selected as the seal of *Tagiom*:

This portion of the procedure is concluded with the construction of a "magic square" comprised of the Name טגנאום, and locating the "magical seal" in the very centre of the square. The final result is the "*Tagiom Kamea*":

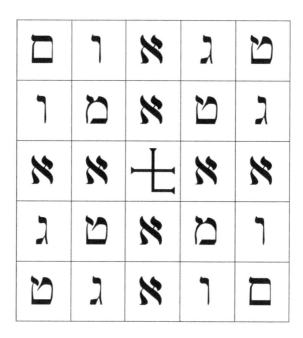

The amulet needs to simply be carried on ones person for it to be effective, but some might prefer to personalise or, as it were, "empower" it. One way of doing this is to follow the procedure of "Identification with the Elements" delineated in the first volume of this series.[55] In this regard, we work with the Elements employed in the construction of the amulet in their exact order of appearance, i.e. first Fire, then Air, and concluding with Water. Here is a description of the complete action applied to our current intention of "empowering" the amulet.

To commence the practice you need to place your "*Tagiom* square" centrally on a little table or cupboard, where you can easily view it. Next, you need to establish "lines of force" linking yourself to the said "magic square." This practice is again the same as the one explicated in "*The Book of Self Creation*,"[56] which is as follows:

1. Focus on your body, and select the following bodily zones, one at a time:

    1. Forehead
    2. Throat
    3. Heart
    4. Navel
    5. Sex organ

2. On an inhalation imagine you are drawing "Divine Spiritual Force" in the form of golden light into the chosen locale inside your body, i.e. the forehead.

3. Next, focus your attention on, i.e. look at, the amulet, and while puckering your mouth and whispering "*OO*" as you exhale, feel the force flow directly out of the chosen area in which it was focussed inside your body, simultaneously imagining or rather feeling how you are projecting a line of force, like a laser beam, from that part of the body from which you are exhaling, and how this line attaches itself to the amulet. There is no need to visualise this thread, since it happens automatically anyway when you look at something. You are only doing it consciously and strengthening the bond.

4. Since you are working this procedure with only one bodily zone at a time, you need to repeat the exercise with each of

the respective areas of your body mentioned above, projecting strands of "Spiritual Force" which link all five locales with the very centre of the *"Tagiom* square" on the surface of the table or cupboard.

5.   On completion, raise your hands and point your fingers or the palms of your hands at the object. Do not tense the hands or fingers, but point in a relaxed manner. Applying the same technique employed in creating the "lines of force" from the previously mentioned bodily organs, project the same "force threads" from your fingers or hands, again imagining them becoming attached to the centre of the amulet. It is possible that you might achieve this with one breath only, however, until you have reached a fair level of proficiency, it is good to employ several breaths in executing this task.

When these golden "lines of power" are established, and all the lines of force are conjoined on the central magical glyph of the *"Tagiom"* amulet, you may commence the earlier mentioned procedure of "Identification with the Elements," focussing first on the Element of Fire. Here is the full procedure:

1.   Select an Element. Bring to mind an image associated with that element, e.g. glowing red coals for Fire (Light); billowing orange clouds for Air (Life); and a deep cool blue pond or lake for Water (Love). Smile warmly at your chosen Element, and feel the warmth of your smile linking with the Element. This should be experienced as intensely as you possibly can.

2.   Keep focussing on the image of your chosen Element, and sense the specific quality associated with that Element, these being "warmth" for Fire, "lightness" for Air, and "coolness" for Water. In this regard, you should encourage a "feeling appreciation" rather than a "thinking" one about each quality. Attempt to keep the "cage of logic" out of this practice. While continuing to smile warmly inside yourself, keep sensing the quality of the Element in question until

you feel you are becoming it. What you should allow to happen, is the sense of being absorbed into, or turning into, the image and quality of that Element.

3.   Continue smiling warmly, and focus your attention fully on the centre of the amulet. During successive inhalations draw the image and quality of the Element into your body, whilst on the exhalations you, as it were, breathe the elemental force along all the "lines of force" established between yourself and the amulet whilst whispering intensely the name "*Tagiom*." Direct the "spirit force" into the very centre of the *Kamea*, i.e. let the fiery, airy or watery element flow into the amulet, which is now turning into a "power object." Repeat this portion of the procedure as many times as you desire, or until you feel that you have, as it were, "charged" the object with the selected Element.

4.   Repeat the full procedure separately with each Element.

On conclusion of these activities, smile warmly at the *Kamea* and keep looking without blinking at the very centre of the object, employing a sort of soft stare in which you perceive the full image in absolute detail with your eyes focussed on the centre. It is bit like looking at someone's nose and seeing the entire face peripherally in absolute detail. This is sometimes called the "soft look," in which you will stare unblinkingly to allow the full image of the object to imprint itself in your eyes and mind, doing so in a surrendered fashion without employing undue force.

      Do this for several minutes, then, when ready, breathe in whilst imagining that you are absorbing the image into your head, close your eyes and for a couple of seconds experience the afterimage inside your head (colours reversed). Take another breath, and on exhalation breathe the image through your forehead into the blackness of the universal infinity whilst whispering the name "*Tagiom*." In this manner you have not only "empowered" the amulet, but have also "internalised" it and linked it with the "Infinite Oneness" of the "All-in-All" and "All-with-All."

Conclude this activity by keeping your eyes closed and invoking in your own being the presence of the "Spirit Force" acting through the *Kamea*, as you utter the following Hebrew incantation:

1. (Say aloud with a deep, stong and resonant voice) *Tagiom, ani mashbi'acha ba-guf* (טגאום אני משביעך בגוף)
   Feeling the whole body resonate with the sound, chant: *Tah–gee–ommmmm*
   Pause and feel the "Presence" inside your body. This is a "feeling appreciation" in which no visualisation is necessary.

2. As before, say aloud *Tagiom, ani mashbi'acha ba-Nefesh* (טגאום אני משביעך בנפש)
   With attention focussed on your solar plexus, or the liver, which in old Kabbalistic teaching is the locale of the Instinctual Self [*Nefesh*], whisper intensely *Tah–gee–ommmmm*
   Pause and feel the "Presence" inside your very gut.

3. As before, say aloud *Tagiom, ani mashbi'acha ba-Ruach* (טגאום אני משביעך ברוח)
   With attention focussed on the heart, the locale of the "Awake Self" [*Ruach*], exhale from your mouth without verbalising anything, as you think in your heart *Tah–gee–ommmmm*
   Pause and feel the "Presence" inside your heart.

4. As before, say aloud *Tagiom, ani mashbi'acha ba-Neshamah* (טגאום אני משביעך בנשמה)
   In total silence and in perfect peace, think above the eyes inside the forehead *Tah–gee–ommmmm*
   Pause and feel yourself being "*Tagiom*." Do absolutely nothing, but simply *be* "*Tagiom*."

5. Conclude the incantation saying the standard: *Baruch Shem K'vod Malchuto l'Olam Va'ed*

The pause between point 4 and the concluding statement is extremely important. You are "*Tagiom.*" You *are* the magic that you are working. This is the point where the "magician" and the "magic" are "One." If the practitioner can achieve the realisation that this specialised "form of force," which was created from the Fire, Air and Water elements, is in fact him or herself, the magic is done and the end result a *fait accompli!*

Do not forget to remove the "*Tagiom Kamea*" from the table top, and carry it on your person, e.g. inside your pocket, wallet, handbag, etc. You only need to quickly think or whisper the concluding incantation every now and again, in order to re-invoke and re-empower the "spirit force" acting through this unique *Kamea.*

. ...When the frog was about to leave, he said to the couple: 'May the Good Lord bless you and be good to you for all the work and trouble you had with me. After all, you didn't even ask who I am. But I will tell you the secret'... ... .

Chapter 7
Shabetai — Saturn
PATTERNS, SHAPES
&
SIZES

A. *Chabusa:* Six-petalled Rosette

I marvel at how people simply "buy" into the most preposterous rubbish, and it would seem they actually relish being led by the nose. I have lost count of the number of times correspondents have tried to convince me of the verity of the most blatant nonsense, by informing me that "it is the absolute truth" since they have seen it written "in black and white." In the current instance it was on Wikipedia, which my correspondent maintained is "a most reliable resource." As it is, Wikipedia certainly offers information but can hardly be construed trustworthy. In numerous instances this resource is dishing up the biggest boloney as fact.

I am presently specifically referring to the ramblings of an individual who styles himself the direct descendent of the biblical *Melchizedek*, and who claims grand galactic origins as well as an equally grand design for himself. Of course, this character is certainly not the first amongst a number of 20th century would-be "messiahs," who have commandeered and abused the identity of the legendary biblical Priest-King. However, he is apparently the first to have misappropriated an ancient, simple, and very popular geometric design, newly styled the "flower of life," to which he assigned a lot of browbeating pseudo-scientific twaddle. It would seem that subsequently all and sundry are satisfied to dance merrily to the crazy rhythms of this off-beat tune!

Now, the image in question is generally known as the six-petalled rosette, a most popular ancient geometric design, carved on ancient Middle Eastern sarcophagi, ossuaries, etc.[1] It was also employed as a decorative design in Jewish legal documents like *Ketubot* [marriage agreements]; prayer books; illuminated manuscripts, etc.,[2] as well as in a variety of Hebrew amulets.[3] In fact, it is the simplest geometric design which can be drawn with any flat circular object. I constructed it when I was six years old with the aid of a lid of a canned fruit bottle, and was very proud of my "discovery" only to be later greatly disappointed at my lack of originality, when the very same image was shown to me in published format.

As it is, the design in question is widely used in traditional folk art, some even calling it a "hex" sign.[4] It appears in both the most simple format, and in more complex and expanded versions as shown in the examples below:

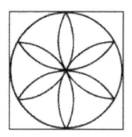 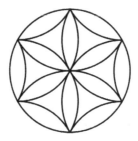 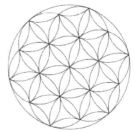

As hinted above, throughout the ages the popularity of these designs is due to the fact that the basic image is easily drawn with any circular object, i.e. the edge of a cup, etc. Researching its inclusion in Hebrew amulets, I have recently perused various examples of its uses in the arts and crafts of Kurdistani Jews, which include magical items like amulets.[5] These people referred to this image as a *Chabusa*, i.e. a "quince" design. The Hebrew for the quince-fruit is *chabush*, which the Kurdistanis thought this image represented. Others called it an "apple" design, and others still thought it representative of a lily, the six-petalled *Shoshan* on which, it has been claimed, the "*Magen David*" (Shield of David) is based. In fact, the design in question and the hexagram often complemented each other on the walls of ancient synagogues, like the famous one of *Kfar Nachum* (Capernaum); or the synagogue of *Kfar Shura* near Rosh Pina in Israel; etc.[6]

So, in contrast to the many fanciful notions regarding the derivation of the six-petalled rosette, its origins are really quite simple and far removed from all the fictitious "extraterrestrial" jabber. Be that as it may, a very beautiful 18/19th century silver necklace from Kurdistan, comprised of a set of five circular amulets, which is currently part of the Feuchtwanger collection of *Kameot*, is a magnificent example of the employment of the six-petalled rosette in Hebrew amulets.[7] The following illustration is a graphic representation of the central main *Kamea*:

This amulet is comprised of the "Forty-two Letter Name of God" including the abbreviation בשכמלו, the latter being a reference to the oft mentioned standard concluding phrase *Baruch Shem K'vod Malchuto l'Olam Va'ed*; ארגמן (*Argaman*) which we noted is an acronym constructed from the initials of the names of the archangels אוריאל (*Ori'el*), רפאל (*Rafa'el*), גבריאל (*Gavri'el*), מיכאל (*Micha'el*) and נוריאל (*Nuri'el*); and concluding with the Name שדי (*Shadai*).

Perusing certain amulets, an individual might think they are much too large to wear as a pendant, yet the size of the amulet is not important at all. In fact, you can make it as small as you like. The only real proviso I have regarding metal amulets, pertains to the edges. These should be rounded and worked in a manner so as not to cut or hurt the one who wears it under a garment against his or her body.

Another personal recommendation is that the writing on the amulet should comprise proper, square Hebrew lettering, as shown above. Some would insist that the glyphs should be *ashurit*, and an amulet of this nature could be made of any metal really, though I would personally construct or have it constructed in silver, always in accordance with exact specifications. Of course, a little ring has to be added to the top of the amulet if it is to worn like a pendent around the neck.

In the case of a young child being introduced to wearing an amulet, I would suggest that the youth don it for brief periods when in the company of a parent. The amulet should however be removed when the child is on his or her own. Otherwise the *Kamea* could be pinned on the inside of clothes, say to the inside of the vest so that it rests against the body, where it would not be bothersome and constantly remind the youth of its presence. It is important to remember that children should wear amulets under their clothes where nobody sees them. When they become teenagers, they may wear them more openly if circumstances allow and if they so wish.

B. *MENORAH:* Seven-branched Candelabrum

Next to the *Magen David* (Star of David), the *Menorah* ranks amongst the most common iconographic designs employed in the ornamentation of synagogues, as well as in *Shiviti* meditational plaques and amulets.[8] As indicated earlier, *Psalm 67*, the "*Menorah Psalm*," is often arranged in the format of the seven-branched candelabrum, which I mentioned is extensively employed in a variety of Hebrew amulets. However, it should be noted that the *Menorah* Psalm often appears in conjunction with other prayers, etc., all presented in *Menorah* formats. Amongst these the most popular is *Psalm 121*, the *menorah* format of which we have addressed earlier, and the well known "*Ana Bechoach*" prayer, the latter appearing many times in the following arrangement in *Shiviti* amulets:

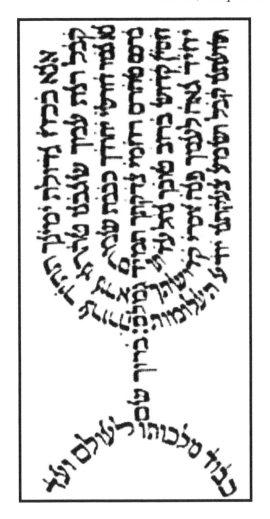

The "*Ana Becho'ach*" prayer reads:

אנא בכח גדולת ימינך תתיר צרורה
קבל רינת עמך שגבנו טהרנו נורא
נא גבור דורשי יחודך כבבת שמרם
ברכם טהרם רחמי צדקתך תמיד גמלם
חסין קדוש ברוב טובך נהל עדתך
יחיד גאה לעמך פנה זוכרי קדושתך
שועתנו קבל ושמע צעקתנו יודע תעלומות
ברוך שם כבוד מלכותו לעולם ועד

Transliteration:

> *Ana Becho'ach G'dulat Yemincha Tatir Tz'rurah*
> *Kabel Rinat Am'chah Sagvenu Taharenu Nora*
> *Na Gibor Dorshei Yichudcha Kevavat Shomrem*
> *Bar'chem Taharem Rachamei Tzidkatcha Tamid Gomlem*
> *Chasin Kadosh B'rov Tuvcha Nahel Adatecha*
> *Yachid Ge'eh Le'am'cha Pneh Zochrei K'dushatecha*
> *Shav'atenu Kabel Ushma Tza'akatenu Yode'a Ta'alumot*
> *Baruch Shem K'vod Malchuto l'Olam Va'ed*

Translation:

> Please now with might, with the strength of your right, untie the bound.
> Accept our song, strengthen us, purify in awe.
> Awesome in grace, we who see you as One, guard from harm.
> Cleanse us and bless, mix mercy with justice, and always redeem.
> Holy power, in your great goodness, guide your people.
> Exalted unique, turn to us, who recall your holiness.
> Receive our cry, hear our plea, you know what is hidden.
> Blessed is the Name, glorious your kingdom, throughout space and time.[9]

As mentioned in the previous volume of this series, the *Ana Becho'ach* prayer is attributed to the Talmudic mystic Rabbi Nechunia ben Hakanah, however it originated at a much later date. As noted previously, the prayer comprises forty-two words, the initials of which spell the "Forty-two Letter Name of God." The concluding stanza was appended "as an affirmation of the entire prayer."[10]

As noted, several Psalms and prayers have been employed in the format of the *Menorah*, sometimes singly and at times conjointly as shown in the following set of six *Menorah* constructs, which were employed collectively in a single *Shiviti* amulet:

This collection of *menorah* shaped Psalms/Prayers comprises, from left to right, *Psalms 23*; *126*; *67*; the *"Ana Bechoach"* Prayer; *Psalm 121* and *Psalm 54*.

C. *MAGEN DAVID:* Shield of David

The hexagram (*Magen David*) is extensively employed in Hebrew amulets, as you have undoubtedly noticed from several *Kameot* shared in this tome. As it is, the six-pointed star has been doing the rounds for several millennia. We are told that it "appears as early as the Bronze age and is at home in cultures and civilizations widely removed in time and geographic area," and it is speculated that it might have always had "magical connotations."[11] However, it would seem that, despite its appearance in the stonework of ancient synagogues,[12] Hebrew manuscripts, etc., until the 18th century it had no distinctly "Jewish symbolic connotation."[13]

Whatever the case may be, whether termed "hexagram," "Shield of Solomon," or "Star of David," this symbol is acknowledged as a most important symbol in the magical traditions of various nations. It features equally prominently also in Jewish Magic, and assuredly counts amongst the most popular symbols employed in Hebrew amulets. Whilst the six-pointed star is employed as the single symbol indicating our identity as Jews, I have noted elsewhere that "the two interlaced triangles of the hexagram comprise the symbol of *Metatron*, the holy intermediary between heaven and earth."[14] In this regard, the hexagram is employed as a *Kamea*, with or without accompanying Divine Names.

The most important Divine Name employed in conjunction with the *Magen David* is the earlier addressed Name שׁדי (*Shadai*). In numerous metal amulets, i.e. pendants, lockets, bracelets, rings, etc., this Divine Name is engraved in the centre of the "Star of David." As noted earlier, This Divine Name is at times represented by a single שׁ (*Shin*) located similarly, as shown below:

Whilst these "*Shadai*" amulets are mostly quite simple, some are comprised of several Divine Names and Hebrew phrases employed in conjunction with the Divine Name שׁדי (*Shadai*), as shown below:

In this instance, the construct is comprised of the Divine Names טפטפיה (*Taftafyah*), שׁדי (*Shadai*), צבאות (*Tzva'ot*), and the earlier mentioned phrase על צבא על מגן (*al tz'va al magen*).

Whilst we have considered the hexagram from the perspective of a simple line drawing, the image itself is at times comprised of Divine Names. In this regard, consider the following *Kamea* which is employed to protect one against any sickness and any other malevolent matter which one may encounter in the world.[15]

We are instructed to write this *Kamea* on a piece of deerskin parchment, or clean paper. This is done by:

1.   first outlining the "Magen David" and circle in light pencil lines.

2.   Next, commencing at the top of the upper triangle of the hexagram and tracing downwards along the left angle, write the first three full spellings of the Ineffable Name pertaining to the four worlds, i.e. יוד הי ויו הי [ע״ב–*AV* (*Atzilut*—Emanation)]; יוד הי ואו הי [ס״ג–*SaG*) (*Bri'ah*—Creation)]; and יוד הא ואו הא [מ״ה–*MaH* (*Yetzirah*—Formation)].

3.   Then, in the manner depicted in the illustration, continue by adding the fourth full spelling of the Ineffable Name along the bottom line, i.e. יוד הה וו הה [ב״ן–*BaN* (*Asiyah*—Action)].

Complete the bottom line by adding three full spellings of יהו״, i.e. יוד הא ואו, יוד הי ויו, and יוד הה וו.

4. Finally, conclude tracing the upper triangle of the hexagram, by writing in the manner depicted, from the bottom right corner upwards towards the top of the triangle the three permutations of אהיה (*Ehyeh*), i.e. אלף הה יוד הה; אלף הי יוד הי; and אלף הא יוד הא.

5. Next, commencing at the top right corner, trace from right to left the three lines of the lower triangle by writing the three permutations of אלהים (*Elohim*) respectively along the three lines, these being (top) אלף למד הי יוד מם; (left down) אלף למד הה יוד מם; and ending with (right up) אלף למד הא יוד מם. This concludes the construction of the "Shield of David."

6. Turn your attention to writing the Name יאהדונהי (*YAHDVNHY*) in the centre of the seal, which is the earlier addressed intertwined combination of יהוה (*YHVH*) and אדני (*Adonai*).

7. In conclusion the hexagram is encircled with the seven six-letter portions of the "Forty-two Letter Name of God," these being again:

אבגיתצ קרעשטן נגדיכש בתרצתג חקבטנע
יגלפזק שקוצית

Starting top centre, write the seven letter sets comprising this Name down the left and up the right, ending again centre top.

If you should write the *Kamea* for a certain individual, you should keep his or her name in mind whilst writing the Divine Names, so as to achieve a "Divine Union" between that individual and the Eternal One. In fact, prior to writing the amulet, you should say the following adjuration:

יהי רצון מלפניך יהוה אלהי ואלהי אבותי שתשגיח בעין
החמלה על [פלוני בן פלוני] נושא קמיע זה עליו בכח
שמותיך הקדושים הכתובים בחותם הזה ותעשה לו דבר
זה כאשר תרצה לעשות לטוב וא להיפך

Transliteration:

> *Y'hi ratzon milfanecha YHVH elohai v'elohei avotai shetashgiach b'ayin ha-chemlah al [.....Ploni ben Ploni.....] nose kamea zeh alav b'koach shmotecha ha-kadoshim ha-k'tuvim b'chotam ha-zeh v'ta'aseh lo davar zeh kasher tirtzeh la'asot l'tov o l'hefech*

Translation:

> May it be your will *YHVH* my God and God of my father, to oversee with your merciful eye [.....insert the name of the individual.....] who bears this amulet, in the power of your Holy Names written on this magical seal, and to do this in accordance with your will, acting for good or for the contrary.

Just prior to putting pen to paper, say:

הרי אני כותב קמיע זה לשם [פלוני בן פלוני]

Transliteration:

> *Harei ani kotev kamea zeh l'shem [.....Ploni ben Ploni.....]*

Translation:

> I am here writing this amulet in the name of [.....insert the name of the individual.....]

You are also required to fast and purify yourself by taking a ritual bath (*Mikveh*), wear clean clothing, and you must focus your intention on the portion of the "Name of Seventy-two Names" applicable to the day on which you are writing the amulet.[16] If you should not know which portion of the latter Divine Name applies to the day on which you are composing the *Kamea* in question, you could simply recite the entire "Name of Seventy-two Names."

This concludes the construction of this amulet, however important actions remain. The *Kamea* could also be employed as an object of contemplation. Hence the owner might attempt to comprehend the inner mysteries of the Divine Names employed, as well as their association with the "Holy Palace," i.e. the totality

Patterns, Shapes & Sizes / 393

of dimensions termed the "Four Worlds," as well as their union within the very being of the owner of the amulet.

It is worth noting that this *Kamea* is employed for every sickness in the world; to change bad fate, i.e. a "bad decree from heaven," so to speak; for the resolution of any problematic situation, i.e. to avert the "Evil Eye," for a woman to fall pregnant, or for any other purpose whatsoever. In other words, the adjuration uttered prior to constructing the amulet could more generally read:

יהי רצון מלפניך יהוה אלהי ואלהי אבותי שתשגיח
בעין חמלתך על [.....פלוני בן פלוני] בזכות אלו שמותיך
הקדושים

Transliteration:

> *Y'hi ratzon milfanecha YHVH elohai v'elohei avotai shetashgiach b'ayin chemlat'cha al [.....Ploni ben Ploni.....] biz'chut elu shmotecha ha-kadoshim*

Translation:

> May it be your will *YHVH* my God and God of my father, to oversee with your merciful eye [.....insert the name of the individual.....] in the merit of these your Holy Names.

In the case of wanting to cause a woman to fall pregnant, you could say:

שתפקדנה ל'[.....פלונית בת פלונית] ותפתח רחמה

Transliteration:

> *Shetepak'dena l'[.....Plonit ben Plonit.....] v'tiftach rachmah*

Translation:

> Approach [command] [.....insert the name of the individual.....] and open her womb.

If you also intend the prevention of a miscarriage, you might add שתשמור פרי בטנה שלא תפיל וכן לכל דבר (*Shetishmor pri bitnah shelo tapil v'chen l'chol davar*—"Safeguard the fruit of her belly against miscarriage and for everything." If you wish to avert the "Evil Eye," i.e. jealousy, hatred, etc., you would say הרע שתצילהו מעין (*Sh'tatzilehu mi'ayin ha-ra*—"save him from the 'Evil Eye'); etc.[17]

Now, in the following illustration of an 18th century double sided Persian protection *Kamea*, the front comprises a "Star of David" constructed from Hebrew expressions rather than Divine Names:[18]

Side A

Side B

The centre of the front side of this *Kamea* comprises a large hexagram constructed from the following words:

Upper Triangle

[Bottom] על צבא קשטיאל חרב

[Right] צבא על צבא מגן על

[Left] מגן צנה פחד

Transliteration:

[Bottom] *al tz'va Kashti'el cherev.....*

[Right] *tz'va al tz'va magen al.....*

[Left] *magen tzinah pachad.....*

Translation:

[Bottom] of the host [army] of *Kashti'el* sword.....

[Right] host of host shield of.....

[Left] shield and buckler of fear.....

Lower Triangle

[Top] על צבא קשטיאל חרב

[Left] צבא על צבא מגן צנה

[Right] פחד על צבא

Transliteration:

[Top] *al tz'va Kashti'el cherev.....*

[Left] *tz'va al tz'va magen tzinah.....*

[Right] *pachad al tz'va.....*

Translation:

[Top] of the host of *Kashti'el* sword.....

[Left] host of host shield and buckler.....

[Right] fear of host.....

The term צנה (*tzinah*) means "cold" or "chill," but in the Bible it refers to a "buckler." In this regard, we read in *Ezekiel 23:24* צנה ומגן וקובע (*tzinah u'magen v'kova*—"buckler and shield and helmet"). As it is, I believe all the phrases comprising the *Magen David* should be read as a continuous whole.

The centre of the amulet is occupied by the Divine Name שדי (*Shadai*), as well as the Angelic names מטטרון (*Metatron*) and יהואל (*Yeho'el*). As mentioned elsewhere in this study, the "shield" in the phrase אל צבא על מגן (*al tz'va al magen*—"on the host of the shield"), is the "Shield of David" which we noted is the symbol of *Metatron*. The Name *Yeho'el* is said to be the first of the seventy names of *Metatron*,[19] and we are told that יהואל (*Yeho'el*) is the leader of the *Serafim* (the "Burning Ones"). Likewise this Spirit Intelligence has rulership over fire.[20] Furthermore, *Yeho'el* is said to be the lofty "judge" ruling with the Eternal One, way beyond all the ministering angels.[21]

As an aside, we are reminded that the *gematria* of יהואל (*Yeho'el* [י = 10 + ה = 5 + ו = 6 + א = 1 + ל = 30 = 52]) is equal to that of כלב. This word could be read *Kelev* meaning "dog," however it could also be read *Kol Lev* ("all heart"). All dog lovers will tell you that this is exactly what a dog is. Both interpretations apply in the current instance, since the angel *Yeho'el* is said to "bark" and spread the "Law," and reveals it to infants directly in their innermost selves, i.e. their hearts.[22] It should be noted that the Name יהואל comprises the letters of the name אליהו (*Eliyahu*—"Elijah"), hence it is understood that Elijah reveals himself to everyone through the power of יהואל (*Yeho'el*) and אלהינו (*Eloheinu*—"our God").[23] All these Hebrew terms are comprised of different permutations of the same letters.

The numerical value of the name יהואל is also equal to that of the Ineffable Name repeated twice, i.e. יהוה יהוה [י = 10 + ה = 5 + ו = 6 + ה = 5 + י = 10 + ה = 5 + ו = 6 + ה = 5 = 52]. The double expression of the Ineffable Name is understood to be a reference to the Eternal One and *Yeho'el*, and it is said that when a woman suffers difficulties during childbirth the *Sar ha-Panim* ("Prince of the Presence") is dispatched to rescue her.[24] Of course, *Yeho'el* is *Metatron* who is the "Prince" of the "Divine Presence." Regarding *Metatron*, I noted elsewhere "that the Name of the Almighty 'is in Him' (*Exodus 23:21*), and hence he is designated.....'*The Lesser YHVH*' whose 'throne' is next to that of the Eternal One."[25]

The combination *Shadai–Metatron–Yeho'el* in the centre of the *Kamea* we are addressing is extremely important. Not only is *Metatron* and *Yeho'el* different appellatives for one and the same Spirit Intelligence, the *gematria* of the Divine Name שדי

(*Shadai*—"Almighty" [ש = 300, ד = 4, י = 10 = 314]) equates with that of the name מטטרון (*Metatron* [מ = 40, ט = 9, ט = 9, ר = 200, ו = 6, ן = 50 - 314]).[26] It is in this regard that the great Abraham Abulafia wrote "Behold God's name *Shadai*. This is *Metatron*. He is the 'Prince of Names' (*Sar HaShemot*), who speaks the 'authority of the Name' [*Reshut HaShem*]."[27] I noted that, "the understanding that the power of *Shadai* is within *Metatron*, would also mean that every time one invokes this Divine Name for protection, etc., one automatically also calls upon the 'Angel of the Divine Presence'."[28] The importance of the archangel *Metatron* in the current *Kamea* we are addressing, is further emphasized by the six letters located in the six corners of the hexagram, and which spell the Divine Name אזבוגה (*Azbogah*). I mentioned earlier that this Name is also said to be one of the seventy Names of *Metatron*.

Now, the central *Magen David* construct is enclosed on three sides by [top] יוחך כלך (*Yohach Kalach*); [right] אגלא (*Agala'a*) and [left] ארגמן (*Argaman*). The Divine Name construct below the hexagram, כמיל לבד, is an abbreviation of *Psalm 91:11* reading כי מלאכיו יצוה לך לשמרך בכל דרכיך (*ki malachav yitzaveh lach lishmor'cha b'chol d'rachecha*—"For He will give His angels charge over thee, to keep thee in all thy ways").[29]

The rear of the amulet in question is divided into two panels. Located centrally at the top, between these divisions we find the Ineffable Name and the Name שדי (*Shadai*). The panel to the right is headed by בטר (*Bitaro*) and צתג (*Tzatag'*), the seventh and eighth tri-letter portions of the "Forty-two Letter Name." The inclusion of these portions are particularly interesting, since "the *gematria* of בטר [ב = 2 + ט = 9 + ר = 200 = 211] is equal to that of the words ארי (*Ari*—"lion" [א = 1 + ר = 200 + י = 10 = 211]) and צחצחיה (*Tzachtzachyah* [צ = 90 + ח = 8 + צ = 90 + ח = 8 + י = 10 + ה = 5 = 211])."[30] We are told *Tzachtzachyah* is one of the Names of *Metatron*, and clearly this Spirit Intelligence features particularly prominently in the amulet we are addressing.

Regarding צתג (*Tzatag'*), the eighth portion of the "Forty-two Letter Name" located in the space directly below בטר

(*Bitaro*), we are told that it pertains "to the thirteen חלונות (*Chalonot*—'windows') on the celestial 'Throne of Glory,' which "are opened by the ministering angels associated with this Divine Name."[31] There are exactly thirteen *Digrammaton* (י״ה) in the panel below צ״תג (*Tzatag'*), all arranged along the left, right and bottom borders of the main portion of the right panel. Ten of these are written upright, and three to the left are upside down.

All of this pertains to a "mystery" involving the "*Shem Vayisa Vayet*" construct, which we know is in *Chesed*, and of which the "source is said to be the Name י״ה."[32] As noted elsewhere, "two principles are basically being addressed here, i.e. י (*Yod—Abba* ["Father"]) and ה (*Heh—Imma* ["Mother"]), respectively associated with *Chochmah* (Wisdom) and *Binah* (Understanding)," these being "two sources within the lofty 'beard,' specifically the higher 'channels'."[33] These "divine channels" comprise what is termed the thirteen strands or thirteen "attributes" of Divine Mercy. In this regard, Kabbalistic tradition has it that the Infinite One relates with creation by means of thirteen spiritual "channels," which for us are what is termed the thirteen "rectifications." In the current *Kamea* all of this is indicated by the thirteen presentations of י״ה (*Yah*).

Regarding the actual placement of the thirteen *Digrammaton* in the amulet, it would seem to indicate the *sefirot* of *Chochmah*–Wisdom and *Binah*–Understanding, respectively top right and left. From *Binah* (left) we witness the drawing down of "Force" into "Form" in the lower five *Digrammaton*, and the return flow back up to *Chochmah* (right). Of course, there are all sorts of explications regarding the division of the thirteen "strands" of the "Holy Beard" applicable here, but for me "the entire process is a union, as it were a 'play' between 'force' and 'form'."[34] Hence I have previously noted "that the 'beard' of the Holy One," is said to be "drawn downwards because of the sacred union of *Chochmah* and *Binah*."[35] Thus I believe the inclusion of the thirteen *Digrammaton* in conjunction with the (*Tzadag'*) portion of the "Forty-two Letter Name of God," is meant to direct the loftiest blessings into the life of the one who bears the amulet in question.

As noted earlier, the *gematria* of י״ה (*Yah*) is 15, and this Divine Name has been associated with the "Magic Square of the

Third Order," each individual row, column and diagonal of which equally totals 15. Hence it is no surprise that located centrally between the thirteen *Digrammaton*, is the threefold magic square. Considering its attribution to שבתאי (*Shabetai*—Saturn), makes the מאדים (*Madim*—"Mars") header to appear somewhat odd. Maybe the power of the threefold square to alleviate fear, is meant to balance the fierceness of *Madim*. On the other hand, the presence of the Hebrew name for the planet Mars, could also mean the "drawing down," as it were, of its "strength." In this regard, the forces channelled by the threefold square, are "enhanced" by מאדים (*Madim*—"Mars").

Be that as it may, we need to consider the left panel on the rear portion of the *Kamea* we are addressing. As in the case of the right panel, the left one commences with a double header comprised of the Divine Name שדי (*Shadai*), listed three time in the amulet, and below it the curious Hebrew letter combination הימצצעמיה. Once again it is the *Digrammaton* (הי) features prominently here. This הימצצעמיה construct, said to pertain to the sphere of *Binah*—Understanding on the sefirotic tree, is a palindrome beginning and ending with הי יה (*HY YH*).

Adjacent this Divine Name pair we trace מצ צמ (*MTz TzM*), and, whilst one might be tempted to read all sorts of meanings into the two constructs comprising this portion of the Divine Name construct, this Hebrew two-letter pair is the combination הי יה transposed by means of *Temurah* (תמורה), the Hebrew method of codes. In the present instance the *Atbash* cipher was applied to transform הי יה into מצ צמ.[36] The Divine Name construct is completed with the inclusion of the letter ע (*Ayin*), the עטרה (*Atarah*—"Crown") in the centre, which is said to imply the Divine Presence (*Shechinah*).[37] The presence of the הימצצעמיה construct in the current amulet is for the bearer to find kindness and favour in the eyes of all he or she may meet.

However, the "secret" of the combination הימצצעמיה is said to pertain to actually acquiring something you may desire from some or other individual. In this regard, the instruction is to write this Divine Name construct on a piece of parchment, then to hold it in your hand whilst approaching the individual with whom you wish to find favour, and from whom you wish to acquire whatever you want. However, it is also said that if you wish to acquire something rather large from someone, then you should inscribe the הימצצעמיד construct either on a silver or golden disc, which is likewise carried in your hand as you approach the said individual in this regard.[38]

Be that as it may, located beneath this Divine Name construct in the amulet we are addressing, is the main portion of the left panel, which is the earlier addressed *Ehyeh*/Ineffable Name square. This adds good health, fertility, Divine protection against the evil which could be afflicted by a human or demonic spirits, and bring other good qualities into the life of the bearer. However, it would seem that despite all the life benefits packed into this amulet, the fundamental intention is "Divine Protection," hence the concluding two terms located bottom centre of this portion of the item, which read לשמירת נוקז. The second term is an abbreviation of the phrase נושא קמיע זה (*nose kamea zeh*), thus the whole reads "for the protection of the bearer of the *Kamea*."

D. THE HAND

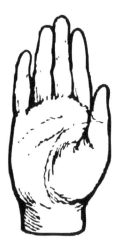

Much of Jewish "magical customs," e.g. *Kameot* (amulets), sympathetic magic practices, incantations, divination, etc., were preserved and continued amongst Jewish communities who lived in Arab lands. In this regard I find the magical customs of Jews of Tunisia which Nahum Slouschz encountered and reported during his *"Travels in North Africa,"*[39] to be of particular personal fascination. In his curious travel report Shlouschz referenced some of the standard Jewish "magical" activities found the world over, e.g. the "many kinds of *kameot*, talismans and amulets, which the Jewish child wears from the day of its birth. First comes the hand (or hand of Fatma) with five fingers, worked in metal with strange designs. This hand is found engraved in all the house of the more backward Jews."[40]

I wonder what Shlouschz would make of not so backward and quite well positioned Jews owning a nice *Chamsa*, the "hand" amulet he was referring to. There is a very nice one in my own home, and, what is more, I am quite satisfied that it is efficacious, whatever the arguments against its use may be. In this regard I certainly have not bothered to argue with those who deemed *Chamsot* "superstitions," in fact, we have ascertained a long time ago that the teeth of foolish argument tear at everything until nothing is left.

Be that as it may, Nahum Slouschz reported that the hand amulet "is worn as an amulet round the neck or on the heart. Children wear besides a horn of coral, a collar containing a small cypress to protect them from evil, a little bag of black cumin, incense, grains of carob, and silver plates with the words *Shaddai*, *Siman Tov*, etc. On account of the hand, which is also named *hamsa* (five), they avoid uttering the number five, and say instead four-and-one, or several, etc."[41] It is worth noting that in Hebrew the number 5 is indicated by the letter *Heh*, the fifth letter of the Hebrew alphabet, and that even on its own, this letter is considered a Divine Name. It often appears singly on amulets. Some believed that its power could be even more enhanced by engraving it five times on an amulet.

This reminds us of the *Chamsa* amulet. As noted elsewhere "the terms *Chamsa* and *Chamesh* (popularly *Hamsa*) respectively refer to the number five in Arabic and Hebrew, which is a direct reference to the shape of the amulet, constructed to show the flat palm and extended five fingers of a hand. Literally the open hand and five fingers which traditionally pushes an enemy away."[42] Since

I have addressed the origins of the *Chamsa* in some detail in the previous volume of this series, I need only reiterate that in Islam this amulet "is believed to be representative of the hand of Fatima, the daughter of the Prophet Mohammed, whilst amongst Jewry it is thought to represent the hand of Miriam, the sister of Moses." However, historical evidence indicates the item to be portraying the hand of an ancient Middle Eastern goddess, "warding off malevolent glances."[43] Next to the *Magen David*, the *Chamsa* is probably the most popular amulet amongst Jewry and others charmed by its simple lines depicting the palm of a hand with its extended fingers.

The open flat surface of the item invites inscription and embellishment. In this regard, this item has been inscribed with a variety of Divine Names, symbols and decorative designs, ranging from the very simple to the most exotic. The most popular comprises the evil eye, a *Magen David*, and the Divine Name שׁדי (Shadai).

As said elsewhere, "today most people carrying a *Chamsa* believe that it represents the protecting hand of the Almighty. Others who feel that this notion might be somewhat blasphemous (remember the injunctions about 'graven images' and 'worshipping false gods,' and so forth?), tell us it is the hand of a 'representative of God,' e.g. one of a Rabbi who raises his hand in blessing, and so directs, as it were, the infinite abundance of Divinity in our direction'."[44] Hand of God or that of a revered Rabbi, we are told "the hand is a symbol of strength and action."[45] It has the power to halt evil, and redirect it back to its originator. Ones own hands could fulfill this very function, if they were raised with the intention to banish evil.

In this regard, I have spotted a while back the following *Shmirah* amulet for sale on the internet, and marveled at its beauty and simplicity. In fact, it makes an excellent template, which anyone could employ in constructing a personal protection *Kamea* comprised of a tracing of his/her own hands:

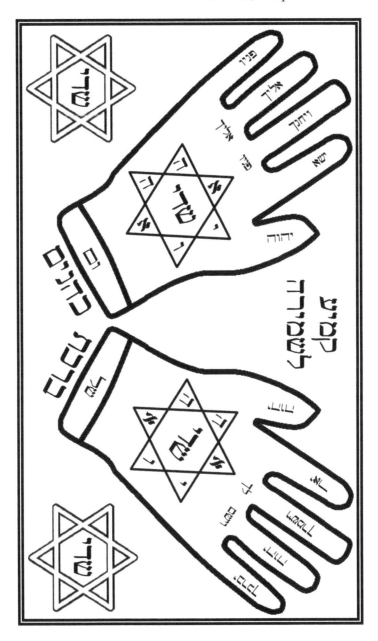

This *Kamea* opens with the header קמיע לשמירה (*Kamea l'shmirah*—"amulet for protection"). As in the case of most protection amulets, the Divine Name שד"י (*Shadai*) features very prominently. It is positioned in the centre of the four hexagrams, two of which are located in the lower right and left corners of the amulet, and two in the palms of the hands. The six corners of the latter two comprise six letters. When read from the upper or lower א (*Alef*) in a zigzag manner downwards or upwards, the successive letters trace two very important Divine Names, i.e. אהיה (*Ehyeh*) and יהוה (*YHVH*).

We also trace the Divine Name אהוה (*Ah'v'hi* or *'havi*) in the pattern of the mentioned six letters. However, since this Divine Name construct does not really feature in Hebrew amulets, I believe its appearance in the amulet to be perhaps "accidental." Incidental or not, there is something good to be had from its appearance in the *Kamea*. The Name אהוה (*Ah'v'hi* or *'havi*) was derived from the words את השמים ואת הארץ (*et ha-shamayim v'et ha-aretz*—"the heavens and the earth") (*Genesis 1:1*), and this very lofty Divine Name is said to be higher than אהיה (*Ehyeh*).[46] The *gematria* of אהוה [א = 1 + ה = 5 + ו = 6 + ה = 5 = 17] is equal to that of the word טוב (*Tov*—"good" [ט = 9 + ו = 6 + ב = 2 = 17]), hence we are told אהוה (*Ah'v'hi*) grants us complete mercy.[47]

Now, below the wrists we trace the words ברכת כהנים (*Birchat Kohanim*— "Priestly Blessing"). This is a reference to *Numbers 6:24–28*, the words of which are written on the two "Priestly Hands" illustrated in the position of blessing in the *Kamea*. Commencing at the little fingers of each hand and reading inwards towards the thumb, then along the upper palms, and concluding with the wrists we trace:

יברכך יהוה וישמרך יאר יהוה [Right Fingers]

פניו אליך ויחנך ישא יהוה [Left Fingers]

פניו אליך [Left Palm]

וישם לך [Right Palm]

שלום [Both Wrists]

"*YHVH* bless thee, and keep thee, *YHVH* make His face to shine upon thee, and be gracious unto thee, *YHVH* lift up His countenance upon thee, and give thee peace."

E. Printed Amulets

שמירה לילד וליולדת

This *Kamea* derives from Casablanca, Morocco. It is attributed to the Baal Shem Tov, the founder of the *Chasidim* in Poland. As it is, the Baal Shem Tov was a wonder worker in the great tradition of the *Baalei Shem*, the "Masters of the Name," and *Kameot* certainly featured in the "magical practices" he employed in service to the Jewish community of his homeland.[48] However, it is highly unlikely that the amulet in question originated with the Baal Shem Tov. As is the case with several of these printed *Shmirah Kameot*, the intention of which is protection of mothers and infants, the header reads:

שמירה לילד וליולדת

Transliteration:
> *Shmirah l'yeled ul'yoledet*

Translation:
> Protection for a child and for women in confinement.

Centrally, below the header, we find the mentioned attribution of this amulet to the Baal Shem Tov. The inscription reads:

מהרב הקדוש רבי ישראל בעל שם טוב זצלה"ה
[זכר צדיק לחיי העולם הבא] בשם יהוה אלהי
ישראל גדול ונורא

Transliteration:
> *m'ha-rav ha-kadosh rabbi Yisra'el ba'al shem tov, zachar tzadik l'chayei ha-olam ha-ba, b'shem YHVH Elohei Yisra'el gadol v'nora*

Translation:
> From the holy master rabbi Israel Baal Shem Tov, may the memory of the *Tzadik* (righteous individual) be for life in the World to Come, in the Name *YHVH Elohei* Israel great and awesome.

In the two blocks on either side of this inscription we read:

[Right] בסימן טוב
[Left] ובמזל טוב

Transliteration:
  [right] *b'siman tov* [left] *ub'mazel tov*
Translation:
  [right] in good fortune [left] and in good luck

The incantation written on both sides of the "Hand of Protection" in the centre of the amulet, and which is standard in "*Shmirah Kameot*," is a slightly expanded version of the earlier mentioned one comprising the saga of the Prophet Elijah's chance meeting with *Lilit*.

Centred directly below the open hand is again the whole of *Psalm 121* arranged in seven rows, and underneath the psalm the earlier mentioned שדי קרע שתן (*Shadai K'ra Satan*—"Shadai rend Satan"). Below these three words we read סנוי (*Sanoi*) [right]; וסנסנוי (*v'Sansanoi*) [centre] and וסמנגלוף (*v'Semangelof*) [left], i.e. the names of the earlier addressed angels protecting against the malevolence of *Lilit*. In turn, located underneath these are the earlier addressed names of the Hebrew Patriarchs and their respective spouses, i.e. אברהם ושרה (*Avraham v'Sarah*— Abraham and Sarah) [right]; יצחק ורבקה (*Yitzchak v'Rivkah*— Isaac and Rebecca) [centre]; and ולאה יעקב (*Ya'akov v'Leah*— Jacob and Lea) [left].

Located centrally below, is a framed and emboldened expression reading אדם חוה פנימה (*Adam v'Chavah p'nimah*—Adam and Eve within). Directly underneath the names of the Patriarchs/Matriarchs located to the right and left, and on either side of the enhanced names of the primordial ancestors, we trace again the earlier addressed six permutations of the three words comprising *Exodus 22:17*. The written part of the amulet is concluded with a reference regarding the demoness *Lilit* located at the very bottom of the *Kamea*, reading לילית וכת דילה חוץ (*Lilit v'kat dilah chutz—Lilit* and her cohorts [sect] out!). Located below the image of a fish which signifies fertility, it is quite appropriate to include the phrase banishing spirit forces considered resolute killers of infants.

Now, besides the image of an open hand indicating "halt," we notice two small hexagrams, as well as the mentioned image of a fish included in this *Shmirah* amulet. Of course, the symbol of the fish dates back to the whole of the ancient Far and Near East, not forgetting ancient Greece, the Roman empire, ancient Europe, Scandinavia, etc.[49] It certainly predates Christianity by many centuries. Regarding its employment in identifying Christians, the popularity of the fish is witnessed today in its prominent display on businesses, vehicles, websites, etc., most of which belong to Christians of the fundamentalist type.[50] On questioning its display on a keyring, the owner informed me that since it is the sign of the Christian Saviour, the keys can never be lost or stolen. In this regard, I can only imagine how many Christians are employing their "Jesus Fish" for other than symbolic purposes.

Be that as it may, the symbol of the fish is popularly acknowledged in Jewish circles as "a symbol of both good luck and fertility."[51] The Talmud (*Talmud Bavli Berachot 20*) tells us the "Evil Eye" has no effect on fish, hence the popularity of this symbol in amulets against the "Evil Eye."[52] In this regard images of fish at one time featured quite prominently at the entrances of private residences, e.g. those of the Jews in Djerba, North Africa.[53] On the other hand, we are told that the fish is a symbol of immortality, and that "the Jewish motif of the Feast of Leviathan might reflect the actual practice, in various religious traditions, of a fish dinner as a foretaste of immortality," hence its appearance on graves and ancient synagogues.[54]

Amongst the North African Jewish folk customs, which the earlier-mentioned Nahum Slouschz deemed "superstitions," he made reference to "a whole series of beliefs which have sprung from the cult of the fish, a cult the traces of whose ancient predominance may be found scattered across the whole Mediterranean. Thus, the Jewish fortune-tellers practise divination with fish. At Tunis, even at Tangiers, there are certain kinds of fish which it is forbidden to eat, on account of their use in divination. It is not in good taste to use the word 'hut' (fish), its use is replaced by the phrase *Mta el hara* or *el bahra* (beings of the sea)."[55]

Interestingly enough, I have investigated an amulet in which fish scales feature rather prominently. It is said this amulet is good for everything. In this instance the following eighteen tri-letter combinations should be written on one side of the skin of a fish with its scales still intact, i.e. one tri-letter combination per scale:

פוא רית הוה ודם וגם רופ ורי ווט מבי לבך אקא ורמ
אבל תהא האי ארה רצו צהא

Afterwards, the following word square is written on the opposite side of the same skin:

ישׁשׁא	הראל	ואלת
הלתם	אידע	לתאם
הןשׁו	יארכ	יתשׁי

The letter combinations in the magic square comprise an arrangement of a phrase derived from *1 Samuel 1:17*. It reads:

יהוה אלהי ישראל יתן את שאלתך אשר
שאלת כי מעמו

Transliteration:
> *YHVH Elohei Yisra'el yiten et she'altech asher sha'alt ki mei'imo*

Translation:
> *YHVH* God of Isra'el grant thy petition that thou hast asked of Him.

In this instance the Ineffable Name was added as a prefix to the biblical phrase, and there have been some minor adjustments in the component words in alignment with the basic intention of the *Kamea* in question, which is plainly the granting of an earnest request.[56] However, there is no instruction on what to do with the fish skin afterwards. I surmise one might place it in a little bag to be carried on ones person.

Considering the importance of the symbol of the fish in Jewish magic, it should come as no surprise that it should be employed in custom made jewellery, as well as on printed and metal *Kameot*. In this regard, consider the following graphic image of an unique, privately owned amulet:

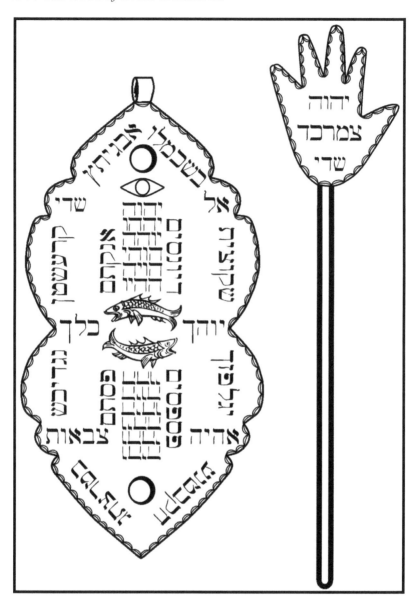

There are two components to this amulet. The large pendant portion on the left comprises two sectors, these being partitioned by two fishes, the symbol of fertility located centrally. Each half is sort of molded into two convex shapes with the centre slightly indented, in order to allow the hand-pin portion of the *Kamea* to fit through two holes, these being respectively located top and bottom centre of the main item.

The graphic eye located beneath the upper hole, as well as the "hand" portion of this *Kamea*, show the construct to be for protection against the "Evil Eye." However, the broad range of Divine Names employed in this instance indicate the amulet to be of the "all purposes" variety, i.e. for protection, health, wealth, fertility and fortune.

The contents of the main item include the following earlier addressed Divine Names:

1. MAIN ITEM
a. Ineffable Name

The twelve permutations of the Ineffable Name are located centrally, six in the upper and six in the lower half of the amulet. The upper six are placed in a column reading the downwards, whilst the concluding six are located similarly upside down and reading upwards.

(Top)

יהוה

יההו

יוהה

הוהי

הויה

ההיו

(Bottom)

והיה

וההי

ריהה

היהו

הויה

ההוי

b. Twenty-two Letter Name

Bordering the left and right of the listed sets of permutations of the Ineffable Name, is the "Twenty-two Letter Name," which, as indicated earlier, is comprised of the phrase:

אנקתם פסתם פספסים דיונסים

Transliteration:
Anaktam Pastam Paspasim Dionsim

c. Forty-two Letter Name

Commencing left of the upper aperture and reading downwards, we trace the first four six-letter combinations of the "Forty-two Letter Name" comprising the left border of the amulet. In turn, continuing from the right of the lower aperture and reading upwards, we trace the remaining three six-letter combinations of this Divine Name, as well as the abbreviation of the concluding phrase traditionally employed in the "*Ana B'choach*" prayer. This portion of the *Kamea* reads:

אבגיתצ קרעשטנ נגדיכש בטרצתג (Top down)

חקבטנע יגלפזק שקוצית בשכמלו (Bottom up)

Transliteration:
Avgitatz Karastan Nagdichesh Batratztag Yaglefzok Shakutzit BShKMLV [Baruch Shem K'vod Malchuto le'Olam Va'ed]

d. Divine Name Pairs

The main portion of the *Kamea* is completed with three Divine Name pairs, two of which are located in the four small niches separating the upper dome and the bottom of the amulet from the large central section. The third Divine Name pair establishes, in conjunction with the pair of fish, the dividing line between the upper and bottom portion of the main construct. These are as follows:

אל שדי (Upper right/left)

יוהך כלך (Centre right/left)

אהיה צבאות (Bottom right/left)

Transliteration:
El Shadai (Upper right/left)
Yohach Kalach (Centre right/left)
Ehyeh Tzva'ot (Bottom right/left)

2. HAND-PIN

The separate hand-pin portion of the amulet, comprising the open palm of a left hand with fingers extended, displays three Names:

יהוה (Top)
צמרחד (Centre)
שדי (Bottom)

Transliteration:
YHVH (Top)
Tzamarchad (Centre)
Shadai (Bottom)

As might be expected, neither the symbol of the fish nor the image of a hand, feature in all printed amulets, whether derived from North Africa or Eastern Europe. Some are decorated with crowns; chalices; roosters; lions; sphinxes; images pertaining to the Zodiac; visual portrayals of biblical scenes and personages; images of sacred sites in the Holy Land; and an assortment of other images. All of these are considered symbolical and significant, e.g. the crown is a symbol of the *Torah*, kingship and priesthood; the lion is a symbol of strength, dominion, and the Jewish People (Lion of Judah); etc.[57]

Whilst many amulets comprise text enhancing floral borders, etc., some are a lot less adorned than others, as indicated by the following fairly simple printed *Kamea* for "good luck" and divine protection against evil of both the spirit and human kind:

✿ למזל טוב ✿

בשם יהוה אלהי ישראל גדול ונורא

שיר למעלות אשא עיני אל ההרים מאין
יבא עזרי עזרי מעם ה" עושה שמים וארץ אל
יתן למוט רגלך ואל ינים שומרך הנה לא
ינים ולא ישן שומר ישראל ה" שומרך ה"
צלך על יד ימינך יומם השמש לא יככה
וירח בלילה ה" ישמרך מכל רע ישמר את
נפשך ה" ישמר צאתך ובואך מעתה ועד
עולם

שדי קרע שטן

וסמנגליו וסנסיניו סיניו
יעקב ולאה יצחק ורבקה אברהם ושרה

תהיה לא מכשפה   מכשפה לא תהיה
מכשפה תהיה לא   תהיה מכשפה לא
לא מכשפה תהיה   לא תהיה מכשפה

 אדם וחוה פנימה

•••• לילת וכת דילה חוצה ••••
לתא"ר ולי"ב

This printed amulet is fairly straightforward. It opens with the header למזל טוב (*l'mazel tov*—"for good fortune"), below which is a subheader reading בשם יהוה אלהי ישראל גדול ונורא (*b'shem YHVH Elohei Yisra'el gadol v'nora*—"In the Name of *YHVH* God of Israel great and awesome"). The large blocked upper portion comprises again *Psalm 121*, which we noted is an important defence against demons and the evil eye, and also for protecting mothers, the unborn and infants, as well as the home.

This *Kamea* includes standard Divine and Angelic Names found in printed amulets of this nature, and the appellatives of the primordial ancestors, and those of the Hebrew Patriarchs and Matriarchs, all of which we have earlier addressed in some detail. In fact, the amulet is purely an unadorned version of the earlier addressed printed *Kamea* for the protection of mothers and infants. In the current instance the intention is "Good Luck" generally, hence the saga of Elijah and *Lilit*, as well as the associated adjuration, were excluded. The abbreviations לתא״ר ולי״ב at the bottom of the amulet comprise the previously mentioned the initials of *Psalm 91:10*.

Now, amongst the most interesting printed amulets are those attributed to Rabbi Moshe Teitelbaum (1759–1841), the famous *Chasid* and "Wonder Worker." Nicknamed the "*Yishmach Moshe*" ("Moses Rejoiced") after the title of one of his works, he signed himself "*Tamar*," this Hebrew term being equivalent to the Yiddish "*Teitelbaum*" (*Dattelbaum* in German), all referring to the date palm. He commenced his rabbinical career in Przemysl, his birth city in south-eastern Poland, and was later appointed Rabbi of nearby Sieniawa. In 1808 he migrated to the Hungarian town of Satoralja-Ujhely, where he spent the rest of his days, and his descendents became the founders of the *Sighet* and *Satmar* chassidic dynasties.

Rabbi Teitelbaum was considered a most remarkable miracle rabbi, i.e. wonder-working *tzaddik* or simply a "practical kabbalist." We might recall the saga of his meeting with the nine year old Lajos Kossuth, who was destined for greatness in his native Hungary, and whom the good Rabbi cured of a childhood illness. It is said the good Rabbi did not only cure young Lajos Kossuth, but that he placed his hands on the head of the child and blessed him with *Psalm 60:4 [6]*, the Hebrew text reading:

נתתה ליראיך נס להתנוסס מפני קשט סלה

Transliteration:

Natatah lirei'echa nes l'hitnoses mipnei koshet Selah

Translation:

Thou hast given a banner to them that fear Thee, that it may be displayed because of the truth *Selah*.

It is said that the *Yishmach Moshe* was punning on the term *"Koshet"* ("truth") in reference to the surname of the boy, i.e. "Kossuth." We are further informed that Rabbi Teitelbaum also prophesied the future greatness of Kossuth, who became Governor General of Hungary in 1848, and then leader of the Hungarian Revolution. As an aside, Lajos Kossuth is not only considered a great hero, but was greatly beloved for his fair behaviour towards all citizens of his country, Jews and gentiles alike.

Getting back to Rabbi Teitelbaum and his activities as "Practical Kabbalist," we are informed that the Rabbi wrote amulets amongst the many services he rendered to the community. We might note that Rabbi Teitelbaum's amulet writing skills did not always result in good returns, so to speak. In 1822 he was accused of supplying amulets to individuals jailed on libel charges, in order to aid them in escaping their incarceration. When confronted with this matter, the *Yishmach Moshe* responded that the amulets were actually substitutes for *Mezuzot*, the purpose of which were to protect those who carried them against dark forces, e.g. demons.

In this regard consider the following, virtually "all purpose," *Kamea*, which we are told was written by this remarkable "wonder worker." As shown below, it mainly comprises a written incantation, plainly inscribed under a header announcing its purpose, without any additional decorative embellishments:

סגולה לפרנסה להצלחה ולשמירה מהגאון בעהמ"ח
ישמ"ח משה בשם ההה"ק אור העולם מרן הבעש"ט זצ"ל

ביראה אתו תעבודו, סגולה הזאת בכל פתח ביתך דבקו, בכל מקום אשר
תדורו, שידנוהלת, רהנוהכתא, שוקע, ואהאוא, לומוממא, עדי, משלוממם, הויה
בזה השער לא יבא צער, בזה הפתח לא יבא רצוו, בהלימהתויהעביעי, הויה
הימל הויהתהצמ, הויהבבהומסקאהוומם, הויהשסנזוואמבובפיו, טפטפיה, שדיכהת
מוהל, אופילה, הויהאימאיר, הויהבאש, הויהיהכם הויהבעשעת, הויהאגלאהוטא
קרושיאל, נוריאל, ועדואל, תדבימי, צמרכד, אדלי, מהלי נעורירון לו
גדשניאל, לעשן, דמוטירון, לצלהלין, גיפמיאל, השהמהמ, אופלא
לומיטוכ איתיאל, פניאל, ואוריאל, דכה, כל עדי הוד
טפטפיה, רזם, זעתמפעטרת תזס, אליהו זכור לטוב, ורז חנכון
אבג יתצ קרע שטן נגד בטר צתג חקב טנע יגל פזק שקו צית בשכמלו
ובלגבב"א

The header of this amulet reads:

סגולה לפרנסה להצלחה ולשמירה מהגאון בעהמ"ח
[בעל המחבר] ישמח משה בשם ההה"ק [החכם הקדוש]
אור העולם מרן הבעש"ט [הבעל שם טוב] זצ"ל [זכר
צדיק לברכה]

Transliteration:

> *Segulah l'parnasah l'hatzlachah v'l'shmirah m'ha-gaon [ba'al ha-m'chaber] Yishmach Mosheh b'shem [ha-Chacham ha-Kadosh] Or ha-Olam maran [ha-Ba'al Shem Tov] [zecher tzadik livrachah]*

Translation:

> A charm for good livelihood, for success and for protection, from the gaon, the author of *Yishmach Mosheh*, in the name of the holy wise person, light of the world, our master, the *Ba'al Shem Tov*, may the memory of the righteous one be a blessing

Below this opening statement, we trace the main body of the *Kamea*, which is comprised of a written incantation containing a number of both regular and incredible Divine and Angelic Names:

ביראה אתו תעבודו סגולה הזאת בכל פתח ביתך דבקו
בכל מקום אשר תדורו שיהודלת רהוהוכתא שקש ואהאוא
לומוממא שדי משלוימם הויה [יהוה] בזה השער לא יבא
צער בזה הפתח לא יבא רצח בהלימהויהעביש הויה
הימל הויהתצמ הויהבהוסקאהווממ הויהשסנחואמבובפיו
טפטפיה שדי כהת מוהל אופילה הויהאיימאיר הויהבאש
הויהיהכם הויהבששת הויה אגלא רוטא קדושיאל נוריאל
ועדואל [ועדאל] תדבימי צמרכד אדלו מהלי נעורירון
לו גדשניאל [גדשנאל] לעשן דמוטירון לצלהלץ גיפמיאל
השהמהמ אופלא לומיטוב איתיאל פניאל ואוריאל תכה
כלעד יהוה טפטפיה רחם חשתמפשרת תחס אליהו זכור
לטוב זרח – חנכון – חנבון – אבג יתצ קרע שטן נגד יכש בטר צתג
חקב טנע יגל פזק שקו צית בשכמלו

Transliteration:

> *b'yirah ito ta'avodu segulah ha-zot b'chol petach beitecha davko, b'kol makom asher taduru, ShYHVHLT, RHVHVKTA, ShKSh, VAHAVA, LVMVMMA, Shadai, MShLVYMM, HVYH [YHVH], b'zeh ha-sha'ar lo yavo tza'ar, b'zeh ha-petach lo yavo retzach, BHLYMHVYHABYSh, HVYH, HYML, HVYHTTzM, HVYHBHVMKAHVVMM, HVYHShSNChVAMBVBPYV, Taftafyah, Shadai kahet mohal,Ofilah, HVYHAYYMAYR, HVYHBASh, HVYHYHKM, HVYHBShShT, HVYH, Agala'a, Ruta, Kadoshi'el, Nuri'el, Vadu'el [Vad'el], TDBYMY, Tzamarchad, ADLV, MHLY NAVRYRVN LV, G'dashni'el [G'dashn'el], l'ishen, DMVTYRVN, LTzLHLTz, GYPMYAL, HShHMHM, Ofila, LVMYTVK, Iti'el, Pani'el,v'Ori'el, takeh, k'la'ad YHVH, Taftafyah, rachem, ChShTMPShRT, TChS, Eliyahu zachor latov Zerach – Chanchon – AViGe YaToTzi KaRo' SaTaN' NaGiDa YeiCheiSha BiTaRo TzaTaG' CheKeVa Tin'I YaGaLi P'Z'Kei ShuKoVa TzoYaT' BShKMLV [Baruch Shem K'vod Malchuto le'Olam Va'ed]*

Translation:

> In fear you must work this charm at every door of your house. You must hang this in every space you live in, *ShYHVHLT, RHVHVKTA, ShKSh, VAHAVA, LVMVMMA,*

Shadai, MShLVYMM, HVYH [*YHVH*], through this gate let no sadness enter, through this portal let no murder enter, *BHLYMHVYHABYSh, HVYH, HYML, HVYHTTzM, HVYHBHVMKAHVVMM, HVYHShSNChVAMBVBPYV, Taftafyah Shadai* darkness dilute, *Ofilah, HVYHAYYMAYR, HVYHBASh, HVYHYHKM, HVYHBShShT, HVYH, Agala'a, Ruta, Kadoshi'el, Nuri'el, Vadu'el* [*Vad'el*], *TDBYMY, Tzamarchad, ADLV, MHLY NAVRYRVN LV, G'dashni'el* [*G'dashn'el*], to smoke out, *DMVTYRVN, LTzLHLTz, GYPMYAL, HShHMHM, Ofilah, LVMYTVK, Iti'el, Pani'el, v'Ori'el*, strike, forever *YHVH, Taftafyah*, Mercy, *ChShTMPShRT, TChS,* Elijah of good memory, *Zerach – Chanchon – AViGe YaToTzi KaRo' SaTaN' NaGiDa YeiCheiSha BiTaRo TzaTaG' CheKeVa Tin'I YaGaLi P'Z'Kei ShuKoVa TzoYaT'*, Blessed be the Name of His glorious Kingdom throughout eternity.

The amulet concludes with a footnote written in Yiddish, in which "the Gaon, the Holy and Righteous Rabbi Moshe Teitelbaum." is acknowledged for having passed this *Kamea* on to the "Jewish folk of the Baal Shem Tov of blessed memory."

This is certainly one of the most elaborate amulets in which we recognise several of the Divine Names addressed in this tome. Whilst many of the standard Divine Names employed in Jewish Magic are clearly distinguishable, others are just too complex to analyse in any great detail in this study. I do believe dividing the large Divine Name constructs into smaller components, will afford a greater understanding of their exact meaning. This task I will leave for other "devotees" of Practical Kabbalah, since it would make this volume overly long if we were to discuss all of the difficult and obscure Divine and Angelic Name listed in this amulet. As it is, I included this amulet in this practical investigation of *Kameot*, since I thought some readers might want to avail themselves of its services.

Be that as it may, the concluding *Kamea* in this tome was printed in the hometown of Rabbi Teitelbaum, and is said to have been "tested and proven" as authentic by the *Yishmach Mosheh* himself. It is certainly a lot easier to explain, than the above amulet which we are informed was penned by the good Rabbi in person:

Printed in the hometown of Rabbi Teitelbaum, the *Kamea* opens with the header ב״ה, abbreviation of בעזרת השם (*B'ezrat ha-Shem*—"with the help of the Divine One [Ineffable Name]"). Below this is a banner headline announcing the purpose of the amulet, this being שמירה למגפה ר״ל (*Shmirah l'Magefah R"L*

[abbreviation of רחמנא לצל״ן—*Rachamana litzlan*] "Protection from the Plague, the Merciful One [God] forbid"). Directly beneath this is an inscription referencing the originator of this *Kamea*. It reads in two lines:

בדוק ומנוסה מהרב הצדיק מהור״ר [מורי הגדול
ורב רבין] משה טייטעלבוים זצללה״ה [זכר צדיק
לברכה לחיי העולם הבא]

Transliteration:

> *Baduk v'menuseh m'harav ha'tzadik [mori ha-gadol v'rav ravi] Moshe Teitelbaum [zecher tzadik livrachah l'chayei ha-olam ha-ba]*

Translation:

> Checked and proven by the Rav, the righteous, the great teacher and rabbi, Moshe Teitelbaum [may the memory of the Righteous One be blessed for life in the World to Come.]

Next, set inside a floral border, we trace the following three rhyming phrases:

לא יבוא צער   בזה השער
לא יבוא בהלת   בזה הדלת
לא יבוא רצח   בזה הפתח

Transliteration:

> *b'zeh ha-sha'ar   lo yivo tza'ar*
> *b'zeh ha-delet   lo yavo bahelet*
> *b'zeh ha-petach   lo yavo retzach*

Translation:

> Through this gate   let no sadness enter
> Through this door   let no fear enter
> Through this portal   let no murder enter

The listed sentences are variations of phrases from the *Birkat ha-Bayit*, the traditional "Blessing of the Home," the latter being often inscribed on *chamsot* and magnificent wall plaques. Affixed to a wall near the front entrance of a home, such objects are employed as amulets to protect the occupants of the house, and to keep evil forces of both the human and spirit kind at bay. The original version reads:

> ברכת הבית
>
> בזה השער   לא יבוא צער
> בזאת הדירה   לא תבוא צרה
> בזאת הדלת   לא תבוא בהלה
> בזאת המחלקה   לא תבוא מחלקת
> בזה המקום תהי   ברכה ושלום

Transliteration:
> *Birkat ha-bayit.*
> *b'zeh ha-sha'ar*   *lo yavo tza'ar*
> *b'zot ha-dirah*   *lo tavo tzarah*
> *b'zot ha-delet*   *lo tavo bahalah*
> *b'zot ha-machlakah*   *lo tavo machloket*
> *b'zeh ha-makom tehi*   *b'rachah v'shalom*

Translation:
> Blessing of the House
> Through this gate   let no sadness enter
> In this dwelling   let no trouble enter
> Through this door   let no fear enter
> In this locale   let there be no conflict
> In this place let there   be blessings and peace

The blocked portion in the centre of the amulet under discussion, comprises the earlier addressed Divine Name construct of *Psalm 106:30*, and underneath this a statement commencing with the header רבש״ע, i.e. the abbreviation of רבונו של עולם (*Ribono shel olam*— "Master of the Universe"). It reads:

> כשם שפסחת על בתי בני ישראל במצרים ולא נתת
> המשחית לבוא אל בתיהם כן תעצור המשחית מלבוא
> אל בתינו ובבתי כל ישראל אמן סלה ועד

Transliteration:

> *K'shem shepasachti al batei b'nei Yisra'el b'Mitzraim v'lo natata ha-mash'chit lavo el bateihem ken ta'atzor ha-mash'chit milavo el bateinu v'b'batei chol Yisra'el Omein Selah Va'ed*

Translation:

> Just as I passed over the houses of the children of Israel in Egypt, rather than letting the destroyer enter their homes, so the destroyer will stop coming into our homes and the residences of all of Israel. *Amen Selah* Forever.

The final blocked portion at the bottom of the amulet comprises the following references:

: אימי דאברהם אבינו

: אמתלאי בת כרנבו

: ושם בת אשר סרח [שרח]

Transliteration:

> : *Imi d'Avraham Aveinu*
> : *Amtalai bat Karnavu*
> : *v'shem bat Asher Sarach* [*Numbers 26:46*]

Translation:

> : Mother of our Father Abraham
> : *Amtalai bat Karnavu*
> : And the name of the daughter of *Asher* was *Sarach*

At the bottom of the *Kamea* is a Yiddish phrase regarding the contents of the amulet having been tried and tested. This amulet has been reprinted many times in different locales around the globe, sometimes with slight variations. Notwithstanding this, it is worth noting that this is still considered a most important and equally most potent amulet.

F. Disposing of Discarded Amulets

The usual way of disposing of *Kameot* is to deposit them in a *Genizah*, that is if one is readily available. However, I have been given some written instructions in this regard more than thirty years ago and have tried to locate these in the mishmash comprising my archives. I wish I was better organized in my filing system, instead of depositing everything in boxes. Anyway, the gist of it is that one should deal with them in the same manner as one would with a *pasul* (unusable) *Torah* scroll. Rather than being burned or destroyed, it is given a sacred burial. I was told to do the same with *Kameot*, and it would seem that this custom was also followed in ancient times — judging by the number of amulets dug up all over the Middle East.

Again some years back I knew an individual who created a kind of "mini *Genizah*" for himself, which was a plain metal box buried in his back garden, which he would dig up now and again to dispose of worn out sacred texts and amulets. Whilst that might be fine in dry climates, I would think it problematic elsewhere. On the other hand, the aim would be to allow them to disintegrate naturally as one would a deceased body.

Personally I have followed the advice of burying the *Kameot* I no longer require, i.e. treating them as reverently as one would a *Torah* scroll which has become *pasul* ("invalid").

. ...'I am the son of Adam, and he had me with Lilith during the hundred and thirty years that he was separated from Eve. The Lord God gave me the power to change shape at will'."

"He put his vessel on his table. Upon opening it, he found a second vessel inside, and within it there was a frog..... Haninah built a room for the frog..... He fattened him up with the best and finest foods until he had spent all he possessed..... Haninah and his wife went into the frog's room and said to him: 'Dear friend, to our great sorrow we can no longer keep you.....'

The frog opened his mouth and began to speak. 'Dear Haninah, don't grieve. Since you've been taking care of me and feeding me all this time, you can now ask something of me.....' Haninah said: 'There is only one thing I desire. Teach me the entire Law'..... The frog took a piece of paper, wrote down several charms, and then told Haninah to swallow it. In this way, he promptly knew the entire Torah and the seventy languages.....

Next the frog turned to Haninah's wife and said: '....I would like you to accompany me as far as the Forest of Trees'..... And so they went into the woods with him and, upon arriving, the frog emitted a loud croak, calling together all the beasts in the forest..... The frog ordered each of them to bring as many jewels and pearls as he could carry. In addition, they were to bring all kinds of herbs and roots to cure the ill..... Meanwhile, he taught Haninah and his wife the virtues of each specific, and then ordered the animals to bring everything back to Haninah's house.....

When the frog was about to leave, he said to the couple: 'May the Good Lord bless you and be good to you for all the work and trouble you had with me. After all, you didn't even ask who I am. But I will tell you the secret. I am the son of Adam, and he had me with Lilith during the hundred and thirty years that he was separated from Eve. The Lord God gave me the power to change shape at will'."... ... .

— The Mayse-Book
(Haninah and the Frog)

REFERENCES
&
BIBLIOGRAPHY

INTRODUCTION

1. **Idel, M.:** *Messianic Mystics*, Yale University Press, New Haven & London 2000.
2. *Ibid.*
3. **Karo, J.:** *Sefer Maggid Mesharim*, Y. ben Y. ha-Kohen, Jerusalem 2006.
    Gordon, H.L.: *The Maggid of Caro,* Pardes Publishing House, New York 1940.
    Werblowsky, R.J.Z.: *Joseph Karo: Lawyer and Mystic*, Oxford University Press, Oxford 1962.
4. *Refuah v'Chayim mi-Yerushalayim*, Hotza'at Backal, Jerusalem.
    Segulot ha-Avanim ha-Tovot, Yarid ha-Sefarim, Jerusalem 2004.
    Avraham Rimon of Granada: *Brit Menuchah*, Machon Ramchal, Jerusalem 1998.
    Vital, Chaim: *K'tavim Chadashim l'Rabbi Chaim Vital*, Machon l'Hotsa'at Sefarim v'Kitve-yad Ahavat shalom, Jerusalem 1988.
    Bacharach, N.: *Emek ha-Melech*, Yerid ha-Sefarim, Jerusalem 2003.
    Moshe ben Ya'akov of Kiev: *Sefer Shoshan Sodot*, Drukeray Y. A. Kriger, Koretz 1784.
    Halevi, B. ben Meir: *Sefer Zechira ve-Einei Segulah*, Novly Dvor, 1798.
    Azulai, C.Y.D.: *Sefer Avodat ha-Kodesh*, Jerusalem 1841.
    —*Midbar Kedemot*, Mayan ha-Chochmah, Jerusalem 1957.
    —*Shem ha-Gedolim*, Yerid ha-Sefarim, Jerusalem 2004.
    Kratchin, B. Beinish: *Amtachat Binyamin*, Hotza'at Backal, Jerusalem 1966.
    Badrashi, Y.: *Yalkut Moshe*, Munkatch 1894.
    B'ruk, Y.S.: *S'dei b'Samim*, Buchdruckerei "Grafia," Munkatsh.
    Chamui, A.: *Devek Me'Ach*, Yarid ha-Sefarim, Jerusalem 2005.
    —*He'Ach Nafshenu*, Yarid ha-Sefarim, Jerusalem 2007.
    —*Nifla'im Ma'asecha*, Hotza'at Backal, Jerusalem 1972.

—*Avi'ah Chidot*, S. Belforti va-chavero, Livorno 1879.

—*Avi'ah Chidot*, Hotza'at Backal, Jerusalem 1996.

Keter, S.: *Nechash ha-Nechoshet*, Baruch Keter, Jerusalem 1990.

Beinish, B.: *Amtachat Binyamin, Op. cit.*

Zacutto, M.: *Shorshei ha-Shemot*, Hotzaat Nezer Shraga, Jerusalem 1999.

Ba'al Shem, E.; Ba'al-Shem, J.; ha-Kohen, N. ben I.; & Katz, N.: *Mifalot Elokim*, Mechon Bnei Yishachar, Jerusalem 1994.

Ba'al Shem, E.; Ba'al-Shem, J. & Hillel, M.: *Sefer Toldot Adam*, Machon Bnei Yishaschar, Jerusalem 1994.

Reuven ben Avraham: *Sefer ha-Segulot*, Jerusalem 1865; Mukatch 1906.

Lifshitz, S.: *Sefer Segulot Yisrael*, Kahn & Fried, Munkatch 1905; Mosdot Hifchadeti Shomrim, Jerusalem 1992.

Heller, S.: *Sefer Refuot vi-Segulot*, Jerusalem 1907.

Sharabi, S.; Duwayk, H.S.; & Legimi, E.Y.: *Sefer Benayahu Ben Yehoyada*, Jerusalem 1911.

Ba'al Livushei Sarad: *Refuot*, J. Schlensinger Buchhandlung, Vienna 1926.

Tzubeiri, Y.: *Emet v'Emunah*, Machon Shtilei Zeitim, Ramat Gan 2002.

Rosenberg, Y.: *Rafael ha-Malach*, Asher Klein, Jerusalem 2000.

Shauli, M.C.: *Marpeh ha-Bosem*, Merkaz Ruchani, Ashdod.

Mizrachi, E.A.: *Refuah v'Chayim m'Yerushalayim*, Defus Yehudah vi-Yerushalayim, Jerusalem 1931.

Trachtenberg, J.: *Jewish Magic and Superstition: A Study in Folk Religion*, Behrman's Jewish Book House Publishers, New York 1939.

Lustig, D.: *Pela'ot Chachmeh ha-Kabbalah: v'He'avar ha-Kadum*, Hotza'at David ben Ze'ev, Tel Aviv 1987.

—*Wondrous Healings of the Wise Kabbalists and the Ancient Physicians*, D. Lustig, Tel Aviv 1989.

Ruderman, D.B.: *Kabbalah, Magic and Science: The Cultural Universe of a Sixteenth-Century Jewish Physician*, Harvard University Press, Cambridge 1988.

Isaacs, R.J.: *Divination, Magic, and Healing: The Book of Jewish Folklore*, Jason Aronson Inc., Northvale 1998.

Tirosh-Rothschild, H.: *Between Worlds: The Life and Thought of Rabbi David ben Juda Messer Leon*, SUNY Press, Albany 1991.

428

Nigal, G.: *Magic, Mysticism, and Hasidism: The Supernatural in Jewish Thought*, Jason Aronson Inc., Northvale 1994.

Idel, M.: *The Magical and Neoplatonic Interpretations of the Kabbalah in the Renaissance* in **Cooperman, B.D.:** *Jewish Thought in the Sixteenth Century*, Harvard University Press, Cambridge 1983.

—*Golem: Jewish Magical and Mystical Traditions on the Artificial Anthropoid*, SUNY Press, Albany 1990.

—*Hasidism: Between Ecstasy and Magic*, SUNY Press, Albany 1995.

Nigal, G.: *Magic, Mysticism, and Hasidism, Op. cit.*

Kanarfogel, E.: *Peering Through the Lattices: Mystical, Magical, and Pietistic Dimensions in the Tosafist Period*, Wayne State University Press, Detroit 2000.

Winkler, G.: *Magic of the Ordinary*, North Atlantic Books, Berkeley 2003.

Etkes, I.: *The Besht: Magician, Mystic and Leader*, Brandeis University Press, Lebanon 2005.

5. **Karo, J. ben E.:** *Shulchan Aruch: Yoreh De'ah*, 2 Volumes, Y. Bodnar, Hebron 1950.

6. See Introduction note 4.

7. *Sefer Shimmush Tehillim*, Éliás Békéscsaba Klein, Budapest.
    Sefer ha-Kanah/Sefer ha-Pli'ah, Koretz 1784.
    Sefer Raziel ha-Malach, Yarid ha-Sefarim, Jerusalem 2003.
    Sefer Mishpatei ha-Olam & *Sefer ha-Mivcharim*, Hotza'at Backal, Jerusalem.
    Sepher ha-Razim: The Book of the Mysteries, transl. M.A. Morgan, Society of Biblical Literature, 1983.
    Sefer ha-Malbush, MS Oxford-Bodleian 1960; MS London British Library OR. 6577 (Margoliouth III, 736)
    Sefer ha-Malbush v'Tikun me'il ha-Tzedakah, MS British Museum, Margoliouth 752.
    Refuah v'Chaim mi-Yerushalayim, Op cit.
    Segulot ha-Avanim ha-Tovot, Op cit.
    Havdalah d'Rabbi Akiva, Hotza'at Backal, Jerusalem 1996.
    Avraham Rimon of Granada: *Brit Menuchah, Op. cit.*
    Zacutto, M.: *Shorshei ha-Shemot, Op. cit.*

8. **Cordovero, M.:** *Pardes Rimmonim*, Yarid ha-Sefarim, Jerusalem 2000.

9. **Karo, J.:** *Sefer Maggid Mesharim, Op. cit.*
    Gordon, H.L.: *The Maggid of Caro, Op. cit.*
    Werblowsky, R.J.Z.: *Joseph Karo: Lawyer and Mystic, Op. cit.*

10. **Gordon, H.L.:** *Ibid.*

11. **Zacutto, M.:** *Shorshei ha-Shemot, Op. cit.*
12. **Zacutto, M.:** *Sefer ha-Sodot she-Kibbalti mi Rabbotai,* referenced in **Chajes, J.H.:** *Between Worlds: Dybbuks, Exorcists, and Early Modern Judaism,* University of Pennsylvania Press, Philadelphia 2003.
13. **Chajes, J.H.:** *Ibid.*
14. *Ibid.*
15. **Swart, J.G.:** *The Book of Sacred Names,* The Sangreal Sodality Press, Johannesburg 2011.
16. **Cordovero, M.:** *Pardes Rimmonim, Op. cit.*
17. Translated in **Idel, M.:** *"Jewish Magic from the Renaissance Period to Early Hasidism"* published in **Neusner, J.; Frerichs, E.S. & Flesher, P.V.M.:** *Religion, Science, and Magic: In Concert and in Conflict,* Oxford University Press, New York 1989.
18. **Swart, J.G.:** *The Book of Sacred Names, Op. cit.*
19. **Eleazar ben Yehudah of Worms:** *Sefer ha-Chochmah,* MS Oxford-Bodleian 1568, relevant portions transl. in **Idel, M.:** *Kabbalah: New Perspectives,* Yale University Press, New Haven & London 1988.
20. **Abulafia, A.:** *Sefer Chayei ha-Olam ha-Ba,* Aharon Barazani, Jerusalem 2001.
     —*Or ha-Sechel,* Aharon Barazani, Jerusalem 2001.
     —*Sefer ha-Tzeruf,* Aharon Barazani, Jerusalem 2003.
     —*The Path of Names,* transl. B. Finkel, J. Hirschman, D. Meltzer and G. Scholem, Trigram, Berkeley 1976.
     Idel, M.: *Kabbalah: New Perspectives, Op. cit.*
     —*The Mystical Experience in Abraham Abulafia,* SUNY Press, Albany 1988.
     Kaplan, A.: *Meditation and Kabbalah,* Samuel Weiser Inc., York Beach 1988.
     Cooper, D.: *Ecstatic Kabbalah,* Sounds True Inc., Louisville 2005.
21. **Albotini, Y.:** *Sulam ha-Aliyah,* Machon Sha'arei Ziv, Machon Sha'arei ziv, Jerusalem 1989.
     —Chapters transl. in **Blumenthal, D.R.:** *Understanding Jewish Mysticism: A Source Reader - The Philosophic Mystical Tradition and the Chassidic Tradition,* Volume II, KTAV Publishing House Inc., New York 1982.
22. **Vital, Chaim:** *Sefer Sha'ar Ru'ach ha-Kodesh,* Hotsa'at Kitve Rabeinu ha-Ari, Tel Aviv 1962; Mosdat Nehar Shalom, Jerusalem 1999.
     —*Pri Etz Chaim, Hotsa'at Eshel,* Tel Aviv 1961.

430

—Sefer Sha'arei Kedushah, Aharon Barazani, Tel Aviv, 1995; Hotza'at Yeshivat ha-Shamash, Jerusalem 1997.
—K'tavim Chadashim l'Rabbi Chaim Vital, Op. cit.
—Sha'ar ha-Kavvanot, Yeshivat ha-shalom, Jerusalem 1997.
Kaplan, A.: *Meditation and Kabbalah, Op. cit.*
Epstein, P.: *Kabbalah: The Way of the Jewish Mystic*, Doubleday & Company, New York 1978.
Besserman, P.: *The Shambhala Guide to Kabbalah and Jewish Mysticism*, Shambhala, Berkeley, 1997.
Cooper, D.: *Ecstatic Kabbalah, Op. cit.*

23. **Vital, Chaim:** *Sidur Tefilah mi-Kol ha-Shanah*, 3 Volumes, Zolkova.
Koppel, Y.: *Siddur m'ha-Arizal ha-Nikra b'Shem Kol Ya'akov*, Yaakov Koppel, Lemberg 1859.
Weinstock, B.M.Y.: *Siddur ha-Gaonim v'ha-Mekubalim*, 21 Volumes, Defus Shraga Weinfeld, Jerusalem 1970.

24. **Wolf, L.:** *Practical Kabbalah: A Guide to Jewish Wisdom for Everyday Life*, Three Rivers Press, New York 1999.

25. **Gray, W.G.:** *Magical Ritual Methods*, Helios Book Service Ltd., Cheltenham 1969.
—A Self Made by Magic, Samuel Weiser Inc., New York 1976.
—Qabalistic Concepts: Living the Tree, (Previously *Concepts of Concepts*, Sangreal Sodality Series, Volume 3), Samuel Weiser Inc., York Beach, 1997.
—A Beginners Guide to Living Kabbalah, The Sangreal Sodality Press, Parkmore 2009.

26. **Stewart, R.J.:** *The Miracle Tree: Demystifying the Qabalah*, New Page Books, Franklin Lakes 2003.

27. *Rabbi Abuhatzeira Bore the Burden of Evil Decrees*, Arutz Sheva, 29 July 2011, IsraelNationalNews.com.

28. **Yagna, Y. & Ettinger, Y.:** *Thousands Attend Murder of Rabbi Abuhatzeira: Man from Ultra-Orthodox City Held*, Haaretz, 31 July 2011, Haaretz.com.

29. **Mae West:** *She Done Him Wrong*, 1933 Paramount Films 1933.

30. **Swart, J.G.:** *The Book of Self Creation*, The Sangreal Sodality Press, Johannesburg 2009.
—The Book of Sacred Names, Op. cit.

31. *Ibid.*

CHAPTER 1

1.   **Swart, J.G.:** *The Book of Self Creation, Op. cit.*
2.   **Chouraqui, A.N.:** *Between East and West: A history of the Jews of North Africa*, translated from the French by Michael M. Bernet, The Jewish Publication Society of America, 1968.
3.   *Ibid.*
4.   **Gikatilla, J.:** *Gates of Light: Sha'are Orah*, transl. Avi Weinstein, Alta Mira Press, Walnut Creek 1998.
      Zacutto, M.: *Shorshei ha-Shemot, Op. cit.*
      Swart, J.G.: *The Book of Sacred Names, Op. cit.*
5.   **Zacutto, M.:** *Ibid.*
      Davis, E. & Frenkel, D.A.: *Ha-Kami'a ha-Ivri: Mikra'i Refu'i Kelali im Tatzlumim v'Iyurim Rabim*, Machon l'Mada'e ha-Yahadut, Jerusalem 1995.
      Green, A.: *Judaic Artifacts: Unlocking the Secrets of Judaic Charms and Amulets*, Astrolog Publishing House, Hod Hasharon 2004.
      Swart, J.G.: *Ibid.*
6.   **Zacutto, M.:** *Ibid.*
7.   *Ibid.*
8.   **Shachar, I.:** *Jewish Tradition in Art: The Feuchtwanger Collection of Judaica*, transl. R Grafman, The Israel Museum, Jerusalem 1981.
9.   **Rosenberg, Y.:** *Rafael ha-Malach, Op. cit.*
10.   **Schrire, T.:** *Hebrew Amulets*, Routledge & Kegan Paul, London 1966.
11.   **Zacutto, M.:** *Shorshei ha-Shemot, Op. cit.*
12.   **Rosenberg, Y.:** *Rafael ha-Malach, Op. cit.*
13.   **Zacutto, M.:** *Shorshei ha-Shemot, Op. cit.*
14.   **Schrire, T.:** *Hebrew Amulets, Op. cit.*
15.   **Zacutto, M.:** *Shorshei ha-Shemot, Op. cit.*
16.   *Sefer Raziel ha-Malach, Op. cit.*
17.   *Ibid.*
18.   **Maller, A.S.:** *God, Sex and Kabbalah: Messianic Speculations*, Ridgefield Publications Co., Los Angeles 1983.
19.   *Ibid.*
20.   **Zacutto, M.:** *Shorshei ha-Shemot, Op. cit.*
21.   *Ibid.*

22. *Ibid.*
23. *Ibid.*
24. **Swart, J.G.:** *The Book of Sacred Names, Op. cit.*
25. **Zacutto, M.:** *Shorshei ha-Shemot, Op. cit.*
    Schrire, T.: *Hebrew Amulets, Op. cit.*
26. **Zacutto, M.:** *Ibid.*
27. **Bartolocci, G.:** *Bibliotheca Magna Rabbinica*, Vol. 4, Sacrae Congregationis de Propaganda Fide, Rome 1675-94.
    Kircher, A.: *Oedipus Aegyptiacus*, Vol. 2, Ex Typographia Vitalis Mascardi, Rome 1653.
    Findlen, P.: *Athanasius Kircher: The Last Man Who Knew Everything*, Routledge, New York 2004.
28. **Bartolocci, G.:** *Ibid.*
29. **Kircher, A.:** *Oedipus Aegyptiacus, Op. cit.*
30. **Schrire, T.:** *Hebrew Amulets, Op. cit.*
31. **Swart, J.G.:** *The Book of Self Creation, Op. cit.*
    —*The Book of Sacred Names, Op. cit.*
32. **Bartolocci, G.:** *Bibliotheca Magna Rabbinica, Op. cit.*
33. **Swart, J.G.:** *The Book of Sacred Names, Op. cit.*
34. **Schrire, T.:** *Hebrew Amulets, Op. cit.*
    Patai, R.: *The Hebrew Goddess*, Third enlarged edition, Wayne State University Press, Detroit 1990.
    Azulai, C.Y.D.: *Sefer Avodat ha-Kodesh, Op. cit.*
35. **Ariel, D.S.:** *The Mystic Quest*, Schocken Books Inc., New York 1992.
36. *Ibid.*
    Leet, L.: *The Universal Kabbalah: Deciphering the Cosmic Code in the Sacred Geometry of the Sabbath Star Diagram*, Inner Traditions, Rochester 2004.
    Jacobs, L.: *Hasidic Prayer*, Schocken Books, New York 1972.
    Eilberg-Schwartz, H.: *People of the Body: Jews and Judaism from an Embodied Perspective*, State University of New York Press, Albany 1992.
37. **Eilberg-Schwartz, H.:** *Ibid.*
38. **Vital, Chaim:** *Sidur Tefilah mi-Kol ha-Shanah, Op. cit.*
    Koppel, Y.: *Siddur m'ha-Arizal ha-Nikra b'Shem Kol Ya'akov, Op. cit.*
    Weinstock, B.M.Y.: *Siddur ha-Gaonim v'ha-Mekubalim, Op. cit.*
    Schrire, T.: *Hebrew Amulets, Op. cit.*
    Shachar, I.: *Jewish Tradition in Art, Op. cit.*
    Shwartz-Be'eri, O.: *The Jews of Kurdistan: Daily Life,*

433

Customs, Arts and Crafts, The Israel Museum, Jerusalem 2000.
Varetz, T.S.: [with A. Sutton] *California Kabbalah: A Contemporary Initiation into Kabbalistic Meditation & Practice*, Zechariah Tzvi Shamayim V'aretz, eText 2001.

39. **Zacutto, M.:** *Shorshei ha-Shemot, Op. cit.*
40. **Schrire, T.:** *Ibid.*
     Shachar, I.: *Ibid.*
     Shwartz-Be'eri, O.: *Ibid.*
     Davis, E. & Frenkel, D.A.: *Ha-Kami'a ha-Ivri, Op. cit.*
41. **Schrire, T.:** *Ibid.*
     Azulai, C.Y.D.: *Sefer Avodat ha-Kodesh, Op. cit.*
42. **Swart, J.G.:** *The Book of Sacred Names, Op. cit.*
43. **Shachar, I.:** *Jewish Tradition in Art, Op. cit.*
     Davis, E. & Frenkel, D.A.: *Ha-Kami'a ha-Ivri, Op. cit.*
44. **Trachtenberg, J.:** *Jewish Magic and Superstition, Op. cit.*
45. **Shachar, I.:** *Jewish Tradition in Art, Op. cit.*
     Davis, E. & Frenkel, D.A.: *Ha-Kami'a ha-Ivri, Op. cit.*
46. **Ba'al Shem, E.; Ba'al-Shem, J. & Hillel, M.:** *Sefer Toldot Adam, Op. cit.*
47. **Zacutto, M.:** *Shorshei ha-Shemot, Op. cit.*
48. **Swart, J.G.:** *The Book of Sacred Names, Op. cit.*
49. **Zacutto, M.:** *Shorshei ha-Shemot, Op. cit.*
50. *Ibid.*
     Mizrachi, E.A.: *Refuah v'Chayim m'Yerushalayim, Op. cit.*
51. **Zacutto, M.:** *Ibid.*
52. *Ibid.*
53. *Ibid.*
54. *Ibid.*
55. **Schrire, T.:** *Hebrew Amulets, Op. cit.*
     Josephy, M.R. & Maurice Spertus Museum of Judaica: *Magic & superstition in the Jewish Tradition: An Exhibition Organized by the Maurice Spertus Museum of Judaica*, Spertus College of Judaica Press, Chicago 1975.
     Peursen, W.T. van & Dyk, J.W.: *Tradition and Innovation in Biblical Interpretation: Studies presented to Professor Eep Talstra on the Occasion of his Sixty-Fifth Birthday*, Koninklijke Brill NV, Leiden 2011.
56. **Zacutto, M.:** *Ibid.*
57. **Schrire, T.:** *Hebrew Amulets, Op. cit.*
58. **Zacutto, M.:** *Shorshei ha-Shemot, Op. cit.*
     Palagi, C.: *Refuah v'Chayim*, Machon l'Hotza'at Sefarim v'Cheker Kitvei Rabotenu ha-Kadmonim, Jerusalem 1997.
59. **Zacutto, M.:** *Shorshei ha-Shemot, Op. cit.*

60. *Ibid.*
61. *Ibid.*
62. **Palagi, C.:** *Refuah v'Chayim, Op. cit.*
    Davis, E. & Frenkel, D.A.: *Ha-Kami'a ha-Ivri, Op. cit.*
63. **Zacutto, M.:** *Shorshei ha-Shemot, Op. cit.*
64. *Ibid.*
65. **Avraham Rimon of Granada:** *Brit Menuchah, Op. cit.*
    Zacutto, M.: *Ibid..*
    Swart, J.G.: *The Book of Sacred Names, Op. cit.*
66. **Swart, J.G.:** *Ibid.*
67. **Zacutto, M.:** *Shorshei ha-Shemot, Op. cit.*
68. **Swart, J.G.:** *The Book of Sacred Names, Op. cit.*
    Avraham Rimon of Granada: *Brit Menuchah, Op. cit.*
    Zacutto, M.: *Ibid.*
69. **Cordovero, M.:** *Sefer Gerushin,* Achuzat Yisrael, Jerusalem 1962.
70. **Swart, J.G.:** *The Book of Sacred Names, Op. cit.*
71. **Zacutto, M.:** *Shorshei ha-Shemot, Op. cit.*
72. *Midrash Tanchuma,* Makor, Jerusalem 1971.
73. **Zacutto, M.:** *Ibid.*
    Swart, J.G.: *The Book of Sacred Names, Op. cit.*
74. **Zacutto, M.:** *Ibid.*
75. *Ibid.*
76. *Ibid.*
77. *Ibid.*
78. *Ibid.*
79. *Ibid.*
80. *Ibid.*
81. *Ibid.*
82. *Ibid.*
83. **Swart, J.G.:** *The Book of Sacred Names, Op. cit.*
84. *Ibid.*
    Zacutto, M.: *Shorshei ha-Shemot, Op. cit.*
85. **Swart, J.G.:** *Ibid.*
86. *Ibid.*
    Zacutto, M.: *Shorshei ha-Shemot, Op. cit.*
87. **Shachar, I.:** *Jewish Tradition in Art, Op. cit.*
88. **Zacutto, M.:** *Shorshei ha-Shemot, Op. cit.*
89. **Swart, J.G.:** *The Book of Sacred Names, Op. cit.*
90. **Zacutto, M.:** *Shorshei ha-Shemot, Op. cit.*
91. *Ibid.*
92. *Ibid.*
    Swart, J.G.: *The Book of Sacred Names, Op. cit.*
93. **Zacutto, M.:** *Ibid.*

94. **Swart, J.G.:** *The Book of Sacred Names, Op. cit.*
95. **Zacutto, M.:** *Shorshei ha-Shemot, Op. cit.*
96. *Ibid.*
97. **Mathers, S.L. Macgregor:** *Key of Solomon the King: Clavicula Salomonis*, Routledge & Kegan Paul, London 1974.
    Gollancz, H.: *Sepher Maphteah Shelomo* (*Book of the Key of Solomon*), Oxford University Press, London 1914.
98. **Zacutto, M.:** *Shorshei ha-Shemot, Op. cit.*
99. *Ibid.*
100. *Ibid.*
101. *Ibid.*
102. *Ibid.*
    Swart, J.G.: *The Book of Sacred Names, Op. cit.*
103. **Zacutto, M.:** *Ibid.*
104. **Swart, J.G.:** *The Book of Self Creation, Op. cit.*
105. **Zacutto, M.:** *Shorshei ha-Shemot, Op. cit.*
    Swart, J.G.: *The Book of Sacred Names, Op. cit*
106. **Zacutto, M.:** *Ibid.*
107. *Ibid.*
108. *Ibid.*
109. **Agrippa, H.C.:** *De Occulta Philosophia*, 3 Vols., Apud Godfridum & Marcellum, Beringos 1550.
    —*Three Books of Occult Philosophy*, transl. J. Freake [John French], Gregory Moule, London 1651.
110. **Zacutto, M.:** *Shorshei ha-Shemot, Op. cit.*
111. **Swart, J.G.:** *The Book of Sacred Names, Op. cit.*
112. **Zacutto, M.:** *Shorshei ha-Shemot, Op. cit.*
113. *Ibid.*
114. **Schrire, T.:** *Hebrew Amulets, Op. cit.*
115. **Zacutto, M.:** *Shorshei ha-Shemot, Op. cit.*
    Chamui, A.: *Avi'ah Chidot, Op. cit.*
116. **Zacutto, M.:** *Ibid.*
117. *Ibid.*
118. **Swart, J.G.:** *The Book of Sacred Names, Op. cit.*
119. **Zacutto, M.:** *Shorshei ha-Shemot, Op. cit.*
120. **Swart, J.G.:** *The Book of Sacred Names, Op. cit.*
121. *Ibid.*
122. **Zacutto, M.:** *Shorshei ha-Shemot, Op. cit.*
123. **Swart, J.G.:** *The Book of Sacred Names, Op. cit.*
124. **Zacutto, M.:** *Shorshei ha-Shemot, Op. cit.*
125. **Shachar, I.:** *Jewish Tradition in Art, Op. cit.*
    Shwartz-Be'eri, O.: *The Jews of Kurdistan, Op. cit.*
126. **Swart, J.G.:** *The Book of Sacred Names, Op. cit.*
127. **Shachar, I.:** *Jewish Tradition in Art, Op. cit.*

128. *Ibid.*
129. *Ibid.*
130. *Ibid.*
131. *Ibid.*
132. *Ibid.*
133. *Ibid.*
134. *Ibid.*
135. *Ibid.*
136. *Ibid.*
137. *Ibid.*
138. *Ibid.*
139. *Ibid.*
140. *Ibid.*
141. **Rothenberg, J.; Lenowitz, H. & Doria, C.:** *A Big Jewish Book: Poems & Other Visions of the Jews from Tribal Times to Present,* Anchor Press, New York 1978.
142. **Swart, J.G.:** *The Book of Sacred Names, Op. cit.*
143. *Ibid.*
144. **Vital, Chaim:** *Sefer Sha'ar Ru'ach ha-Kodesh, Op. cit.*
    Kaplan, A.: *Meditation and Kabbalah, Op. cit.*
145. **Swart, J.G.:** *The Book of Sacred Names, Op. cit.*
146. *Ibid.*
147. **Gikatilla, J.:** *Gates of Light: Sha'are Orah, Op. cit.*
148. **Swart, J.G.:** *The Book of Sacred Names, Op. cit.*
149. *Ibid.*
150. *Ibid.*
151. *Ibid.*
152. *Ibid.*
153. **Zacutto, M.:** *Shorshei ha-Shemot, Op. cit.*
154. *Ibid.*
155. *Ibid.*
156. *Ibid.*
157. *Ibid.*
158. *Ibid.*
159. **Shachar, I.:** *Jewish Tradition in Art, Op. cit.*
160. **Zacutto, M.:** *Shorshei ha-Shemot, Op. cit.*
    Stern, A.Y. bar J: *Sefer Roshei Teivot,* A. Kaufman, Sighetul-Marmatiei 1926.
161. **Zacutto, M.:** *Ibid.*
    Schrire, T.: *Hebrew Amulets, Op. cit.*
    Shachar, I.: *Jewish Tradition in Art, Op. cit.*
    Davis, E. & Frenkel, D.A.: *Ha-Kami'a ha-Ivri, Op. cit.*
    Green, A.: *Judaic Artifacts, Op. cit.*
162. **Swart, J.G.:** *The Book of Sacred Names, Op. cit.*

163.   *Ibid.*
164.   **Mathers, S.L. Macgregor:** *Key of Solomon the King, Op. cit.*
       Gollancz, H.: *Sepher Maphteah Shelomo, Op. cit.*
165.   **Swart, J.G.:** *The Book of Sacred Names, Op. cit.*
166.   **Gikatilla, J.:** *Gates of Light: Sha'are Orah, Op. cit.*
167.   **Zacutto, M.:** *Shorshei ha-Shemot, Op. cit.*
168.   **Shachar, I.:** *Jewish Tradition in Art, Op. cit.*
169.   **Swart, J.G.:** *The Book of Sacred Names, Op. cit.*
170.   **Davis, E. & Frenkel, D.A.:** *Ha-Kami'a ha-Ivri, Op. cit.*
       Green, A.: *Judaic Artifacts, Op. cit.*
171.   **Zacutto, M.:** *Shorshei ha-Shemot, Op. cit.*
172.   *Ibid.*
173.   *Ibid.*
174.   *Ibid.*

CHAPTER 2

1.   **Zacutto, M.:** *Shorshei ha-Shemot, Op. cit.*
2.   **Schrire, T.:** *Hebrew Amulets, Op. cit.*
        Shachar, I.: *Jewish Tradition in Art, Op. cit.*
        Naveh, J. & Shaked, S.: *Amulets and Magic Bowls: Aramaic Incantations of Late Antiquity*, The Magnes Press, Jerusalem 1985.
        —*Magic Spells and Formulae: Aramaic Incantations of Late Antiquity*, The Magnes Press, Jerusalem 1993.
        Davis, E. & E.: *Jewish Folk Art over the Ages: A Collector's Choice*, R. Mass, Jerusalem 1977.
        Davis, E. & Frenkel, D.A.: *Ha-Kami'a ha-Ivri, Op. cit.*
3.   **Zacutto, M.:** *Shorshei ha-Shemot, Op. cit.*
        Seligmann, S.: *Der Böse Blick und Verwandtes: Ein Beitrag zur Geschichte des Aberglaubens aller Zeiten und Völker*, Hermann Barsdorf Verlag, Berlin 1910.
4.   **Zacutto, M.:** *Ibid.*
        Seligmann, S.: *Ibid.*
        Naveh, J. & Shaked, S.: *Amulets and Magic Bowls, Op. cit.*
5.   **Zacutto, M.:** *Ibid.*
6.   *Ibid.*
        Mizrachi, E.A.: *Refuah v'Chayim m'Yerushalayim, Op. cit.*
7.   **Zacutto, M.:** *Ibid.*
8.   **Davis, E. & Frenkel, D.A.:** *Ha-Kami'a ha-Ivri, Op. cit.*
        Green, A.: *Judaic Artifacts, Op. cit.*
9.   **Zacutto, M.:** *Shorshei ha-Shemot, Op. cit.*
        Schrire, T.: *Hebrew Amulets, Op. cit.*
        Davis, E. & Frenkel, D.A.: *Ha-Kami'a ha-Ivri, Op. cit.*
10.   **Mathers, S.L. MacGregor:** *The Book of Sacred Magic of Abramelin the Mage*, Thorsons Publishers Limited, Wellingborough, Northamptonshire 1976.
11.   **Dehn, G.:** *The Book of Abramelin*, Ibis Press, Lake Worth 2006.
12.   **Patai, R.:** *The Jewish Alchemists: A History and Source Book*, Princeton University Press, Princeton 1994.
13.   **Dehn, G.:** *The Book of Abramelin, Op. cit.*
14.   **Patai, R.:** *The Jewish Alchemists, Op. cit.*
15.   *Ibid.*
16.   **Emden, Y.:** *Sefer Torat ha-Kenaot v'hu kevutsat ma'amarim v'k'tuvim neged Shabetai Tzvi u-mete sodo*, Amsterdam 1752.

            Eibeshutz, Y.: *Luchot Edut*, Altona 1755.

17.   **Eibeshutz, Y.:** *Ibid.*

18.   *Ibid.*

19.   **Wahshih, A. bin A. bin & Hammer, J.**: *Ancient Alphabets and Hieroglyphic Characters Explained*, W. Bulmer and Co., London 1806.

            Rodkinson, M.L.: *History of Amulets, Charms and Talismans*, New York 1893.

            Elworthy, F.T.: *The Evil Eye: An Account of this Ancient & Widespread Superstition*, John Murray, London 1895.

            Blau, L.: *Das Altjüdische Zauberwesen*, K.J. Trübner, Strassburg 1898.

            Gollancz, H.: *A Selection of Charms from Syriac Manuscripts*, London 1898.

            Hanauer, J.E.: *Folk-Lore of the Holy Land: Moslem, Christian and Jewish*, Duckworth & Co., London 1907.

            Reisner, M.G.: *Catalogue Général des Antiquités Égyptiennes du Musée du Caire*, Institut Français d'Archéologie Orientale, Cairo 1907.

            Thompson, R.C.: *Semitic Magic: Its Origins and Development*, Luzac & Co., London 1909.

            Montgomery, J.A.: *Aramaic Incantation Texts from Nippur*, University Museum, Philadelphia 1913.

            Flinders Petrie, W.M.: *Amulets: Illustrated by the Egyptian Collection in University College*, London, Constable & Company Ltd., London 1914.

            Kunz, G.F.: *The Magic of Jewels and Charms*, J.B. Lippincott Company, Philadelphia & London 1915.

            Ahrens, W.: *Hebräische Amulette mit Magischen Zahlenquadraten*, Louis Lamm, Berlin 1916.

            Thomas, W. & Pavitt, K.: *The Book of Talismans, Amulets and Zodiacal Gems*, William Rider & Son Ltd., London 1922.

            Trachtenberg, J.: *Jewish Magic and Superstition, Op. cit.*

            Morgan, H.T.: *Chinese Symbols and Superstitions*, P.D. and Ione Perkins, South Pasadena 1946.

            Bonner, C.L: *Studies in Magical Amulets: Chiefly Graeco-Egyptian*, University of Michigan Press, Ann Arbor 1950.

            Bing, G.: *"Picatrix" das Ziel des Weisen von Pseudo-Magriti*, The Warburg Institute University of London, London 1962.

            Atallah, H.: *Picatrix (Ghayat al-Hakim): The Goal of the Wise, edited by W. Kiesel*, 2 Volumes, Ouroboros Press, Seattle 2002.

Greer, J.M. & Warnock, C.: *The Latin Picatrix*, Book I & II, Renaissance Astrology Press, 2009.
— *The Picatrix*, Adocentyn Press, 2011.
Wallis Budge, E.A.: *Amulets and Talismans*, University Books, New York 1968.
Wippler González, M.: *The Complete Book of Amulets & Talismans*, Llewellyn Publications, St. Paul 1991.
Gager, J.G.: *Curse Tablets and Binding Spells from the Ancient World*, Oxford University Press, Oxford & New York 1992.
Spier, J.: Medieval Byzantine Magical Amulets and Their Tradition, Journal of the Warburg and Courtauld Institutes, Vol. 56, London 1993.
Naveh, J. & Shaked, S.: *Amulets and Magic Bowls, Op. cit.*
—*Magic Spells and Formulae, Op. cit.*
Meyer, M.W. & Smith, R.: *Ancient Christian Magic: Coptic Texts of Ritual Power, Princeton University Press*, Princeton 1999.
MacLeod, M. & Mees, B.: *Runic Amulets and Magic Objects*, The Boydell Press, Woodbridge 2006.
Skemer, D.C.: *Binding Words: Textual Amulets in the Middle Ages*, Pennsylvania State University Press, Pennsylvania 2006.
Macleod, M. & Mees, B.: *Runic Amulets and Magic Objects, Op. cit.*
20.   **Agrippa, H.C.:** *De Occulta Philosophia, Op. cit.*
—*Three Books of Occult Philosophy, Op. cit.*
Barrett, F.: *The Magus or Celestial Intelligencer, being a Complete System of Occult Philosophy in Three Books*, University Books Inc., New York 1967.
Papus: *Traité Élémentaire de Magie Pratique*, Chamuel, Paris 1893.
Wallis Budge, E.A.: *Amulets and Talismans, Op. cit.*
Sepharial: *The Book of Charms and Talismans*, W. Foulsham & Co., London 1923.
Poinsot, M.C.: *Encyclopédie des Sciences Occultes*, Les Éditions Georges-Anquetil, Paris 1925.
Shah, S.I.: *The Secret Lore of Magic: Books of the Sorcerers*, Frederick Muller Ltd., London 1957.
Regardie, I.: *How to Make and Use Talismans*, The Aquarian Press, Wellingborough 1972.
—*The Complete Golden Dawn System of Magic*, Falcon Press, Santa Monica 1987.
MacLean, A.: *A Treatise on Angel Magic*, Phanes Press, Grand Rapids 1990.

441

Pennick, N.: *Magical Alphabets*, Weiser Books, York Beach 1992.

Fanger, C.: *Conjuring Spirits: Texts and Traditions of Medieval Ritual Magic*, Sutton Publishing, Stroud 1998.

Farrell, N.: *Making Talismans: Living Entities of Power*, Llewellyn Publications, St. Paul 2001.

Lehrich, C.I.: *The Language of Demons and Angels: Cornelius Agrippa's Occult Philosophy*, Koninklijke Brill NV, Leiden 2003.

21. **Tzayach, J.:** *Even ha-Shoham*, Ms. 8° 416, Jerusalem.
     —*Sheirit Josef*, Ms. 260. Vienna.
     Patai, R.: *The Jewish Alchemists, Op. cit.*
     Kaplan, A.: *Meditation and Kabbalah, Op. cit.*
22. **Kaplan, A.:** *Ibid.*
23. **Tirshom, J. ben E.:** *Shoshan Yesod Olam* in *Collectanea of Kabbalistic and Magical Texts*, Bibliothèque de Genève: Comites Latentes 145, Genève.
     Zacutto, M.: *Shorshei ha-Shemot, Op. cit.*
     Horowitz, Y.: *Shnei Luchot ha-Brit*, Vol. 2, Warsaw 1930. *Moroccan Kabbalah manuscript.*
     Ba'al Shem, E.; Ba'al-Shem, J. & Hillel, M.: *Sefer Toldot Adam, Op. cit.*
     Beinish, B.: *Amtachat Binyamin, Op. cit.*
     Refuah v'Chayim mi-Yerushalayim, Op. cit.
     Mizrachi, E.A.: *Refuah v'Chaim mi-Yerushalayim, Op. cit.*
     Davis, E. & Frenkel, D.A.: *Ha-Kamia ha-Ivri, Op. cit.*
     Schrire, T.: *Hebrew Amulets, Op. cit.*
     Ahrens, W.: *Hebräische Amulette mit Magischen Zahlenquadraten, Op. cit.*
     Shachar, I.: *Jewish Tradition in Art, Op. cit.*
24. **Tirshom, J. ben E.:** *Ibid.*
25. **Ibn Ezra, A.:** *Sefer Hashem,*
26. **Ahrens, W.:** *Hebräische Amulette mit Magischen Zahlenquadraten, Op. cit.*
27. **Zacutto, M.:** *Shorshei ha-Shemot, Op. cit.*
     Davis, E. & Frenkel, D.A.: *Ha-Kamia ha-Ivri, Op. cit.*
28. *Segulot, Hashva'ot v'Goralot*, Yemenite script, MIC. #8988, Jewish Theological Seminary.
     Seligmann, S.: *Der Böse Blick und Verwandtes, Op. cit.*
29. See note 20.
30. *Ibid.*
     Zacutto, M.: *Shorshei ha-Shemot, Op. cit.*

31. **Zacutto, M.:** *Ibid.*
32. See note 20.
33. *Ibid.*
     Zacutto, M.: *Shorshei ha-Shemot, Op. cit.*
34. See note 20.
35. **Agrippa, H.C.:** *De Occulta Philosophia, Op. cit.*
     —Three Books of Occult Philosophy, Op. cit.
     Lehrich, C.I.: *The Language of Demons and Angels, Op. cit.*
36. *Ibid.*
     Zacutto, M.: *Shorshei ha-Shemot, Op. cit.*
37. **Agrippa, H.C.:** *Ibid.*
38. **Davis, E. & Frenkel, D.A.:** *Ha-Kamia ha-Ivri, Op. cit.*
39. **Zacutto, M.:** *Shorshei ha-Shemot, Op. cit.*
40. See note 20.
41. *Mazalot v'Goralot,* Jerusalem - The National Library of Israel
     Ms. Heb. 28°3987.
42. **Atallah, H.:** *Picatrix* (*Ghayat al-Hakim*)*, Op. cit.*
     Greer, J.M. & Warnock, C.: *The Picatrix, Op. cit.*
43. **Zacutto, M.:** *Shorshei ha-Shemot, Op. cit.*
44. *Ibid.*
45. *Ibid.*
46. *Ibid.*
     Chamui, A.: *Liderosh Elohim,* Mosdot "Mishpatim Yesharim,"
     Bnei Barak 2011.
47. **Miller, C. & Schneerson, M.M.:** *The Gutnick Edition
     Chumash: Exodus,* Kol Menachem, Brooklyn 2004-2005.
48. **Zacutto, M.:** *Shorshei ha-Shemot, Op. cit.*
49. *Ibid.*
50. *Ibid.*
51. *Ibid.*
52. *Ibid.*
53. *Ibid.*
54. **Rosenberg, Y.:** *Rafael ha-Malach, Op. cit.*
55. **Octavius, M.:** quoted in *Proceedings of the Society of
     Antiquaries of London*, Vol. 4, Society of Antiquaries of
     London, London 1859.
56. *Ibid.*
57. **Fanger, C.:** *Conjuring Spirits, Op. cit.*
58. *Ibid.*
59. **MacLean, A.:** *A Treatise on Angel Magic, Op. cit.*
60. **Agrippa, H.C.:** *De Occulta Philosophia, Op. cit.*
     See note 20.
61. **Lehrich, C.I.:** *The Language of Demons and Angels, Op. cit.*
62. *Mazalot v'Goralot, Op. cit.*

63. **Atallah, H.:** *Picatrix* (*Ghayat al-Hakim*), *Op. cit.*
    Greer, J.M. & Warnock, C.: *The Picatrix, Op. cit.*
64. **Ba'al Shem, E.; Ba'al-Shem, J. & Hillel, M.:** *Sefer Toldot Adam, Op. cit.*
65. **Patai, R.:** *The Jewish Alchemists, Op. cit.*
66. **Ba'al Shem, E.; Ba'al-Shem, J. & Hillel, M.:** *Sefer Toldot Adam, Op. cit.*
67. **Ahrens, W.:** *Hebräische Amulette mit Magischen Zahlenquadraten, Op. cit.*
68. *Mazalot v'Goralot, Op. cit.*
69. **Ahrens, W.:** *Hebräische Amulette mit Magischen Zahlenquadraten, Op. cit.*
70. **Vital, Chaim:** *Sefer Sha'ar Ru'ach ha-Kodesh, Op. cit.*
71. *Refuah v'Chayim mi-Yerushalayim, Op. cit.*
    Mizrachi, E.A.: *Refuah v'Chaim mi-Yerushalayim, Op. cit.*
72. **Zacutto, M.:** *Shorshei ha-Shemot, Op. cit.*
    Refuah v'Chayim mi-Yerushalayim, Op. cit.
    Mizrachi, E.A.: *Refuah v'Chaim mi-Yerushalayim, Op. cit.*
    Shachar, I.: *Jewish Tradition in Art, Op. cit.*
    Davis, E. & Frenkel, D.A.: *Ha-Kami'a ha-Ivri, Op. cit.*
73. **Zacutto, M.:** *Shorshei ha-Shemot, Op. cit.*
74. *Ibid.*
75. *Mazalot v'Goralot, Op. cit.*
76. **Agrippa, H.C.:** *De Occulta Philosophia, Op. cit.*
77. **Zacutto, M.:** *Shorshei ha-Shemot, Op. cit.*
    Refuah v'Chayim mi-Yerushalayim, Op. cit.
    Mizrachi, E.A.: *Refuah v'Chaim mi-Yerushalayim, Op. cit.*
78. *Ibid.*
79. *Ibid.*
80. *Ibid.*
81. *Ibid.*
82. **Shachar, I.:** *Jewish Tradition in Art, Op. cit.*
83. **Zacutto, M.:** *Shorshei ha-Shemot, Op. cit.*
84. **Ba'al Shem, E.; Ba'al-Shem, J. & Hillel, M.:** *Sefer Toldot Adam, Op. cit.*
85. See note 20.
86. **Atallah, H.:** *Picatrix* (*Ghayat al-Hakim*), *Op. cit.*
    Greer, J.M. & Warnock, C.: *The Picatrix, Op. cit.*
87. **Agrippa, H.C.:** *De Occulta Philosophia, Op. cit.*
    —*Three Books of Occult Philosophy, Op. cit.*
88. **Fanger, C.:** *Conjuring Spirits, Op. cit.*
89. **Agrippa, H.C.:** *De Occulta Philosophia, Op. cit.*
    —*Three Books of Occult Philosophy, Op. cit.*
90. **Patai, R.:** *The Jewish Alchemists, Op. cit.*

91. **Ahrens, W.:** *Hebräische Amulette mit Magischen Zahlenquadraten, Op. cit.*
92. **Agrippa, H.C.:** *De Occulta Philosophia, Op. cit.*
   —Three Books of Occult Philosophy, Op. cit.
93. *Ibid.*
94. **MacLean, A.:** *A Treatise on Angel Magic, Op. cit.*
95. **Fanger, C.:** *Conjuring Spirits, Op. cit.*
96. *Liber Cabbalae Operativae* (1401–1500), Biblioteca Medicea Laurenziana, Firenze, IT-FI0100. Plut.44.22
97. **Ahrens, W.:** *Hebräische Amulette mit Magischen Zahlenquadraten, Op. cit.*
98. **Agrippa, H.C.:** *De Occulta Philosophia, Op. cit.*
   —Three Books of Occult Philosophy, Op. cit.
99. **Ahrens, W.:** *Hebräische Amulette mit Magischen Zahlenquadraten, Op. cit.*
100. **Agrippa, H.C.:** *De Occulta Philosophia, Op. cit.*
   —Three Books of Occult Philosophy, Op. cit.
101. *Ibid.*
102. **Patai, R.:** *The Jewish Alchemists, Op. cit.*
103. *Ibid.*
104. **Agrippa, H.C.:** *De Occulta Philosophia, Op. cit.*
   —Three Books of Occult Philosophy, Op. cit.
105. *Ibid.*
106. **Fanger, C.:** *Conjuring Spirits, Op. cit.*
107. **Agrippa, H.C.:** *De Occulta Philosophia, Op. cit.*
   —Three Books of Occult Philosophy, Op. cit.
108. *Ibid.*
109. *Ibid.*
110. **Stern, A.Y. bar J:** *Sefer Roshei Teivot, Op. cit.*
111. **Agrippa, H.C.:** *De Occulta Philosophia, Op. cit.*
   —Three Books of Occult Philosophy, Op. cit.
   See note 20.
112. **Bischoff, E.:** *The Kabbalah, an Introduction to Jewish Mysticism and Its Secret Doctrine*, Samuel Weiser Inc., York Beach 1985.
113. **Ahrens, W.:** *Hebraeische Amulette mit Magischen Zahlenquadraten, Op. cit.*
114. *Liber Cabbalae Operativae, Op. cit.*
115. **Ba'al Shem, E.; Ba'al-Shem, J. & Hillel, M.:** *Sefer Toldot Adam, Op. cit.*
116. **Chamui, A.:** *Nifla'im Ma'asecha, Op. cit.*
117. *Ibid.*
118. **Ahrens, W.:** *Hebräische Amulette mit Magischen Zahlenquadraten, Op. cit.*

119. *Ibid.*
120. **Agrippa, H.C.:** *De Occulta Philosophia, Op. cit.*
    —*Three Books of Occult Philosophy, Op. cit.*
121. **Fanger, C.:** *Conjuring Spirits, Op. cit.*
122. **Agrippa, H.C.:** *De Occulta Philosophia, Op. cit.*
    —*Three Books of Occult Philosophy, Op. cit.*
    See note 20.
123. **Patai, R.:** *The Jewish Alchemists, Op. cit.*
124. **Tzayach, J.:** *Even ha-Shoham, Op. cit.*
    —*Sheirit Josef, Op. cit.*
125. **Kaplan, A.:** *Meditation and Kabbalah, Op. cit.*
126. *Liber Cabbalae Operativae, Op. cit.*
127. **Bischoff, E.:** *The Kabbalah, Op. cit.*
128. **Ahrens, W.:** *Hebräische Amulette mit Magischen Zahlenquadraten, Op. cit.*
129. **Agrippa, H.C.:** *De Occulta Philosophia, Op. cit.*
    —*Three Books of Occult Philosophy, Op. cit.*
130. *Ibid.*
131. *Ibid.*
132. *Ibid.*
133. **Fanger, C.:** *Conjuring Spirits, Op. cit.*
134. *Ibid.*
135. **Tzayach, J.:** *Even ha-Shoham, Op. cit.*
    —*Sheirit Josef, Op. cit.*
136. *Ibid.*
    Kaplan, A.: *Meditation and Kabbalah, Op. cit.*
137. See note 20.
138. **Agrippa, H.C.:** *De Occulta Philosophia, Op. cit.*
    —*Three Books of Occult Philosophy, Op. cit.*
139. **MacLean, A.:** *A Treatise on Angel Magic, Op. cit.*
140. **Fanger, C.:** *Conjuring Spirits, Op. cit.*
141. *Ibid.*
142. **Morgan, O.:** in *Proceedings of the Society of Antiquaries of London*, Vol. 4 – November 1856 to June 1859, The Society of Antiquaries, London 1859.
143. *Ibid.*

CHAPTER 3

1. **Trachtenberg, J.:** *Jewish Magic and Superstition, Op. cit.*
2. **Akko, I. ben Samuel:** *Me'irat Einayim*, Jerusalem 1975.
3. **Rosenberg, Y.:** *Rafael ha-Malach, Op. cit.*
4. *Ibid.*
5. **Swart, J.G.:** *The Book of Sacred Names, Op. cit.*
6. **Koppel, Y.:** *Siddur m'ha-Arizal ha-Nikra b'Shem Kol Ya'akov, Op. cit.*
7. **Asher, Y.Y. ben:** *Toldot Yitzchak*, Vol. 1, Bilgoraj 1909.
   Davis, E. & Frenkel, D.A.: *Ha-Kami'a ha-Ivri, Op. cit.*
   Shniori: *Mikra'i Refu'i Kelali im Tatzlumim v'Iyurim Rabim Ner Mitzvah b'Torah Or*, New York 2003.
8. **Daitch, C. Yom Tov L.:** *Mishnayot Masechet Mikva'ot*, Vol. 4, New York 1972.
   Paprish, M. ben Yehudah: *Or Tzadikim v'Derech Se'udah*, Defus Y. Unterhendler, Warsaw 1889.
9. **Hanauer, J.E.:** *Folk-Lore of the Holy Land, Op. cit.*
   Schrire, T.: *Hebrew Amulets, Op. cit.*
   Shachar, I.: *Jewish Tradition in Art, Op. cit.*
   Davis, E. & Frenkel, D.A.: *Ha-Kami'a ha-Ivri, Op. cit.*
   Green, A.: *Judaic Artifacts, Op. cit.*
10. **Shachar, I.:** *Jewish Tradition in Art, Op. cit.*
11. *Ibid.*
12. *Ibid.*
13. **Cardozo, A.M. & Halperin, D.J.:** *Abraham Miguel Cardozo: Selected Writings*, Paulist Press, Mahwah 2001.
14. *Ibid.*
15. *Ibid.*
16. *Ibid.*
17. *Ibid.*
18. *Ibid.*
19. *Ibid.*
20. *Ibid.*
21. *Ibid.*
22. *Ibid.*
23. *Ibid.*
24. **Hammer, R.:** *Entering the High Holy Days: A Guide to Origins, Themes, and Prayers*, Jewish Publication Society, Philadelphia 1998.

Eisenberg, R.L.: *The JPS Guide to Jewish Traditions*, The Jewish Publication Society, Philadelphia 2004.

Sperling, A.I.: *Reasons for Jewish Customs and Traditions*, transl. A. Mats, Bloch Publishing Company, New York 1968.

25. **Zacutto, M.:** *Shorshei ha-Shemot, Op. cit.*

26. *Sefer Raziel ha-Malach*, Amsterdam 1701.
     Zacutto, M.: *Ibid.*

27. **Zacutto, M.:** *Ibid.*

28. **Schrire, T.:** *Hebrew Amulets, Op. cit.*

29. **Zacutto, M.:** *Shorshei ha-Shemot, Op. cit.*

30. *Ibid.*

31. *Ibid.*

32. *Ibid.*

33. *Ibid.*

34. *Ibid.*

35. *Ibid.*

36. *Ibid.*

37. *Ibid.*

38. *Siddur T'filah: Complete Prayer Book*, Shapiro, Vallentine & Co., London 1931.

39. *Sefer Shimmush Tehillim, Op. cit.*

40. **Foreiro, F.:** *Novus Index Librorum Prohibitorum, juxta decretum Sacrae Congregationis Illustriss. S.R.E. Cardinalium à S.D.N. Urbano Papa VIII Sanctaq. Sedé Apostolica publicatum, Romae 4 Febr. 1627 auctus; primum auctoritate Pij IV. P.M. editus, deinde à Sixto Vampliatus, tertio à Clemente VIII recognitus; praefixis regulis, ac modo exéquendae prohibitionis per R.P. Franciscum Foretium Ord. Praed. à deputatione S.S. Trid. Synodi Secretarium; ante quemlibet librum noviter prohibitum praefixum est signun*, Apud Antonii Boetzeri Haeredes, Coloniae Agrippinae 1627.

41. **Raz, U.:** *Shimmush Tehilim & Sepher Yetzira*, Message #3685, http://groups.yahoo.com/group/ Kabbalahconcepts/

42. *The Sixth and Seventh Books of Moses or, Moses' Magical Spirit-art, known as the Wonderful Arts of the Old Wise Hebrews, taken from the Mosaic books of the Cabala and the Talmud, for the good of mankind. Translated from the German, word for word, according to Old Writings, with Numerous Engravings*, The Arthur Westbrook Co., 1870.

43. **Selig, G.A.:** *Secrets of the Psalms: A Fragment of the Practical Kabala, with Extracts from other Kabalistic writings, as translated by the author*, Dorene, Arlington 1929.

44.   *Sefer Shimmush Tehillim, Op. cit.*
45.   **Selig, G.A.:** *Secrets of the Psalms, Op. cit.*
46.   *Sefer Shimmush Tehillim, Op. cit.*
47.   *Ibid.*
48.   *Ibid.*
49.   *Sefer Raziel ha-Malach, Op. cit.*
      Zacutto, M.: *Shorshei ha-Shemot, Op. cit.*
      Schrire, T.: *Hebrew Amulets, Op. cit.*
50.   **Trachtenberg, J.:** *Jewish Magic and Superstition, Op. cit.*
51.   **Appel, G. & Ganzfried, S. benJ.:** *The Concise Code of Jewish Law: compiled from Kitzur Shulchan Aruch and Traditional Sources : a New Translation with Introduction and Halachic Annotations based on Contemporary Responsa*, Ktav Publishing Inc., New York 1991.
      Becher, M.: *Gateway to Judaism: The What, How and Why of Jewish Life*, Shaar Press, Brooklyn 2005.
      Isaacs, R.H.: *Bubbe Meises: Jewish Myths, Jewish Reality*, Ktav Publishing House Inc., Jersey City 2008.
52.   **Trachtenberg, J.:** *Jewish Magic and Superstition, Op. cit.*
53.   *Ibid.*
54.   *Ibid.*
55.   *Sefer Raziel ha-Malach, Op. cit.*
      Tirshom, J. ben E.: *Shoshan Yesod Olam, Op. cit.*
      Zacutto, M.: *Shorshei ha-Shemot, Op. cit.*
      Rosenberg, Y.: *Rafael ha-Malach, Op. cit.*
      Schrire, T.: *Hebrew Amulets, Op. cit.*
      Shachar, I.: *Jewish Tradition in Art, Op. cit.*
      Davis, E. & Frenkel, D.A.: *Ha-Kami'a ha-Ivri, Op. cit.*
      Green, A.: *Judaic Artifacts, Op. cit.*
56.   *Ibid.*
57.   *Ibid.*
58.   *Sefer Shimmush Tehillim, Op. cit.*
59.   *Ibid.*
60.   *Ibid.*
61.   **Shadur, J. & Shadur, Y.:** *Traditional Jewish Papercuts: An Inner World of Art and Symbol*, University Press of New England, Hanover 2002.
62.   **Cosman, Madeline P. & Jones, Linda G.:** *Handbook To Life In The Medieval World*, Vol. 2, Facts on File Inc., New York 2008.
63.   **Scholem, G.:** *Kabbalah*, Keter Publishing House, Jerusalem 1974.

Klein, M.: *Not to Worry: Jewish Wisdom & Folklore, The Jewish Publication Society,* Philadelphia 2003.

64. **Zion, N. & Spectre, B.:** *A Different Light: The Big Book of Hanukkah,* Devora Publishing, New York 2000.

65. **Idelsohn, A.Z.:** *Jewish Liturgy and Its Development,* Shocken Books, New York 1967.
   Kitov, E.: *The Book of Our Heritage: The Jewish Year and Its Days of Significance,* Feldheim Publisher, Jerusalem 1997.
   Fine, L.: *Judaism in Practice: From the Middle Ages through the Early Modern Period,* Shocken Books, Princeton University Press, Princeton 2001.
   Brettler, M.Z.: *My People's Prayer Book: Traditional Prayers, Modern Commentaries,* edited by Hofmann, L.A., Volume 9, Jewish Light Publishing, Woodstock 2005.

66. **Chamui, A.:** *Bet El,* Eliyahu ben Amozeg va-chavero, Livorno 1878.

67. **Chamui, A.:** *Avi'ah Chidot, Op. Cit.*
   —*Li-Derosh Elohim,* Eliyahu ben Amozeg va-chavero, Livorno 1879.
   —*Yimlat Nafsho,* E.M. Devich ha-Kohen, Calcutta 1884.
   —*Niflaim Ma'asecha, Op. cit.*
   —*Devek Me'ach, Op. cit.*

68. **Schrire, T.:** *Hebrew Amulets, Op. cit.*
   Patai, R.: *The Hebrew Goddess, Op. cit.*
   Azulai, Chaim Y.D.: *Sefer Avodat ha-Kodesh, Op. cit.*

69. **Swart, J.G.:** *The Book of Self Creation, Op. cit.*

70. **Schrire, T.:** *Hebrew Amulets, Op. cit.*
   Patai, R.: *The Hebrew Goddess, Op. cit.*
   Azulai, Chaim Y.D.: *Sefer Avodat ha-Kodesh, Op. cit.*

71. **Zacutto, M.:** *Shorshei ha-Shemot, Op. cit.*
   Schrire, T.: *Ibid.*
   Davis, E. & Frenkel, D.A.: *Ha-Kami'a ha-Ivri, Op. cit.*
   Green, A.: *Judaic Artifacts, Op. cit.*

72. **Zacutto, M.:** *Shorshei ha-Shemot, Op. cit.*
   Swart, J.G.: *The Book of Sacred Names, Op. cit.*

73. **Davis, E. & Frenkel, D.A.:** *Ha-Kami'a ha-Ivri, Op. cit.*
   Green, A.: *Judaic Artifacts, Op. cit.*

74. **Zacutto, M.:** *Shorshei ha-Shemot, Op. cit.*

75. **Green, A.:** *Judaic Artifacts, Op. cit.*
   Shachar, I.: *Jewish Tradition in Art, Op. cit.*

76. **Davis, E. & Frenkel, D.A.:** *Ha-Kami'a ha-Ivri, Op. cit.*
   Green, A.: *Ibid.*
   Shachar, I.: *Ibid.*

77. **Schechter, S.:** *Studies in Judaism*, Vol. 2, Books for Libraries Press, Freeport 1972.
78. **Swart, J.G.:** *The Book of Sacred Names, Op. cit.*
79. **Schrire, T.:** *Hebrew Amulets, Op. cit.*
     Shachar, I.: *Jewish Tradition in Art, Op. cit.*
     Davis, E. & Frenkel, D.A.: *Ha-Kami'a ha-Ivri, Op. cit.*
     Green, A.: *Judaic Artifacts, Op. cit.*
80. **Zacutto, M.:** *Shorshei ha-Shemot, Op. cit.*
     Rosenberg, Y.: *Rafael ha-Malach, Op. cit.*
     Davis, E. & Frenkel, D.A.: *Ibid.*
     Green, A.: *Ibid.*
81. **Davis, E. & Frenkel, D.A.:** *Ibid.*
     Green, A.: *Ibid.*
82. **Zacutto, M.:** *Shorshei ha-Shemot, Op. cit.*
     Schrire, T.: *Hebrew Amulets, Op. cit.*
     Green, A.: *Ibid.*
83. **Vukosavović, F.:** *Angels and Demons: Jewish Magic through the Ages*, Bible Lands Museum Jerusalem, Jerusalem 2010.
84. **Ba'al Shem, E.; Ba'al-Shem, J. & Hillel, M.:** *Sefer Toldot Adam, Op. cit.*
85. **Ochanah, R. ben C.:** *Sefer Mareh ha-Yeladim*, Yerid ha-Sefarim, Jerusalem 1990.
     Patai, R.: *The Hebrew Goddess, Op. cit.*
86. **Zacutto, M.:** *Shorshei ha-Shemot, Op. cit.*
87. *Ibid.*
     Heschel, A.Y.: *Shemirot uSegulot Niflot*, Warsaw 1913.
     Palagi, C.: *Refuah v'Chayim, Op. cit.*
88. **Zacutto, M.:** *Ibid.*
     Avraham, R. ben: *Sefer ha-Segulot, Op. cit.*
     Sifrin, Y.Y.Y.: *Sha'ar Sefer Adam Yashar*, Lemberg.
     Lifshitz, S.: *Segulot Yisrael, Op. cit.*
     Mi-Yerushalayim, R. ben A.: *Sefer Segulot*, Kahn & Fried, Munkatch 1906.
     Ochanah, R. ben C.: *Sefer Mareh ha-Yeladim, Op. cit.*
89. *MS Heb. A 19*, Wellcome Library, London.
90. **Zacutto, M.:** *Shorshei ha-Shemot, Op. cit.*
     Rosenberg, Y.: *Rafael ha-Malach, Op. cit.*
     Heschel, A.Y.: *Shemirot uSegulot Niflot, Op. cit.*
     Palagi, C.: *Refuah v'Chayim, Op. cit.*
     Schrire, T.: *Hebrew Amulets, Op. cit.*
     Shachar, I.: *Jewish Tradition in Art, Op. cit.*
     Davis, E. & Frenkel, D.A.: *Ha-Kami'a ha-Ivri, Op. cit.*
     Green, A.: *Judaic Artifacts, Op. cit.*

91.   Wellcome Library, London.
92.   *MS Heb. A 19, Op. cit.*
93.   **Rosenberg, Y.:** *Rafael ha-Malach, Op. cit.*
94.   *Ibid.*
95.   *Ibid.*
96.   *Ibid.*
97.   **Wasserfall, R.R.:** *Women and Water: Menstruation in Jewish Life and Law*, Bandeis University Press, Hanover 1999.
        Philip, T.S.: *Menstruation and Childbirth in the Bible: Fertility and Impurity*, Peter Lang Publishing Inc., New York 2006.
98.   **Rosenberg, Y.:** *Rafael ha-Malach, Op. cit.*
99.   *Ibid.*
        Vital, Chaim: *Shaar ha-Yichudim*, Koretz 1783.
100.   **Zacutto, M.:** *Shorshei ha-Shemot, Op. cit.*
101.   *Ibid.*
        Davis, E. & Frenkel, D.A.: *Ha-Kami'a ha-Ivri, Op. cit.*
        Green, A.: *Judaic Artifacts, Op. cit.*
102.   **Zacutto, M.:** *Ibid.*
103.   *Ibid.*
104.   *Ibid.*
        Davis, E. & Frenkel, D.A.: *Ibid.*
        Green, A.: *Judaic Artifacts, Op. cit.*
105.   **Zacutto, M.:** *Ibid.*
        Vital, Chaim; Ha Cohen, S.; Heilprin, M.M. & Musayuv, S.: *Zeh Sefer Shaar ha-Kavanot*, Jerusalem 1902.
106.   **Zacutto, M.:** *Ibid.*
107.   *Ibid.*
108.   *Ibid.*
109.   *Ibid.*
110.   *Ibid.*
        Rosenberg, Y.: *Rafael ha-Malach, Op. cit.*
        Davis, E. & Frenkel, D.A.: *Ha-Kami'a ha-Ivri, Op. cit.*
        Green, A.: *Ibid.*
111.   **Rosenberg, Y.:** *Ibid.*
112.   **Zacutto, M.:** *Shorshei ha-Shemot, Op. cit.*
113.   *Ibid.*
114.   **Rosenberg, Y.:** *Rafael ha-Malach, Op. cit.*
115.   **Davis, E. & Frenkel, D.A.:** *Ha-Kami'a ha-Ivri, Op. cit.*
        Green, A.: *Judaic Artifacts, Op. cit.*
116.   **Schrire, T.:** *Hebrew Amulets, Op. cit.*
        Green, A.: *Ibid.*
117.   **Rosenberg, Y.:** *Rafael ha-Malach, Op. cit.*
118.   **Vital, Chaim:** *Shaar ha-Yichudim, Op. cit.*

119. **Chouraqui, A.N.**: *Between East and West, Op. cit.*
120. *Ibid.*
121. *Ibid.*
122. *Ibid.*
123. **Hanauer, J.E.**: *Folk-Lore of the Holy Land, Op. cit.*
124. **Gerchikov, Y.H. bar S.S.**: *Divrei ha-Rabanim*, 1905.
125. **Vital, Chaim**: *Shaar ha-Yichudim, Op. cit.*
126. **Swart, J.G.**: *The Book of Sacred Names, Op. cit.*
127. **Zacutto, M.**: *Shorshei ha-Shemot, Op. cit.*
128. *Ibid.*
129. **Davis, E. & Frenkel, D.A.**: *Ha-Kami'a ha-Ivri, Op. cit.*
     Green, A.: *Judaic Artifacts, Op. cit.*
130. **Green, A.**: *Ibid.*
131. **Davis, E. & Frenkel, D.A.**: *Ha-Kami'a ha-Ivri, Op. cit.*
     Green, A.: *Ibid.*
132. **Zacutto, M.**: *Shorshei ha-Shemot, Op. cit.*
133. **Swart, J.G.**: *The Book of Sacred Names, Op. cit.*
134. **Davis, E. & Frenkel, D.A.**: *Ha-Kami'a ha-Ivri, Op. cit.*
     Green, A.: *Judaic Artifacts, Op. cit.*
135. *Sefer Shimmush Tehillim, Op. cit.*
     Zacutto, M.: *Ibid.*
     Schrire, T.: *Hebrew Amulets, Op. cit.*
     Shachar, I.: *Jewish Tradition in Art, Op. cit.*
     Davis, E. & Frenkel, D.A.: *Ha-Kami'a ha-Ivri, Op. cit.*
     Green, A.: *Judaic Artifacts, Op. cit.*
     Peursen, W.T. van & Dyk, J.W.: *Tradition and Innovation in Biblical Interpretation, Op. cit.*
136. **Zacutto, M.**: *Ibid.*
137. *Sefer Shimmush Tehillim, Op. cit.*
138. **Schrire, T.**: *Hebrew Amulets, Op. cit.*
     Klein, M.: *A Time to Be Born: Customs and Folklore of Jewish Birth*, The Jewish Publication Society, Philadelphia 1998.
139. **Schrire, T.**: *Ibid.*
140. **Green, A.**: *Judaic Artifacts, Op. cit.*
141. *Sefer Shimmush Tehillim, Op. cit.*

CHAPTER 4

1. **Postel, W.:** *De Originibus seu de Hebraicae Linguae & Gentis Antiquitate, deque variarum linguarum affinitate liber*, Apud Dionysium Lescuier, Paris 1538.

2. **Gaffarel, J.:** *Curiositez Inouyes hoc est Curiositates Inauditae de Figuris Persarum Talismannicis, Horoscopo Patriarcharum et Characteribus Coelestibus*, Gothofredum Schultzen: Hamburg; Janssonio Waesbergios: Amsterdam 1676.

3. **Agrippa, H.C.:** *De Occulta Philosophia, Op. cit.*

4. *Ibid.*

5. **Gaffarel, J.:** *Curiositez Inouyes hoc est Curiositates Inauditae de Figuris Persarum Talismannicis, Horoscopo Patriarcharum et Characteribus Coelestibus, Op. cit.*

6. **Barrett, F.:** *The Magus or Celestial Intelligencer, Op. cit.*

7. **Müller, A.:** *Alphabeta ac Notae Diversarum Linguarum pene Septuaginta tum & Versiones Orationis Dominicae prope centum collecta olim & illustrata ab Andrea Mullero*, Johann Lieberman, Berlin 1703.

8. *Chochmat Shlomo ha-Melech*, Ms. Heb. 28°1875, National Library of Israel, Jerusalem.

9. **Zacutto, M.:** *Shorshei ha-Shemot, Op. cit.*

10. *Ibid.*

11. *Ibid.*

12. *Ibid.*

13. *Ibid.*

14. **Tirshom, J. ben E.:** *Shoshan Yesod Olam, Op. cit.*
    Zacutto, M.: *Ibid.*

15. **Bartolocci, G.:** *Bibliotheca Magna Rabbinica, Op. cit.*
    Gettings, F.: *Dictionary of Occult, Hermetic and Alchemical Sigils*, Routledge & Kegan Paul Ltd., London 1981.
    Pennick, N.: *Magical Alphabets, Op. cit.*

16. **Bohak, G.:** *The Charaktêres in Ancient and Medieval Jewish Magic* in *Acta Classica Universitatis Scientiarum Debreceniensis*, Vol. 47, Univ Debreceniensis, Debrecen 2011.

17. **Tirshom, J. ben E.:** *Shoshan Yesod Olam, Op. cit.*
    Zacutto, M.: *Shorshei ha-Shemot, Op. cit.*

18. **Zacutto, M.:** *Ibid.*

19. **Bartolocci, G.:** *Bibliotheca Magna Rabbinica, Op. cit.*
20. **Tirshom, J. ben E.:** *Shoshan Yesod Olam, Op. cit.*
    Zacutto, M.: *Shorshei ha-Shemot, Op. cit.*
21. **Tirshom, J. ben E.:** *Ibid.*
22. **Zacutto, M.:** *Shorshei ha-Shemot, Op. cit.*
23. **Tirshom, J. ben E.:** *Shoshan Yesod Olam, Op. cit.*
24. *Ibid.*
    Davis, E. & Frenkel, D.A.: *Ha-Kami'a ha-Ivri, Op. cit.*
25. *Ibid.*
26. **Bartolocci, G.:** *Bibliotheca Magna Rabbinica, Op. cit.*
27. **Tirshom, J. ben E.:** *Shoshan Yesod Olam, Op. cit.*
28. **Zacutto, M.:** *Shorshei ha-Shemot, Op. cit.*
29. **Tirshom, J. ben E.:** *Shoshan Yesod Olam, Op. cit.*
30. *Ibid.*
31. Anonymous Manuscript.
32. **Tirshom, J. ben E.:** *Shoshan Yesod Olam, Op. cit.*
33. **Zacutto, M.:** *Shorshei ha-Shemot, Op. cit.*
34. *Ibid.*
    Tirshom, J. ben E.: *Shoshan Yesod Olam, Op. cit.*
    Davis, E. & Frenkel, D.A.: *Ha-Kami'a ha-Ivri, Op. cit.*
35. **Tirshom, J. ben E.:** *Shoshan Yesod Olam, Op. cit.*
36. **Zacutto, M.:** *Shorshei ha-Shemot, Op. cit.*
37. *Ibid.*
38. **Balmes, A. Ben M. de:** *Mekanah Avraham*, Venice 1523.
    Schickard, W.: *Bechinath Happeruschim, hoc est Examinis Commentationum Rabbinicarum in Mosen prodromus vel sectio prima, complectens generalem protheriam, de 1. Textu Hebraico, 2. Targum Chaldaico, 3. Versione Graeca, 4. Masóreth, 5. Kábbalah, 6. Peruschim, cum indicibus locorum scripturae, rerumq; memorabilium*, Johan-Alexandri Cellii, Tübingen 1624.
39. **Bartolocci, G.:** *Bibliotheca Magna Rabbinica, Op. cit.*
40. **Agrippa, H.C.:** *De Occulta Philosophia, Op. cit.*
    Barrett, F.: *The Magus or Celestial Intelligencer, Op. cit.*
41. **Müller, A.:** *Alphabeta ac Notae Diversarum Linguarum, Op. cit.*
42. *Ibid.*
43. Anonymous Manuscript.
44. **Agrippa, H.C.:** *De Occulta Philosophia, Op. cit.*
45. **Bartolocci, G.:** *Bibliotheca Magna Rabbinica, Op. cit.*
    Müller, A.: *Alphabeta ac Notae Diversarum Linguarum, Op. cit.*

46. **Barrett, F.:** *The Magus or Celestial Intelligencer*, *Op. cit.*
47. Contemporary True Type Font.
48. **Agrippa, H.C.:** *De Occulta Philosophia*, *Op. cit.*
49. **Bing, G.:** *"Picatrix" das Ziel des Weisen von Pseudo-Magriti*, *Op. cit.*
    Atallah, H.: *Picatrix (Ghayat al-Hakim): The Goal of the Wise*, *Op. cit.*
    Greer, J.M. & Warnock, C.: *The Picatrix*, *Op. cit.*
50. **Tirshom, J. ben E.:** *Shoshan Yesod Olam*, *Op. cit.*
51. **Walker, D.P.:** *Spiritual and Demonic Magic: From Ficino to Campanella*, The Warburg Institute, University of London, London 1958.
    Yates, F.A.: *Giordano Bruno and the Hermetic Tradition*, Routledge & Kegan Paul, Henley-on-Thames 1964.
    Idel, M.: *Kabbalah in Italy 1280-1510: A Survey*, Yale University Press, New Haven 2011.
52. **Scholem, G.:** *Kabbalah*, *Op. cit.*
    Cooperman, B.D.: *Jewish Thought in the Sixteenth Century*, Harvard University Center for Jewish Studies, Harvard University Press, Cambridge 1983.
    Idel, M.: *Ibid.*
    —*Hasidism: Between Ecstasy and Magic*, *Op. cit.*
    —*Enchanted Chains: Techniques and Rituals in Jewish Mysticism*, Cherub Press, Los Angeles 2005.
53. **Schwartz, D.:** *Central Problems of Medieval Jewish Philosophy*, Koninklijke Brill NV, Leiden 2005.
54. **Zacutto, M.:** *Shorshei ha-Shemot*, *Op. cit.*
55. *Ibid.*
56. **Weinstock, I.:** *Temirin: Mekorot u-mech'karim b'Kabbalah v'Chasidut*, Mosad ha-Rav Kook, Jerusalem 1972.
57. **Scholem, G. & Werblowsky, R.J.Z.:** *Origins of the Kabbalah*, Jewish Publication Society [Princeton University Press], Princeton 1990.
58. *Ibid.*
59. **Weinstock, I.:** *Temirin*, *Op. cit.*
60. *Ibid.*
61. *Pirke Avot: Sayings of the Fathers*, Behrman House Inc., Springfield 1945.
62. **Swart, J.G.:** *The Book of Sacred Names*, *Op. cit.*
63. **Trachtenberg, J.:** *Jewish Magic and Superstition*, *Op. cit.*
64. **Swart, J.G.:** *The Book of Self Creation*, *Op. cit.*
65. *Ibid.*

66. **Fleg, E.:** *The Life of Moses*, E.P. Dutton & Co., New York 1928.
67. **Swart, J.G.:** *The Book of Self Creation, Op. cit.*
68. *Ibid.*
69. *Ibid.*
70. **Levi, E.:** *The History of Magic: including a clear and precise Exposition of its Procedure, its Rites and its Mysteries*, transl. by A.E. Waite, Rider & Co., London 1913.
    Baine Harris, R.: *Neoplatonism and Contemporary Thought: Part 2*, State University of New York Press, Albany 2002.
71. **Hubbard, E. & Hubbard, B.:** *The Note Book of Elbert Hubbard*, W.H. Wise & Co., New York 1927.
72. **Mordell, P:** *Sefer Yetsirah*, P. Mordell, Philadelphia, 1914.
    Stenring, K.: *The Book of Formation*, KTAV, New York 1968.
    Kalisch, I.: *The Sepher Yetzirah: A Book of Creation*, L.H. Frank & Co., New York (Reprinted by the AMORC, San Jose, California, 1974.)
    Westcott, W.W.: *Sepher Yetzirah*, Occult Research Press, New York, 1887. Reprinted by Samuel Weiser, New York 1975.
    Suares, C.: *The Sepher Yetzirah: Including the Original Astrology according to the Qabala and its Zodiac,"* Shambhala Publications Inc., Boulder 1976.
    Friedman, I.: *The Book of Creation: Sefer Yetzirah*, Samuel Weiser Inc., New York 1977.
    Blumenthal, D.R.: *Understanding Jewish Mysticism: A Source Reader*, Volume I, KTAV Publishing House Inc., New York 1978.
    Kaplan, A.: *Sefer Yetzirah: The Book of Creation In Theory and Practice*, Samuel Weiser Inc., York Beach 1990 (Revised edition with index 1997).
    Hyman, A.P.: *Sefer Yesira*, Mohr Siebeck, Tübingen 2004.
73. **Vital, Chaim:** *Sha'ar ha-Gilgulim*, edited Yehudah Ashlag, Eshel, Tel Aviv 1961.
74. **Kaplan, A.:** *The Aryeh Kaplan Anthology I: Illuminating Expositions on Jewish thought and Practice by a Revered Teacher*, National Conference of Synagogue Youth/Union of Orthodox Jewish Congregations of America, New York 1991.
75. **Zacutto, M.:** *Shorshei ha-Shemot, Op. cit.*
    Swart, J.G.: *The Book of Sacred Names, Op. cit.*
76. **Swart, J.G.:** *Ibid.*
77. *Ibid.*
78. **Swart, J.G.:** *The Book of Self Creation, Op. cit.*
79. **Levi Yitzhak of Berdichev** in **Buber, M.:** *Tales of the Hasidim:*

457

The Early Masters, Thames and Hudson, London 1956.

80. **Besserman, P.:** *The Shambhala Guide to Kabbalah and Jewish Mysticism, Op. cit.*
81. **Weinstock, I.:** *Temirin, Op. cit.*
82. *Ibid.*
83. *Ibid.*
    Jacob ben Moses Kohen of Yonova: *Minchot Ya'akov Solet,* Willhelmsdorf 1731, transl. in **Etkes, I.:** *The Besht: Magician, Mystic and Leader, Op. cit.*
84. **Tirshom, J. ben E.:** *Shoshan Yesod Olam, Op. cit.*
    Zacutto, M.: *Shorshei ha-Shemot, Op. cit.*
    Keter, S.: *Nechash ha-Nechoshet, Op. cit.*
    Ba'al Shem, E.; Ba'al-Shem, J.; ha-Kohen, N. ben I.; & Katz, N.: *Mifalot Elokim, Op. cit.*
    Ba'al Shem, E.; Ba'al-Shem, J. & Hillel, M.: *Sefer Toldot Adam, Op. cit.*
    Reuven ben Avraham: *Sefer ha-Segulot, Op. cit.*
    Lifshitz, S.: *Sefer Segulot Yisrael, Op. cit.*
    Tzubeiri, Y.: *Emet v'Emunah, Op. cit.*
    Mizrachi, E.A.: *Refuah v'Chayim m'Yerushalayim, Op. cit.*
    Schrire, T.: *Hebrew Amulets, Op. cit.*
    Shachar, I.: *Jewish Tradition in Art, Op. cit.*
    Sepher ha-Razim: The Book of the Mysteries, Op. cit.
    Naveh, J. & Shaked, S.: *Amulets and Magic Bowls, Op. cit.*
    —*Magic Spells and Formulae, Op. cit.*
    Shiffman, L.H. & Swartz, M.D.: *Hebrew and Aramaic Incantation Texts from the Cairo Genizah,* Sheffield Academic Press, Sheffield 1992.
    Davis, E. & Frenkel, D.A.: *Ha-Kami'a ha-Ivri, Op. cit.*
85. *Sefer Raziel ha-Malach, Op. cit.*
86. *Ibid.*
    Trachtenberg, J.: *Jewish Magic and Superstition, Op. cit.*
87. **Zacutto, M.:** *Shorshei ha-Shemot, Op. cit.*
88. *Ibid.*
89. *Ibid.*
90. *Ibid.*
91. *Ibid.*
92. *Sefer Raziel ha-Malach, Op. cit.*
    Zacutto, M.: *Ibid.*
    Davis, E. & Frenkel, D.A.: *Ha-Kami'a ha-Ivri, Op. cit.*
93. **Zacutto, M.:** *Ibid.*

94. **Bar Meir, M.:** *Sefer Segulot*, Ms. hebr. oct. 131, Universitätsbibliothek JCS, Frankfurt am Main.
95. *Ibid.*
96. **Zacutto, M.:** *Shorshei ha-Shemot, Op. cit.*
97. *Ibid.*
98. *Ibid.*
99. *Ibid.*
100. *Ibid.*
101. *Ibid.*

CHAPTER 5

1. **Rappoport, A.S.:** *The Folklore of the Jews*, The Soncino Press, London 1937.
2. **Swart, J.G.:** *The Book of Self Creation, Op. cit.*
3. **Tillich, P.:** *The Eternal Now*, Charles Scribner's Sons, New York 1963.
4. *Yalkut Chadash* quoted in **Cassels, W.R.:** *Supernatural Religion: An Inquiry into the Reality of Divine Revelation* Vol. 1, Longmans Green & Co., London 1874.
5. **Cassels, W.R.:** *Supernatural Religion, Ibid.*
6. *The Zohar*, transl. D.C. Matt (Pritzker edition), Vol. 1 to 5, Stanford University Press, Stanford 2003–2009.
   Zacutto, M.: *Shorshei ha-Shemot, Op. cit.*
   Charles, R.H.: *The Book of Enoch*, (Ethiopic Enoch/Enoch 1), The Clarendon Press, Oxford 1912.
   Odeberg, H.: *3 Enoch or The Hebrew Book of Enoch*, Cambridge University Press, London 1929.
   Sepher ha-Razim: The Book of the Mysteries, Op. cit.
   Avraham Rimon of Granada: *Brit Menuchah, Op. cit.*
   Cordovero, M.: *Pardes Rimmonim, Op. cit.*
   Bacharach, N.: *Emek ha-Melech, Op. cit.*
   Ginzburg, L.: *The Legends of the Jews*, Philadelphia: Jewish Publication Society, Philadelphia, 1913.
   Margaliot, R.: *Malachei Elyon: ha-Muzkarim b'Talmud Bavli v'Yerushalmi b'chol ha-Midrashim Zohar v'Tikunim Targumim v'Yalkutim im Tziyunim l'Sifre Kodesh shel ha-Kabbalah*, Mosad ha-Rav Kook, Jerusalem 1945.
   Davidson, G.: *A Dictionary of Angels: Including the Fallen Angels*, The Free Press, New York 1971.
7. **Maimonides, M. & Rosner, F.:** *Moses Maimonides' Treatise On Resurrection*, Ktav Publishing House Inc., New York 1982.
8. **Nachman, M. ben; Blinder, Y.; & Kamenetsky, Y:** *Torah with Ramban's Commentary translated, annotated and elucidated: Devarim/Deuteronomy*, Mesorah Publications, New York 2008.
9. **Gutmann, J.:** *Hebrew Manuscript Painting*, George Braziller, Inc., New York 1978.
   Shachar, I.: *Jewish Tradition in Art, Op. cit.*
   Arba Hagadot – 4 Haggadot: me-osef bet ha-sefarim ha-le'umi veha-universitai bi-yerushalayim, V. Turnowsky, Tel Aviv 1989.

10.	**Swart, J.G.:** *The Book of Sacred Names, Op. cit.*
11.	**Zacutto, M.:** *Shorshei ha-Shemot, Op. cit.*
12.	**Mathers, S.L. Macgregor:** *Key of Solomon the King, Op. cit.*
	Gollancz, H.: *Sepher Maphteah Shelomo, Op. cit.*
13.	**Zacutto, M.:** *Shorshei ha-Shemot, Op. cit.*
14.	**Swart, J.G.:** *The Book of Sacred Names, Op. cit.*
15.	*Sefer Raziel ha-Malach, Op. cit.*
16.	**Zacutto, M.:** *Shorshei ha-Shemot, Op. cit.*
17.	*Sefer Raziel ha-Malach, Op. cit.*
18.	**Zacutto, M.:** *Shorshei ha-Shemot, Op. cit.*
19.	*Ibid.*
20.	*Ibid.*
21.	*Ibid.*
22.	**Pietersma, A. & Wright, B.G.:** *A New English Translation of the Septuagint and the Other Greek Translations Traditionally Included under That Title*, Oxford University Press, Oxford and New York 2007.
23.	**Schrire, T.:** *Hebrew Amulets, Op. cit.*
24.	**Odeberg, H.:** *3 Enoch or The Hebrew Book of Enoch, Op. cit.*
25.	*Ibid.*
26.	**Charles, R.H.:** *The Book of Enoch, Op. cit.*
27.	*Ibid.*
28.	*Ibid.*
29.	**Zacutto, M.:** *Shorshei ha-Shemot, Op. cit.*
	Avraham Rimon of Granada: *Brit Menuchah, Op. cit.*
30.	**Charles, R.H.:** *The Book of Enoch, Op. cit.*
31.	**Zacutto, M.:** *Shorshei ha-Shemot, Op. cit.*
32.	*Ibid.*
33.	*Ibid.*
	Swart, J.G.: *The Book of Sacred Names, Op. cit.*
34.	*Ibid.*
35.	*Ibid.*
36.	**Zacutto, M.:** *Ibid.*
37.	**Thompson, R.C.:** *Semitic Magic, Op. cit.*
38.	*Ibid.*
	Rappoport, A.S.: *The Folklore of the Jews, Op. cit.*
	Proceedings of the Society of Biblical Archaeology, Vol. 9 November 1886 to June 1887, The Offices of the Society, Bloomsbury 1887.
39.	**Cassels, W.R.:** *Supernatural Religion, Op. cit.*
40.	**Patai, R.:** *The Hebrew Goddess, Op. cit.*
41.	**Hanauer, J.E.:** *Folk-Lore of the Holy Land, Op. cit.*
42.	**Patai, R.:** *The Hebrew Goddess, Op. cit.*

43. **Boulay, R.A.:** *Flying Serpents and Dragons: The Story of Mankind's Reptillian Past*, The Book Tree, Escondido 1999.

44. **Neusner, J.:** *A History of the Jews in Babylonia: Later Sasanian Times*, E.J. Brill, Leiden 1970.
    Klein, M.: *A Time to Be Born, Op. cit.*
    Isaacs, R.H.: *Ascending Jacob's Ladder: Jewish Views of Angels, Demons, and Evil Spirits*, Jason Aronson, Northvale 1998.
    Hurwitz, S.: *Lilith-The First Eve: Historical and Psychological Aspects of the Dark Feminine*, Daimon Verlag, Einsiedeln 1999.
    Schwartz, H., Loebel-Fried, Ginsburg, E.K.: *Tree of Souls: The Mythology of Judaism*, Oxford University Press Inc., New York 2004.
    Silverman, E.K.: *From Abraham to America: A History of Jewish Circumcision*, Rowman & Littlefield Publishers Inc., Lanham 2006.

45. *Encyclopedia Judaica*, Vol. 11, The Macmillan Company, New York 1970.

46. **Thompson, R.C.:** *Semitic Magic, Op. cit.*
    Montgomery, J.A.: *Aramaic Incantation Texts from Nippur, Op. cit.*
    Hurwitz, S.: *Lilith-The First Eve, Op. cit.*
    Khanam, R.: *Demonology: Socio-religious Belief of Witchcraft*, Global Vision Publishing House, Delhi 2003.
    Scurlock, J. & Andersen, B.R.: *Diagnoses in Assyrian and Babylonian Medicine*, University of Illinois Press, Urbana 2005.

47. **Hurwitz, S.:** *Ibid.*
    Koltuv, B.B.: *The Book of Lilith*, Nicolas-Hays, York Beach 1986.
    Patai, R.: *The Hebrew Goddess, Op. cit.*
    Isaacs, R.H.: *Ascending Jacob's Ladder, Op. cit.*
    Schwartz, H., Loebel-Fried, Ginsburg, E.K.: *Tree of Souls, Op. cit.*
    Dennis, G.W.: *The Encyclopedia of Jewish Myth, Magic and Mysticism*, Llewellyn Publications, Woodbury 2007.

48. **Nitzan, B.:** *Qumran Prayer and Religious Poetry* Vol. 12, E.J. Brill, Leiden 1994.
    Porter, S.E. & Evans, C.A.: *The Scrolls and the Scriptures: Qumran Fifty Years After*, Sheffield Academic Press, Sheffield 1997.
    Elledge, C.D.: *The Bible And the Dead Sea Scrolls*, Koninklijke Brill NV, Leiden 2005.

49.   **Conybeare, F.C.:** *The Testament of Solomon* in **Abrahams, I.:** *The Jewish Quarterly Review*, Vol. 11, October 1898.
        Duling, D.C.: *Testament of Solomon* in **Charlesworth, J.H.:** *The Old Testament Pseudepigrapha*, Vol. 1, Doubleday, New York 1983.
        Whittaker, M.: *The Testament of Solomon* in **Sparks, H.F.D.:** *The Apocryphal Old Testament*, Clarendon Press, Oxford 1984.
50.   **Eisenstein, J.D.:** *Alpha Beta Ben Sira* in *Otsar Midrashim*, Vol. 1, J.D. Eisenstein, New York 1915.
        Sirach; Haberman, A.M. & Hacker, J.: *The Alphabet of Ben Sira*: Facsimile of the Constantinople 1519 Edition, Valmadonna Trust Library, London 1997.
51.   **Rappoport, A.S.:** *The Folklore of the Jews, Op. cit.*
52.   **Montgomery, J.A.:** *Aramaic Incantation Texts from Nippur, Op. cit.*
        Blau, L.: *Das Altjüdische Zauberwesen, Op. cit.*
53.   **Dennis, G.W.:** *The Encyclopedia of Jewish Myth, Magic and Mysticism, Op. cit.*
54.   **Schwartz, H., Loebel-Fried, Ginsburg, E.K.:** *Tree of Souls, Op. cit.*
55.   **Witton Davies, T.:** *"Magic" Back and White, Charms and Counter Charms, Divination and Demonology among the Hindus, Hebrews, Arabs and Egyptians*, de Laurence, Scott & Co., Chicago 1910.
56.   *Ibid.*
57.   *Ibid.*
58.   *Ibid.*
59.   *Ibid.*
60.   **Montgomery, J.A.:** *Aramaic Incantation Texts from Nippur, Op. cit.*
61.   **Witton Davies, T.:** *"Magic" Back and White, Op. cit.*
62.   **Thompson, R.C.:** *Semitic Magic, Op. cit.*
        Rappoport, A.S.: *Myth and Legend of Ancient Israel*, Vol. 1, The Gresham Publishing Company Ltd., London 1927.
63.   **Thompson, R.C.:** *Ibid.*
64.   **Tziyoni, M. ben M.:** *Tzefunei Tziyoni*, Shalom ha-Kohen Weiss, Brooklyn 1985.
        Huss, B.: *Demonology and Magic, Kabbalah: Journal for the Study of Jewish Mystical Texts 10*, 2004.
65.   **Tziyoni, M. ben M.:** unpublished passage in *Sefer Tziyoni* translated in **Huss, B.:** *Ibid.*
66.   **Swart, J.G.:** *The Book of Self Creation, Op. cit.*
67.   *Sefer Raziel ha-Malach, Op. cit.*
68.   **Skemer, D.C.:** *Binding Words, Op. cit.*

69.   **Recanati, M.:** quoted in **Chill, A.:** *The Mitzvot: The Commandments and their Rationale*, Bloch Publishing Co., New York 1974.

70.   **Trachtenberg, J.:** *Jewish Magic and Superstition, Op. cit.*

71.   *Ibid.*

72.   *Ibid.*

73.   *Ibid.*

74.   *Ibid.*

75.   *Ibid.*

76.   **Zacutto, M.:** *Shorshei ha-Shemot, Op. cit.*

77.   *Ibid.*

78.   **Swart, J.G.:** *The Book of Sacred Names, Op. cit.*

79.   **Zacutto, M.:** *Shorshei ha-Shemot, Op. cit.*

80.   *Ibid.*

81.   *Ibid.*

82.   *Ibid.*

83.   *Ibid.*

84.   *Ibid.*

85.   *Ibid.*
       Bischoff, E.: *The Kabbalah, Op. cit.*
       WallisBudge, E.A.: *Amulets and Talismans, Op. cit.*

86.   **Zacutto, M.:** *Ibid.*

87.   *Ibid.*

88.   **Yisrael, M. ben:** *Nishmat Chayim*, Amsterdam 1652.
       Emden, Y.: *Torat ha-Kenaot, Op. cit.*
       Maaseh Nora, Thorn 1865.
       Chazan, B.M.: *Maaseh Nora shel ha-Ruach*, Jerusalem 1904.
       Deitchman, C.A.: *Emunat Tzadikim*, Warsaw 1900.
       Petayah, Y.: *Minchat Yehudah*, Baghdad 1933.
       Chajes, J.H.: *Between worlds: Dybbuks, Exorcists, and Early Modern Judaism*, University of Pennsylvania Press, Philadelphia 2003.
       Nigal, G.: *Magic, Mysticism, and Hasidism, Op. cit.*

89.   **Zacutto, M.:** *Shorshei ha-Shemot, Op. cit.*

90.   **Swart, J.G.:** *The Book of Self Creation, Op. cit.*

91.   *Ibid.*

92.   *Sefer Shimmush Tehillim, Op. cit.*

93.   **Zacutto, M.:** *Shorshei ha-Shemot, Op. cit.*

94.   **Ba'al Shem, E.; Ba'al-Shem, J. & Hillel, M.:** *Sefer Toldot Adam, Op. cit.*

95.   *Ibid.*

96.   **Swart, J.G.:** *The Book of Sacred Names, Op. cit.*

97.   *Ibid.*

98.   *Ibid.*
       Zacutto, M.: *Shorshei ha-Shemot, Op. cit.*

99.   **Zacutto, M.:** *Ibid.*

100.   *Ibid.*

101.   **Mizrachi, E.A.:** *Refuah v'Chayim m'Yerushalayim, Op. cit.*

102.   **Zacutto, M.:** *Shorshei ha-Shemot, Op. cit.*

103.   **Ba'al Shem, E.; Ba'al-Shem, J. & Hillel, M.:** *Sefer Toldot Adam, Op. cit.*

104.   **Zacutto, M.:** *Shorshei ha-Shemot, Op. cit.*

105.   **Avraham Rimon of Granada:** *Brit Menuchah, Op. cit.*
Tikunei ha-Zohar, Jerusalem 1909.
Tikunei Zohar im m'forshim, Jerusalem.
Landau, R.: *Tikunei ha-Zohar*, Lublin 1927.
Vital, Chaim: *Sefer Sha'ar Ru'ach ha-Kodesh, Op. cit.*
Ba'al Shem, E.; Ba'al-Shem, J. & Hillel, M.: *Sefer Toldot Adam, Op. cit.*
Ba'al Shem, E.; Ba'al-Shem, J.; ha-Kohen, N. ben I.; & Katz, N.: *Mifalot Elokim, Op. cit.*
Rosenberg, Y.: *Rafael ha-Malach, Op. cit.*
Mizrachi, E.A.: *Refuah v'Chayim m'Yerushalayim, Op. cit.*
Roth, A.: *Ahavat ha-Bore*, Jerusalem 1959.
Ades, Y.: *Divrei Yaakov: b'Kitvei ha-Ari*, Yarid Ha-Sefarim, Jerusalem 2010.
—*Divrei Yaakov: b'Shemot ha-Kodesh*, Yarid Ha-Sefarim, Jerusalem 2010.
—*Divrei Yaakov: Kabalat ha-Gra*, Vol. 1& 2, Yarid Ha-Sefarim, Jerusalem 2010.
—*Divrei Yaakov: b'Shaar ha-Kavvanot*, Part 2, Yarid Ha-Sefarim, Jerusalem 2010.
—*Divrei Yaakov: Ketuvot Kidushin*, Yarid Ha-Sefarim, Jerusalem 2010.

106.   **Zacutto, M.:** *Shorshei ha-Shemot, Op. cit.*

107.   **Ades, Y.:** *Divrei Yaakov: Kabalat ha-Gra*, Vol. 2, *Op. cit.*

108.   **Roth, A.:** *Ahavat ha-Bore, Op. cit.*

109.   **Rosenberg, Y.:** *Rafael ha-Malach, Op. cit.*

110.   **Vukosavović, F.:** *Angels and Demons, Op. cit.*

CHAPTER 6

1.   **Swart, J.G.:** *The Book of Sacred Names, Op. cit.*
2.   **Bischoff, E.:** *The Kabbalah, Op. cit.*
    WallisBudge, E.A.: *Amulets and Talismans, Op. cit.*
    Hastings, J.: *Encyclopaedia of Religion and Ethics* Vol. 3, T. & T. Clarke, Edinburgh 1910.
    Trachtenberg, J.: *Jewish Magic and Superstition, Op. cit.*
    Isaacs, R.H.: *Divination, Magic and Healing, Op. cit.*
    Schrire, T.: *Hebrew Amulets, Op. cit.*
    Nigal, G.: *Magic, Mysticism, and Hasidism, Op. cit.*
3.   **Swart, J.G.:** *The Book of Sacred Names, Op. cit.*
4.   **Ba'al Shem, E.; Ba'al-Shem, J.; ha-Kohen, N. ben I.; & Katz, N.:** *Mifalot Elokim, Op. cit.*
    Zacutto, M.: *Shorshei ha-Shemot, Op. cit.*
5.   *Ibid.*
6.   **Zacutto, M.:** *Ibid.*
    Isaacs, R.: *Divination, Magic and Healing, Op. cit.*
7.   **Isaacs, R.:** *Ibid..*
8.   **Zacutto, M.:** *Shorshei ha-Shemot, Op. cit.*
9.   *Ibid.*
10.   *Sefer Raziel ha-Malach, Op. cit.*
11.   **Zacutto, M.:** *Shorshei ha-Shemot, Op. cit.*
12.   **Swart, J.G.:** *The Book of Sacred Names, Op. cit.*
13.   **Zacutto, M.:** *Shorshei ha-Shemot, Op. cit.*
14.   *Ibid.*
15.   *Ibid.*
16.   *Ibid.*
17.   *Ibid.*
18.   *Ibid.*
19.   *Ibid.*
20.   *Ibid.*
21.   *Ibid.*
22.   *Ibid.*
23.   *Ibid.*
24.   *Ibid.*
25.   *Ibid.*
    Chamui, A.: *Aviah Chidot, Op. cit.*
26.   **Ochanah, R. ben C.:** *Sefer Mareh ha-Yeladim, Op. cit.*
    Palagi, C.: *Refuah v'Chayim, Op. cit.*

27. **Heschel, A.Y.:** *Shemirot uSegulot Niflot, Op. cit.*
28. **Ochanah, R. ben C.:** *Sefer Mareh ha-Yeladim, Op. cit*
29. *Ibid.*
30. **Heschel, A.Y.:** *Shemirot uSegulot Niflot, Op. cit.*
31. **Ochanah, R. ben C.:** *Sefer Mareh ha-Yeladim, Op. cit.*
32. **Zacutto, M.:** *Shorshei ha-Shemot, Op. cit.*
33. **Heschel, A.Y.:** *Shemirot uSegulot Niflot, Op. cit.*
34. **Zacutto, M.:** *Shorshei ha-Shemot, Op. cit.*
    Rosenberg, Y.: *Rafael ha-Malach, Op. cit.*
    Chamui, A.: *Aviah Chidot, Op. cit.*
    Ochanah, R. ben C.: *Sefer Mareh ha-Yeladim, Op. cit*
    Palagi, C.: *Refuah v'Chayim, Op. cit.*
    Mizrachi, E.A.: *Refuah v'Chayim m'Yerushalayim, Op. cit.*
    Heschel, A.Y.: *Shemirot uSegulot Niflot, Op. cit.*
    Rubenstein, Y.Y.: *Zichron Yakov Yoshef*, Defus Yehudah vi-Yerushalayim, Jerusalem 1931.
35. **Maller, A.S.:** *God, Sex and Kabbalah, Op. cit.*
36. **Zacutto, M.:** *Shorshei ha-Shemot, Op. cit.*
37. *Sefer Raziel ha-Malach, Op. cit.*
38. **Rosenberg, Y.:** *Rafael ha-Malach, Op. cit.*
39. **Zacutto, M.:** *Shorshei ha-Shemot, Op. cit.*
40. *Sefer Shimmush Tehillim, Op. cit.*
41. **Swart, J.G.:** *The Book of Sacred Names, Op. Cit.*
42. See Chapter 4 Note 69.
43. **Regardie, I.:** *The Complete Golden Dawn System of Magic*, Op. cit.
44. **Hall, M.P.:** *The Secret Teachings of All Ages: An Encyclopedic Outline of Masonic, Hermetic, Qabbalistic, and Rosicrucian Symbolical Philosophy*, Philosophical Research Society, Los Angeles 1988.
    Ponce, C.: *Kabbalah: An Introduction and Illumination for the World Today*, The Garnstone Press Ltd., London 1974.
45. **Halevi, Z. Ben S.:** *Kabbalah: Tradition of Hidden Knowledge*, Thames & Hudson Ltd., London 1979.
    Davis A. & Dunn-Mascetti, M.: *Judaic Mysticism*, Hyperion, New York 1997.
46. **Davis, A. & Dunn Mascetti, M.:** *Ibid.*
47. **Gray, W.G.:** *Magical Ritual Methods, Op. cit.*
48. **Hyman, A.P.:** *Sefer Yesira, Op. cit.*
49. See Chapter 4 Note 69.
50. **Swart, J.G.:** *The Book of Self Creation, Op. cit.*
51. See Chapter 4 Note 69.
52. **Schrire, T.:** *Hebrew Amulets, Op. cit.*

467

53. **Agrippa, H.C.:** *De Occulta Philosophia, Op. cit.,*
   Barrett, F.: *The Magus or Celestial Intelligencer, Op. cit.*
   Mathers, S.L. MacGregor: *The Kabbalah Unveiled,* Routledge & Kegan Paul Ltd., London 1954.
   Westcott, W.W.: *Numbers: Their Occult Power and Mystic Virtue: Being a Résumé of the Views of the Kabbalists, Pythagoreans, Adepts of India, Chaldean Magi and Medieval Magicians*; Theosophical Publication Society, London 1911.
54. **Swart, J.G.:** *The Book of Sacred Names, Op. cit.*
55. **Swart, J.G.:** *The Book of Self Creation, Op. cit.*
56. *Ibid.*

CHAPTER 7

1.   **Figueras, P.:** *Decorated Jewish Ossuaris,* Koninklijke Brill N.V., Leiden 1983.
     Hachlili, R.: *Ancient Jewish Art and Archaeology in the Diaspora,* Koninklijke Brill N.V., Leiden 1998.
     —*Jewish Funerary Customs, Practices And Rites In The Second Temple Period,* Koninklijke Brill N.V., Leiden 2005.
     —*Ancient Mosaic Pavements: Themes, Issues and Trends,* Koninklijke Brill N.V., Leiden 2009.
2.   **Roth, C.:** *Jewish Art: An Illustrated History,* McGraw-Hill Book Co., New York 1961.
     Huberman, I.: *Living Symbols: Symbols in Jewish Art and Tradition,* Modan Publishers Ltd., Jerusalem 1996.
     Shwartz-Be'eri, O.: *The Jews of Kurdistan, Op. cit.*
3.   **Shachar, I.:** *Jewish Tradition in Art, Op. cit.*
     Davis, E. & Frenkel, D.A.: *Ha-Kamia ha-Ivri, Op. cit.*
     Shwartz-Be'eri, O.: *Ibid.*
4.   **Yoder, D. & Graves, T.E.:** *Hex Signs: Pennsylvania Dutch Barn Symbols & Their Meaning,* Stackpole Books, Mechanicsburg 2000.
5.   **Shwartz-Be'eri, O.:** *The Jews of Kurdistan, Op. cit.*
6.   **Sapir, B. & Neeman, D.:** *Capernaum (Kfar-Nachum): History and Legacy, Art and Architecture,* Historical Sites Library, Tel Aviv 1967.
     Urman, D. & McCracken Flesher, P.V.: *Ancient Synagogues: Historical Analysis and Archaeological Discovery,* Koninklijke Brill N.V., Leiden 1994.
     Huberman, I.: *Living Symbols, Op. cit.*
7.   **Shachar, I.:** *Jewish Tradition in Art, Op. cit.*
     Shwartz-Be'eri, O.: *The Jews of Kurdistan, Op. cit.*
8.   **Schrire, T.:** *Hebrew Amulets, Op. cit.*
     Bialer, Y.L. & Fink, E.: *Jewish Life in Art and Tradition: Based on the Collection of the Sir Isaac and Lady Edith Wolfson Museum, Hechal Shlomo,* Jerusalem, G.P. Putnam's Sons, New York 1976.
     Ungerleider, J.G.; Gottlieb, F. & Lessing, E.: *Jewish Folk Art: From Biblical Days to Modern Times,* Summit Books, New York 1986.
     Shachar, I.: *Ibid.*

469

Frankel, E. & Teutsch, B.P.: *The Encyclopedia of Jewish Symbols*, Jason Aronson, Northvale 1992.
Davis, E. & Frenkel, D.A.: *Ha-Kamia ha-Ivri, Op. cit.*
Shwartz-Be'eri, O.: *Ibid.*
Shadur, J. & Shadur, Y.: *Traditional Jewish Papercuts, Op. cit.*
Slapak, O.: *The Jews of India: A Story of Three Communities*, The Israel Museum, Jerusalem 2003.
Wertkin, G.C.: *Encyclopedia of American Folk Art*, American Folk Art Museum, Routledge, London & New York 2004.
Boustan, R.S.; Kosansky, O., & Rustow, M.: *Jewish Studies at the Crossroads of Anthropology and History: Authority Diaspora Tradition*, University of Pennsylvania Press, Philadelphia 2011.
Calò, G.: *About Paper: Israeli Contemporary Art*, Postmedia Srl, Milano 2012.

9. **Chefitz, M.:** *The Seventh Telling: The Kabbalah of Moshe Katan*, St. Martin's Press, New York 2001.
10. **Swart, J.G.:** *The Book of Sacred Names, Op. cit.*
11. **Gutmann, J.:** *Iconography of Religions XXIII, 1: The Jewish Sanctuary*, Institute of Religious Iconography, State University Groningen/E.J. Brill, Leiden 1983.
12. *Ibid.*
Huberman, I.: *Living Symbols, Op. cit.*
13. **Gutmann, J.:** *Ibid.*
Stern, S.: *Jewish Identity in Early Rabbinic Writings*, E.J. Brill, Leiden 1994.
Huberman, I.: *Ibid.*
Scholem, G.: *The Curious History of the Six Pointed Star*, published in *Commentary Vol. 8*, December 1949.
Scholem, G.; Hasan-Rokem, G. & Shapira, A.: *Magen David: Toldotov shel Semel*, Mishkan le-Omanut, Ein Harod 2008.
14. **Swart, J.G.:** *The Book of Sacred Names, Op. cit.*
Epstein, M.M.: *Dreams of Subversion in Medieval Jewish Art and Literature*, The Pennsylvania State University Press, Pennsylvania 1992.
15. **Zacutto, M.:** *Shorshei ha-Shemot, Op. cit.*
16. *Ibid.*
17. *Ibid.*
18. **Shachar, I.:** *Jewish Tradition in Art, Op. cit.*
19. **Odeberg, H.:** *3 Enoch or The Hebrew Book of Enoch, Op. cit.*
20. **Avraham Rimon of Granada:** *Brit Menuchah, Op. cit.*
Zacutto, M.: *Shorshei ha-Shemot, Op. cit.*
Davidson, G.: *A Dictionary of Angels, Op. cit.*

21.   **Zacutto, M.:** *Ibid.*
22.   *Ibid.*
23.   *Ibid.*
24.   *Ibid.*
25.   **Swart, J.G.:** *The Book of Sacred Names, Op. cit.*
26.   *Ibid.*
      Zacutto, M.: *Shorshei ha-Shemot, Op. cit.*
27.   **Abulafia, A.:** *Sefer Chayei ha-Olam ha-Ba,* transl. in **Kaplan, A.:** *Meditation and Kabbalah, Op. cit.*
28.   **Swart, J.G.:** *The Book of Sacred Names, Op. cit.*
29.   **Davis, E. & Frenkel, D.A.:** *Ha-Kamia ha-Ivri, Op. cit.*
      Green, A.: *Judaic Artifacts, Op. cit.*
30.   **Swart, J.G.:** *The Book of Sacred Names, Op. cit.*
      Zacutto, M.: *Shorshei ha-Shemot, Op. cit.*
31.   *Ibid.*
32.   *Ibid.*
33.   *Ibid.*
34.   *Ibid.*
35.   *Ibid.*
36.   **Zacutto, M.:** *Ibid.*
37.   *Ibid.*
38.   *Ibid.*
39.   **Slouschz, N.:** *Travels in North Africa, Op. cit.*
40.   *Ibid.*
41.   *Ibid.*
42.   **Swart, J.G.:** *The Book of Sacred Names, Op. cit.*
43.   *Ibid.*
44.   *Ibid.*
45.   **Dennis, G.W.:** *The Encyclopedia of Jewish Myth, Magic and Mysticism, Op. cit.*
46.   **Avraham Rimon of Granada:** *Brit Menuchah, Op. cit.*
      Zacutto, M.: *Shorshei ha-Shemot, Op. cit.*
47.   **Zacutto, M.:** *Ibid.*
48.   **Etkes, I.:** *The Besht: Magician, Mystic and Leader, Op. cit.*
49.   **Knight, R.P.:** *Symbolical Language of Ancient Art and Mythology,* J.W. Bouton, New York 1892.
      Eisler, R.: *Orpheus - the Fisher: Comparative Studies in Orphic and Early Christian Cult Symbolism,* J.M. Watkins London 1921.
      Cirlot, J.E.: *A Dictionary of Symbols,* translated from the Spanish by Jack Sage, Routledge & Paul, London 1962.
      Black, J.A.; Green, A. & Rickards, T.: *Gods, Demons and Symbols of Ancient Mesopotamia: An Illustrated Dictionary,* University of Texas Press, Austin 1992.

Jung, C.G. & Stein, M.: *Jung on Christianity: Selected & Introduced by Murray Stein*, Princeton University Press, Princeton 1999.

Beer, R.: *The Handbook of Tibetan Buddhist Symbols*, Shambhala, Boston 2003.

Ornan, T.: *The Triumph of the Symbol: Pictorial Representation of Deities in Mesopotamia and the Biblical Image Ban*, Academic Press Fribourg, Vandenhoeck & Ruprecht, Fribourg & Göttingen 2005.

Welch, P.B.: *Chinese Art: A Guide to Motifs and Visual Imagery*, Tuttle Publishing, North Clarendon 2008.

50. **Beine, D. & Pittle, K.:** *Hooked on The Fish: The Christian Sign of The Fish (and Co-Option Thereof) as Symbolic Capital*, SIL International 2009.

51. **Dennis, G.W.:** *The Encyclopedia of Jewish Myth, Magic and Mysticism, Op. cit.*

52. *Ibid.*

53. **Huberman, I.:** *Living Symbols, Op. cit.*

54. **Wineman, A.:** *Mystic Tales from the Zohar*, The Jewish Publication Society of America, 1997.

55. **Slouschz, N.:** *Travels in North Africa, Op. cit.*

56. **Zacutto, M.:** *Shorshei ha-Shemot, Op. cit.*

57. **Frankel, E. & Teutsch, B.P.:** *The Encyclopedia of Jewish Symbols, Op. cit.*

Huberman, I.: *Living Symbols, Op. cit.*

also published by The Sangreal Sodality Press

Shadow Tree Series
Volume 1

THE BOOK OF
SELF CREATION

Jacobus G. Swart

'*The Book of Self Creation*' is a study guide for all who seek God within and who prefer to steer the course of their lives in a personal manner. The doctrines and techniques addressed in t his book will aid practitioners in the expansion of personal consciousness and spiritual evolution. Combining the principles and teachings of Kabbalah and Ceremonial Magic, the book offers step by step instructions on the conscious creation of physical life circumstances, such being always in harmony with the mind-set of the practitioner.

'The Book of Self Creation is a rich and resourceful workbook of practical kabbalah from the hands of a master kabbalist who is both compassionate and insightful.'
Caitlin Matthews, author of *Walkers Between the Worlds* and *Sophia, Goddess of Wisdom*.

The 'Shadow Tree Series' comprises a unique collection of Western Esoteric studies and practices which Jacobus Swart, spiritual successor to William G. Gray, has actuated and taught over a period of forty years. Regarding the author of this series, William Gray wrote 'It is well to bear in mind that Jacobus Swart is firstly and lastly a staunchly practicing member of the Western Inner Tradition and perforce writes from that specific angle alone. Moreover, he writes well, lucidly, and absolutely honestly.'

ISBN 978-0-620-42882-2   *Paperback*

also published by The Sangreal Sodality Press

Shadow Tree Series
Volume 2

THE BOOK OF SACRED NAMES

Jacobus G. Swart

'*The Book of Sacred Names*' is a practical guide into the meditational and magical applications of ancient Hebrew Divine Names. Perpetuating the tenets of traditional Kabbalists who recognised the fundamental bond between 'Kabbalah' and 'Magic,' Jacobus Swart offers step by step instructions on the deliberate and conscious control of personal life circumstances, by means of the most cardinal components of Kabbalistic doctrines and techniques—Divine Names!

The material addressed in this tome derives from the extensive primary literature of 'Practical Kabbalah,' much of which is appearing in print for the first time in English translation.

The 'Shadow Tree Series' comprises a unique collection of Western Esoteric studies and practices which Jacobus Swart, spiritual successor to William G. Gray and co-founder of the Sangreal Sodality, has actuated and taught over a period of forty years. Having commenced his Kabbalah studies in Safed in the early 1970's, he later broadened his 'kabbalistic horizons' under the careful guidance of the famed English Kabbalist William G. Gray.

ISBN 978-0-620-50702-8   *Paperback*

also published by The Sangreal Sodality Press

THE LADDER OF LIGHTS
(OR QABALAH RENOVATA)

William G. Gray

The Tree of Life works in relation to consciousness somewhat like a computer. Data is fed in, stored in associative banks, and then fed out on demand. The difference between the Tree and a computer, however, is that a computer can only produce various combinations of the information that has been programmed into it. The Tree, operating through the intelligent consciousness of living beings, whether embodied in this world or not, acts as a sort of Universal Exchange throughout the entire chain of consciousness sharing its scheme, and the extent of this is infinite and incalculable.

The Tree of Life is a means and not an end. It is not in itself an object for worship or some idol for superstitious reverence. It is a means, a method, a map and a mechanism for assisting the attainment of the single objective common to all creeds, systems, mysteries and religions—namely, the mystical union of humanity and divinity. With this end in view, this book is an aid to whoever desires to climb the Tree of Life.

'.....the most original commentary on basic Kabbalistic knowledge that I have read for God knows how many years.'
Israel Regardie

'.....beautifully presented and set in excellent marching order.....For one new to the subject, this is a fine text and an exceptionally lucid introduction to a veiled and meditative lore which is still being enlarged from year to year.'
Max Freedom Long (*Huna Vistas*)

ISBN 978-0-620-40303-0   *Paperback*

also published by The Sangreal Sodality Press

AN OUTLOOK ON OUR INNER WESTERN WAY

William G. Gray

'*An Outlook on Our Inner Western Way*' is a unique book. This is no dusty, quaint grimoire — it is a sane and simple method of true attainment for those who seek communion with their higher selves.

In this book, William Gray shows simply and lucidly, how to *live* the Western Inner Tradition. Tracing the cosmology of Western magic, he substantiates its vitality and urgency for our future.

William G. Gray is rated one of the most prolific — and controversial — occultists today. Blending keen insight, modern psychological models and an overall sense of practicality, his books have torn at the mouldy veils of so-called occult secrets, laying out a no-non sense foundation by which modern Western humanity may once again regain its precious magical soul.

ISBN 978-0-620-40306-1   *Paperback*

also published by The Sangreal Sodality Press

Sangreal Sodality Series
Volume 1

WESTERN INNER WORKINGS

William G. Gray

The '*Sangreal Sodality Series*' is a home study course comprising the fundamental text books of the Sangreal Sodality, that revives the instrumentality inherent in our western Tradition. The series makes available to us, in our own cultural symbolism, a way to enlightenment that we can practice on a daily basis.

'*Western Inner Workings*' provides a practical framework for the western student's psycho-spiritual development. Each day includes a morning meditation, a mid-day invocation, evening exercises, and a sleep subject. Incorporating symbols that are 'close to home,' these rituals increase consciousness in comfortable increments.

ISBN 978-0-620-40304-7   *Paperback*

also published by The Sangreal Sodality Press

A BEGINNERS GUIDE TO LIVING KABBALAH

William G. Gray

This compendium comprises six Kabbalistic works by William G. Gray, some of which are appearing here in print for the first time. The texts included in this compilation are ranging from the simplest introduction to the Spheres and Paths of the Kabbalistic Tree of Life system, to related meditation techniques and associated ritual magical procedures, to an advanced system of what could be termed 'inter-dimensional spiritual communication.'

The title 'A Beginners Guide to Living Kabbalah' is perhaps somewhat misleading, as this compilation equally contains works of an advanced nature, and the ritual and meditation techniques addressed in this tome, pertain to both beginners as well as advanced practitioners of 'Practical Kabbalah.'

ISBN 978-0-620-42887-3   *Paperback*

Milton Keynes UK
Ingram Content Group UK Ltd.
UKHW021526260724
1051UKWH00086BA/1563

9 780620 596985